Constitutional Law in Greece

Fourth Edition

Philippos C. Spyropoulos
Theodore P. Fortsakis

This book was originally published as a monograph in the International Encyclopaedia of Laws/Constitutional Law.

Founding Editor: Roger Blanpain
General Editor: Frank Hendrickx
Volume Editors: André Alen & David Haljan

Wolters Kluwer

Published by:
Kluwer Law International B.V.
PO Box 316
2400 AH Alphen aan den Rijn
The Netherlands
E-mail: lrs-sales@wolterskluwer.com
Website: www.wolterskluwer.com/en/solutions/kluwerlawinternational

Sold and distributed by:
Wolters Kluwer Legal & Regulatory U.S.
920 Links Avenue
Landisville, PA 17538
United States of America
Email: customer.service@wolterskluwer.com

ISBN 978-94-035-0427-8

e-Book: ISBN 978-94-035-0437-7
web-PDF: ISBN 978-94-035-0447-6

The Authors

Philippos C. Spyropoulos was born in Athens in 1952. He is Professor Emeritus at the Law School of the National and Kapodistrian University of Athens. He studied Law at the University of Athens (LLB, 1974), the London School of Economics and Political Science (LSE) of the University of London (LLM, 1978) and the University of Freiburg i. Br. (Dr iur. 1979). He has taught courses on public law and especially constitutional law and human rights and has numerous publications in the field of constitutional law and theory.

He also practises law, mainly as an advocate before the Greek Council of State (Administrative Supreme Court).

He has been an advisor to the Presidency of the Republic (1981–1983), Secretary General of the Ministry to the Prime Minister (1989) and of the Ministry of Justice (1990–1991), legal advisor to the Ministerial Committee for Privatization (1992–1993), and member of the Hellenic Telecommunications and Post Commission (2000–2005). He recently served as the Minister of Justice of the caretaker Government (2023).

Theodore P. Fortsakis was born in Athens in 1954. He studied law in Greece and in France (University of Nancy (DEUG, 1975)), University of Athens (LLB, 1978), University of Paris 2 (Doctorat d'Etat en droit, 1985). He is Professor at the Law School of the National and Kapodistrian University of Athens. He is a corresponding member of the French Academy of Moral and Political Sciences (Institut de France). He was a member of the Greek Parliament (2015–2019). Previously, he was the Rector of the National and Kapodistrian University of Athens (2014–2015). He has served as the Dean of the Law School of Athens (2009–2014), Deputy Dean (2007–2009) and Director of the Department of Public Law (2009–2014).

Since 1990, he has been a lecturer in constitutional law, administrative law and tax law. He has also been a Visiting Professor for over a decade at the Sorbonne

(Paris 1: 2003–2013, Paris 2: 2010–2011 & 2012–2013) and at the University Paul Cézanne – Aix-Marseille (2002–2003, 2006–2007, 2008–2010).

Professor Fortsakis has also served as an advisor to the Prime Minister on issues of Public Law (1990–1991); as an expert of the Council of Europe (Strasbourg) on issues of administrative law and organization of administrative justice (1998–2003); a member of the Hellenic Competition Commission (2000–2003); a member of the National Commission for Human Rights (2003–2006); a member of the Board of Directors of the National Library (2008–2011). He has also been a member of the Special Supreme Court of Greece (2012–2013); Chairman of the Board of Directors of the State Orchestra of Athens (2012–2014); Chairman of the Consulting Committee of the General Secretariat of Public Revenues (Ministry of Finance) (2013–2014); Chairman of the Supervisory Board of the Public Television (NERIT) (2013–2014), and a member of numerous committees of different ministries for the preparation of legislative and regulatory bills and decrees.

Since 2010, he is Chairman of the Association Franco-Hellénique (Lycée français Eugène Delacroix).

He practises law as a barrister (member of the Athens Bar Association since 1981) mainly before the Greek Administrative Supreme Court. He is a founding partner of the law firm 'FDM&A' (www.fdmalaw.com).

He is the author of numerous books and more than 150 scientific articles on all fields of public law (in Greek, French, English and German). He is a member of numerous international and Greek scientific associations for public and tax law and sits on many of their Boards of Directors.

Professor Fortsakis has received the distinction of 'Chevalier de l'Ordre des Palmes académiques' by decree of the French Prime Minister (2006); the distinction of 'Officier de l'Ordre des Palmes académiques' by decree of the French Prime Minister (2012); the distinction of 'Officier de la Légion d'honneur' by decree of the French President (2015); the distinction of 'Archon Guardian of Law (Dikaiophylax)' of the Greek Orthodox Patriarchate of Alexandria and All Africa (2009).

Table of Contents

List of Abbreviations

AEAP	Annuaire Européen d'Administration Publique
AIFP-IISA	*Association Internationale de la Fonction Publique* – Institut International de Sciences Administratives
AIJC	*Annuaire International de Justice Constitutionnelle*
CJEU	Court of Justice of the EU
CNRS	Centre National de la Recherche Scientifique
CRA	Centre de recherches administratives
EAM	National Liberation Front (Εθνικό Απελευθερωτικό Μτωπο, Ethnikó Apeleftherotikó Métopo
ECHR	European Convention on Human Rights
ECtHR	European Court of Human Rights
ELAS	Greek People's Liberation Army (Ελληνικός Λαικός Απελευθερωτικός Στρατός, Ellinikós Laïkós Apeleftherotikós Stratós)
ERE	National Radical Union
ERT	Hellenic Broadcasting Corporation
EU	European Union
GDPR	General Data Protection Regulation
HDPA	Hellenic Data Protection Authority
JöR	Jahrbuch des öffentlichen Rechts
MCC	Municipal and Communal Code
PPP	Public-Private Partnership
PSI	Private Sector Involvement
RDP	Revue du Droit Public et de la Science Politique en France et a l'Étranger
REDP	Revue Européenne du Droit Public (European Review of Public Law/Europäische Zeitschrift des öffentlichen Rechts / Rivista Europea di Diritto Pubblico)
RFDA	Revue Française de Droit Administratif
RHDH	Revue Hellénique des Droits de l'Homme

List of Abbreviations

RHDI	Revue Hellénique du Droit International (Hellenic International Law Review)
SLLGAs	Second-Level Local Government Agencies
SLLGC	Second-Level Local Government Code
TEU	Treaty on the European Union
TFEU	Treaty on the Functioning of the European Union

Glossary

Act of Parliament	(nomos) νόμος, (typikos nomos) τυπικός νόμος, (nomothetiki praxi) νομοθετικ πρξη
Acts with a legislative content	(Praxeis nomothetikou periehomenou), Πρξεις Νομοθετικο Περιεχομνου
Administrative act	(Dioikitiki praxi), Διοικητικ πρξη
Individual (administrative) act	(Atomiki dioikitiki praxi), Ατομικ (διοικητικ) πρξη
Regulatory (administrative) act	(Kanonistiki dioikitiki praxi), Κανονιστικ (διοικητικ) πρξη
Administrative Recourse	
Simple Administrative	(Apli Dioikitiki Prosfigi), Απλ Διοικητικ Προσφυγ
Special Administrative	(Eidiki Dioikitiki Prosfigi), Ειδικ Διοικητικ Προσφυγ
Quasi-judicial	(Endikofanis Prosfigi), Ενδικοφανς Προσφυγ
Administrative supervision	(Dioikitiki epopteia), Διοικητικ εποπτεα
Appeals Committee	(Epitropi Prosfygon), Επιτροπ Προσφυγν
Asylum Service	(Ypiresia Asylou), Υπηρεσα Ασλου
Auditor of Legality	(Elegktis nomimotitas) Ελεγκτς νομιμότητας
Bill	(Nomoshedio), Νομοσχδιο
Civil Courts	
Justices of Peace	(Eirinodikeia), Ειρηνοδικεα

Glossary

One-member district courts	(Monomeli Protodikeia), Μονομελ Πρωτοδικεα
Three-member district courts	(Polimeli protodikeia), Πολυμελ Πρωτοδικεα
Court of Appeal(s)	(Efeteio), Εφετεο
Civil Rights	(atomika dikaiomata), Ατομικ Δικαιματα
Court of Audit/Auditors	(Elegktiko Sinedrio), Ελεγκτικό Συνδριο
Commission for the quality of life	(Epitropi poiotitas zois), Επιτροπ ποιότητας ζως
Commune	(Koinotita), Κοινότητα
Conference of Parliamentary Chairmen	(Diaskepsi ton Proedron), Δισκεψη των Προδρων
Consenting Opinion	(simfoni gnomi), σμφωνη γνμη
Council of State	(Simvoulio Epikrateias), Συμβολιο Επικρατεας
Decentralization	(Apokentrosi), Αποκντρωση
Decentralized Administration	(Apokentromeni Dioikisi), Αποκεντρωμνη Διοκηση
Deputy Minister	(Anaplirotis Ypourgos), Αναπληρωτς Υπουργός
Executive Commission	(Ektelestiki epitropi), Εκτελεστικ Επιτροπ
Financial Commission	(Oikonomiki Epitropi), Οικονομικ Επιτροπ
General Secretary of the Decentralized Administration	(Genikos Grammateas tis Apokentromenis Dioikisis), Γενικός Γραμματας της Αποκεντρωμνης Διοκησης
Hierarchical control	(Ierarhikos eleghos), Ιεραρχικός λεγχος
Independent administrative authorities	
Hellenic Competition Commission	(Epitropi Antagonismou), Επιτροπ Ανταγωνισμο
Hellenic Telecommunications and Post Commission (EETT)	(Ethniki Epitropi Tilepikoinonion kai Tahidromion), Εθνικ Επιτροπ Τηλεπικοινωνιν και Ταχυδρομεων (EETT)

Regulatory Authority for Energy	(Rithmistiki arhi energeias), Ρυθμιστικ Αρχ Ενργειας
Independent authorities	
Hellenic Authority for the information and Communication Security and Privacy	(Arhi diasfalisis tou aporritou ton epikoinonion), Αρχ Διασφλισης του Απορρτου των Επικοινωνιν
(ADAE)	(ADAE)
Hellenic Data Protection Authority	(Arhi prostasias prosopikon dedomenon), Αρχ Προστασας Προσωπικν Δεδομνων
Ombudsman	(Synigoros tou Politi), Συνγορος του Πολτη
National Radio and Television Council	(Ethniko Symvoulio Radiotileorasis), Εθνικό
(NRTVC)	Συμβολιο Ραδιοτηλεόρασης (ΕΣΡ)
Supreme Council for Civil Personnel Selection	(Anotato symboulio epilogis prosopikou), Αντατο Συμβολιο Επιλογς Προσωπικο (ΑΣΕΠ)
Independent Supervisory Agency	(Aftotelis Ypiresia Epopteias), Αυτοτελς Υπηρεσα Εποπτεας
Judicial Remedy	(Endiko voithima), νδικο βοθημα
Action	(Agogi), Αγωγ
Application for annulment	(Aitisi akyrosis), Ατηση Ακρωσης
Civil servants' recourse	(Ypalliliki prosfygi), υπαλληλικ προσφυγ
Defence (Opposition)	(Anakopi), Ανακοπ
Objection	(Enstasi), νσταση
Petition for reversal	(Aitisi anairesis), Ατηση αναρεσης (application for reversal, final appeal)
Recourse Law	(prosfygi), προσφυγ (nomos), νόμος
Executive statute, law, Act	(ektelestikos nomos), εκτελεστικός νόμος
	'Formal' law, ordinary law, law, Statute, Act of Parliament, Act or

Glossary

legislative act or legislative text	(tipikos nomos, koinos nomos, nomos, nomothetiki praxi, nomothetiko keimeno), τυπικός νόμος, κοινός νόμος, νόμος, νομοθετικ πρξη, νομοθετικό κεμενο
Framework statute	(nomos-plaisio), νόμος-πλασιο
Material law	(ousiastikos nomos), ουσιαστικός νόμος
Law Proposal	(Protasi Nomou), πρόταση νόμου
Legal Council of State	(Nomiko Symvoulio tou Kratous), Νομικό Συμβολιο του Κρτους
Local communities	(Topiko diamerisma), Τοπικό Διαμρισμα
Mayor	(Dimarhos), Δμαρχος
Minister	(Ypourgos), Υπουργός
Municipal council	(dimotiko simvoulio), Δημοτικό Συμβολιο
Municipal Community	(Dimotiko Koinotita), Δημοτικ Κοινότητα
Municipality	(Dimos), Δμος
National Schism	(Ethnikos Dihasmos), Εθνικός Διχασμός
Ordinary administrative courts	(Taktika dioikitika dikastiria), Τακτικ Διοικητικ Δικαστρια
Administrative courts of first instance	(Dioikitika protodikeia), Διοικητικ Πρωτοδικεα
Administrative courts of appeal	(Dioikitika efeteia), Διοικητικ Εφετεα
President of the Republic	(Proedros tis dimokratias), Πρόεδρος της Δημοκρατας
Presidential Decree	(Proedriko Diatagma), Προεδρικό Διταγμα
Prime Minister	(Prothipourgos), Πρωθυπουργός
Private Law Legal Persons (Private Law Legal Entities)	(Nomika Prosopa Idiotikou Dikaiou), Νομικ Πρόσωπα Ιδιωτικο Δικαου

Public Enterprises and Organizations	(Dimosies epiheiriseis kai organismoi), Δημόσιες Επιχειρσεις και Οργανισμο
Public Law Legal Persons (Public Law Legal Entities)	(Nomika Prosopa Dimosiou Dikaiou), Νομικ Πρόσωπα Δημοσου Δικαου
Public Legal Persons (Public Legal Entities)	(Dimosia nomika prosopa), Δημόσια Νομικ Πρόσωπα
Regions	(Perifereies), Περιφρειες
Regulatory Act	(KanonistikiPraxi), Κανονιστικ πρξη
Salary Court	(Misthodikeio), Μισθοδικεο
Second Level Local Government Agencies, SLLGAs	(Nomarchiakes aftodioikiseis), Νομαρχιακς Αυτοδιοικσεις
Special Highest Court (or Supreme Special Court)	(Anotato Eidiko Dikastirio), Αντατο Ειδικό Δικαστριο
Standing Orders (Regulations of Parliament)	(Kanonismos tis Voulis), Κανονισμός της Βουλς
State Deputy	(Bouleytis epikrateias), Βουλευτς Επικρατεας
Statute, Act	(typikos nomos) τυπικός νόμος
Supreme Civil and Criminal Court	(Areios Pagos), ρειος Πγος
Undersecretary	(Ifipourgos), Υφυπουργός

Glossary

Note

Work on this fourth edition was carried out by Professor Theodore P. Fortsakis and approved by Professor Philippos C. Spyropoulos (July 2023). The three previous, restructured and much-enlarged editions were also written by Professor Fortsakis. The first edition was based on an earlier work, which was written by Professor Philippos C. Spyropoulos (The Hague, London, Boston, Athens: Kluwer/Sakkoulas, 1995, 172 pages). It was originally published as a monograph in the International Encyclopaedia of Laws/Constitutional Law (Kluwer, 1995). The numbering of the paragraphs in the current edition has changed in comparison with the previous editions.

The present monograph refers extensively to a bibliography in English, French and German. Greek bibliography has not been included, since access to such bibliography for Greek-speaking persons is easy.

The main Greek textbooks concerning Hellenic constitutional law, referring to the Greek Constitution of 1975/1986/2001/2008/2019, are:

Chryssogonos, K., *Constitutional Law*, 2nd ed., Athens – Thessaloniki: Sakkoulas, 2014;
Dimitropoulos, A., *Constitutional Law System*, 2nd ed., Athens – Thessaloniki: Sakkoulas, 2011;
Georgopoulos, K., *Concise Constitutional Law*, 12th ed., Athens – Komotini: Ant. N. Sakkoulas, 2001;
Manesis, A., *Constitutional Law I*, Athens – Komotini: Ant. N. Sakkoulas, 1980;
Manitakis, A., *Greek Constitutional Law I*, Athens – Thessaloniki: Sakkoulas, 2004;
Mavrias, K., *Constitutional Law*, 6th ed., Athens: P. N. Sakkoulas, 2022;
Pantelis, A., *Constitutional Law Handbook*, 5th ed., Athens: Livanis, 2020;
Raikos, A., *Constitutional Law*, Vol. I, 5th ed., Athens: Nomiki Bibliothiki, 2018; Vol. II, 4th ed., Athens: Nomiki Bibliothiki, 2012;
Spyropoulos, Ph. et al. (eds.), *Constitution: A Commentary*, Athens – Thessaloniki, Sakkoulas, 2017;
Spyropoulos, Ph., *Constitutional Law*, 2nd ed., Athens – Thessaloniki: Sakkoulas, 2020;
Tsatsos, D., Constitutional Law, Vol. A, 4th ed., Athens – Komotini: Ant. N. Sakkoulas, 1994; Vol. B, Athens – Komotini: Ant. N. Sakkoulas, 1992;
Venizelos, E., *Courses in Constitutional Law*, Athens – Thessaloniki: Sakkoulas, 2021.

Note

The main textbooks concerning human rights, referring to the Constitution of 1975/1985/2001/2008/2019, are:

Chryssogonos, K./ Vlachopoulos, S., *Civil and Social Rights*, 4th ed., Athens: Nomiki Bibliothiki, 2017;
Dagtoglou, P.D., *Constitutional Law: Human Rights*, 4th ed., Athens – Thessaloniki: Sakkoulas, 2012;
Dimitropoulos, A., *Constitutional Rights*, 2nd ed., Athens – Thessaloniki: Sakkoulas, 2008;
Manesis, A., Constitutional Rights, Athens – Thessaloniki: Sakkoulas, 1978;
Raikos, A., *Constitutional Law: Fundamental Rights*, Vol. III, 4th ed., Athens: Nomiki Bibliothiki, 2011;
Spyropoulos, Ph., *Introduction to Constitutional Law: Fundamental Rights – General Part*, Vol. II, Athens: Themis – N. A. Sakkoulas, 2012.
Tsatsos, D., Constitutional Law, Vol. C, Athens – Komotini: Ant. N. Sakkoulas, 1987;

In the present monograph, Greek terminology has been translated in accordance with the official English version of the Constitution of the Hellenic Republic, published by the Hellenic Parliament. The provisions of the Constitution are cited from the same official translation (*see* http://www.parliament.gr/en/).

Acknowledgements

For the fourth edition, Professor Theodore P. Fortsakis is greatly indebted to Nikolaos Vadivoulis, LLM (NYU '23).

Acknowledgements

General Introduction

§1. The Form of Government

1. The Hellenic Republic (*'Ελληνική Δημοκρατία'*, *'Elliniki Demokratia'*) is a unitary State. Its form of government as a parliamentary democracy is mainly laid down in the first article of the Constitution: '1. The form of government of Greece is that of a parliamentary republic. 2. Popular sovereignty is the foundation of government. 3. All powers derive from the People and exist for the People and the Nation; they shall be exercised as specified by the Constitution.'

2. Traditionally in legal scholarship, a distinction is made between the 'form of government' in the narrow sense, on the one hand, and its fundamental principles, on the other. The decisive criterion regarding the 'form of government' of a state is still the Aristotelian one; according to this, states are divided into monarchies, oligarchies, or democracies (Pol. 1279a 22 et seq.), depending on the number of persons constituting the supreme organ of the State. In this sense, democracy is explicitly defined in the Constitution as the form of government of Greece. On the other hand, the fundamental principles underpinning the form of government constitute the so-called organizational bases of the democratic state, which determine and conceptualize the core rules for the organization and exercise of state power. In the constitutional framework of the Greek legal order, these principles are the principle of representation, the parliamentary system of government, the separation of powers principle, the rule of law (*état de droit*) and the welfare state principles, as well as political pluralism, mainly manifested in the right of founding and joining political parties (*see infra* No. 441).

I. The Democratic Principle

3. According to the classic definition given by Aristotle in his Politics: 'there are two things that are sought to be defining features of democracy, the sovereignty of the majority and liberty' (Pol. 1310a 28 et seq.), meaning the 'egalitarian liberty' (Pol. 1317b 17). Both these elements of democracy are enshrined in the Constitution: on the one hand, through the establishment of a universal, regular, and free electoral system; on the other hand, through the protection of fundamental rights and freedoms, notably human dignity, free development of the personality and religious freedom, in terms of equality. They thus form barriers against any arbitrary action by the State, since as rigid elements of the Constitution, they are not subject to any kind of revision (*see infra* No. 51).

4. In particular, the democratic principle is enshrined in the first article of the Constitution, which, *inter alia*, confers a high degree of institutional symbolism because, until the present Constitution, the first article referred to religious issues (the prevailing religion of the nation, the status of the Orthodox Church, religious freedom, etc.). Nevertheless, the democratic principle is further guaranteed through several other constitutional clauses.

First, Article 50 introduces the principle of legality by explicitly restricting the powers of the President of the Republic, as Head of State, to those provided by the Constitution and the laws laid in accordance with it. This restrictive clause is *a fortiori* applicable to every organ of the State, mainly to those of the Executive, which are totally bound by the principle of legality.

Second, Article 51 paragraph 3 and Article 52 guarantee universal suffrage as well as the free and unfalsified expression of the will of the people.

Third, (the newly revised) Article 73 paragraph 6 vests, for the first time, the power of legislative initiative in the people, providing that the signatures of five hundred thousand (500 000) citizens have been collected. The proposed draft legislation may not relate to budgetary, foreign policy and national defence matters.

Lastly, Article 110 refers to the revision of the Constitution, and provides that it may only be decided by two subsequent Parliaments, making thus recourse to the popular vote indispensable.

II. The Principle of Representation

5. The Constitution establishes the system of representative democracy (Articles 51 et seq.). State power is not directly exercised by the people, but either through elected representatives with a free mandate (*mandat libre* or *représentatif*) or through other legitimized officials dependent on the confidence of Parliament or acting subject to their authority and competence according to the laws. In Greece, the system of representation is unicameral. In the past, under the Constitutions of 1844 and 1927, there were provisions for the function of a second chamber, called the 'Senate'. Since then, there have been proposals from time to time that the second chamber be revived, but none of these has borne fruit.

6. An exception to the principle of representation is the institution of the referendum (Article 44 paragraph 2 of the Constitution). However, since the introduction of the Constitution, only one referendum has been held: the one of July 2015. The voters were asked to approve or reject the draft proposal of the European Commission, the European Central Bank and the International Monetary Fund, which was addressed to the Greek government and contained their terms for the continuance of their financial assistance to Greece (*see infra* Nos 512 et seq.). In the referendum only 62.15% of registered voters (6,161,338 out of 9,914,244) participated; 61.31% of the voters answered 'no' to the draft proposal while 38.69%

answered 'yes'. Surprisingly, a few days later, the Greek government concluded an agreement with the aforementioned institutions which mainly adopted the terms of the draft proposal.

The announcement of the Prime Minister's intention to hold a referendum provoked turmoil in Greece and abroad. A number of substantial arguments were raised that it did not accord with constitutional provisions, mainly from opposition parties as well as from prominent members of the academic community, e.g., the Athens Bar Association, the largest scientific association in Greece. Briefly, opponents of the referendum advanced the following three arguments. First, the referendum violated Article 44 paragraph 2 a of the Constitution, since it did not concern 'crucial national matters' but purely fiscal matters. Second, the time between its announcement and its conduct was extremely short, only one week, and therefore did not allow reflection on the subject matter. Third, its content was extremely obscure and confusing. Despite these objections, the referendum took place. The Full Bench of the Council of State held, in its Ruling 2787/2015, that the related Act of the Cabinet of 26 June 2015 regarding the proposal to hold a referendum as well as the Presidential Decree 38/2015 regarding the announcement of the referendum were government acts and, consequently, were not subject to judicial examination.

III. The Non-hereditary Head of State: The 'Presidential' Dimension in the Parliamentary Republic

7. It may sound peculiar to define the democratic form of government in Greece as presidential and parliamentary at the same time; peculiar because the relationship between the Legislature and the Executive is basically different in a presidential system of government on the one hand and in a parliamentary system on the other. What the Greek Constitution lays down is a parliamentary republic in contrast to a parliamentary monarchy, which was the system of government in most Greek Constitutions of the past.

8. It was a decision of the framers of the Constitution (belonging to the government majority) to include the word 'presidential' in the declaration of the form of government in the first article of the Constitution, in order to emphasize one of the basic differences of the new Constitution from its predecessors, that is, an elected President of the Republic and not a hereditary king. It is to be noted that the official English translation of the Greek term 'presidential parliamentary democracy' of Article 1 paragraph 1 of the Constitution is 'parliamentary Republic'.

The opposition in Parliament criticized this decision of the government majority. It is true that the Constitution created a powerful Executive and especially a strong President of the Republic by granting him authority and powers which might well have been assigned to Parliament or the Government. During the framing of the Constitution, the parliamentary opposition claimed that by expanding the definition of the form of government (parliamentary democracy) by addition of the word 'presidential' in Article 1 of the Constitution – a provision which may not be amended – the government majority actually aimed to make constitutional amendment of the competences of the President of the Republic impossible. The majority, while drafting the Constitution, assured critics that such an interpretation would exceed the aims of Article 1. The opposition's objections proved to be unjustified when the time came for the Constitutional Revision of 1985/1986, which focused exclusively on the competences and powers of the President of the Republic. There were no serious legal claims that the amendment was unconstitutional as a whole, owing to the term 'presidential' in Article 1.

IV. The Parliamentary System of Government

9. Two basic articles of the Constitution form the foundation of the parliamentary system of government. The first one, concerning the relationship between Parliament and government, is enshrined in Article 84: '1. The Government must enjoy the confidence of Parliament. The Government shall be obliged to request a vote of confidence by Parliament within fifteen days of the date the Prime Minister shall have been sworn in and may also do so at any other time … 2. Parliament may decide to withdraw its confidence from the government or from a member of the government … .'

10. The second main provision on parliamentarism, concerning the relationship between the President of the Republic and the Government, is laid down in Article 37: '1. The President of the Republic shall appoint the Prime Minister and, on his recommendation, shall appoint and dismiss the other members of the Cabinet and the Undersecretaries. 2. The leader of the party having the overall majority of seats in Parliament shall be appointed Prime Minister. If no party has the absolute majority, the President of the Republic shall give the leader of the party with a relative majority an exploratory mandate, in order to ascertain the possibility of forming a government enjoying the confidence of the Parliament … .'

11. The procedure to be followed in appointing a government is set out so explicitly and in such detail in the above provision that the powers and competences of the President of the Republic in this respect are strictly defined and limited; essentially his role in appointing a Prime Minister and Ministers is confined to simply following the steps set out in the procedure. Further provisions of Article 37 on the process of forming a government will be mentioned in the Chapter on the Executive (*see infra* Nos 183 et seq.). What is important to emphasize here is that parliamentarism is understood as being two-dimensional. It concerns with almost equal gravity the relationship between the Government and Parliament on the one hand and between the Government and the Head of State on the other.

12. The dependence of the Government on the Parliament's confidence has been the major pole and the core of Greek parliamentarism, and the major concern of legal scholars has been to make this dependence an exclusive one. The Government should be recognized to have no other dependence, such as, for example, a dependence on the confidence of the Head of State.

Historically, under the Constitution of 1864, which was based on the system of parliamentary democracy, governments had been dependent on the Crown as well.

This led Prime Minister Charilaos Trikoupis to declare the principle of pure or authentic parliamentarism in 1875, which was recognized as a constitutional convention. It acquired the force of a constitutional rule in the Constitution, which for the first time established explicitly the obligation of the President of the Republic to appoint as Prime Minister the leader of the party holding the majority in Parliament.

The process leading to pure parliamentarism was concluded in 1986 by a constitutional amendment, which abolished the discretionary power of the President of the Republic to dismiss the Government after consulting with the 'Council of the Republic'. This institution was created by the Constitution following the old model of the 'Council of the Crown'. The 'Council of the Republic' had been criticized in constitutional writings as a 'camouflage' for the President's wide discretionary powers, which ultimately resulted in its abolition under the Revision of 1986.

This historical background explains in a sense the meticulous constitutional provisions on the appointment of the Prime Minister and of the Cabinet (*see infra* Nos 183 et seq.).

V. The Separation of Powers Principle

13. Provision is made for the separation of powers in all Greek Constitutions, dating back to the time of the War of Independence. In the current Constitution, the principle of the separation of powers is enshrined in Article 26 of the Constitution, as follows: '1. The legislative powers shall be exercised by the Parliament and the President of the Republic. 2. The executive powers shall be exercised by the President of the Republic and the Government. 3. The judicial powers shall be exercised by courts of law, the decisions of which shall be executed in the name of the Greek people.'

The Constitution uses, by way of accurate translation, the terms 'legislative function', 'executive function' and 'judicial function' instead of 'powers' (legislative, executive, judicial). Though it apparently underlines the functional separation of the three main directions of state activity, it does not underestimate their organic separation that is, the assignment of the three different functions of the State to separate organs. As a matter of fact, Article 26 is mainly interpreted as a guarantee of the organic separation of powers.

14. The separation of powers, as in every parliamentary system of government, is not absolute but relative, regarding the relationship between the Legislative and the Executive Branches which are not 'independent' but 'interdependent'. Article 26 itself is referred to the President of the Republic as an organ of both the Legislative and Executive Branches. Other provisions of the Constitution determine the interdependence between the legislative and the executive power, *inter alia*, by assigning legislative jurisdiction to the Government, such as legislative initiative, and jurisdiction for administrative acts or judicial jurisdiction to Parliament, such as impeachment proceedings for members of the Government.

15. The 'interdependency' of powers, of course, does not involve judicial power, which is institutionally separate and independent. The practical importance of the separation of powers principle lies nowadays primarily in the independence of the Judiciary. Its main consequence is that irrevocable court rulings may not be altered even by statute. In fact, both the Constitution (Articles 94 paragraph 4, and 95 paragraph 5) and ordinary Greek legislation (Act 3068/2002 and the Codes of Civil and Administrative Procedure, Article 198 of the Administrative Court Procedure Code and Article 50 of the Presidential Decree 18/1989) contain provisions for the compulsory enforcement of judicial decisions and the compliance of the executive power with such decisions.

VI. The Rule of Law Principle

16. The rule of law principle is explicitly declared in Article 25 paragraph 1 of the Constitution. In particular, it states, 'The rights of the human being as an individual and as a member of the society and the principle of the welfare state rule of law are guaranteed by the State. All agents of the State shall be obliged to ensure the unhindered and effective exercise thereof. These rights also apply to the relations between individuals to which they are appropriate. Restrictions of any kind which, according to the Constitution, may be imposed upon these rights, should be provided either directly by the Constitution or by statute, should a reservation exist in the latter's favour, and should respect the principle of proportionality.'

17. Until the Revision of 2001, the rule of law principle was not explicitly mentioned in the Constitution as part of the form of government. Its content was, nevertheless, guaranteed through several other constitutional clauses, not subject to any form of revision. Thereby, an almost full catalogue of fundamental rights and freedoms, including social rights (Articles 2, 4 et seq.) is sufficiently guaranteed in the Constitution. Accordingly, the obligation of State organs to respect fully fundamental rights and freedoms is shown to be the most important element of the rule of law principle. Nevertheless, the Constitution imposes the separation of powers with the independence of the Judiciary as its main consequence and establishes a hierarchy of norms and the duty of the Judiciary to review the constitutionality of laws (Article 93 paragraph 4) as well as to review administrative action (Articles 94 and 95). It also guarantees every person's right of access to a court (Article 20 paragraph 1).

VII. The Welfare State Principle

18. The rule of law principle is supplemented by the welfare state principle. The Constitution contains several provisions on social rights and social limitations of fundamental rights and freedoms.

19. Indicatively, it is provided that the State shall protect the family, motherhood and childhood, as well as the poor and the homeless, ensuring that all citizens enjoy a decent standard of living by means of a system of a minimum guaranteed income. It furthermore imposes on the State an obligation to care for the creation of conditions of employment for all citizens, and to make provision for health, social security and free education. It also contains provisions on the so-called economic constitution. In its revised form, the Constitution explicitly enshrines the principle of the welfare State in Article 25 paragraph 1. This explicit statement of the principle complements and supports the protection of other social rights, apart from those already safeguarded by the Constitution.

§2. State Territory

20. Greece occupies the southern part of the Balkan peninsula of southern Europe. It comprises a mainland and islands and covers an area of 131,957 km^2. Of the total area, 25,166 km^2 is made up of 169 inhabited islands and almost 6000 uninhabited islets. Greece shares borders with Albania, North Macedonia, Bulgaria and Turkey.

The territory of Greece was acquired gradually from 1830, when the modern Greek State was first recognized by the international community (*see infra* No. 24), to 1947, when the Treaty of Paris united Greece with the Dodecanese Islands (for a more detailed account of the formation of Greek territory, *see* the chapter on constitutional history *infra* Nos 24 et seq.).

§3. Population

21. The 2021 census results have not yet been published. According to the previous census of 18 March 2011, the Greek population (Greek citizens and foreigners who have permanent residence in the country) was 10,816,286. Males make up 49.0% of the population, while females, 51.0%. The average age of the population was estimated at 41.9 years and 91.6% of the population were of Greek nationality. According to Eurostat (2014), the population density was 83.3 per km^2. According to the World Bank Group (2015), the urban population amounts to 78% approximately, given that a constant movement to urban centres has taken place over the last forty years. Athens, the capital city of Greece, with its surrounding area (Attica), has 3,828,434 inhabitants (35.39% of the total population, 2011 census).

22. In 2015 over 800,000 refugees and migrants entered Greece from Turkey through irregular channels (UN Refugee Agency). The majority of them left Greece in order to settle in another country. Nevertheless, there are still tens of thousands of refugees and migrants who have been stranded in Greece since Greece's neighbours decided to close their borders. The European Union (EU) is currently trying to address the problem through the implementation of a special agreement with Turkey, concerning the management of refugees and migrant flows, as well as an ambitious resettlement scheme.

23. According to the latest statistics provided by the General Secretariat for Greek abroad, more than 5,000,000 persons of Greek origin live abroad in 140 countries (United States of America, with about 3,000,000; Europe, with about 1,000,000; Australia with 650,000 to 700,000; Canada, with about 350,000; Asia-Africa, with about 100,000; and Central and South America, with about 60,000). During the period 2008–2013, 427,000 residents of Greece left the country permanently due to the financial crisis (Bank of Greece). Many of them were highly educated and had professional experience (a 'brain drain'). The Constitution (Article 108 paragraph 1) provides for a special duty of care by the Greek State towards expatriate Greeks. 'The State must take care for emigrant Greeks and for the maintenance of their ties with the Fatherland. The State shall also attend to the education, the social and professional advancement of Greeks working outside the State.'

Part I. Constitutional History, Sources of Constitutional Law, Codification and Interpretation

Chapter 1. An Outline of Greek Constitutional History

24. The declaration of the Greek Revolution in 1821, the lengthy war and its successful outcome with the establishment of an independent State inaugurated changes that introduced Greek society to the modern era. These changes occurred in all sectors of social, political, and economic life, and gradually dominated in different ways and at different times. The changes which characterize the whole Greek society of the nineteenth century became more apparent in the years of the Revolution. From the First National Assembly and the Provisional Constitution of Epidaurus (1822) procedures of political unification and integration began with the introduction of modern institutions and machinery: the formation of a constitution, the separation of powers and the establishment of a governmental infrastructure.

However, the introduction of modern political institutions was often accompanied by elements that belonged to a different, traditional political culture. This was reflected in a society which acknowledged itself and its future in a different way from the past and which consequently sought new forms of existence.

In particular, during the period 1897–1922, very important events and headlong developments determine the evolution of Greece and decisively contribute to its formation as a modern state. It is a period of spectacular changes, critical choices, acute crises and a ten-year war, which ends up in the territorial expansion of Greece on the one hand and the dramatic termination of the Asia Minor Campaign on the other hand and aims at the formation of a state radically different from that of the past.

Subsequently, the period between 1923 and 1940 (between the Catastrophe of Asia Minor and the entrance of the country into the Second World War) could be defined as the Greek 'inter-war period', in contrast to its European counterpart. The defeat of Greek forces in Asia Minor signalled the end of a decade of continuous wars, but also the cancellation of the 'Great Idea' after a hundred years of territorial expansion and population integration. The demands of domestic re-organization, on the basis of new political-social agendas, were to become fundamental characteristics of the times. In addition, this period – perturbed as it was and full of contradictions and retrogressions – is fundamental for a deeper understanding of how modern Greek society was formed. For the first time, the Greek State would include within its borders the maximum percentage of Greek people. Out of the ruins of the Catastrophe, a period of transition was born without any dominant ideological binding fabric.

The involvement of Greece in the Second World War began on 28 October 1940 when Italy declared war on Greece. From this date, the Greek-Italian war began in the mountains of Albania, which turned into a major focal point of national unanimity, determination and anti-Fascist spirit and ended in a series of impressive and unexpected successes that at the same time constituted the first victory of the Allies against the Axis. Greece was liberated in October 1944, but the euphoria of liberation was immediately succeeded by an impasse created by domestic political conflicts. As well as liberation from conquerors, the Greek resistance struggle was aimed at social and political reforms that would apply after the departure of the invader from the country, expressing the demand of the Greek people for a better future and the restoration of democratic legality. However, the disparity of these political aims, the legacy of the friction of the inter-war period and the instability of institutions, escalated into a bitter civil war which lasted until 1949. Its consequences were immediate, long-lasting and disastrous for the political, social and institutional development of Greece.

The following years (1945–1960) began soon after the termination of the Civil War, establishing a critical period marked by the course of polarization between the two superpowers, the USA and the USSR, producing the Cold War. The consequences of conflicts inside Greece on the one hand and of international tensions on the other underscored the social-political developments in Greece for several decades. On the one hand, large-scale changes took place, such as urbanization, industrial development and emigration. In parallel with these changes, reactions were engendered inside a torn society, which often refused to negotiate with its past and was unable to rationalize its dilemmas (e.g., the Cyprus problem, political prisoners).

During the 1960s, the country was shaken by conflicts among parties and by violent social confrontations, which were sealed by the military coup in 1967. However, these institutional aberrations had begun much earlier and concerned election frauds, political assassinations and, mainly, the arbitrariness of the throne. At the same time, rapid strides were made on the economic front. Developments in the Western world were also reflected in Greek society in various fields, such as the mobilization of young people, musical culture, fashion, and so on.

The 1970s were marked by the transition from the junta to parliamentary democracy, which for the first time after 1974 existed without social exclusions. In the second half of the decade, with the complete restoration of social liberties, the country became politically stable and Europe-oriented (exemplified by the accession of Greece to the European Economic Community). In the following years (1980–1990), changes in governing subverted the establishment and consolidated hierarchies of decades past. Change, which constituted the principal slogan of that time, did not concern the materialization of real proclamations, but rather the undeniable fact of social reforms being introduced and of new strata emerging that altered the profile of Greek society.

Finally, during the most recent decades, the entire world – and Greece along with it – was shaken by rapid changes in politics, society and economy. The end of the

Cold War, the European integration course and the political-ideological convergence formed the new conditions in which the country entered during the time of globalization. The modernization of the State, the position of the country in a constantly changing world, but also the determination of the national identity are the open issues at stake that the country faces since the dawn of the twenty-first century.

The evolution of Greece's constitutional institutions is inseparably linked with her turbulent history as a modern State. The opening of Greek society to modernity indeed represented a new departure at the time and a new experience for the people. Between the outbreak of the War of Independence and 1974, there have been no fewer than twenty-six changes in the country's system of government. These innovations resulted in general changes in political life, which were expressed on different levels. First, there were changes in the institutions through which the political autonomy of the Greek nation was achieved. Secondly, there were changes which involved the formation of new political hierarchies, that is the social origin and composition of the personnel that staffed and operated the new institutions.

These profound changes which affected the whole of Greek society reversed the pre-revolutionary established institutions, hierarchies and procedures formed during the Ottoman occupation. The pulling down of a world and the building of a new one provoked social reversals and produced antagonisms which often took the form of conflicts in the age-long struggle for freedom. Through these conflicts, the new institutions prevailed and offered the possibility of the unification and modernization of the social-political arena, which was inaugurated by the Greek Revolution.

§1. The Period of the Struggle for Independence (1821–1833): The First Hellenic Republic

I. Local Constitutions

25. The establishment of central, modern, western-type political institutions was probably as great an undertaking on the part of the Greek Revolution as that of political independence. It is worth mentioning that as early as 1797 (that is, before the War of Independence had begun) the Greek intellectual Rigas Velestinlis-Pheraios had prepared a draft Constitution, inspired by the French Constitutions of 1793 and 1795. In this document, Rigas proposed the organization of all the subjugated Balkan peoples into one single State, framed according to the principle of popular sovereignty. Furthermore, the preamble of the draft Constitution contained a declaration of human rights. Although this draft was never formally adopted it did exert a significant influence on the subsequent development of Greek constitutional ideology.

Certain local political formations or constitutions already functioned in the first years of the Revolution and facilitated provisional government and military set-ups, until the eventual establishment of the 'Assembly of the Nation'. They suggest the communal institutions formed from the time of Ottoman rule, and as a result showed up primarily in the Peloponnese (Achaean Government, Messenian Senate or the

Senate of the Argolis and others which were soon joined to the Peloponnesian Senate), in west-central Greece (Organization of West Mainland-Greece) and east-central Greece (Legal Provision of east-central Greece-*Areios Pagos*), as well as in Crete (Regime of Crete).

Nevertheless, certain islands, which enjoyed a regime of more or less extended communal administration before the Revolution, followed the existing forms of communal administration. Samos was an exception since Lykourgos Logothetis had consolidated a local regime on the island.

It should be mentioned that one important element in the establishment of these early local constitutions is the initial and perhaps incomplete manifestation of political self-determination and individual freedom. They were in fact imperfect legal texts, in the form of declarations, with a low degree of enforceability.

II. The Constitution of Epidaurus of 1822

26. The formation of a central political scene and the focusing of political procedures in this administration signified primarily and principally the end of local and regional political centres and of the political-administrative organizations that had been formed in all the rebellious regions in the first months of the Revolution.

In December 1821, the First National Assembly opened its proceedings at Piada (ancient Epidauros). Representatives from the most rebellious regions attended the assembly. Most of the representatives were local notables and clergymen from Morea, Rumeli and the islands. Although they had actually never been elected, their capacity to act as such was never disputed. These were the pre-revolutionary social elites to which the Phanariotes and scholars, who had reached the rebellious districts in the first months of the Revolution, were added. Conversely, Dimitrios Ypsilantis and the most prominent chieftains from Rumeli and the Peloponnese were absent.

The most significant act of the assembly was the *Provisional Constitution of Epidaurus*, that is to say, the first Constitution of the rebellious Greeks, in which the *Declaration of Independence* was included. The Provisional Constitution, a work of the Italian Gallina, included the liberal and democratic principles of the French revolutionary Constitutions (1793 and 1795), as well as those of the Constitution of the United States of America (1787).

Most of its one hundred and ten (110) paragraphs concerned the organization of the State on a multi-central model. It provided for two annual bodies: a Legislative Branch and an Executive Branch, whose duties were nevertheless not clearly defined. They had the same rank of authority and powers, as far as legislation was concerned.

An eleven-member Supreme Court was also established, the members of which were to be appointed both by the Legislative and the Executive Branches. The Executive – a five-member Head of State, not an actual government – appointed the eight Secretaries of State.

The Epidaurus Constitution was only partially put into effect, owing to difficulties arising from the struggle for independence, as well as the emerging tensions between politicians and the military.

III. The Constitution of Astros of 1823 ('The Law of Epidaurus')

27. Two years after the declaration of the Revolution in the Peloponnese, in March 1823, the proceedings of the Second National Assembly opened at Astros, Kynouria. In the time that elapsed between the First and Second National Assembly, the successful military operations kept pace with the worsening of the political controversies. In the framework of political factions, the attendants of the National Assembly issued a restricted revision of the constitution, which confirmed the basic principles of the Provisional Constitution of Epidaurus.

The Assembly amended the Constitution of 1822, naming it 'Law of Epidaurus', in order to emphasize its continuity with the preceding one. In the framework of political factions, the attendants of the National Assembly issued a restricted revision of the Constitution, which confirmed the basic principles of the Provisional Constitution of Epidaurus. At the same time, it made an explicit provision for the formal precedence of the Constitution over ordinary legislation, while it reinforced the protection of fundamental rights and freedoms which had been insufficiently safeguarded in the preceding Constitution. It had also been decided to convene anew after two years, in order to proceed with further necessary amendments.

However, this Constitution was not put into place without difficulty. The decision on the abolition of the regional local-administrative organizations may have given the power to organs of the central administration (mainly the Legislative Branch), but it placed them in the middle of political contests. In the summer of 1823 open hostility broke out between the Legislature and the Executive Branches, led by the islanders and the military leaders respectively. This civil conflict continued until the end of 1824, when the islanders finally prevailed, offering though to the foreign powers their first pretext to involve themselves in Greek affairs. From that time onwards, such involvement would be continuous.

IV. The Constitution of Troizina of 1827 ('The Political Constitution of Greece')

28. The Third National Assembly took place under different conditions than the two previous ones. The civil conflicts of 1824 had terminated, without however solving the organizational weaknesses of the central administration, while the persecutions of the defeated continued even when Ibrahim had landed in the Peloponnese (beginning of 1825). The preparations for the organization of a National Assembly which had begun in September 1825 did not advance in these conditions. Conversely, the rival factions were reorganized, creating renewed tension. Finally, the Third National Assembly opened its proceedings on 6 April 1826 at Piada but was soon interrupted because of the fall of Missolongi. In the meantime, it was decided that the Greeks had to appeal to Great Britain to intervene and determine the terms of the negotiation, while a new administration, called 'the Administrative Committee', was formed. In the autumn of the same year (1826) attempts were made to call another National Assembly, but without success. Conversely, small-scale civil conflicts broke out in Corinthia and Nauplion while at the beginning of 1827 the rival factions organized separate assemblies at Aegina and

Ermioni. Finally, the assemblies were united at Troizina at the end of March 1827, thus expressing the wish of both sides to achieve a common political agreement.

The 'Political Constitution of Greece', which would no longer be provisional, redefined the terms of negotiation with the Ottoman Empire seeking independence and not autonomy. This Constitution manifests an attempt to introduce strong central authority in order to overcome the problems of too many separate centres of power, without compromising the democratic and liberal character of the system of government. Thus, many provisions of the new Constitution were devoted to the protection of fundamental rights and freedoms, such as religious freedom, freedom of education, property rights, equality and non-discrimination.

Further enacted was the separation of powers principle. Parliament, whose members would be elected every three years, was to exercise legislative power. On the other hand, the head of the executive power would be placed in a single-member administrative organ, namely the Governor. Count Ioannis Kapodistrias was chosen for this position with a seven-year term of office. In August of the same year (1827), Kapodistrias accepted the proposition of the National Assembly. Until his arrival, a special Vice-Governmental Committee would assume his duties as it was formed for this purpose.

V. Ioannis Kapodistrias' Authoritarian Regime

29. During the five year-period 1823–1827, the various political groups and factions were engaged in incessant political antagonism which sometimes took the form of armed conflict. The divided political field and the fluid character of political alliances did not allow the winners to impose their dominance with any degree of permanency. The fluidity of the political situation favoured the successive reversal of power. Furthermore, this situation affected the negotiating ability of the Greeks in a period (1827) when Britain and Russia seemed to seek, each one for its own reasons, a favourable resolution for the rebellious Greeks. Under these conditions, the unanimous selection of Kapodistrias as Governor during the proceedings of the Third National Assembly was associated with his experience as a diplomat. His post in the top rank of the Russian Ministry of Foreign Affairs and in a period (1815–1822) in which the Art of Diplomacy had reached high levels revealed that he had the qualifications to carry out the complex and fine diplomatic manipulations that the promulgation of Greek claims required. The political groups and factions that had chosen him needed the diplomat Kapodistrias. Thus, at the time of the formation of the Constitution of Troizina, they ensured that the work of the Governor was subjected to the control of the Parliament, which was controlled by themselves.

Ioannis Kapodistrias arrived in Greece in January 1828 and was welcomed by the people with great enthusiasm. Using his prestige and reputation – and probably surprising the political groups and factions – Kapodistrias achieved right from the beginning the suspension of the Constitution, the self-dissolution of the Parliament and the concentration of all powers into the hands of the Governor. With the cooperation of Parliament, he immediately suspended the Constitution of 1827. Parliament resigned and surrendered all its powers to the Governor. An interim advisory body consisting of twenty-seven members, the 'Panhellenium', was formed until the election of a new Parliament. In legal terms, the suspension of the Constitution and the dissolution – by its own decision – of the Parliament constituted a coup d'état. The Fourth National Assembly convened in Argos from 11 July to 6 August of 1829, ratified the powers concentrated in the hands of the Governor, and legitimized the suspension of the Constitution. It accepted that in the prevailing circumstances and until the fate of Greece was definitely settled, the country could not be governed in the framework of a permanent constitution. Also, it established a 'Senate' instead of the 'Panhellenium', consisting also of twenty-seven members. Its competence was advisory too. The Assembly empowered the Government to draft a new Constitution in consultation with the Senate on the basis of the same principles of the Constitutions of 1822, 1823 and 1827.

Kapodistrias was undoubtedly an important political personality, who managed to lay the foundations of the new State, starting from scratch. The reforms he attempted in the organization and function of the regional administration were the first systematic intervention in the direction of the creation of a modern state. His primary concern was the abolition of regional autonomy from which the traditional but also the newly established political groups of Greek society drew their economic power and socio-political force. The number of administrative districts was reduced whereas the organs of regional administration and the persons that staffed them were subjected to the control of the central power. These measures, which led to a rupture between Kapodistrias and the local social elites of Greek society, were fundamentally similar to those adopted by the regency and Otto a few years later.

Finally, as Governor he put his diplomatic skills in favour of the Nation. From September 1828 the ambassadors of Great Britain, France and Russia were holding counsel at Porus in order to decide on the frontiers of the new Greek State. Their suggestion was made after taking into account, to a certain extent, the claims of the Greek side, as these were expressed in the memorials that Kapodistrias had sent on 11/23 September and 30 October/11 November. Thus, they suggested that the Greek territory should include the regions of Central Greece situated south of the borderline running from the Gulf of Amvrakikos in the west to the Pagasitikos Gulf in the east. Despite this decision and as the conference at Porus was not yet completed the British Minister of Foreign Affairs and the ambassadors of the other two countries were signing a protocol in London. This protocol (4–16 November 1828) excluded Central Greece from the Greek territory. The frontiers of the new Greek State that were in formation included only the Peloponnese and the Cyclades. However, some months later, the propositions of the three ambassadors at Porus at the conference were accepted. The frontier line Amvrakikos-Pagasitikos was adopted by the Great Powers in the Protocol of 10–22 March 1829, which was signed in London. Crete was not included in the Greek territory. In September of the same year, the Ottoman Empire was obliged to accept this protocol, in the context of capitulating with Russia (Treaty of Adrianople).

At the beginning of the following year, specifically in the period 22 January–3 February 1830, the three Great Powers proceeded with the signing of a new protocol, again in London, known as the Treaty of London for Greek Independence. It was the first official international act which acknowledged Greece as an independent sovereign state and not a state obliged to pay tribute to the Ottoman Empire.

This important decision was accompanied by the definition of a new borderline. The regions between the River Achelous in the west and Sperchios in the east were included in the territory of the new state. The newly formed State had at that time an area of 47,546 km^2, while its population was estimated at 753,400 inhabitants.

VI. The 'Hegemonic' Constitution of 1832

30. Kapodistrias was assassinated in September 1831. The Senate nominated three persons to form a Governmental Committee. The Committee convoked a National Assembly which assigned executive power to Avgoustinos Kapodistrias, brother of the assassinated Governor, ousting the opponents of Kapodistrias from power. The Assembly also enacted the Constitution of 1832, known as the 'Hegemonic Constitution', because the office of Head of State was hereditary and its holder bore the title 'Hegemone'.

The Constitution of 1832 was never implemented. On being excluded from office the anti-Kapodistrian party withdrew from the Assembly. The clash of opinions led to civil conflict, which ended in a victory for the 'constitutional' party, that is, those opposed to Kapodistrias. They appointed a seven-member Committee, which convoked another Assembly in 1832. The Assembly endorsed the decision of the 'protecting powers' (England, France and Russia) that Otto, second son of King Ludwig I of Bavaria, would become 'King of Greece'. The Assembly also started drafting a new Constitution. However, the protecting powers insisted that the Constitution ought to be drafted with the cooperation of the King. Thus, in August 1832, elements controlled by the 'protecting' powers dissolved the National Assembly and work on drafting the new constitutional charter came to nothing.

§2. The Period of Absolute Monarchy (1833–1843)

31. King Otto arrived in Greece in January 1833, and his arrival was greeted with lively celebrations. Despite being a minor he did not assume his duties until June 1835. In the meantime, royal power was exercised by a three-member regency. During the first decade of Otto's reign, there was no kind of constitutional text in force. There were no legal constraints on the power of the Regent, or the King when he entered his majority. There was no Parliament; personal freedoms were diminished. Power was exercised on the basis of the Treaty of London of 1832, not the wishes of the Greek people or their representatives. Key positions were occupied by Bavarians; the regime came to be known as the '*Bavarokratia*', the rule of the Bavarians. Opposition to the regime grew and culminated in the 'revolution' of 1843 and later in the dethronement of Otto (1862).

Despite its despotic nature, the period of absolute monarchy was characterized by a quick and efficacious organization of the State. It was during these years that a regular army was formed, and the administrative functions of the State were organized. Expanded legislation, the basis of the later development of the Greek legal system, was introduced, to a great extent the result of a task successfully undertaken by Georg Ludwig von Maurer, a professor of law at the University of Munich, who came to Greece as a member of the regency.

§3. The Period of Constitutional Monarchy (1843–1862) and the Constitution of 1844

32. On 3 September 1843, troops from the Athens garrison surrounded the palace and, with the support of the people, demanded a constitution. Otto was forced by the circumstances to proclaim elections to a National Assembly, which would proceed to draw up a constitution. A draft Constitution, which was prepared by a parliamentary committee, was voted on in February 1844. The Constitution was submitted to King Otto who sanctioned and promulgated it.

The Constitution of 1844 was in its essence a pact between the monarch and the people. It was not a product of a sovereign constituent assembly but a '*charte octroyée*', which acquired legal force by the act of royal ratification. In other words, the monarch was essentially the only holder of constitutional authority but agreed to limit his powers through the drafting of a Constitution in order to retain his throne.

The monarch was the supreme organ of the State; it was up to the people, not the monarch, to prove competence in any field. He was the head of the Executive, while also participating in the exercise of legislative power since he had the right of legislative initiative. He was also competent to appoint the members of the Upper House (Senators) and judges. Ministerial responsibility for the actions of the monarch was also introduced.

The Constitution recognized the principle of the separation of powers and guaranteed fundamental rights and freedoms (as defined by the French Revolution). These provisions provided the necessary basis for the working of a parliamentary system, but the conditions were not yet ripe for this potential to be realized. The Constitution of 1844 was monarchical, not democratic, even though the power of the monarch was now limited. It was also an absolutely rigid Constitution; there was no provision for its revision.

Apart from the Constitution the Assembly also enacted a very remarkable electoral law, revolutionary for its time, even by European standards. It introduced universal direct suffrage – although without, of course, granting the vote to women.

The Constitution of 1844 was never fully implemented. Otto endeavoured to regain his previous unrestricted powers by making Parliament subject to his political will, intervening in all sorts of ways in the electoral process, exerting influence on the press and prosecuting opponents. Although in the beginning, he had enjoyed indisputable popularity, thanks to his 'great idea' of reviving the Byzantine Empire, his continual interference in the workings of the State, preventing the political institutions from running smoothly, generated new popular opposition to him, which continued to increase.

§4. The First Period of Parliamentary Monarchy (1862–1924)

I. The Election of King George and the Constitution of 1864

33. In October 1862 the people and the army of Athens revolted against King Otto and dethroned him and the dynasty. The revolutionary directory convoked a Constituent Assembly to reconstitute the State and proclaimed the election of a new King by the people. Prince Alfred of England was elected 'King of the Greeks'. He did not accept the election, because, under Article 3 of the London Protocol of 1830, which was signed by England, France and Russia and which recognized Greece as an independent monarchy, members of the royal families of the great powers signatory to the Protocol could not get involved with the Greek throne. Thus, in March 1863, at the proposal of Great Britain, the Assembly unanimously elected Prince George Christian Wilhelm of Denmark as 'King George, King of the Greeks', not as 'King of Greece' like Otto. This differentiation was meant to underline that the new dynasty stemmed from the will of the people. The proposed candidacy of George was accompanied by the ceding of the Ionian Islands to Greece by the British. Greek territory was thus enlarged to 50,211 km^2.

In the meantime, the Assembly was working on the new Constitution. Though it was originally decided that the Constitution would not be sanctioned by the King, the Assembly submitted it to him. King George suggested two alterations, one concerning the revision clause of the Constitution and another concerning the citizenship of Roman Catholic priests. The Assembly deleted the provision that Roman Catholic functionaries should have Greek citizenship but did not consent to the proposal of the King to make the revision procedure more flexible. At all events, the 1864 Constitution did not represent a 'deal' between the two sides but was the work of the sovereign constituent assembly. The King played no formal role in its drafting, nor did he sign its ratification, as with the Constitution of 1844.

The new Constitution, influenced by the previous Constitution of 1844 as well as by the Belgian Constitution of 1831 and to a lesser extent by the Danish Constitution of 1845, was democratic and liberal. The form of government was that of a parliamentary monarchy based on national sovereignty and on the principle of the separation of powers with an independent Judiciary. It also introduced the system of the single Parliament, rejecting the institution of the Senate – a groundbreaking move at that time. The list of fundamental rights and freedoms was enlarged. Finally, the competences and powers of the King were restricted to those explicitly laid down in the Constitution. It thereby established the principle that the burden of proving competence in any area should lie with the King, not with the people. The 1864 Constitution provided the nucleus on which all subsequent Constitutions were based.

This new Constitution was not implemented without some degree of upheaval. The socioeconomic structures and political traditions of the country made it hard for the ideals of democracy and liberty to be rapidly assimilated and put into effect. During the first decade after the introduction of the 1864 Constitution, the practice was followed of appointing governments selected by the King, while the palace continued to insist on playing a more general political role.

Continual interference by the palace in political life ran counter to the institutional strengthening of the Parliament and caused great discontent in the political community. One mouthpiece of this displeasure was Charilaos Trikoupis. King George I, wishing to appease this opposition, appointed Trikoupis Prime Minister in 1875 and proclaimed the principle of 'declared confidence' (a system of pure parliamentarism), namely that the Government appointed would be that which enjoyed the demonstrated confidence of the majority of the representatives of the nation. Thus the parliamentary system was introduced to Greece.

During the period in which the 1864 Constitution remained in force, its inherent liberalism led to recognition in case law of its higher legal force; in a groundbreaking development judicial control of the constitutionality of the laws was introduced, on the model of the American system (Rulings 18/1871 and 23/1897 of the *Areios Pagos* [the Supreme Civil and Criminal Court]).

During the reign of George I Greece was awarded by the Congress of Berlin (1878) and the ambassadorial summit of Constantinople (1881) the regions of Thessaly and part of Epirus; thus, the territorial area was increased to 63,606 km^2. However, in 1897, following a failed military campaign by Greece against the Ottoman Empire, the country was obliged to return to the latter a small part of these territories. From 1875 onwards the country was in dire straits: maladministration and nepotism, economic crisis culminating in the bankruptcy of 1893, the military defeat of 1897 and the imposition of international financial control in 1898. The situation was exacerbated by the departure from politics of Charilaos Trikoupis in 1895.

II. The Revolt of 1909, the 'Revision' of the Constitution in 1911 and the 'National Schism'

34. A long crisis dominating Greek politics even after 1875 was interrupted by a revolt in Athens in the year 1909. The revolt was organized by a part of the army inspired by liberal and nationalist ideals, along the lines of the uprising of the Young Turks in 1908, and was assisted by political parties and the people. The rebels were not demanding the entire overturning of the political system, but simply reforms of the army and administration. Eleftherios Venizelos, a well-known high-ranking politician from Crete (which was not yet part of Greece but enjoyed autonomy, having broken away from the Ottoman Empire) was asked to form a government. Eleftherios Venizelos came to Greece and, without assuming an official government post, proposed that an election be held to allow the Revision of the 1864 Constitution. The country went to the polls in 1910 and the Parliament thus elected acted to revise the Constitution. The revision was completed in 1911, but the procedure for the revision, as laid down in Article 110 of the Constitution of 1864, was violated. For this reason, the so-called Revision of 1911 was as a matter of fact a product of a constituent will.

The 1911 revision of the Constitution entailed numerous innovations, chief among them the delegation to a special court, and no longer to Parliament, of responsibility for verifying the validity of parliamentary elections, the introduction of permanent tenure for civil servants, the strengthening of the independence of the judiciary, the establishment of free and mandatory basic education, simplification of procedures for legislation and revision of legislation, and greater protection for civil rights.

On completion of its work of revision, the Parliament was dissolved. There followed the election of March 1912, won by the party of. Venizelos with an overwhelming majority. It was thus under the leadership of Venizelos that Greece took part, in 1912–1913, in the two Balkan Wars, the first against the Ottoman Empire, and the second against Bulgaria. By the time these hostilities were over Greece had doubled her population and extended her territory to embrace part of Epirus, Macedonia, the islands of the eastern Aegean, Crete and part of Thrace. The surface area of the country had now increased to 127,000 km^2.

It was not long before the new Constitution ran into difficulties. In 1913 King George was assassinated and succeeded by Constantine. The disagreement between the new King and Venizelos on the Greek stance in the First World War led to the emergence of the so-called National Schism. The stubborn refusal of Constantine (whose wife was Sophia, sister of Kaiser Wilhelm II, the German Emperor) to approve Greece's involvement in the war on the side of Britain, France and Russia led to the resignation of the Venizelos government, which felt unable to accept royal interference in matters of foreign policy. In the ensuing election (31 May 1915) the party of Venizelos was returned to power. However, Parliament was again dissolved in October 1915, when the Venizelos government resigned once more. An election was called for December 1915 but Venizelos' party, in protest at the continuing violations of the Constitution by the monarch, refused to participate. Venizelos refused to acknowledge the result of the election and departed for Thessaloniki, where he formed a government separate from the administration elected in Athens. Thus for a short period of time, Greece was governed by two governments, one in Athens and one in Thessaloniki (1916–1917). The administration set up by the party of Venizelos in Thessaloniki declared that Greece would enter the war. In 1917, after British and French troops had disembarked in Piraeus and trained their artillery on the palace, Constantine abdicated in favour of his second son Alexander, who appointed Venizelos as Prime Minister of a reunited Greece. Thus the crisis was brought to a formal conclusion, although the national schism would continue to have disastrous consequences for Greek constitutional and political life for decades.

During the period 1917–1920, Venizelos engaged in intense diplomatic activity, culminating in the Treaty of Sevres of 1920, a triumphant outcome for Greece. Under the Treaty Greece would acquire eastern Thrace as far as the Black Sea, as well as the islands of Imbros and Tenedos. Although Smyrna and its surrounding region were to remain formally under Turkish sovereignty, Greece was to administer the region and be permitted to station military forces there. The Treaty included provision for a plebiscite, to be held after five years, on whether Smyrna should become part of Greece. The Dodecanese were assigned to Italy, which later ceded them to Greece. Thus the great dream was realized, if only temporarily, of a Greece straddling five seas and two continents. The surface area of the country was now over 150,000 km^2.

In 1920 the administration of Venizelos called an election for a Parliament to revise the Constitution of 1911. However, the revision never took place, since the 1920 election was won by the opposition. A month before the country went to the polls, in October 1920, Alexander died and the duties of Regent were assumed on a temporary basis by Admiral Koundouriotis. At the end of the same year a referendum was held, as a result of which Constantine re-ascended the throne, while Venizelos went into voluntary political exile in France. It is more than likely, however, that the plebiscite had been rigged: it was claimed that 99% of those voting had supported the return of Constantine!

The year of the Asia Minor catastrophe was 1922 – a tragedy for Greece and her people. The Greek army, having advanced deep into the Turkish interior, was unable to resist the forces of Kemal Ataturk. The catastrophe had the most dire military, political and social consequences for the country, with a tidal wave of refugees from the lost territories pouring into Greece. Officers loyal to Venizelos organized a movement known as the Revolution of 1922, under the leadership of Nikolaos Plastiras. Constantine was forced by a revolutionary government to resign once again in 1922, in favour of his first son George II. Antiroyalists reacted again by forcing King George II to leave the country in December 1923. The Treaty of Lausanne in 1923 brought the conflict between Greece and Turkey officially to an end, but Greece lost substantial territories acquired under the Sevres Treaty, namely eastern Thrace, Smyrna and the surrounding area, Imbros and Tenedos. The Dodecanese were returned to Italy. The surface area of the country now amounted to 129,281 km^2. The Treaty also provided for a significant exchange of populations between the two countries.

§5. The Second Hellenic Republic (1924–1935) and the Constitution of 1927

35. A Constituent Assembly was convoked in January 1924. Plastiras willingly gave all revolutionary powers to Assembly and to the newly formed government. The Assembly officially dethroned the King and the dynasty and voted for the republican form of government. This development was endorsed by a popular referendum.

The constitutional work of the Government proceeded slowly. The instability of the administration led to a new coup, under General Pangalos (1925). The Pangalos government compelled the Assembly to grant it a vote of confidence. A parliamentary committee was also set up, chaired by Alexandros Papanastasiou, to draft a constitution. After completing its work the committee, in the same year, submitted a draft constitution for publication in the Official Gazette. The Constitution was unlawfully modified by the Pangalos regime but was in fact never implemented. Pangalos dissolved Parliament and instituted a period of dictatorship, overturned in 1926 by a new coup led by General Kondylis. The latter restored the original Constitution of 1925, as voted by the Assembly, and called an election. An all-party government was formed, which in 1927 approved and promulgated the new Constitution of 1927.

This new Constitution revived the provisions of its predecessor of 1925, with minimal amendments. It established republican democracy as the form of government. The parliamentary system was now explicitly established and ceased to be a mere 'convention' of the system of government. The President of the Republic was to be elected by the Parliament and the Senate in a common session for a term of five years. He was only accountable for high treason and for intentional violation of the Constitution. His competences were restricted in comparison to those of the King in the previous Constitutions. A Senate was established with legislative competences as well as competences with regard to the revision of the Constitution, the dissolution of Parliament, and so on. Specifically, the dissolution of Parliament could not be effectuated by the President of the Republic without the Senate's consent. This provision was a result of the political experience of the 'national schism'.

Other main provisions of the Constitution of 1927 pertained to the Council of State as the Supreme Administrative Court, which was established in 1929, to guarantee on local government and decentralization, as well as to social rights such as the right to work, the right of promotion of arts, literature and science, the protection of marriage and the family, etc. It also explicitly established (*see supra* No. 33) judicial review of the constitutionality of the laws.

The Constitution of 1927 was well-crafted, democratic and liberal in spirit. However, re-emerging political tensions prevented its smooth implementation. In 1928, the Liberal Party returned to power under Venizelos, who governed until 1932 (the 'four-year government'), while in 1933 power passed to the opposition.

The party of Venizelos, under Plastiras, reacted to their opponents' victory with an unsuccessful coup d'état, in March 1933. The old political and constitutional crises revived. The country was declared to be in a state of siege (emergency) and the Government, under Panagis Tsaldaris abolished, suspended and amended in an unconstitutional manner provisions of the Constitution of 1927 concerning the Senate, the Judiciary, and universities, the civil service, the army, among others.

§6. The First Period of Authoritarian Regimes (1935–1946)

36. Another coup d'état in October 1935, led by General Kondylis, restored the Crown and brought into force the Constitution of 1911. King George II returned to Greece after the changes in the form of government had been endorsed by a popular referendum. The result of this referendum was never in doubt, since the Kondylis administration had removed all its Venizelist and left-wing opponents. George II appointed a new government under the moderate anti-Venizelist, K. Demertzis, dissolved the National Assembly and called an election. When Demertzis died the office of Prime Minister was taken by Ioannis Metaxas. All the parties put up candidates in the election but none of them secured a large enough majority to form a government not dependent on other parties. The Revisionary Parliament, as it was called, did not attempt its work of constitutional revision, but after approving the appointment of Metaxas as Prime Minister suspended its proceedings and authorized Metaxas to legislate on its behalf. The way was now clear for a dictatorship. On 4 August 1936, the King issued two royal decrees, on the recommendation of the Metaxas government, suspending basic constitutional guarantees of civil rights and dissolving Parliament.

The regime of Metaxas – close to fascism in its ideology – was essentially a monarchical dictatorship, which lasted until the country was occupied by the Italians and Germans. In October 1940 fascist Italy launched an attack on Greece, an attack which the Greeks victoriously counter-attacked until the German invasion of May 1941. The King and government, under Tsouderos (Metaxas had died in January 1941 and his successor Koryzis had committed suicide in April of the same year) fled to Crete and then to Egypt, where they remained throughout the occupation of Greece by the enemy forces of three nations: Germans, Italians and Bulgarians (who had annexed part of Thrace). During the occupation the Germans assumed virtually total control of the country: they appointed the Governments, which were more in the nature of administrative authorities. The King and the Government of Greece during the occupation, residing in London and later in Cairo, decided to proclaim elections for the designation of a Constituent Assembly after liberation. This decision was backed by all political parties. King George II himself did not oppose it. He promised that the people would freely decide by way of a referendum whether the form of government would be a monarchic or a republican democracy.

Athens was liberated in October 1944 by English troops disembarking in Piraeus. The rest of the country was liberated by the resistance forces. As soon as the Cairo government, under Prime Minister. Papandreou, returned to Athens they demanded that the various organizations set up to resist the occupying forces, which were largely controlled by the Communist Party, should lay down their arms and dissolve themselves. King George II was to remain abroad until a referendum had been held on how the country should be governed. A civil war then broke out between government forces and the resistance fighters controlled by the communist party. During the first phase of this civil conflict, in December 1944, there were clashes in the centre of Athens between the Greek and British forces on the one hand, supporting the Government, and the communist forces of EAM/ELAS on the other. These clashes became known as the '*Dekemvriana*' (Events of December) or the 'Battle of Athens'. The first phase of the civil war came to an end in February 1945, with the Varkiza Agreement, which envisaged, *inter alia*, an end to the military activities of ELAS and the granting of an amnesty for political offences. The disarmament of ELAS gave the opportunity to right-wing extremist groups to apply retaliation measures against the members of EAM/ELAS, especially in the Hellenic countryside.

In March 1946, the people went to the polls to elect a government which would hold the referendum mentioned above. The Communist Party declined to contest the election, as being far from equal and fair. In fact, the parties of the left attempted to disrupt the election, organizing strikes and even perpetrating acts of violence in certain areas. The election went ahead and the subsequent referendum of September 1946 brought the return of George II to Greece. He died one year later and was succeeded by his brother Paul.

The second phase of the Civil War began in late 1947 after ELAS had been disarmed and many persons on the left had been prosecuted or driven into exile; this time the fighting, in the spirit of the cold war, involved military aid of the USA and of the communist satellites of the USSR respectively. It was not until August 1949 that the hostilities finally ceased with the victory of the government forces (the Battles of Grammos and Vitsi). These five years of civil strife seriously delayed the recovery of the country from the Second World War and postponed the normalization of political and constitutional life.

During the turmoil of the civil war, a set of constitutional acts and decrees were promulgated which became known as the *Parasyntagma* or Para-constitution. They comprise emergency provisions such as deportation orders, certificates of good citizenship, deprivation of nationality, purging of civil servants, confiscations of property, etc. Such measures continued to be taken after the end of the Civil War and the voting of the new Constitution. In 1951 Parliament ruled that these measures should henceforth have no enhanced formal force, but should remain in effect as ordinary statutes, even where their content ran counter to the new Constitution. In their highly specific application to particular cases, these para-constitutional provisions often supplanted the regular operation of the Constitution. This state of affairs prevented the establishment of the proper rule of law because it indefinitely prolonged the implementation of a host of unconstitutional provisions dating from the period of civil strife, while also undermining the regulatory authority of the 1952 Constitution. It was not until 1975 that this 'Para-constitution' was finally rescinded.

§7. The Second Period of Parliamentary Monarchy (1946–1967) and the Constitution of 1952

37. The Parliament, which was elected in 1946, was a Revisionary Parliament, not a Constituent one, as was initially intended. It empowered a committee to draft the revision of the Constitution of 1864/1911. After two parliamentary elections the amended Constitution was voted in December 1951 and brought into force in January 1952.

The Constitution of 1952 established a parliamentary monarchy, based on the principle of the separation of powers. The King, despite the antagonisms of the past between the Crown on the one hand and Parliament and government on the other, still retained the legislative initiative and was competent to sanction statutes enacted by Parliament; he could furthermore issue legislative decrees with the consent of a committee of representatives if Parliament was not in session (*see infra* No. 81) and he was competent to dissolve Parliament.

In the domain of fundamental rights and freedoms, the Constitution was relatively anachronistic; it did not even include provisions on social rights, though it could have been used as a model for the Constitution of 1927.

In reality, the Constitution of 1952 was, like the former one of 1911, a new Constitution, not a revision, since it was issued in violation of the revision clause of the Constitution of 1911.

During the life of the 1952 Constitution, the reins of power in Greece were held first by General Alexandros Papagos and later, mainly, by Constantine Karamanlis, a successful young politician who was the surprise choice of the King in 1955 to succeed the late General Papagos, selected in preference to the traditional 'barons' of his party. Karamanlis remained in power until 1963, thanks to three successive election victories (in 1956, 1958 and 1961) of the party he had himself created – the National Radical Union (ERE). The 1961 election was particularly interesting, in that Karamanlis found himself opposed by the newly established Union of the Centre party (*Enosis Kentrou*), led by George Papandreou. When it lost the election the Union of the Centre challenged the result, claiming the poll had been rigged. It embarked on the so-called Relentless Struggle, boycotting the opening of Parliament and organizing popular rallies. Meanwhile, Karamanlis had fallen out with the King and eventually resigned in June 1963. An election was called for November of the same year and won by the Union of the Centre; George Papandreou was now Prime Minister. He resigned just two months later but was re-elected once more in February 1964.

King Paul died in March 1964 and was succeeded by his son, Constantine II. In the early days of his reign, while the Constitution of 1952 was still in place, another political crisis of major constitutional dimensions took place, known as the '*Iouliana*'– the Events of July. The popular Prime Minister George Papandreou asked that the King allow him to occupy the post of Minister for Defence as well as that of Prime Minister. But the King was adamant in his refusal, on the grounds that the Prime Minister's son, Andreas Papandreou, was at that time being investigated on suspicion of organizing a military movement. Finally, the Prime Minister resigned in July 1965. In constitutional terms, this time the issue was whether the royal 'prerogative' to appoint Ministers was a matter of discretion of the King or a decision of the Prime Minister, binding for the King, who merely had to formally issue the decree. King Constantine II unjustifiably claimed the political decision for the throne. The resigning Prime Minister stuck to his guns, but without seeking the dissolution of Parliament and holding of a new election. The King called on three politicians in succession to try to form a government: first, the Speaker, Georgios Novas, deputy leader of the Union of the Centre, which continued to be led by Papandreou; then Ilias Tsirimokos, also from the Union of the Centre. Both men failed to secure the necessary vote of confidence in Parliament. Despite this failure, and the clear popular support for Papandreou, amid continual demonstrations and political turmoil, the King persisted in his attempts to appoint a new Prime Minister without resorting to an election – a line of conduct verging on the unconstitutional. Finally, in September 1965, the King issued the instruction to form a government to Stefanos Stefanopoulos, who, with Novas and Tsirimokos as his deputies, secured a vote of confidence in Parliament. At the end of 1966, following a secret agreement between Panayiotis Kanellopoulos, leader of the opposition party (ERE) and G. Papandreou, on the holding of an election and regularization of the situation, the former withdrew his party's support for the Government. An interim Government was then appointed (December 1966) under Ioannis Paraskevopoulos in order to hold elections, but subsequently overturned by Panayiotis Kanellopoulos when it was slow to organize an election. Over the objections of George Papandreou, Kanellopoulos was appointed Prime Minister in April 1967. His administration, which never sought a vote of confidence in Parliament, was overturned just eighteen days later in the military coup of 21 April 1967.

§8. The Second Period of Authoritarian Regimes (1967–1974)

38. On the night of 21–22 April 1967, a number of politicians, including Prime Minister P. Kanellopoulos, and ordinary citizens were arrested by supporters of the coup. That same night the King, surrounded by men involved in the coup, under the control of a group of colonels who had come to the palace, was persuaded to instruct the Prosecutor of the Supreme Civil and Criminal Court, K. Kollias, to form a government. Military officers were to assume posts in this new government, which, of course, did not and could not secure a vote of confidence from Parliament. In December 1967, the King attempted to organize his own military coup against this administration but failed and decided to leave the country. A new government was then formed under the true moving spirit behind the dictatorship, Colonel George Papadopoulos.

The dictatorship remained in power until July 1974, sustained by the threat and actual use of force. First, it abolished the Constitution of 1952 and introduced absolute government. The 'Constitution' of 1968, which was drafted by a twenty-member committee and amended by the dictator George Papadopoulos and his advisors, was merely a polite fiction. It retained the system of monarchical democracy and contained a list of fundamental rights and freedoms. However, in its transitional provisions, it stated that the clauses on civil rights and those concerning elections were suspended. This Constitution was conceived from the very beginning by the great majority of the Greek population as a piece of paper and nothing more. Parliament was never elected and fundamental rights and freedoms were systematically violated. The dictators denounced the European Convention on Human Rights (ECHR) after Norway, Sweden and Denmark, in a joint application, and the Netherlands in a separate one, had referred the 'Greek Case' to the European Commission of Human Rights for serious breaches of the provisions of the Convention.

The Constitution of 1968 was revised by the same dictatorship in 1973. The new Constitution of 1973 replaced 'parliamentary monarchy' and 'King' with 'republican democracy' and 'President of the Republic' respectively. In 1973, the first mass demonstrations against the junta took place. The uprising by students at the Law School was followed, in May 1973, by a movement led by naval officers in support of the monarchy. It was believed that the King, who had been out of the country since 1967, was implicated in this movement. In June 1973, the Government decided to declare a non-monarchical republic, its President to be none other than the dictator George Papadopoulos. A rigged referendum held in July of the same year sanctioned the new system of government. A government was formed, under S. Markesinis, to hold a general election. There followed the uprising by students of the Polytechnic School, in November 1973, in support of political demands rather than the usual student issues. The army was called in to suppress the student movement, and troops entered the grounds of the Polytechnic. Immediately after this, a new coup ousted Papadopoulos and placed Brigadier Ioannidis at the head of an even more oppressive regime.

The military regime disintegrated in July 1974 after it had provoked the Turkish invasion of Cyprus. It left behind a national tragedy (Cyprus) and an institutional wasteland (Greece).

§9. The Third Hellenic Republic (1974–present)

I. The Constitution

39. Constantine Karamanlis, an experienced conservative politician enjoying high esteem, who had served as Prime Minister from 1955 to 1963 (*see supra* No. 37) and had resigned because of a disagreement with the King, after the disintegration of the junta formed a government of 'national unity', in collaboration with the parties of the centre ground. The Government immediately proceeded to revoke the dictatorial Constitutions of 1968 and 1973, replacing them with the Constitution of 1952 – minus those provisions which defined the system of government. The new administration also granted amnesty for all political crimes, allowed all parties, including the Communist Party, which had been banned since the time of the Civil War, to resume activity, and re-ratified the ECHR. By the popular referendum of December 1974, the form of government was decided to be a republican democracy.

The new Constitution, which was brought before Parliament as a draft in January 1975, was voted in June of the same year. The Constitution was in reality a product of a constituent, not a revisionary will, though the Parliament was officially called 'revisionary'. The Constitution is still in force today, as amended in the revisions of 1986, 2001 and 2008. A new revision is currently under consideration. It is based on the principles of popular sovereignty, the rule of law and the separation of powers. Its main innovations are as follows:

- explicit safeguarding of the parliamentary system;
- fuller protection for fundamental rights and freedoms;
- safeguarding of a series of social rights;
- explicit acknowledgement of the precedence of international law over domestic legislation;
- safeguarding of the institution of political parties;
- possibility of adhesion to the European Communities.

The opposition parties (PASOK and the other left-wing parties) abstained from the vote on adoption of the new Constitution, in protest at the strengthening of the role of the President of the Republic.

It is true that the President of the Republic was entrusted, with a range of competences: he could dismiss Cabinet, even though it enjoyed the confidence of Parliament, he could decide on the dissolution of Parliament and on the sanctioning of statutes enacted by Parliament. He could further proclaim referenda and address messages to the people even without ministerial countersignature and he could also declare a 'state of siege (emergency)'. This strengthening of the role of the President of the Republic has led some scholars to characterize the form of government as 'semi-presidential' or 'bipolar parliamentarianism' (the one pole being the President, the other being the Cabinet).

II. The Revision of 1986

40. The Constitution was applied for a decade without institutional turbulence. It was the basic tool for a difficult but, retrospectively, smooth and altogether successful transition to democracy. The political and theoretical critics of the Constitutional Charter were not vindicated. The aforementioned competences of the President of the Republic were in practice never exercised vis-à-vis Parliament or the Government. The two Presidents of the Republic, C. Tsatsos (1975–1980) and C. Karamanlis (1980–1985, 1990–1995), confined themselves to exercising their symbolic powers as 'regulators' of the system. The fact is that during the eleven years in which the Constitution was in force before its revision in 1986, the conditions never arose in which the real presidential powers would need to be exercised. All the general elections of this period (1977, 1981 and 1985) produced solid, one-party governments – and there was thus no need for the President of the Republic to intervene.

Nevertheless, in March 1985, a constitutional revision was proposed in Parliament, by the governing PASOK party, for party-political reasons. It was limited to the revision of eleven articles of the Constitution. They all involved the competences of the President of the Republic, though could certainly involve other issues as well, for example, the advancement of the protection of fundamental rights and freedoms, of political and social institutions, and of the independence of the Judiciary. The proposal was aimed, according to its declaration, at the strengthening of the role of Parliament, thereby establishing a purely parliamentary system.

The amendment was rapidly completed and passed in March 1986. It is the first constitutional revision in Greek constitutional history which has been completed in accordance with the revision clause of the Constitution, in conditions of constitutional and political normality.

The Constitutional Revision of 1986 has actually strengthened the role of the Prime Minister. It has been an important step for future avoidance of eventual collisions between the main organs of the State.

III. The Revision of 2001

41. In 1993 the New Democracy government under Prime Minister Constantine Mitsotakis raised the prospect of another revision of the Constitution. However, no further action was taken since the weakness of its parliamentary majority obliged it to dissolve Parliament and call an election for October of that year.

The need for revision was accepted by the newly elected PASOK government. The process of revision took no fewer than eight years and the new revised text was finally passed by the VII Revisionary Parliament in 2001. The work of revision was carried out in the context of the procedure envisaged in Article 110 of the Constitution, and took place in undisturbed political conditions, with broad political consensus between the two major parties. The revision was extraordinarily wide-ranging in terms of the number of provisions to be amended: four new articles were added and forty-eight were modified, more than one-third of the total content of the Constitution. The Greek Constitution is now one of the most comprehensive and detailed in Europe. However, in terms of real content, the revision did not entail any serious changes in the machinery of the political system. Its most important elements were as follows:

- Adaptation of the Constitution to new technological developments and expansion of the area of human rights. The Constitution enshrined such new rights as the right to information and participation in the information society (Article 5a), protection of personal data (Article 9a) and the right to protection of genetic identity (Article 5 paragraph 5).
- Prohibition on any precipitate change in electoral law (Article 54 paragraph 1).
- Amendment of the provisions on disqualifications and incompatibilities of Members of Parliament, the most important being the introduction of the general principle of professional incompatibility (Articles 56 and 57).
- Enshrining in the Constitution of five independent administrative authorities, the Ombudsman, the National Radio and Television Council, the Hellenic Data Protection Authority (HDPA or Authority), the Supreme Council for Civil Personnel and the Hellenic Authority for Communication Security and Privacy (*see infra* Nos 215 et seq.).

IV. The Revision of 2008

42. The governing party of New Democracy had announced since 2004 its intention for a new and quite extensive revision of the Constitution, suggesting the revision of twenty-nine articles in all, regarding the founding of a Constitutional Court, the general principle of parliamentary incompatibility, the protection of the environment, the founding of private universities, etc. With the completion of five years after the entry into force of the revised Constitution of 1975/1986/2001, both New Democracy as a party of the governing majority and PASOK as a party of the main opposition, i.e., the two parties that had at that time the required minimum number of fifty deputies, submitted to the Parliament a proposal for the revision of the Constitution (on the revisionary procedure *see infra* Nos 52 et seq.).

The procedure was completed in May 2008, with PASOK (the main opposition party) not participating in the revision process. Finally, the Parliament that had emerged from the elections of 16 September 2007, acting as the 8th Revisionary Parliament, adopted only four minor changes. The most significant among them was the abolition of the parliamentary incompatibility with the exercise of any profession (*see infra* No. 138).

V. The Revision of 2019

43. The process that resulted in the 2019 Revision, even though the relevant political discussions had begun as early as 2013, that is five years since the Revision of 2008, was initiated only in 2018 with the proposal submitted by the governing party of SYRIZA. This was followed by the submission of a respective proposal by the main opposition party of New Democracy.

It was preceded, on the initiative of the Government, by the establishment of an 'extra-parliamentary' committee to conduct a 'public consultation' for the revision of the Constitution, although the Government – as has already been pointed out – is not an organ that participates in the revision process, nor does it have any revisionist initiative.

The main topic of discussion during the first phase of the revisionary procedure was the issue of whether or not the following Parliament (i.e., the Revisionary Parliament) is bound by the 'directions' of the first Parliament, meaning the delimitation of the revisionary competence of the Revisionary Parliament.

Although the Revision of 2019 covered relatively few amendments, these were of great significance regarding the function of the State. Specifically, apart from the abolition of the transitional provisions of Articles 113–115, given they had already become obsolete, the most important elements of the 2019 Revision were as follows:

- The provision that the State shall ensure that all citizens enjoy a decent standard of living by means of a system of minimum guaranteed income (Article 21, paragraph 1).
- The abolition of the provision on automatic dissolution of the Parliament due to failure to elect a President of the Republic (Article 32, paragraph 4).
- The facilitation of the voting process regarding the Greeks living abroad (Article 54, paragraph 4).
- The granting to the opposition of the right to establish two, at the maximum, Committees of Inquiry per parliamentary term (Article 68).
- The introduction of the institution of legislative initiative, following a relevant proposal made by five hundred thousand citizens at minimum (Article 73, paragraph 6).
- The adoption of limitations to certain privileges recognized in favour of ministers (Article 86) and deputies (Article 62), regarding their criminal liability and their immunities respectively.
- The facilitation of the appointment process of members of Independent Authorities (Article 101A).

Chapter 2. Sources of Constitutional Law

44. The term 'sources of constitutional law' means the ways in which rules of constitutional law are generated; that is, all different types of legal norms referring to the Constitution in its material sense, namely the rules concerning the formation and organization of state power as well as its relation to individuals, groups of individuals and society as a whole.

The Constitution as the supreme law of the State has also a formal sense: it refers to the rules which are placed at the top of the hierarchy of legal norms and which can only be changed following a strict procedure, if at all.

45. Constitutional rules in the formal sense are usually also constitutional rules in the material sense; but there are formal constitutional rules which do not simultaneously pertain to the material Constitution, for example, the provision on the protection of foreign capital imported into the country (Article 107 of the Constitution). Conversely, there are a large number of rules pertaining to the material Constitution which are not simultaneously part of the Constitution in its formal sense. They refer to the organs of the State and to fundamental rights and freedoms but are not placed at the top of the hierarchy of legal norms. They appear in the form of statutes, international treaties, administrative regulations, etc.

The term 'sources of constitutional law' may also refer to the socio-political background which led the legislator to produce concrete norms. Though of great significance, this dimension of the sources of constitutional law will not be dealt with here; it is a matter of history of law, political science and sociology of law.

46. The sources of Greek constitutional law are:

- the written Constitution (called in Greek 'formal' Constitution) (section 1);
- Constituent Acts and Resolutions (section 2);
- the unwritten constitution, that is, constitutional custom and the conventions of the political system, as well as the general principles of constitutional law (section 3);
- the Statutes or Acts of Parliament (called in Greek 'laws' or 'formal laws' or 'ordinary' laws) (section 4);
- the Standing Orders (Regulations of Parliament) (section 5);
- the Regulatory Acts of the Executive Branch (section 6);
- acts of legislative content (section 7);
- the legislative decrees and emergency laws of the past, as well as the arbitrary regulatory administrative acts under the current Constitution (section 8);
- certain decisions by the Special Highest Court and the upper courts, especially the Council of State (section 9);
- international law (section 10);
- the law of the EU (section 11).

§1. THE CONSTITUTION

I. Hierarchy

47. Greece has always had a written and rigid Constitution as its supreme law.

48. The Constitution in force contains several provisions which place it at the top of the hierarchy of legal norms. These are the following:

(1) Article 110 prohibits revision of several constitutional provisions and prescribes a certain procedure for the revision of all others.
(2) Article 93 paragraph 4 as well as Article 87 paragraph 2 entrusts the judiciary with the duty of review of legislation contrary to the Constitution.
(3) Article 111 paragraph 1 provides for the abrogation of any previous legal rules contrary to the Constitution.

49. A specific issue of hierarchy of legal rules is that of the relationship between constitutional norms and norms of European law. The Council of State, exercising its advisory competence to elaborate on Presidential Decrees of a regulatory nature (*see infra* No. 77), followed the jurisprudence of the Court of Justice of the European Union (CJEU) on the primacy of European law (Council of State Advice 406/1980). But the Council of State itself, as the Supreme Administrative Court, exercising its judicial competences (Ruling 297/1985), held that the Constitution recognizes the primacy of international treaties solely vis-à-vis statutes; Greece's accession to and membership of the European Communities did not alter the situation. Consequently, there may be no priority of any legal system over the Constitution. The case law has confirmed this position (*see* Council of State Rulings 1809/1997 and 3242/2004). Specifically, in Ruling 3242/2004 the Supreme Administrative Court issued a majority ruling that the sending of a pre-judicial question to the CJEU concerning the compatibility or otherwise of a provision of the Constitution (specifically, Article 14 paragraph 9) with European law would be pointless since in any case the Greek judge is obliged to apply the Constitution. It thus ruled that in the current phase of development of European law, and until a common European constitutional text is in place, it is not permissible for any rule to be recognized, whatever its provenance, as taking precedence over the Constitution. The case in question was referred to the Plenary Session of the Council of State, in view of the importance of the matter at issue, and the Plenary Session referred the case to the European Court of Justice (Council of State Ruling 3670/2006), which did not take a position on the matter (*see infra* No. 400). However, there are certain rulings which ascribe precedence to European law over the Constitution (Council of State Ruling 249/1997, referring the case in question to the Full Bench, which preferred, however, not to rule on this point).

In other respects, conflicts between European law and constitutional rules are extremely rare. It is important to emphasize that the problem of the relationship between the two legal systems is not mainly a problem of hierarchy of norms but a problem of delimitation of competences.

II. Revision of the Constitution

50. Article 110 of the Constitution refers to its revision. In particular, paragraph 1 thereof specifies the articles which may not be revised, while paragraphs 2–6 determine the amending procedure.

51. Provisions relating to the form of government, on certain fundamental rights and freedoms (i.e., human dignity, equality before the law, access of Greek citizens to public office, prohibition of titles of nobility or distinction, free development of the personality, personal liberty, religious freedom), as well as the separation of powers principle, may not be revised. Furthermore, paragraph 1 of Article 106 may also not be revised; this is not determined in the Constitution itself but it is inferred by the interpretation and the *ratio* of the aforementioned clause.

52. Regarding the amending procedure, a proposal for the revision of the Constitution must be tabled by at least fifty Members of Parliament and approved by two separate majority votes of three-fifths of the entire body. Voting shall be by roll call and at least one month must elapse between the two votes. During this procedure, the provisions to be revised shall be specifically determined (Article 110 paragraph 2). The second phase of the revision is conducted at the first sitting of the next Parliament, which shall vote on the provisions to be revised, in principle, Article by Article and in their entirety (Article 110 paragraph 3). An absolute majority of the entire body is required here. The possibility is envisaged, however, of reversing the majorities required in paragraphs 2 and 3, as long as the three-fifths majority has been achieved in one of the two Parliaments (Article 110 paragraph 4). The revision is deemed completed when published in the Official Gazette, within ten days after it has been voted on in Parliament (Article 110 paragraph 5). The President of the Republic takes no part in the revision procedure, in contrast to the usual legislative process. Finally, there can be no new revision of the Constitution until five years have elapsed since the completion of the previous revision (Article 110 paragraph 6).

In 1985 the proposal for the revision of certain Articles of the Constitution, mainly in relation to the competences of the President of the Republic, included also a draft provision for the amendment of the procedural section of Article 110. It was intended to amend the procedure so that the revision of the Constitution could be concluded in future in one stage instead of two. A theoretical debate which focused on the democratic dimension of the existence of two stages for the revision of the Constitution (*see supra* No. 3) led to withdrawal of this specific draft proposal.

§2. Constituent Acts of the Executive and Resolutions of the Parliament Equivalent to the Constitution

53. De facto (i.e., illegal and authoritarian) regimes of the past have issued acts abrogating, by way of 'revolution' (in the Kelsenian sense), constitutional provisions and introducing new 'constitutional' law. These acts, called 'Constituent Acts', were issued by the Executive.

54. Resolutions of Parliament, on the other hand, have been issued by Constituent or Revisionary Assemblies in order to deal with transitory or procedural matters with a view to the voting of a new Constitution or of a constitutional amendment.

55. The difference between Constituent Acts and Resolutions relates to the organ which issues them as well as their purpose. Constituent Acts are usually the means to abolish the legitimate Constitution, while Resolutions are the means for a return to legitimacy. Nevertheless, Constituent Acts have also been issued by governments pursuing normalization of political and constitutional life.

The Constitution devoted a special provision regarding the validity of Constituent Acts and Resolutions of the past (Article 111): provisions contained, *inter alia,* in Constituent Acts and Resolutions prior to the restoration of democracy (24 July 1974) and contrary to the Constitution were abolished; Constituent Acts and Resolutions issued after 24 July 1974 continued to be valid, even if they were contrary to the Constitution, but they could be abolished or amended by ordinary statutes. If still in force, their applicability is based on the maxim *lex posterior generalis* (i.e., the Constitution) *non derogat legi priori specialis* (i.e., the Constituent Act or the Resolution).

§3. Unwritten Law

I. Constitutional Customs

56. Customs have generally been recognized as a source of law since the Royal Decree of 23 February 1835. Article 1 of the Civil Code, more than a hundred years later (1946), places customs on the same level of hierarchy of rules as ordinary legislation. Nevertheless, Article 2 paragraph 2 of the Legislative Decree of 7–10 May 1946 has amended, as *lex posterior*, this provision of the Civil Code and forbids the abrogation of statutes by customs.

However, due to the rigid character of the Constitution, constitutional customs may not abrogate or alter written constitutional provisions. Otherwise, it would make no sense to produce rules of law, in any form, which will supersede provisions of the Constitution, in a manner different from that strictly defined in the Constitution itself (Article 110). Thus only customs supplementary to the written Constitution are recognized as sources of constitutional law. These supplementary customs have a force equal to the written constitutional provisions.

The existence of constitutional customs presupposes that there is no contrary constitutional rule or even no contrary ordinary rule to avert their gradual creation. Thus, the fact that constitutional customs have the same constitutional status as written constitutional provisions means that constitutional customs may not abrogate constitutional or other legal provisions but do prohibit the enactment of statutory provisions contrary to their content as long as they remain in force. They may only be abrogated or altered by a new written constitutional rule.

Under the Constitution of 1952, case law and legal scholars unanimously considered that there existed a constitutional custom forbidding courts to review the compliance of statutes with the rules of legislative procedure, as well as a constitutional custom prescribing that general elections should be carried out by an interim (non-political) government. Prior to the Constitution of 1952, the legislative delegation to the administration of the power to issue regulatory acts was held to be based on a supplementary constitutional custom (Council of State Ruling 197/1945).

Under the Constitution of 1975/1986/2001/2008/2019, constitutional customs are of no practical importance. The aforementioned constitutional customs have been tacitly set aside by the Constitution of 1975/1986/2001/2008/2019, which contains specific provisions on these matters.

II. Conventions of the Constitution

57. The concept of 'conventions of the Constitution' is not unknown in the Greek legal system. However, they do not have any practical importance. The Constitution makes very detailed provisions for the working of the various organs of the State, and thus there is very little scope for such conventions to develop. The difference with constitutional customs is that they lack the so-called *opinio juris* or *opinio necessitatis*. Conventions of the Constitution are not considered sources of constitutional law, since they do not have any binding force and no sanctions are provided in case of violation.

The parliamentary system of government was initially introduced as a convention of the Constitution (*see supra* No. 12). The insistence on considering it as a convention of the Constitution and not as a constitutional custom is perhaps due to the fact that its violation by the Crown could not entail the imposition of any sanctions.

One current practice which might be described as a convention of the Constitution is the habit of briefing the President of the Republic and/or leaders of the political parties, by the Prime Minister and Ministers, on the Government policy being pursued on important issues.

It might be urged that a recent convention of the Constitution has emerged: the President of the Republic may on the proposal of the Prime Minister bring together the leaders of the political parties represented in the Parliament, in cases of crucial national issues. This 'Council of the Leaders of the political parties' is not expressly provided for in the Constitution. During the first period which followed its appearance, it was rarely convened: the first time in 1992 for consultations in relation to the use of the official name of FYROM (now North Macedonia), and the second time in 2004 to discuss the Anan plan for Cyprus. Nevertheless, during the financial crisis, it has been convened more often. The latest meetings of the Council of the Leaders of the political parties took place in July 2015 concerning the referendum which rejected the proposal of the European Commission, the European Central Bank and the International Monetary Fund for the continuance of the financial assistance of Greece (*see supra* No. 6); in November 2015 concerning the refugee crisis (*see supra* No. 22), the revision of the Constitution, the electoral law, and the reform of the national insurance system, and in March 2016 concerning the refugee crisis. The institution of this Council is similar to the 'Council of political leaders' which is convened by the President of the Republic before elections in order to exhaust all possibilities to form a Government consisting of all political parties (Article 37 paragraph 3 of the Constitution, *see infra* No. 183).

III. General Principles of Law

58. Apart from written and customary rules, law is also regulated by general principles. Being formulated in a general and abstract way, they function as interpretative tools that guide and complement both the adoption and the application of legal rules. General principles, though not set down in a specific constitutional or legislative text nevertheless emerge from legislation as a whole. They are of special interest for the regulation of certain matters regarding the organization and activities of the administrative organs (*see infra* Nos 85 et seq.).

Therefore general principles of law are of major importance, especially for administrative law. Their concrete content is determined in court rulings; they are considered as deriving, though not explicitly, from the spirit of the legal order. The Council of State has recognized as general principles of law the principle of fairness and impartiality of administrative action, the principle of proportionality, the principle of protection of the legitimate (substantive) expectations of the individual, the principle of publication of legal regulations etc. The general principles of administrative law are supplementary to statutes and higher-ranking rules. Thus general principles of law prevail over contrary provisions of regulatory acts of the administration.

§4. Statutes

59. In the Greek language, the term 'law' has two distinguishable meanings: it means either all the norms of the legal order (in Greek 'νόμος' or 'ουσιαστικός νόμος' or 'δίκαιο' or 'ουσιαστικό δίκαιο', translated sometimes as 'substantive law' or 'material law'), or a 'statute' (or Act of Parliament or legislative Act or legislative text; in Greek 'νόμος' or 'νομοθετική πράξη' or 'νομοθετικό κείμενο', translated sometimes as 'formal law' or 'ordinary law', 'τυπικός νόμος' or 'κοινός νόμος') issued by the competent legislative organ. Statutes are produced by the legislative power, that is, normally Parliament; 'substantive' or 'material' laws are legal rules of general and abstract content, irrespective of the organ that issues them.

The Constitution uses the term 'law' in both senses. In some articles reference to a statute is explicitly made (e.g., Article 78 paragraph 1, *see infra* No. 486, Article 100 paragraph 1(e), *see infra* No. 350), in others, a statute is implied (e.g., Article 77, *see infra* No. 65), but in most articles of the Constitution, 'law' may mean either a statute or substantive law.

Substantive laws produced by organs of the Executive will be dealt with in *infra* Nos 71 et seq.

I. Legislative Procedure

60. According to Article 26 paragraph 1 of the Constitution, 'legislative powers shall be exercised by Parliament and the President of the Republic'. The legislative procedure in Parliament is laid down in Articles 70 et seq. of the Constitution. These more or less general rules are specified in Articles 86 et seq. of the Standing Orders. The participation of the President of the Republic in the legislative procedure is provided for in Article 42 of the Constitution. In general terms, the process of generating statutes might be divided into three stages:

(1) Stage of legislative initiative.
(2) SStage of elaboration, discussion and voting on bills or law proposals.
(3) SStage of promulgation and publication of voted statutes.

61. (a) Legislative initiative stage. Legislative initiative is vested in Parliament or the Government (Article 73 paragraph 1 of the Constitution). Since the Revision of 2019, neither the President of the Republic nor the people have the power of legislative initiative. However, according to the newly added paragraph 6 thereof, 'Upon signature by five hundred thousand citizens having the right to vote, up to two bills per parliamentary term may be tabled in Parliament, which shall be referred to the relevant parliamentary committee for processing by decision of the Speaker and shall then be compulsorily submitted to the plenum for debate and voting. The bills of the preceding section may not deal with budgetary, foreign policy or national defence matter. A statute shall specify the terms and conditions of application of this paragraph.' This statute has not yet been enacted.

Parliament, that is, every single Member of Parliament, may submit 'law proposals'. The Government, that is, the competent Minister(s), may submit 'Bills'. Exceptionally, only the Government may introduce Bills on civil service pensions through the Minister of Finance and more generally Bills determining salaries, pensions and general benefits, if they involve spending by the State, local authorities, or public law legal persons (Article 73 paragraphs 2 and 3). Likewise, only at the initiative of the Government can Bills be introduced levying local or special taxes or charges of any nature on behalf of agencies or public or private law legal persons (Article 73 paragraph 5). Adoption by Parliament of law proposals as opposed to Bills is very rare, due to the usual governmental predominance in Parliament.

Bills and law proposals submitted to Parliament must be accompanied by a report stating the reasons for and/or purposes of the legislative initiative. If they entail costs to the Budget, they must be accompanied by a report of the General Accounting Office on the expenditure they entail and how it will be covered. Bills entailing expenditure or diminution of state income must be accompanied by a special report on how this expenditure will be met or loss covered by the Minister for Finance and other competent Ministers. Finally, Bills involving pensions must be accompanied by an opinion from the Court of Audit.

A Bill or law proposal containing provisions not related to its main subject matter shall not be introduced for debate (Article 74 paragraph 5). The same holds for amendments or supplements not related to the main content of the Bill.

62. (b). Stage of elaboration, discussion and voting of Bills or law proposals. Bills or law proposals are referred to the competent parliamentary permanent committee and to the scientific service of Parliament for elaboration. Omission of this procedural stage does not entail nullity or other sanctions (Article 74 paragraphs 1 and 2).

Bills and law proposals are then brought before Parliament to be debated upon and voted, once in principle, then article by article and finally as a whole (Article 76 paragraph 1). Bills and law proposals not subject to the exclusive competence of the plenary session of Parliament may be discussed and voted on by the competent parliamentary committee (Article 72 paragraphs 1 and 2). They are then laid before Parliament as a whole and, in one sitting, voted on in principle, then article by article, and then as a whole (Articles 76 paragraph 1 and 72 paragraph 4). Bills and law proposals which have been voted on by the competent committee with a majority of at least four-fifths are laid before a plenary session of Parliament for a vote without discussion (Article 72 paragraph 4 b of the Constitution, in combination with 108 paragraph 6 of the Standing Orders).

A Bill or law proposal designated by the Government as very urgent shall be introduced for voting after a limited debate in one sitting (Article 76 paragraph 4 of the Constitution, Article 109 of the Standing Orders).

Amendments and additions by both Members of Parliament and Ministers are discussed and voted upon only if tabled at least three days before the commencement of the sitting at which the bill or proposal is to be discussed (Article 74 paragraph 5). If in the course of the debate amendments or additions are accepted, voting as a whole shall be postponed for twenty-four hours from the distribution of the amended Bill or law proposal (Article 76 paragraph 3).

63. (c). Stage of promulgation and publication. Bills or law proposals passed by Parliament are promulgated and published by the President of the Republic within one month of being voted on, according to Article 42 of the Constitution.

By promulgating the Bill or the law proposal the President of the Republic acknowledges that the text of the Bill or proposal is indeed the same as that voted upon by Parliament and that the legislative procedure provided in the Constitution and the Standing Orders has been complied with. This ascertainment of the President of the Republic constitutes an irrebuttable presumption of the formal constitutionality of statutes. Consequently, courts may not review whether statutes have been enacted in compliance with procedural rules (*see supra* No. 56, and *infra* Nos 349).

Publication of the Bill or of the law proposal follows upon the order of the President of the Republic for its publication in the Official Gazette, whence the Bill or the law proposal becomes 'law'.

The Revision of 1986 has abrogated the competence of the President of the Republic to sanction statutes. This competence, which was actually never exercised in Greek constitutional history either by a King or by a President of the Republic, was meant to express the assent of the Head of State to the substance or the content of the enacted statutes.

Under the Constitution, before the revisions, the Head of State could send back a Bill passed by Parliament either because he disagreed with the content of the Bill or because the enactment of the Bill had violated the rules of the legislative procedure. However, the re-enactment of the Bill was binding on the Head of State, who then was obliged to proceed to its sanctioning, promulgation and publication.

The Revision of 1986 has preserved the competence of the President of the Republic to send back Bills, probably for reasons referring to a refusal of promulgation, that is, for violation of the legislative procedure. In the event of the President sending back a Bill or proposal, it is laid again before a full session of Parliament for discussion and voting, twice and in two distinct sittings, at least two days apart, in principle and by article during the first debate, and by article and as a whole during the second (Article 76 paragraph 2). The re-enactment of the Bill by the absolute majority of the parliamentary plenum binds the President of the Republic to sign the Bill within the next ten days (on the right of referring legislation back to Parliament, *see infra* No. 106).

II. Force of Statutes: Retroactive Force of Statutes

64. With the publication in the Official Gazette, the law acquires its 'formal' validity, its formal legal force, that is, it begins to exist in the legal world. It is to be noted that the term 'legal force' of a legal norm has two senses: it means either the fact of the creation of the legal norm or its rank in relation to other norms of the legal order. The 'material' validity of a statute, that is, its binding force, begins, according to Article 103 of the Introductory Statute to the Civil Code, ten days after its publication in the Official Gazette. Statutes may, however, include special provisions concerning the starting point of their 'material' validity. These special provisions amend *in concreto* the general rule of Article 103 of the Introductory Act to the Civil Code.

According to Article 2 of the Civil Code statutes refer to the future. However, this general provision may also be altered *in concreto* by a special clause of the statute. Retroactive force must be explicitly determined by the statute and may not infringe constitutional prohibitions on retroactive force.

65. The Constitution explicitly prohibits retroactive force of statutes in the following cases:

(1) Under Article 7 paragraph 1 a, 'There shall be no crime, nor shall punishment be inflicted unless specified by law in force prior to the perpetration of the act … .' The prohibition on retroactive force concerns statutes establishing or increasing criminal liability, not laws excluding or mitigating criminal liability.
(2) According to Article 78 paragraph 2, 'A tax or any other financial charge may not be imposed by a retroactive statute effective prior to the fiscal year proceeding the imposition of the tax' (*see also infra* Nos 486 et seq.).
(3) Under Article 77 paragraph 2, 'A statute which is not truly interpretative shall enter into force only as of its publication.' This provision concerns the authentic or authoritative interpretation of statutes, which according to Article 77

paragraph 1 of the Constitution 'rests with the legislative power'. The practical importance of this clause is that the legislator may not conceal the retroactive force of statutes by enacting pseudo-authentic interpretative statutes. A truly authentic interpretative statute refers to a previous statute with no clear content and meaning, which according to the Ruling 330/1969 of the Supreme Civil and Criminal Court 'has caused legal disputes and differing interpretations in legal theory and practice'. But the last condition of having caused 'disputes and differing interpretations in theory and jurisprudence' has not been repeated in all later rulings of the court, with the consequence that broader margins of appreciation are left to courts as to the judgment whether the law is a truly authentic interpretative one or not.

(4) Retroactive force of statutes is also prohibited in cases where constitutional rights are infringed. Court rulings refer usually to the right of property (Article 17 of the Constitution) but this rule may extend to the principle of equality (Article 4) as well as to other constitutional rights.

(5) The prohibition on retroactive application of statutes also holds for electoral statutes. Article 54 paragraph 1 of the Constitution states, 'The electoral system and constituencies are specified by statute which shall be applicable as of the elections after the immediately following ones, unless an explicit provision, adopted by a majority of two-thirds of the total number of Members of Parliament, provides for its immediate application as of the immediately following elections.' Thus, the electoral statute is valid for the future in all cases.

III. Types of Statutes

66. (a) Statutes implementing the Constitution ('Executive Statutes'). The Constitution contains in many of its articles a reservation in favour of a statute (*réserve de la loi*). Statutes, the enactment of which is provided for in the Constitution, are called 'Executive Statutes'.

Statutes of organic character (called in Greek 'organic' or 'organizational statutes') form a special category of Executive Statutes; they refer to the main organs and to the essential institutions of the State (elections, referenda, judiciary, etc.). The enactment of such statutes is compulsory, since otherwise, the State organ cannot assume its function and competence. These statutes may not simply be abrogated without a simultaneous enactment of a new statute.

67. (b) Framework Statutes. Article 43 paragraph 4 of the Constitution provides for a special category of statutes: 'Framework Statutes' (*lois-cadres*).

The framework statute is a statute of a very general character. It contains directives to be more specifically defined as legal rules by the administration and thus grants a broad delegation to the President of the Republic to issue Regulatory Decrees upon the proposal of the competent Minister(s). Framework Statutes have first to be passed by the parliamentary plenum, whereas ordinary statutes, with the exception of those provided for in Article 72 paragraph 1 of the Constitution (electoral statutes, statutes on the exercise and protection of human rights, on political parties, etc.), may be passed by the Recess Section. Second, they must provide for temporal limitations for the issuance of the Regulatory Decrees. If the delegation is not implemented within the time limits set by the framework statute, the Regulatory Decrees cannot be issued.

68. (c) Legislation enjoying legal force higher than that of statutes and 'once and for all' statutes. Article 107 paragraph 1 of the Constitution provides for a special category of statutes of a higher rank, that is, higher legal force, than ordinary statutes. These statutes enjoying legal force higher than that of 'ordinary statutes' are the 'Statute on Investment and Protection of Foreign Capital' (Legislative Decree 2687/1953) and extend to the principle of section A, Chapters A to D, of the 'Statute on Taxation of Ships, etc.' (Act 27/1975).

Article 107 paragraph 2 of the Constitution provides for a statute to be promulgated once and for all: 'A statute to be promulgated once and for all within three months of the date of entry into force of this Constitution, shall specify the terms and the procedure for the revision or cancellation of administrative acts [...] or agreements contracted on investment of foreign capital [...]'. Act 141/1975 has been enacted in accordance with this constitutional provision.

Both the higher-ranking statutes and the 'once and for all statutes' enjoy a special constitutional status. They may not be altered or abrogated by ordinary statutes. Nevertheless, an ordinary interpretative statute (Article 12 of Act 1701/1987) with retroactive effect has been considered by the Supreme Civil and Criminal Court as being a truly authentic interpretative statute of the 'once and for all Act 141/1975' (Ruling 4/1989). Thus, according to the ruling of the court, the ordinary statute was not unconstitutional, since the authentic interpretation of a 'once and for all statute' was deemed not to constitute an alteration thereof.

69. (d) Individual Statutes and '*Massnahmegesetze*'. Statutes have general and abstract content. This is not explicitly determined in a constitutional provision but it may be considered a consequence of the principle of equality. If equality or other constitutional rights are not infringed (*see* for instance Article 19 paragraph 1 of the German *Grundgesetz*), an individual statute may be enacted, in order to resolve an individual case.

'*Massnahmegesetze*' (legal measures) are enacted in order to cope with the social and political needs of a temporary character. They differ from individual statutes since they arrange categories of cases and not individual cases. They also differ from ordinary statutes because they are issued under temporary circumstances and have by their own nature a provisional validity.

§5. The Standing Orders (Regulations of Parliament)

70. According to Article 65 paragraph 1 of the Constitution:

> Parliament shall determine the manner of its free and democratic operation by adopting its own Standing Orders; these shall be adopted by the Plenum as specified in Article 76 and shall be published in the Official Gazette on the order of the Speaker.

The main difference between the Standing Orders and statutes, as far as procedure is concerned, is that the former are adopted without any cooperation of the President of the Republic, as is the case with the latter. Even the publication of the Standing Orders is made upon the order of the Speaker and not of the President of the Republic.

The substantial difference between Standing Orders and statutes lies in the fact that they have different domains of reference. Statutes may not regulate the operation of Parliament, since the Constitution reserves this matter to Parliament alone, and the Standing Orders may not refer to any other issue, apart from the determination of the operation of Parliament. In this sense, statutes and Standing Orders do not stand in any hierarchical relationship to one another.

Article 118 of the Standing Orders provides for a special procedure for their amendment as well as for their codification. The relevant proposals, which only Members of Parliament may initiate, are submitted to the competent parliamentary committee for elaboration. They are then brought to the plenum for debate and voting.

The above regulations safeguard the independence of Parliament, allowing it to regulate its own affairs. In this context, Parliament's actions are limited only by the Constitution, since the provisions of the Standing Orders may not under any circumstances run counter to the Constitution.

The current Standing Orders are divided into two parts. The first part regulates the organization and function of the Parliament while the second part concerns its services and staff. Since 2016 an appendix has been added to the first part. It is entitled 'Code of Ethics of the Members of the Parliament' and contains rules of political behaviour. The Standing Orders may not be abrogated without a simultaneous substitution by new Standing Orders. In this aspect, they are similar to 'organic' statutes.

§6. Administrative Regulations

71. The Constitution provides for the Executive to introduce rules of law (regulatory competence). This ability is granted either directly by the Constitution or by legislative act.

The practice of issuing regulatory administrative acts is particularly common today. The main reasons are the, frequently, technical nature of the issues to be regulated, the need to settle certain questions in a limited time frame and the need for rapid and smooth adjustment to continually changing social and economic conditions.

I. Presidential Decrees

72. (a) Categories. Under Article 43 paragraph 1(a) of the Constitution 'the President of the Republic shall issue the decrees required for the execution of statutes'. This provision presupposes the existence of a statute and the need to issue further rules of secondary importance, which specify the application of the statute. The secondary rules established by Presidential Decree are certainly ranked lower than statutes. Presidential Decrees issued according to Article 43 paragraph 1(a) are very rare.

73. Under Article 43 paragraph 2(a) of the Constitution, 'The issuance of general regulatory decrees, by virtue of special delegation granted by statute and within the limits of such delegation, shall be permitted on the proposal of the competent Minister.' The issuance of presidential Regulatory Decrees of this category presupposes the existence of a statute containing a specific and limited delegation of legislative authority. If delegation is broad and general the decree is null and void, though the tendency of the Council of State in reviewing such regulatory administrative action is to enlarge the boundaries of 'specific and limited' delegation (Rulings 2497/1974, 1201/1980 etc.).

74. Under Article 43 paragraph 4 of the Constitution, the 'Framework Statutes' (*lois-cadres*) passed by the parliamentary plenum may grant broad delegation for the issuance of C: 'These statutes shall set out the general principles and directives of the regulation to be followed and shall set time limits within which the delegation must be used.' Delegation by Framework Statutes is not permitted for matters concerning parliamentary elections, the exercise and protection of fundamental rights and freedoms, the operation of political parties, or more generally any issue which must be decided by the plenary session of Parliament (e.g., Articles 43 paragraph 4, and 72 paragraph 1 of the Constitution).

75. Decrees under both Article 43 paragraph 2 and under Article 43 paragraph 4 are equivalent to statutes. However, the difference between decrees under paragraph 2 and decrees under paragraph 4, apart from the broadness of the delegation, is that the former do not have to be issued within certain time limits and they need not be based on a statute passed by the parliamentary plenum; statutes passed by a parliamentary section may also delegate regulatory authority to the President of the Republic, under the condition that the delegation is specific and limited. In any case, sub-delegation is not permitted except where the statute provides otherwise.

76. A specific competence to issue Regulatory Decrees directly conferred by the Constitution on the President of the Republic is provided in Article 54 paragraph 2 of the Constitution: 'The number of Members of Parliament elected in each constituency is specified by presidential decree on the basis of the legal population … .'

77. (b) Procedure of Issuance. All decrees are issued by the President of the Republic on a proposal of the competent Minister, who also countersigns them. The initiative thus belongs solely to the Minister.

The draft decree, before being signed by the President of the Republic, must be submitted to the Council of State for a prior review (Article 95 paragraph 1(d) of the Constitution). This submission is an essential procedural condition of the issuance of the decree, omission of which results in the annulment, upon application, of the decree by the Council of State.

The review of the draft decree by the Council of State is limited to legality and constitutionality. The Council of State will also confirm that it has been drafted correctly in terms of legal technicalities. It does not extend to advisability. Since this review is not a judicial competence of the Council of State but an administrative and advisory one, it is not formally binding on the Minister. But in practice, insistence of a Minister on the draft and non-compliance with the observations of the Council of State would be a rather rare exception.

The President of the Republic does not have discretionary power to issue the decree or not: he is bound to proceed to the issuance as proposed by the Minister. The wording of the constitutional provision (Article 43 paragraph 2(a), '[…] the issuance of general regulatory decrees shall be permitted […]'), creates the impression prima facie that the President has a margin of appreciation as to the issuance of the decree. But what Article 43 paragraph 2 means by the word 'permitted' is that the issuance of Regulatory Decrees is an exception to the rule that legislation is within the competence of the legislative organ of the State. It does not imply any discretionary power of the President.

II. Regulations of Other Administrative Agencies

78. Article 43 paragraph 2(b) of the Constitution provides for administrative regulations by institutions other than the President of the Republic. Examples of such regulations would include Ministerial Decisions, the various acts of the Cabinet, local authorities, regional bodies, public law legal persons or even private law legal persons, provided that through this particular act, they are exercising some public authority.

A specific and limited delegation by a statute is necessary; furthermore, delegation of legislative authority is only permitted in cases 'concerning the regulation of more specific matters or matters of local interest or of a technical and detailed nature'. The criteria are particularly fluid and only given a more specific form by the courts in individual circumstances. However, the practical importance of the ruling on the specific nature of the issue is great, since regulations by other organs of administration are not subject to legislative elaboration to the Council of State. Often the legislature delegates rule-making powers to an administrative body other than the President of the Republic, precisely in order to bypass the procedure at the Council of State. This practice is particularly problematic, since in cases where the court rules that the issue was not of a specific, detailed or technical nature, then the Regulatory Act issued is nullified on the grounds that it rests on an unconstitutional law.

It has been decided that questions of protection of the environment and cultural heritage are never of purely local interest; they can, therefore, only be regulated by statute or Regulatory Decree (Ruling 3661/2005 Council of State).

Sub-delegation of the power to draft regulations to other agencies is prohibited unless the delegating statute determines otherwise.

III. Publication and Validity

79. Decrees must be published in the Official Gazette (Article 35 paragraph 1 of the Constitution). Act 3469/2006 (which replaced Act 301/1976) provides for the publication in the Official Gazette of all regulations as well. An exception is made for regulations of municipalities, which are published in one newspaper of the municipality and are kept in a special file, to which each person has free access.

The Council of State has ruled that Article 2 paragraph 2 of Act 301/1976, according to which regulations may not be published if this would endanger the national defence, is not contrary to the obligation of publication, which derives from a general principle of law of a constitutional rank (Rulings 2124/1977, 4250/1980). The same provision is included in Article 8 paragraph 1 of Act 3469/2006.

Regulations acquire their 'formal' validity with publication. Their 'material' validity usually coincides temporally with their 'formal' validity. In all cases, the 'material' validity starts from the actual date of publication in the Official Gazette. Retroactive application is only permitted in case the delegating statute specifically so provides.

§7. Acts with Legislative Content

80. According to Article 44 paragraph 1 of the Constitution:

> Under extraordinary circumstances of an urgent and unforeseeable need the President of the Republic may, upon the proposal of the Cabinet, issue acts of legislative content. Such acts shall be submitted to Parliament for ratification, as specified in the provisions of Article 72 paragraph 1, within forty days of their issuance or within forty days from the convocation of a parliamentary session. Should such acts not be submitted to Parliament within the above time limits or if they should not be ratified by Parliament within three months of their submission, they will henceforth cease to be in force.

Acts with legislative content, before being ratified by Parliament, are according to the organic criterion of administrative acts. They are, nevertheless, considered equivalent to statutes. Consequently, they may abrogate or amend, even before being ratified by Parliament, statutory provisions enacted according to the ordinary legislative procedure. The content of their provisions is not restricted so long as they do not violate the Constitution.

As they are equivalent to statutes, acts with legislative content are not subject to annulment procedures before the Council of State, as are administrative acts. Nor is judicial review admissible as to the occurrence of 'extraordinary circumstances of an urgent or unforeseeable need' (Full Bench of the Council of State 3636/1989, 2567/2015).

The President of the Republic 'may', according to the wording of Article 44 paragraph 1, 'issue acts with a legislative content'. This does not, however, imply a discretionary power of the President of the Republic, that is, a presidential 'prerogative' to issue or not issue such acts. It simply means that this competence is an exception to the rule of Article 26 paragraph 1, according to which 'Legislative powers shall be exercised by the Parliament and the President of the Republic.' This exception is justified by 'the extraordinary circumstances of an urgent and unforeseeable need' that make recourse to Parliament for quick legislation practically impossible.

The proposal of the Cabinet is binding for the President of the Republic if 'extraordinary circumstances of an urgent and unforeseeable need' are present. But a certain margin of appreciation is left to the President of the Republic as to the occurrence of such circumstances. This is probably the reason why the Constitution provides for a complex organ for the issuance of acts with legislative content, consisting of the Cabinet and the President of the Republic. The appreciation of the President of the Republic minimizes the danger of possible governmental abuse. Possible objections by the President of the Republic must, however, be expressed with caution, in order not to reveal a disagreement with the responsible government. It is a constitutional practice that before undertaking the initiative, the Government consults with the President of the Republic.

Acts with legislative content are also provided for in Article 48 paragraph 5 of the Constitution. This particular category will be dealt with in Part VII (*see infra* No. 507).

Acts with legislative content must be published in the Official Gazette twice – once after their issuance and once after they have been ratified by statute.

§8. Legislative Decrees, Laws of Emergency, Arbitrary Regulatory Administrative Acts

81. According to Article 35 paragraph 1 of the previous Constitution of 1952, 'During the parliamentary term, if Parliament is absent or not in session, the King may proceed with the issuance of legislative decrees in order to deal with matters of extraordinary urgency after a committee of Members of Parliament has expressed its assent.'

Legislative Decrees are not provided for in the Constitution of 1975/1986/2001/2008/2019. But those which were issued in the past under the Constitution of 1952 and are still in force are equivalent to statutes.

82. The issuance of 'emergency laws' by the Executive has been another form of unconstitutional practice of the past exercised mainly by authoritarian governments. The justification was usually sought in the maxim '*salus rei publicae suprema lex*'.

83. A surviving remnant of this unconstitutional practice of the past is the issuance of Regulatory Acts by the Cabinet or of ministerial regulations issued without delegated authority. These acts, which are applied by the public administration, usually contain a final clause providing for their ratification by a future law. They are usually ratified retroactively by a statute. The Council of State has ruled (3596-7/1991) that the issuing of a Ministerial Decision without legislative delegation, and its subsequent ratification by statute, is unconstitutional, contravening Article 43 of the Constitution. Such 'capricious' or 'arbitrary' regulatory acts acquire material validity only after they have been ratified by statute, not retroactively. During the period prior to its ratification, the Ministerial Decision continues to be regarded as an administrative act and as such subject to review and possible annulment by the Council of State.

§9. Case Law

84. Judgments of higher courts enjoy a moral authority and tend to be followed by the lower courts; however, they have never been considered as a formal source of law, even if they form a '*jurisprudence constante*'. An exception is made for the rulings of the Special Highest Court related to the settlement of controversies on whether the content of a statute enacted by Parliament is contrary to the Constitution, or on the interpretation of provisions of such statute when conflicting judgments have been pronounced by the Supreme Administrative Court, the Supreme Civil and Criminal Court or the Court of Audit (Article 100 paragraph 1(e) of the Constitution). If provisions of a statute are declared unconstitutional, they cease to be valid 'as of the date of publication of the respective judgment, or as of the date specified by the ruling' (Article 100 paragraph 4 of the Constitution).

Another exception is the case of annulment by the Council of State of a Regulatory Administrative Act, in accordance with Article 95 paragraph 1(a) of the Constitution. Annulment of the Regulatory Act, and thus of a rule of law, is equivalent to a negative enactment of law.

§10. International Law

85. Under Article 28 paragraph 1(a) of the Constitution:

> Generally recognized rules of international law, as well as international conventions as of the time they are ratified by statute and become operative according to their respective conditions, shall be an integral part of domestic Greek law and prevail over any contrary provision of the law.

Generally recognized rules of international law, that is, the general principles of the law of nations and international customary law, are integrated into domestic law automatically, that is, without any act of domestic law being required. International conventions, on the other hand, specifically conventions on trade, taxation, economic cooperation and participation in international organizations or unions and all others containing concessions for which, according to other provisions of this Constitution, no provision can be made without a statute, or which may burden the Greeks individually, must be ratified by statute in order to acquire validity in Greece. Article 36 paragraph 4 of the Constitution, which also refers to international law (*see infra* Nos 509–510) prohibits delegation of this legislative authority to the administration.

Both the generally recognized rules of international law and international conventions transformed into Greek law are placed in the hierarchy of legal rules between the Constitution and the statutes.

Under Article 100 paragraph 1(f) of the Constitution, the Special Highest Court settles questions of whether rules of international law are generally recognized or not.

Article 28 paragraph 1(b) of the Constitution contains a reservation of reciprocity concerning the application of international law to aliens. Reciprocity must exist in reality, not only in theory (*see* Ruling of the Council of State 2280/1990). Nevertheless, the rights of aliens guaranteed by the Constitution or by international covenants on human rights and fundamental freedoms ratified by statute are protected without the condition of reciprocity.

The importance of generally recognized rules of international law, to which reference was already made in the year 1896 by the Supreme Court of Civil and Criminal Justice (Ruling 14/1896), as forming part of internal law, though no special provisions – constitutional or other – existed at that time, is now emphasized in Article 2 paragraph 2 of the Constitution: 'Greece, adhering to the generally recognized rules of international law, pursues the strengthening of peace and of justice and the fostering of friendly relations between peoples and States.' This provision provides the basis for interpretation of the Constitution as consistently as possible with international law.

§11. EU Law

86. The Hellenic Republic signed its Treaty of Accession to the European Union in 1979. Paragraphs 2 and 3 of Article 28 of the Constitution served as the constitutional basis for the accession. These paragraphs, introduced in the Constitution and included for precisely this purpose, are worded as follows:

> 2. Authorities provided by the Constitution may by treaty or agreement be vested in agencies of international organizations, when this serves an important national interest and promotes cooperation with other States. A majority of three-fifths of the total number of Members of Parliament shall be necessary to vote the law [statute] ratifying the treaty or agreement. –
> 3. Greece shall freely proceed by law [statute] passed by an overall majority of the total number of Members of Parliament to limit the exercise of national sovereignty, insofar as this is dictated by an important national interest, does not infringe upon the rights of man and the foundations of democratic government and is effected on the basis of the principles of equality and under the condition of reciprocity.

The wording of these paragraphs as well as the distinction they make between the recognition of competences of international organizations on the one hand and the limitation of national sovereignty on the other are not technically successful, since the former are a category of the latter. What makes things more confusing is that the statute on the limitation of national sovereignty does not require as large a majority as the recognition of competences of international organizations, though it seems to be of equal, if not of greater, importance.

Act 945/1979 which ratified the European Communities Treaties was voted by a large majority required according to Article 28 paragraph 2 and consequently, the problems of interpretation were avoided in practice.

On 1 January 1981, when the above statute came into force, EU law – both primary law (founding treaties) and derivative law (Regulations, Directives, decisions, opinions, recommendations) – acquired the force of domestic law and henceforth represent a special source of constitutional law.

With the Revision of 2001, an interpretative statement was added to Article 28, according to which, 'Article 28 constitutes the foundation for the participation of the Country in the European integration process.' No real change was effected by the introduction of this statement to the Constitution. It did, however, emphasize the importance of the European perspective, and provide more robust support and guidance for any further transfer of powers to the EU (on the position of European law in the national legal framework, *see supra* No. 49).

Chapter 3. Codification and Interpretation of Legal Rules

§1. Codification

87. The Greek legal system is a continental one. Thus written legislation is of major importance. Several branches of law are codified. Formal constitutional rules form part of a unitary text, the Constitution; equivalent legal rules, that is, Constituent Acts and Resolutions of Parliament still in force (Article 111 of the Constitution, *see supra* No. 55) are to be found separately.

Major codifications of ordinary law include the Civil Code, the Penal Code, the Codes of Civil and Criminal Procedure, and the Military Penal Code. More specific subjects are treated in the Code on Civil Servants, the Municipal and Communal Code (MCC), the Second-Level Local Government Code (SLLGC), the Code of Greek Citizenship, the Agriculture and Forest Codes, the Code on Taxation of Income, the Code on Stamp Taxes, and the Code of Private Maritime Law.

Act 2717/1999 brought together in a single codified text the rules of administrative court procedure concerning the hearing of substantive administrative disputes by administrative courts. This codified law does not apply to disputes concerning annulment, or to cases before the Council of State or the Court of Audit where special laws apply.

Also, Act 2690/1999 ratified the Administrative Process Code, with regulations on the organization and operation of administrative bodies, administrative acts, administrative contracts, and such like. The Code sets out in writing many general principles of administrative law which had already taken shape in case law, for example, the justifying of administrative acts.

Article 76 paragraph 6 of the Constitution provides for a special procedure for the enactment of codes: 'Judicial or administrative codes drafted by special committees established under special statutes may be voted through in the Plenum of the Parliament by a special statute ratifying the code as a whole.' Likewise, according to Article 76 paragraph 7, legal provisions in force may be codified by simple classification.

It is a quite usual practice that statutes contain clauses delegating authority to the administration to codify laws in 'codifying presidential decrees'.

§2. Interpretation

I. Interpretation in General

88. Objective interpretation, that is, the attempt to establish the meaning of the legal rule at the time of interpretation, is unanimously recognized as the correct method of interpretation. Subjective interpretation, that is, the attempt to ascertain the meaning of the rule which the legislator had in mind, is usually of great assistance.

Interpretation aims to reveal the meaning of the rule and its purpose. Therefore, teleological interpretation is the main task of the interpreter. Grammatical, systematic and logical interpretation are certainly of great avail, though the well-known principles of systematic and logical interpretation (*e silentio, e contrario, ubi lex non distinguit nec nostrum est distinguere, a minori ad majus and vice versa,* etc.) are to be applied with caution.

II. Interpretation of the Constitution

89. The property of the Constitution as the supreme law of the land and judicial review of the constitutionality of laws as well as the laconic wording of constitutional provisions make the interpretation of the Constitution an issue *per se*. Furthermore, constitutional law is not only law, subject to positivistic and doctrinal interpretation; it is political law par excellence, for the interpretation of which the interpreter has to take into consideration politics, history, sociology, philosophy of law and State, and so on.

The ultimate limit of the interpretation of the Constitution is the wording of the Constitution itself: there is no interpretation *'contra constitutionem'*. A second limit is freedom: *'in dubio pro libertate'*. A third is the unity of the Constitution: there are no unconstitutional provisions of the Constitution, as the Council of State (292/1984) has explicitly ruled. Consequently, conflicting constitutional provisions must both be applied; neither may be surrendered in favour of the other but they must be balanced in the concrete conditions of their application.

As far as the constitutionality of laws is concerned the unanimous opinion in theory and jurisprudence is that laws are to be interpreted in accordance with the Constitution and are judged unconstitutional only in cases of evident violation of the Constitution: *'in dubio pro lege'*.

III. Authoritative Interpretation of Laws

90. *See supra* Nos 64–65.

Part II. The Head of State

91. The President of the Republic is the Head of State and exercises both legislative and executive power (Article 26 paragraphs 1 and 2 of the Constitution).

Chapter 1. Election and Substitution

§1. Election

I. Eligibility

92. The President of the Republic is elected by Parliament (Article 30 paragraph 1 of the Constitution). A person may be elected as President if they have been a Greek citizen for at least five years; if they are of Greek descent from the father's or, since the 2001 Revision, mother's side; if they have attained the age of 40 and have the capacity to vote (Article 31 of the Constitution). Re-election of the same person as President of the Republic is permitted only once (Article 30 paragraph 5 of the Constitution); in other words, no more than two terms of office are permitted, whether consecutive or divided by an interval. The resignation of the President of the Republic prior to the expiration of their term bars them from standing in the presidential election resulting from their resignation (Article 32 of the Constitution), although they can be re-elected at a later date.

II. Procedure

93. The procedure for the presidential election is as follows (Article 32 of the Constitution). The Speaker convokes Parliament, even if it is not sitting (except due to dissolution), in an ad hoc session at least one month before the expiration of the mandate of the incumbent President. In the case of premature termination (due to resignation, death, etc.), Parliament is assembled to elect the President within the next ten days. If Parliament has been dissolved, the election of the President is postponed until the new Parliament has constituted itself as a body and within twenty days thereof.

The Constitution does not provide for candidacies. However, under Article 140 paragraph 5 of the Standing Orders, parliamentary groups as well as groups of independent deputies have the right to propose candidates. The constitutionality of this provision is not certain, since Article 32 of the Constitution, while not containing any special provision, does not permit any limit on the freedom of Members of Parliament to put forward candidates for the Presidency. In order to protect the authority and prestige of the President of the Republic, Article 140 paragraph 4 of the Standing Orders does not permit debates prior to the election.

Until its revision in 1986, Article 32 paragraph 1 provided for the election of the President of the Republic by secret ballot. This article was revised in 1986 to provide in future for election by roll call. Thus in essence it legitimized the breach of secrecy that had already occurred in March 1985 during the election of Christos Sartzetakis. On that occasion, the Members of Parliament belonging to the socialist and to the communist parties, not one of whose votes could be lost if the necessary minimum majority of 180 was to be secured, had been invited to cast their 'secret' votes using coloured ballot papers!

94. The Constitution provides for several stages of the presidential election (Article 32 paragraphs 3 and 4):

> 3. The person receiving a two-thirds majority of the total number of Members of Parliament shall be elected President of the Republic. Should the said majority not be attained, the ballot shall be repeated after five days. Should the second ballot fail to produce the required majority, the ballot shall once more be repeated after five days; the person receiving a three-fifths majority of the total number of Members of Parliament shall be elected President of the Republic.

The Constitution provided for an automatic dissolution of the Parliament due to failure to elect a President of the Republic. As per the Revision of 2019, the relevant paragraph reads as follows:

> 4. Should the third ballot fail to produce the said qualified majority, the ballot shall be repeated after five days and the person receiving an absolute majority of the votes of the total number of Members of Parliament shall be elected President of the Republic. Should this majority also not be attained, the ballot shall be repeated after five days and the person receiving a relative majority shall be elected President of the Republic. In case of a tie vote, the person receiving the greatest number of votes in the first ballot of the preceding paragraph shall be elected President of the Republic.

Although the Constitution makes detailed provisions for the procedure to be followed in electing the President of the Republic, it does not cover every single eventuality that may arise during the election. For example, there is no provision for what should happen in the event of a tie between the two candidates in the final vote of the second phase. In such circumstances, Parliament would have to be dissolved again and the new Parliament elect a President.

The Constitution does not provide for any judicial review of the election (*see* Council of State Ruling 2862/1985).

95. On the restoration of democracy after the military dictatorship the former President of the Council of State and member of the Academy, Michael Stassinopoulos, was elected as transitional President of the Republic (1975). He was followed by the member of the Academy and Professor at the University of Athens, Constantine Tsatsos (1975–1980), by Constantine Karamanlis, who served two non-consecutive terms (1980–1985, 1990–1995), by the Supreme Civil and Criminal Court judge Christos Sartzetakis, who held office between Constantine Karamanlis' two terms (1985–1990), by Constantine Stephanopoulos, who served for two consecutive terms (1995–2000, 2000–2005), and by the politician Karolos Papoulias, who also served for two consecutive terms (2005–2010, 2010–2015). Afterwards, the office of President of the Republic was held by the politician and professor at the University of Athens Prokopios Pavlopoulos (2015–2020). The office is currently held by, the former President of the Council of State Katerina Sakellaropoulou.

III. Tenure

96. The President of the Republic is elected for a five-year term, commencing upon their swearing-in (Articles 30 paragraph 3, and 32 paragraph 2 of the Constitution). They enter office on the day following the expiration of the term of the outgoing President or, in all other cases, on the day following their election (Article 33 paragraph 1).

Before assuming the exercise of their duties they take an oath 'in the name of the Holy and Consubstantial and Indivisible Trinity' to safeguard and faithfully observe the Constitution and the laws, to defend the national independence and the territorial integrity of the country, to protect the rights and freedoms of the Greeks and to serve the general interest and progress of the people (Article 33 paragraph 2 of the Constitution). This oath is a Christian oath, the wording of which is determined in the text of the Constitution. A matter of interpretation may arise if a non-Christian President is ever elected by Parliament. They will probably have to take an oath, due to the constitutional guarantees of religious liberty (Article 13), according to the form determined by their own religion or to make a declaration invoking their conscience and honour.

The presidential term expires on the day the five-year term is completed. But tenure of office may be extended in case of war until the end of hostilities (Article 30 paragraph 4) as well as in circumstances where the procedure for the election of the new President of the Republic is not completed in due time. The incumbent President continues in both cases to exercise his duties (Article 32 paragraph 6) until the election of the new President.

A premature ending of the presidential term occurs in case of resignation, death, or removal from office, as well as in case of permanent incapacity of the President of the Republic to exercise his duties (Article 32 paragraph 1(b) of the Constitution).

§2. Substitution

97. The Constitution (Article 34 paragraph 1) allows for the replacement of the President of the Republic in the event of their absence abroad for more than ten days, and in the event of their death, resignation, removal from office or any other circumstance preventing them from carrying out their duties. When the incapacity is temporary, replacement shall last only until the return of the President or the ceasing of the circumstances preventing them from carrying out their duties. Should this circumstance, however, continue for more than thirty days, Parliament is convoked, even if it has been dissolved, in order to decide by a three-fifths majority of the total number of its Members whether the situation calls for the election of a new President of the Republic (Article 34 paragraph 2 of the Constitution).

98. In the event of permanent incapacity or premature termination of the President's term of office, the substitute shall hold office until the commencement of the term of the next President. In no circumstances may a replacement last more than six months. Within this six-month period, the election of the new President must take place. During the period of incapacity, the Speaker temporarily replaces the President of the Republic in their duties. If Parliament is not sitting, the Speaker of the former Parliament stands in for the President of the Republic and, should they refuse or not exist, the President is replaced by the Cabinet collectively (Article 34 of the Constitution). This provision entails that the acting Speaker does not have the right to refuse to serve as the replacement for the President. They may only resign from office in order for a new Speaker to be elected, subsequently to take over as the substitute for the President of the Republic. The election of the new President of the Republic may in no case be delayed for more than six months from the commencement of the substitution.

99. The substitute President of the Republic may exercise all constitutional competences and powers of the Head of State with the exception of the dissolution of Parliament, except in the event of no new President being elected (Article 32 paragraph 4 of the Constitution), the dismissal of the Cabinet and the proclamation of referenda (Article 34 paragraph 1(b)). This provision has been obsolete since the constitutional amendment of 1986 as far as the dismissal of Cabinet and referenda are concerned. Dismissal of Cabinet is no longer permitted by the Constitution and the proclamation of referenda is merely a formal competence of the President of the Republic, which is decided and initiated by Parliament and the Cabinet.

Chapter 2. Legal Status

§1. General

100. The President of the Republic participates in the Legislature and in the Executive (Article 26 paragraphs 1 and 2 of the Constitution).

101. Apart from their legislative and administrative competence, the President of the Republic is characterized as a 'mediator' or 'arbitrator'. According to Article 30 paragraph 1(a), they shall regulate the function of the institutions of the Republic ('regulator'); i.e., they intervene in cases of malfunctioning institutions of the Republic, in order to restore the harmonious functioning of the Constitution. The actual exercise of the regulatory role of the Head of State has been the subject of political dispute, mainly inspired by memories of the events of 1965 (*see supra* No. 37).

Thus the regulatory role of the President of the Republic was institutionally apparent before the Revision of 1986 when the President of the Republic disposed over substantial and not merely formal competences. It would have been more consistent with the purposes of the 1986 constitutional amendment if Article 30 paragraph 1(a) of the Constitution had also been deleted. After that amendment, the meaning of Article 30 paragraph 1(a) of the Constitution has shifted to a mere declaratory principle of the authority and prestige that the President of the Republic ought to enjoy. It is questionable if it still has regulatory consequences.

The diminution of the role of the President has left the Greek system excessively focused on the office of the Prime Minister. The leader of the parliamentary majority in reality controls both Parliament, through their parliamentary party, and the Executive, through what is – in essence – their absolute discretion to hire and fire the members of the Government. There is thus no institutional counterweight in the taking of critical political decisions and the handling of important institutional issues – as should be the case in a genuinely parliamentary system.

102. The President of the Republic may not exercise their competences without ministerial countersignature. According to this rule, the responsibility of the Head of State is assumed by the Government. Nevertheless, the Constitution provides for some exceptions: for example, the appointment of the Prime Minister, the discharge of the Government of its duties following a resignation or a vote of censure, the return of a bill to Parliament, and so on, do not need to be countersigned (Article 35 paragraph 2).

§2. Incompatibilities

103. The office of the President cannot be held at the same time as any other office, position or function (Article 30 paragraph 2 of the Constitution). This principle of incompatibility is extremely broad in its application, covering any professional or business activity, public or private. We may ask whether the concept of 'work' embraces the activities of a President as an author, scholar or artist, particularly if such activities yield no financial benefit (as would seem to be suggested by the proceedings of the Plenary Session of the Constitutional Committee of 1975).

104. Constitutional theory was confronted in 1985 with a major issue, known as the 'Alevras vote' concerning the right to vote in the presidential election of the substitute President of the Republic. Ioannis Alevras was the Speaker during the presidential election in 1985. The former conservative President of the Republic, Constantine Karamanlis, had resigned before the expiry of his term (in protest at the conduct of the then socialist Prime Minister Andreas Papandreou, who had broken his promise to support his re-election and instead had proposed Sartzetakis, *see supra* Nos 93 and 95). He was replaced by Alevras, the Speaker, who exercised his right to vote in the presidential election in his capacity as a Member of Parliament. Alevras' vote, without which the President of the Republic would not have been elected and consequently Parliament would have been dissolved according to the Constitution (Article 32 paragraph 4), was considered by the parliamentary majority to be valid.

The 'Alevras vote' bitterly divided both politicians and scholars. Constitutionalists are still concerned, even after so many years have passed, over whether the incompatibilities of the office of the President apply also to the substitute President of the Republic, and whether the presidential election of 1985 proceeded in conformity with or in violation of the Constitution. The debate has transcended its own boundaries: it resulted in a discourse on the political interpretation of the Constitution. What may be remarked here is that the application of the Constitution in 1985 was unfortunately directed by political criteria. Even if the constitutionality of the 'Alevras vote' was not clear, it would have been a desideratum of the interpretation of the Constitution to dissolve Parliament rather than tolerate a possible violation of the Constitution.

Chapter 3. Competence

§1. The Principle of Specific Competence

105. According to Article 50 of the Constitution, 'The President of the Republic shall have no powers other than those explicitly conferred upon them by the Constitution and the laws concurrent herewith.' Consequently, the competences of the President of the Republic[1] (the preferred term here is 'competences', not 'powers' or 'prerogatives' or 'rights') are those which are explicitly assigned to them by the Constitution and the laws in accordance to the Constitution. Article 50 is considered to belong to the group of constitutional provisions which form the core of the principle of democracy and of the principle of legality. As a matter of fact, this provision, which was introduced in the first democratic Constitution of 1864, was intended to restrict the powers of the King. It was meant to underline the basic difference between the democratic Constitution of 1864 and the former monarchic Constitution of 1844. Nowadays, under the predominance of the rule of law, Article 50 seems superfluous: the President of the Republic, like any other organ of the State, only has competences based on law. The specific constitutional provision of Article 50 on the restriction of presidential competences expresses mainly the historical dimension of the evolution to democracy; its crucial normative content is the principle of legality in general.

§2. Legislative Competences

106. The exercise of legislative competences by the President of the Republic is provided for in principle in Article 26 paragraph 1 of the Constitution and is more narrowly defined by a series of other constitutional provisions. Specifically:

(1) The President of the Republic may return a bill to Parliament (Article 42 paragraphs 1 and 2). While the Constitution makes no reference to the reasons for returning a bill, it does state that the President must set out these reasons when they exercise this particular competence. To date, no President of the Republic has returned a bill to Parliament. Some constitutional scholars have claimed that the reasons must be confined to the formal aspects of the procedure for introducing legislation, even the essential unconstitutionality of the law in question; in no case may a bill be returned on grounds of merit (*see also supra* No. 63).
(2) The President of the Republic issues Regulatory Decrees (*see supra* Nos 73 et seq.);
(3) The President of the Republic issues acts with legislative content (*see supra* Nos 80 et seq.).

1. According to the continental legal terminology, the preferred and most accurate term to describe the presidential authority is the term 'competences' rather than 'powers', 'prerogatives' or 'rights'.

(4) The President of the Republic proclaims referenda on matters of crucial national interest and on Bills concerning serious social issues (*see supra* No. 173).
(5) The President of the Republic decrees a 'state of siege' (state of emergency), if Parliament is not sitting or if it is impossible for it to convene, pursuant to Article 48 paragraph 2 (*see infra* Nos 507 et seq.).

§3. Administrative Competences

107. The Constitution lists certain administrative competences of the President of the Republic. Specifically:

(1) The President of the Republic promulgates and publishes statutes (*see supra* Nos 63 et seq.).
(2) The President of the Republic issues individual administrative acts (individual Decrees), a special category of which – the appointment and dismissal of public servants, officers of the armed forces, as well as judges – are provided for in Articles 46 paragraphs 1, 45 and 88 paragraph 1 of the Constitution. Because of the limiting reference to the law, in Articles 45 and 46 paragraph 1 of the Constitution, civil servants and officers of the armed forces may be appointed and dismissed by means of other administrative acts. In the case of judges, there is no such possibility.
(3) The President of the Republic awards decorations and orders according to Article 46 paragraph 2 of the Constitution. The initiative of awarding decorations lies with the Minister for Foreign Affairs, who is advised by the Council for Decorations, and not with the President of the Republic (*see* Executive Statute 106/1975 on Decorations regarding this Article).
(4) The President of the Republic is the head of the armed forces, the command of which is entrusted to the Government according to Article 45 of the Constitution. The entrusting of leadership of the armed forces to the Head of State has its origins in the monarchical period. Since 1975, when the limitation in favour of the Government was introduced into the Constitution, this competence of the President has had purely symbolic significance.

§4. 'Regulatory' Competences

108. The Constitution makes the following provision for regulatory competences of the President of the Republic:

(1) The President of the Republic convokes Parliament in sessions and declares the commencement and the termination of the parliamentary terms according to Article 40 paragraph 1 (*see infra* Nos 164).
(2) The President of the Republic suspends parliamentary sessions according to Article 40 paragraph 2 (*see infra* Nos 164).

(3) The President of the Republic dissolves Parliament, mainly according to Article 41 (*see infra* Nos 169 et seq.).
(4) The President of the Republic appoints the Prime Minister and the Cabinet and discharges them from their duties in case of resignation or of a parliamentary vote of censure according to Articles 37 and 38 (*see infra* Nos 183 et seq.).
(5) The President of the Republic addresses messages to the Greek people under exceptional circumstances after having secured the consent of the Prime Minister (Article 44 paragraph 3 of the Constitution). These messages as official manifestations of the communication of the President of the Republic with the people have to be countersigned by the Prime Minister and are published in the Official Gazette. Informal messages, speeches, and so on of the President of the Republic in everyday political life, even when they sometimes cause constitutional debates as to whether they are permitted or not, do not fall under Article 44 paragraph 3 of the Constitution.

§5. Competences of the President of the Republic Related to their International Role

109. The President of the Republic represents the country in its relations with other nations, in accordance with Article 36 paragraph 1 of the Constitution. He may declare war and enter international undertakings on behalf of the State, concluding and signing international peace treaties, treaties of alliance, economic cooperation and participation in international organizations or associations. Such documents must be countersigned by the appropriate Minister or the Prime Minister.

§6. Judicial Competences

110. The President of the Republic has the right to pardon, alter or reduce punishments pronounced by the courts of law and to remove all consequences at law of punishments pronounced and served, upon the proposal of the Minister of Justice and after consulting with a council composed in its majority of judges. A Presidential pardon of a Minister may only be given with the consent of Parliament (Article 47 paragraphs 1 and 2 of the Constitution).

The functioning of the Council of Pardons is determined by Legislative Decree 68/1968 'On the Council of Pardons – Composition and Procedure' as amended by Legislative Decree 1295/1972.

However, the President of the Republic has no longer the power to grant amnesty for political crimes. Since the constitutional Revision of 1986 amnesty may only be granted by Parliament, voting by a three-fifths majority of all members (Article 47 paragraph 3).

Chapter 4. Liability and Responsibility

§1. General

111. The liability in law of the President of the Republic is determined in Article 49 of the Constitution and in the special Act thereon, Act 265/1976.

That constitutional provision (Article 49 paragraph 1) differentiates between acts related to the exercise of his duties and acts not related thereto. For acts related to the exercise of his competences, the provision exempts the President from all liability, political, civil or criminal. The President of the Republic is only exceptionally liable for 'high treason' and for 'intentional violation of the Constitution'. For acts not related to the discharge of those duties, the President is fully responsible 'but prosecution shall be suspended until the expiration of the presidential term'. The provision refers to the suspension of criminal prosecution only, which means that there is no impediment to the bringing of an action in a civil dispute.

§2. Kinds of Criminal Responsibility

112. Article 49 paragraph 1 of the Constitution refers to the criminal responsibility of the President of the Republic. Accordingly, Article 15 of Act 265/1976 establishes civil liability arising from high treason or intentional violation of the Constitution and provides that for civil claims only civil courts are competent.

The President of the Republic does not have political responsibility. Removal from office, mentioned in Articles 32 paragraph 1(b), and 34 paragraph 1(a) of the Constitution, is a consequence of the criminal sentence imposed by the court (Article 3 of Act 265/1976 'On the Responsibility of the President of the Republic').

§3. Responsibility for High Treason

113. The President of the Republic commits high treason if they abolish, change, or attempt to abolish or change the form of government of the country (Article 2 paragraph 2 of Act 265/1976).

They intentionally violate the Constitution if they behave by acts or omissions contrary to a prescriptive constitutional provision, which assigns to them binding competences with no discretionary power, to be solely exercised by them, and if as a consequence the normal functioning of the Constitution has been seriously breached (Article 2 paragraph 3 of Act 265/1976). This legal definition of the crime of intentional violation of the Constitution restricts the responsibility of the President to such an extent, especially after the constitutional amendment of 1986, that it makes responsibility almost impossible. It seems thus to be unconstitutional.

§4. Criminal Proceedings

114. Criminal proceedings against the President of the Republic are laid down in outline in Article 49 paragraphs 2 and 3, and Article 86 of the Constitution and are specified in Act 265/1976.

Proceedings start with a proposal signed by at least one-third of the total number of the Members of Parliament. The relevant proposal is accepted only if it secures the votes of two-thirds of all members. The session will be held *in camera* and the vote conducted by roll call. The need for an increased majority reflects the gravity of the charge while offering a measure of security to the President of the Republic against frivolous accusations.

Should Parliament decide to proceed with the impeachment of the President of the Republic, it elects a twelve-member investigating committee of deputies, which submits its report to the plenum within a time period of two months (Article 8 of Act 265/1976). The parliamentary plenum finally decides whether to press charges, so that the President of the Republic will be brought to trial (Article 10 of Act 265/1976). After arraignment, the President abstains from the discharge of his duties and is replaced by his substitute (Article 49 paragraph 4 of the Constitution).

The main proceedings take place before the Special Court defined in Article 86 of the Constitution. Article 86 of the Constitution refers to the criminal responsibility of the members of the Government but is also applicable in case of criminal responsibility of the President.

If the President is exculpated they will resume their duties, provided that their term of office has not expired.

Part III. Parliament

115. Legislative power is exercised, pursuant to the Constitution (Article 26 paragraph 1), by a composite organ consisting of the Parliament and the President of the Republic (for the latter, *see* detailed account *supra* Nos 91 et seq.).

Parliament, being the main organ of legislative power and the representative of the people, is designated by election. It has thus a direct democratic legitimacy. The Government is democratically legitimized by virtue of the mechanisms of the parliamentary system. Governmental oversight over administrative agencies as well as parliamentary and judicial controls supply a practical implementation of the constitutional provision that 'all powers derive from the People and exist for the People and the Nation … ' (Article 1 paragraph 3).

Chapter 1. The Organ of State

§1. Unicameral System

116. The bicameral system was established under the Constitutions of 1832, 1844, 1925 and 1927. All the other Greek Constitutions, including that currently in force, have provided for a unicameral system.

Greek constitutional theory considers the unicameral system to correspond to a higher degree to the democratic principle since the Upper House (Senate) has been traditionally characterized by aristocratic or elitist elements.

Greece is furthermore a unitary State, not a federal one; there is thus no need for an Upper House safeguarding the competences of the states vis-à-vis the federation.

§2. Number and Classification of Members of Parliament

117. According to the Constitution, the number of the Members of Parliament is to be specified by statute; it cannot, however, be below two hundred or over three hundred (Article 51 paragraph 1). Electoral legislation traditionally determines the number of deputies as three hundred (Article 2 paragraph 1 of the Presidential Decree 26/2012, 'Codification of Legislation on the Election of Members of Parliament').

118. Members of Parliament are elected in electoral districts. However, Article 54 paragraph 3 of the Constitution states, 'Part of the Parliament, comprising not more than one-twentieth of the total number of its members may be elected throughout the country at large in proportion to the total electoral strength of each party throughout the country, as specified by law [statute].' The electoral statute determines the number of national representatives to be twelve; thus the number of Members of Parliament elected in electoral districts is 288 (Article 2 paragraph 1 of the Presidential Decree 26/2012). Nevertheless, the legal status of all Members of Parliament is the same: they 'represent the nation' (Article 51 paragraph 2 of the Constitution) (*see infra* No. 126).

According to Article 54 paragraph 2 of the Constitution:

> The number of Members of Parliament elected in each constituency is specified by presidential decree on the basis of the legal population thereof, deriving, according to the latest census, from the persons registered in the relevant municipal rolls, as specified by law [statute]. The results of the census are considered to have been published on the basis of the data of the competent service, after one year has elapsed from the last day on which the census was conducted.

The electoral statute further contains specific provisions on how this number is to be determined (Article 2 of Presidential Decrees 26/2012 and 4/2013, 'Determination of parliamentary seats for each constituency concerning general elections').

119. Members of Parliament are also classified into parliamentary groups corresponding to political parties in accordance with the Standing Orders. Groups of independent members are also recognized mainly for the purpose of proportional participation in the sections and committees of Parliament.

§3. Elections

I. The Electoral Body

120. Members of Parliament are elected by the electoral body, that is, all those citizens who have the right to vote. All Greeks aged 17 years or over may vote, provided they are not subject to legal incapacity and have not been convicted (finally, without the possibility of appeal) for certain felonies (Article 4 paragraph 1 and Article 5 of the Presidential Decree 26/2012). Regarding age limits in particular, Article 4 paragraph 2 of the Presidential Decree 26/2012 extends essentially the right to vote to all Greeks aged 16 or over, since it provides that for voting purposes a person is considered to turn 17 not on their birthday itself but on 1 January of the related year. Entry on the electoral register is not a necessary condition of the right to vote but is a necessary condition for the exercising of that right.

II. Constitutional Principles

121. According to the Constitution, election of Parliament is based on the principles of universal, direct, secret, compulsory and individual ballot:

(1) 'Members of Parliament shall be elected through direct, universal and secret ballot by the citizens who have the right to vote […]' (Article 51 paragraph 3 of the Constitution). 'Universal ballot' means that no specific qualifications are required for the right to vote other than those provided for in Article 51 paragraph 3 b, which reads, 'The law cannot abridge the right to vote except in cases where a minimum age has not been attained or in cases of legal incapacity or as a result of irrevocable criminal conviction for certain felonies.' The theory asserts that the legislator may not raise the minimum voting age (*see supra* No. 120) since this would reduce the number of electors and thus render the vote less universal.
(2) 'The exercise of the right to vote is compulsory' (Article 51 paragraph 5).
(3) 'Direct ballot' means that no election through intermediary electors is tolerated.
(4) 'Individual ballot' prescribes that a citizen votes as an individual and not as a member of social, professional, ethnic, religious or other group. This principle derives from Article 51 paragraph 3 of the Constitution according to which the right to vote is granted to citizens.
(5) Under the elect oral law, elections are also based on the principle of a personal vote, which means that voting by a representative or by correspondence is not

permitted. By way of exception, voters who are abroad at the time of an election may exercise their right through a postal vote or other appropriate means (Article 51 paragraph 4, as amd. in 2001). However, the executive order determining the relevant procedure has yet to be issued. The Grand Chamber of the European Court of Human Rights (ECtHR) has ruled that this omission does not violate voting rights, as they are enshrined in Article 3 of the First Protocol of the ECHR (*Sitaropoulos and Giakoumopoulos v. Greece*, Judgment of 15 March 2012, which reversed the earlier and opposite ruling of the First Section of the ECtHR, *Sitaropoulos and others v. Greece*, Judgment of 8 July 2010).

(6) Constitutional theory and jurisprudence have traditionally regarded the equal importance of each vote as a constitutional principle of election. It derives from the universality of ballots and/or the general principle of equality. This principle of equality is to be understood in the numerical sense.

(7) 'Parliamentary elections shall be held simultaneously throughout the Country' (Article 51 paragraph 4 a). Traditionally elections are carried out simultaneously throughout the State on a Sunday. 'Members of Parliament shall be elected for a term of four consecutive years, commencing on the day of the general elections' (Article 53 paragraph 1 a). Parliament is renewed in its entirety. The institutions of re-election or by-election are not contrary to these last two principles. Re-election occurs if the Special Highest Court annuls the election for violations of the electoral law which cast doubt on the results. A by-election is held if a vacancy occurs and there is no substitute to take the vacant seat. Article 53 paragraph 2 of the Constitution provides, however, 'A parliamentary seat that has become vacant during the last year of a parliamentary term shall not be filled by a by-election, where such is required by law, as long as the number of vacant seats does not exceed one-fifth of the total number of the Members of Parliament.'

(8) Secrecy is the exerting of improper influence on voters.

III. Electoral System

122. The electoral system is not defined *expressis verbis* in the Constitution. Article 54 paragraphs 1, 3 and 4, in conjunction with Articles 72 paragraph 1, and 43 paragraph 4 provide for a broad discretion of the Legislature to specify the electoral system. However, legislation passed by Parliament on the electoral system does not in general come into force until the next general election but one, unless an explicit decision taken by the majority of two-thirds of the total number of the Members of Parliament provides for its immediate application (Article 54 paragraph 1 of the Constitution). This is to ensure that the party enjoying a majority in Parliament at any time cannot alter the electoral system to its own advantage.

123. The electoral system in place for most elections under the current Constitution (but also previously, since 1951) has been the system of reinforced proportional representation. The extreme form of proportional representation was used only during the period 1989–1990. Reinforced proportional representation is the system in which seats are distributed in Parliament in proportion to votes cast, with some reinforcing elements. The purpose of this system is to strengthen the first party in order to make it easier to secure an overall parliamentary majority and thereby promote stability of government often featuring mechanisms for levelling out both votes and seats.

The proportional character of the electoral law is usually limited by a provision to exclude from the allocation of seats those parties, which secure less than 3% of the national vote. The constitutionality of this clause has been challenged on the grounds that it militates against single, independent candidates. However, the Special Highest Court deemed it to be constitutional, arguing that it rests on objective and impersonal criteria, intended to prevent the fragmentation of political forces within the Parliament (Rulings 11, 12, 13 and 24/1994, Special Highest Court).

124. The current electoral system is laid down in Act 3231/2004 ('Election of Members of Parliament'), as amended by Acts 3636/2008, 4406/2016, and 4654/2020. The legislation on the election of deputies is found in a multitude of laws, which were codified in a single text, contained in the Presidential Decree 26/2012.

Applied to the general elections of May 2023, Act 4406/2016 established an electoral system based on simple proportional representation, meaning that the seats of each electoral grouping are going to be allocated across the single electoral regions of the country.

However, under the amendments to the electoral law in Act 4654/2020, the system of first-party reinforcement is reintroduced. Thus, following the failure to form a government in May 2023, this electoral system was applied to the elections of June 2023. Under this, if the first party reaches more than or equal to 25% of the valid ballots, then it will receive a bonus of 20 seats, while the remaining 280 seats are to be distributed proportionally among the other parties entitled to seats. From 25% onwards, for every 0.5% the first party will receive an additional bonus of one seat, while the maximum bonus of 50 seats will be received if the party's percentage of valid ballots is at 40%.

The above also applies in the case of a coalition of parties, provided that the average strength of the parties that make up the coalition is greater than the strength of the independent party that has obtained the largest number of valid ballots.

125. According to Act 4648/2019 ('Facilitating the exercise of electoral rights by voters outside the Territory and amending the electoral procedure'), voters who are outside the territory on the day of parliamentary elections, of elections for the European Parliament, and the day of a national referendum may exercise their electoral rights.

A 'voter outside the territory' means any Greek citizen who has the active right to vote, is registered in the electoral rolls and is permanently or temporarily outside Greece on the day of the election.

A prerequisite for registration on the special electoral rolls of voters abroad is that voters must meet the following criteria cumulatively: (a) they have resided for a total of two years within the territory of Greece during the period of the last thirty-five years from the date of submission of the application for registration; and (b) they have submitted a tax return during the current or previous tax year.

126. The Constitution (Article 54 paragraph 3) introduced the system of national candidates, complementing those elected for a particular geographical area. The intention is to attract into politics persons of calibre who do not, however, enjoy a local electoral power base. These Members of Parliament, selected by the various parties, are not elected as representatives of a specific constituency, but in proportion to the overall strength of the parties across the country as a whole. Traditionally the electoral statutes provide for twelve such Members of Parliament. Usually, once they have served their first term, these individuals do not appear again on the list of national candidates, but – assuming they wish to remain in politics – are invited to stand for election as ordinary constituency candidates.

127. An interesting discussion occurred concerning blank ballot papers, namely the question of whether a ballot paper left blank is an authentic expression of popular will. The Special Highest Court pronounced unconstitutional the provisions of an older electoral statute (Presidential Decree 315/2003), which stated that blank ballot papers should not be counted as valid votes in calculating the formula for allocation of seats. The Court ruled that although the blank paper indicates a rejection of all the combinations proposed, it is not legally defective and is entirely valid. Therefore, failure to include blank ballots in the calculation of the total number of valid ballot papers is an impermissible breach of the core principle of popular sovereignty and the equal value of each vote (Ruling 12/2005, Special Highest Court). However, the present electoral statute (Article 98 paragraph 8 of the Presidential Decree 26/2012) stipulates that blank papers should not be counted together with valid papers. The constitutionality of this provision is questionable given that the Special Highest Court has already ruled against it.

IV. Electoral Process

128. Parliamentary elections are proclaimed by Presidential Decree. They have to be held within thirty days from the dissolution of Parliament. This Presidential Decree must also provide for the convocation of the new Parliament in an ordinary session within another thirty days (Articles 53 paragraph 1, and 41 paragraph 3 of the Constitution).

Candidatures are proposed either by the candidate personally or by the candidate's representative or by twelve voters (Article 32 paragraph 1 of the Presidential Decree 26/2012). Candidates stand for election either in lists of political parties or on their own as independent candidates. They stand for election after a decision of the civil Court of First Instance, stating that their candidature has been lawfully proposed (Articles 33 and 94 paragraph 3 of the Presidential Decree 26/2012). Review of legality by the civil court is, however, restricted because of the competence of the Special Highest Court to review the electoral results *ex post.*

In order to facilitate the process of election electoral districts are divided by the decision of the Vice Regional Governor into several electoral centres comprising not more than eight hundred voters each (Articles 51 and 55 of the Presidential Decree 26/2012). Elections are carried out before electoral committees, presided over by a representative of the judiciary, on a Sunday, from sunrise to sunset (Articles 50 and

58 of the Presidential Decree 26/2012). The distribution of seats is done by the 'highest electoral committee' consisting of the President and members of the Supreme Civil and Criminal Court as well as officials of the Ministry of Interior (Article 101 of the Presidential Decree 26/2012). Candidates are declared elected Members of Parliament by the civil courts of first instance (Article 103 paragraph 1 of the Presidential Decree 26/2012).

V. Eligibility

129. Under Article 55 paragraph 1 of the Constitution to be elected as a Member of Parliament one must be a Greek citizen, have the legal capacity to vote (*see supra* No. 120) and have attained the age of twenty-five on the day of the election.

130. Article 56 (as modified radically in the Revision of 2001) establishes certain disqualifications to prevent those holding public positions from exploiting their position in order to promote their candidacy.

According to paragraph 1(a) thereof, there is a prohibition on the candidacy of:

> [s]alaried civil functionaries and servants, other servants of the State, persons serving in the armed forces and the security corps, servants of local government agencies or of other public law legal persons, elected single-member organs of local government agencies, governors, deputy governors or chairmen of the boards of directors or managing or executive directors of public law legal persons or of state-controlled legal entities of private law or of public enterprises or of enterprises whose management the State appoints directly or indirectly by administrative act or by virtue of its capacity as shareholder, or of local government enterprises […].

Persons subject to this prohibition who wish to stand for election must submit their resignation before their official declaration of candidacy. Specifically, this resignation must be submitted in writing and forwarded by an officer of the court to the president of the court responsible for approving the list of candidates, before the day on which the approved list is published. Once the resignation has been formally lodged with the court it is automatically deemed to have been accepted and cannot be withdrawn (Article 30 of the Presidential Decree 26/2012). The Constitution exempts university professors from tendering their resignations under this obligation. Should they eventually be elected they retain their posts but the exercise of their professorial duties is suspended for as long as they serve as Members of Parliament (Article 56 paragraph 2 of the Constitution).

131. The higher elected single-person-organs of local government agencies of the second degree may not stand for election nor be elected to Parliament throughout the term for which they have been elected, even if they resign (Article 56 paragraph 1 of the Constitution). The same ban applies to civil servants and members of the military who, having undertaken the obligation by law to remain in service for a certain period of time, may not stand for election nor be elected to Parliament during the period of such obligation (Article 56 paragraph 4 of the Constitution).

132. The Constitution (Article 56 paragraph 3) also introduces a prohibition of a local nature on certain candidacies. It forbids the candidacy or election of Members of Parliament in the electoral district where they served or in any constituency to which their local powers extended of the following persons:

> (a) Governors, deputy governors, chairmen of the boards of directors, managing and executive directors of public law legal persons, with the exception of associations, of state-owned private law legal persons and of public enterprises or of enterprises whose management the State appoints directly or indirectly by administrative act or by virtue of its capacity as shareholder. (b) Members of independent authorities, which are constituted and operate in accordance with Article 101A, as well as of the authorities designated by law as independent or regulatory. (c) High and highest-ranking officers of the armed forces and the security corps. (d) Salaried servants of the State, of local government agencies and their enterprises, as well as of the legal entities and enterprises falling under case (a) who held the post of head of an organic unit at the level of a directorate or a corresponding post, as specifically provided by law. Servants mentioned in the preceding section who exercise a larger local power are subject to the restrictions of this paragraph concerning constituencies other than those of their seat, only in case they were holding a post of head of unit at the level of general directorate or another corresponding level, as specifically provided by statute. (e) General or special secretaries of ministries or of autonomous secretariats, general or regional administrations and all persons that the law deems equivalent with these.

Those falling within this group must resign at least eighteen months before the end of the four-year parliamentary term. The new constitutional provision gives the candidate certainty about the date by which he must submit his resignation from his service.

The prohibition does not apply to candidates on the national list (i.e., to candidates for State Deputies).

133. The Constitution prohibits (Article 56 paragraph 1 c) the return to active service of military officers who have stood for election. By contrast, anyone not subject to that specific ban who was retired from his post in order to contest an election is allowed to return to active service, and this freedom is not subject to any restriction in respect of time It has been ruled (Athens Administrative Court of Appeal 1779/2010) that police officers are to be classed with military officers for the purposes of Article 56 paragraph 1 of the Constitution. Therefore, they are barred from returning to their duties.

134. Violation of the provisions of Articles 55 and 56 has as a consequence the forfeiture of membership in Parliament, which is declared by the Special Highest Court upon application (Articles 58 and 100 paragraph 1 of the Constitution).

The case law of the Special Highest Court reviewing election results has involved many cases concerning disqualifications. Originally the Court interpreted Article 56 of the Constitution very narrowly, regarding it as laying down exceptions to the general rule of entitlement to stand for election, and therefore limiting the democratic principle (Rulings 6/1982, 4/1995, 67/1997). However, on certain occasions, before the Revision of 2001, the Court had broadened its interpretation of the exceptions, ruling that central civil servants of general competence throughout the country have been considered disqualified to stand for election not only in the electoral district in which they had served but in any electoral district of the country (Rulings 33/1982, 47/1985, 7/2000). This interpretation was adopted by the revisionary legislator (*see* Article 56 paragraph 3(a) of the Constitution).

Chapter 2. Legal Status

§1. Mandate of the Members of Parliament

I. Term of Mandate

135. The tenure of the Members of Parliament begins *ipso iure* with their election and on the day of the election. The exercise of their office starts, however, after the official declaration of their election by the Court of First Instance (civil) and after their swearing-in (Articles 53 paragraph 1, and 59 of the Constitution, Article 3 paragraph 4 of the Standing Orders). According to Article 59 paragraphs 1 and 2 of the Constitution, swearing-in takes place in the Parliament House in a public sitting. The oath is worded as follows: 'I swear in the name of the Holy Consubstantial and Indivisible Trinity to keep faith in my country and in the democratic form of government, obedience to the Constitution and the laws and to discharge conscientiously my duties.' The Constitution refers explicitly only to the oath to be sworn by members of the Eastern Orthodox Church. Those of other religions or persuasions shall take the same oath according to the form of their own religion or creed. No provision is made for atheists or agnostics. In fact, the Standing Orders state that objections to the swearing of the oath are not permitted. Any reservations are to be expressed in a brief written statement (Article 3 paragraph 3 of the Standing Orders). This provision contravenes Article 13 of the Constitution since it introduces discrimination on the ground of religious belief. It should be acceptable, therefore, for those who refuse to swear a religious oath to offer an equivalent promise, invoking their honour and conscience.

Termination of office takes place in case of death, resignation (Article 60 paragraph 2 of the Constitution), expiration of the parliamentary term, forfeiture, and when objections against the election of a Member of Parliament have been admitted by the Special Highest Court.

II. Free (Representative) Mandate

136. Members of Parliament are considered to be representatives of the nation (Article 51 paragraph 2 of the Constitution). Their mandate is a 'free' mandate not an 'imperative' one. Article 60 paragraph 1 of the Constitution is explicit: 'Members of Parliament enjoy unrestricted freedom of opinion and the right to vote according to their conscience.' Moreover, Members of Parliament do not have to represent also their own electoral district, as was the case under previous Constitutions, according to which 'Members of Parliament represent the nation and not only their electoral district.'

§2. Incompatibilities, Immunities and Privileges

I. Incompatibilities

137. Incompatibilities refer either to incompatible offices and functions or incompatible acts. They apply to Members of Parliament once elected and are intended to ensure the impartial and transparent exercise of their parliamentary duties.

Under Article 57 paragraph 1 of the Constitution, the duties of Members of Parliament are incompatible with the position or capacity of owner or partner or shareholder or governor or administrator or member of the board of directors or general manager or a deputy thereof, of an enterprise that:

> (a) Undertakes public works or studies or procurements or the provision of services to the State or concludes with the State similar contracts of a developmental or investment nature. (b) Enjoys special privileges. (c) Owns or manages a radio or television station or publishes a newspaper of countrywide circulation in Greece. (d) Exercises by concession a public service or a public enterprise or a public utility enterprise and (e) Rents for commercial purposes real estate owned by the State.

For the purposes of the application of this paragraph, local government agencies, other public law legal persons, State-owned private law legal persons, public enterprises, enterprises of local government agencies and other enterprises whose management the State appoints directly or indirectly by administrative act or by virtue of its capacity as shareholder, are equated to the State. A shareholder of an enterprise falling within the restrictions of this paragraph is every person possessing more than 1% of its share capital.

In the event of an incompatible office or function predating the parliamentary election, within eight days after their election, Members of Parliament have to declare a choice between their incompatible duties. If they fail to make this statement, they forfeit their parliamentary office (Article 57 paragraph 2 of the Constitution). The Constitution speaks of *ipso jure* forfeiture. Nevertheless, in all cases a decision of the Special Highest Court is required, although that decision shall have retroactive force, applying *ex tunc*, that is, from the time of the circumstance(s) representing the grounds for forfeiture (Rulings 1/1992, 59/1995).

138. The Constitution (Article 57, as revised in 2001) made the holding of parliamentary office incompatible with the performance of any professional activity. Legislation was planned to define the precise details of how this principle of incompatibility would be applied, how Members of Parliament might resume their professional duties, how any compatible activities should be defined, and so on. A bill was laid before Parliament in February 2003 but failed to secure a majority vote. Thus the principle of incompatibility, in accordance with transitional Article 115 paragraph 7 of the Constitution, was applied since 1 January 2003 without exception. A Member of Parliament who continued to exercise any profession subsequent to his or her election had to forfeit his position as Member of Parliament and all relevant contracts or actions had to be annulled.

This interpretation was endorsed by the courts. In its Ruling 11/2003 the Special Highest Court determined that forfeiture must ensue even in the absence of an executive statute. The ruling concerned a Member of Parliament and lawyer who had been declared to have forfeited his parliamentary office; the forfeiture was not affected by the fact that he had not been paid for the provision of legal services. The case was brought before the ECtHR (*Lykourezos v. Greece* 33554/03, 15 June 2006), which ruled that the Special Highest Court decision contravened Article 3 of the First Additional Protocol. Specifically, the ECtHR accepted that there had been a breach of protected confidence (a claim which the Special Highest Court had rejected) since the immediate effect of the general principle of professional and parliamentary incompatibility and its application to Members of the current Parliament essentially overturned the choice of the people and the right of the Member himself to serve his term.

Also, in its Ruling 1/2007, the Special Highest Court ruled a Member of Parliament (a member of the PASOK party elected on the national list) to have forfeited his office because – in violation of the constitutional prohibition (Article 57 paragraph 2) – he had undertaken, through a contract with a business which also undertook studies and provided services for the Greek State, the expert coordination of a community programme providing advice to the Russian government on aspects of economic competitiveness.

The parliamentary incompatibility with the exercise of any profession was finally abolished by the revision of the Constitution in May 2008. Article 57 paragraph 1 as revised provides that a specific statute may define the professional activities, beyond those mentioned here above, which are prohibited to the Members of Parliament.

II. Immunities

139. In order to ensure that Members of Parliament may carry out their duties without impediment and in order to guarantee their freedom to express their opinion and vote without constraint and according to their conscience (as established in Article 60 paragraph 1 of the Constitution), three constitutional immunities are envisaged: (1) parliamentary freedom of speech, (2) parliamentary immunity from criminal process, and (3) the right to refuse testimony.

140. (a) Parliamentary Freedom of Speech. A Member of Parliament shall not be prosecuted or in any way interrogated for an opinion expressed or a vote cast by him in the discharge of his parliamentary duties (Article 61 paragraph 1 of the Constitution). This immunity may not be waived, owing to its nature as an institutional guarantee of the Constitution (*see infra* No. 357).

The immunity extends over criminal, civil, political and disciplinary action. However, the Member of Parliament enjoys the freedom only in respect of his opinions or votes, not in respect of other actions, and only in respect of the exercise of his parliamentary duties, not in respect of actions unconnected with those duties.

An exception to this principle of parliamentary freedom of speech, contrary to the tradition of Greek parliamentarianism, was introduced by the Constitution (Article 61 paragraph 2) following a provision of the dictatorial 'constitutions' of 1968 and 1973:

> A Member of Parliament may be prosecuted only for libel, according to the law, after leave has been granted by Parliament. The Court of Appeals shall be competent to hear the case. Such leave is deemed to be conclusively denied, if Parliament does not decide within forty-five days from the date the charges have been submitted to the Speaker.

As this provision endangers the principle of parliamentary immunity, it must be applied only with the greatest care.

141. (b) Parliamentary Immunity from criminal process. According to Article 62 of the Constitution:

> During the parliamentary term, Members of Parliament shall not be prosecuted, arrested, imprisoned or otherwise confined without prior leave granted by Parliament. Likewise, a member of a dissolved Parliament shall not be prosecuted for political crimes during the period between the dissolution of Parliament and the confirmation of the election of the members of the new Parliament. Leave is granted by Parliament compulsorily if the request of the public prosecutor's office concerns an offense which is not related to the performance of the duties or the political activity of the member of Parliament. Parliament, under the responsibility of its Speaker, shall decide on the request within three months of the date the later was transmitted to the Speaker by the public prosecutor. The three-month limit is suspended during the Parliament's recess. No leave is required when Members of Parliament are caught in the act of committing a felony.

These provisions are the result of the Revision of 2019, which limited certain privileges previously recognised in favour of the members of the Parliament, taking into consideration the relevant case law of the ECtHR.

Parliamentary immunity refers only to criminal prosecution, which means that no impediment stands in the way of civil or disciplinary actions being brought against a Member of Parliament. The immunity from prosecution applies in respect of any crime, whether committed during the exercise of the Member's duties or not. The date on which the crime was committed also has no bearing. The Member enjoys the same immunity whether the crime was committed before or after he was elected to Parliament. However, in contrast to the principle of freedom of speech, this immunity from prosecution is limited in time, protecting the Member only during the term of the Parliament. The period in which the Member enjoys this parliamentary immunity shall not be counted in calculating limitations on liability to prosecution for any offence he may have committed.

The Supreme Civil and Criminal Court (Ruling 904/1980) has held that the beginning of criminal proceedings against a member of Parliament, the collection of evidence, and the acquittal by a judicial council *in camera* do not infringe parliamentary immunity. This ruling has been justifiably criticized as a misinterpretation of the relevant constitutional provision.

Subsequent case law took the opposite direction, accepting that in no case may criminal proceedings be initiated, or existing proceedings be continued, against a person who has been elected to Parliament, without the prior consent of Parliament (Athens Court of Appeal 2819/1993).

142. (c) The Right to Refuse Testimony. According to the Constitution, Members of Parliament can refuse to give testimony on information given to them or supplied by them in the course of the discharge of their duties (Article 61 paragraph 3). In contrast to the other two principles above, which are rules of public order from which no individual may derogate, the question of whether or not to exercise the right to refuse testimony is a matter of the Member of Parliament's discretion.

III. Indemnity and Benefits

143. Members of Parliament are entitled to receive compensation and an expense allowance for the exercise of their duties. They also enjoy exemptions from transportation, post and telephone charges, the extent of which is decided upon by the Parliament itself (Article 63 paragraphs 1 and 2). Resolutions on this subject are not statutes; that is, they do not require the cooperation of the President of the Republic. However, in case of unjustified absence of a Member for more than five sittings per month, one-thirtieth of his monthly compensation shall be withheld for each absence (Article 63 paragraph 3).

Chapter 3. Competence

§1. Legislation

144. In the domain of legislation:

(1) Parliament is exclusively competent to revise the Constitution (*see supra* Nos 50 et seq.).
(2) Parliament enacts statutes (*see supra* Nos 60 et seq.).
(3) Parliament is exclusively competent to enact Standing Orders (*see supra* Nos 70 et seq.) as well as to decide on deputies' indemnities and benefits (*see supra* No. 143).
(4) Parliament decides on implementing the state of siege (emergency) (*see infra* Nos 507 et seq.).
(5) Parliament ratifies international treaties (*see supra*, Nos 155 et seq., and *infra* No. 509) and
(6) Parliament grants amnesty for political crimes (Article 47 paragraph 3 of the Constitution).

§2. Parliamentary Control over the Executive

I. Petitions

145. Article 69 of the Constitution enshrines the right of each citizen to address the legislature, submitting petitions or grievances to the administration. However, no one may appear before Parliament on his own initiative. Petitions to Parliament are either presented through a Member of Parliament, who may adopt them or are addressed to the Speaker. After being registered they are submitted to the competent Minister, who has to answer in writing within twenty-five days, otherwise, they are debated upon like questions (Article 125 of the Standing Orders).

II. Applications for Presentation of Documents

146. Members of Parliament may ask the competent Minister, by written application to Parliament, to make available documents concerning a public matter (Article 133 of the Standing Orders). The Minister must produce the required documents in Parliament within thirty days or otherwise state the reasons for non-presentation. In no circumstances shall a Minister place before Parliament documents containing military or diplomatic secrets or information that might compromise the security of the State. The documents are delivered to the Member of Parliament who has submitted the application unless the documents are original papers from public archives, in which case the Member of Parliament shall be invited to inspect their contents at the offices of the Parliament.

III. Summoning of Ministers

147. Parliament and parliamentary committees may request Ministers and Undersecretaries to be present at debates (Article 66 paragraph 3 of the Constitution). In this respect, the Standing Orders (Article 41A) provide that the standing committees of Parliament, by a decision supported by two-fifth of their total membership, may summon Ministers and Undersecretaries to appear before them. This procedure is designed to assist the work of parliamentary audit and control, as performed by Parliament in plenary session or the Recess Section. Those summoned to appear before the committees are obliged to answer all questions even those related to state secrets, except those pertaining to the subject of current negotiations on matters of national importance.

IV. Questions

148. Questions are put by Members of Parliament and are classed as ordinary or current. Members of Parliament may address written questions to Ministers asking for information on any public matter, what measures the Government intends to take on such matters, and so on. The Minister has to answer in writing within the next twenty-five days, otherwise, the questions are debated (Articles 126 et seq. of the Standing Orders).

Current questions refer to current public issues, are addressed to the Prime Minister or Ministers, and are answered orally, according to Articles 129–132 of the Standing Orders. The Prime Minister must reply to two current questions each week, unless the matter on which a reply is to be given falls within the exclusive competence of a Minister. The Standing Orders envisage a specific procedure for selection of the current questions to be discussed in Parliament. The President of each parliamentary group selects two of the submitted current questions to be discussed during the respective parliamentary sitting.

V. Interpellations

149. The purpose of interpellations is to allow scrutiny of the Government; they are classed as either ordinary or current. Members of Parliament may interpellate Ministers, namely, question their acts or omissions and demand explanations. Ordinary interpellations are always debated according to Articles 134 et seq. of the Standing Orders. Members of Parliament may also submit interpellations when they deem that a Minister's reply to a question was inadequate, or when they have not been given all the documents they have requested in good time.

Current interpellations relate to current public issues. The President of each parliamentary group selects two of the submitted current interpellations and the Conference of Parliamentary Chairmen (*see infra* No. 158) chooses only one to be debated within a week. The rest are debated as ordinary interpellations (Article 138 of the Standing Orders).

VI. Government Announcements and Statements

150. Article 142A of the Standing Orders allows the Government to proceed at any time to make announcements or statements to Parliament on serious matters of public concern. The request to make such an announcement or statement is laid before the Speaker, who informs the leaders of the parliamentary parties. The statement is made in person by the Prime Minister and is followed by a debate with the party leaders.

VII. Debates Held at the Initiative of Members of Parliament

151. Each Member of Parliament is entitled to submit to the Conference of Parliamentary Chairmen at least one issue of general importance or interest to be discussed by Parliament in plenary session. The issues to be debated are selected by lot at the Conference of Parliamentary Chairmen (Article 132A of the Standing Orders).

VIII. Debates with Priority over the Order of the Day

152. Under Article 143 of the Standing Orders, during each parliamentary session, seven debates on national matters or matters of general and major public interest must take place irrespective of the agenda. One issue concerning matters of EU interest is chosen by the Government; two issues are chosen by the largest parliamentary group of the opposition, one by the second largest, one by the third largest, and one by the fourth largest. The issues are introduced for debate following the relevant application by each parliamentary group. The application must be signed by two-thirds of the members of the group, or by its leader.

IX. Investigations

153. The right of investigation, to examine special issues of public interest, is basically provided for in Article 68 paragraph 2(a) and (b) of the Constitution:

> Parliament shall set up investigation committees from among its members by a resolution supported by a majority of the members who are present, which may not be less than two-fifths of the total number of the members of Parliament, on proposal of one-fifth of the total number of its members. A parliamentary resolution adopted by an absolute majority of the total number of members shall be required in order to set up investigation committees on matters related to foreign policy and national defence.

According to the Revision of 2019, Parliament may set up two investigation committees per parliamentary term, should a proposal of at least ten of its members be supported by two-fifths of the total number of the Members of Parliament, regardless of majority. Details pertaining to the composition and operation of such committees are provided by Article 144 paragraph of the Standing Orders.

Investigating committees are granted broad investigating powers in order to reveal the truth of the issue in question. They have all the powers enjoyed by the criminal investigation authorities and prosecutors of the magistrates' courts. They may require information from public authorities and private citizens; they may examine witnesses and carry out investigations *in situ*. On completion of their investigation, they draw up their findings and submit them to Parliament.

X. Vote of Confidence and Motion of Censure

154. The cornerstone of the parliamentary system is the dependence of the Government on Parliament's confidence. Under Article 84 paragraph 1(a) and (b) of the Constitution, 'the Government must enjoy the confidence of Parliament. The Government shall be obliged to request a vote of confidence by Parliament within fifteen days of the date the Prime Minister shall have been sworn in, and may also do so at any other time'.

The Constitution provides thus for two cases in which the Parliament's vote of confidence may be requested. The first is compulsory; the second is up to the Government to initiate.

The appointment of a new Prime Minister and only of a Prime Minister – not a change in the members of the Cabinet, irrespective of whether it occurs after parliamentary elections or otherwise – must be followed by the Government's request for Parliament's confidence, after the programme of government policy has been presented to Parliament by the Prime Minister.

The optional request of the vote of confidence is a means whereby the Government can assure itself of stability for political reasons since the vote will usually be won by the Government, which can impose party discipline on the members of its parliamentary group.

The vote of censure is the ultimate act of parliamentary control. If Parliament decides to withdraw its confidence in the government or in a member of the Government, then the Government has to resign. Theoretically, if confidence is withdrawn from one member of the Government, resignation is obligatory for this member only. But due to the collective responsibility of the Government and the solidarity of its members, resignation will usually be collective.

The main constitutional provisions on the motion of censure (Article 84 paragraphs 2–7) are the following. A motion of censure must be signed by at least one-sixth of the total number of Members of Parliament and must explicitly state the issues on which the debate is to be held. It may not be submitted before the lapse of six months from the rejection by Parliament of a previous motion of censure. But if the motion is signed by the absolute majority of the total number of Members, it may be submitted without temporal limitations.

A motion of censure is considered adopted by Parliament only if it is approved by the absolute majority of the total number of its Members. By contrast, for a motion of confidence to be approved a relative majority, that is, the majority of the

Members of Parliament present, is sufficient, under the condition that this majority is not less than two-fifths of the total number of members (this is the 'vote of tolerance' or 'abstention vote', which allows Members of Parliament not wishing to vote either for or against the Government to absent themselves, *see infra* No. 183). It is obvious that the required absolute majority for the approval of the motion of censure is dictated by the desideratum of governmental stability.

§3. Quasi-Judicial Competences

155. According to the Constitution:

(1) Parliament grants leave for prosecution of Members of Parliament according to Articles 61 paragraphs 2 and 62 of the Constitution (*see supra* Nos 140–141).
(2) Parliament initiates criminal proceedings against the President of the Republic (*see supra* No. 114).
(3) Parliament initiates criminal proceedings against the members of the Government and the Undersecretaries (*see infra* No. 197).
(4) Parliament consents, according to Article 47 paragraph 2 of the Constitution, to the pardoning of a member of the Government or Undersecretary convicted and sentenced for a crime (*see supra* No. 110).

§4. Administrative Competences

156. According to the provisions of the Constitution:

(1) Parliament shall vote on the Budget, financial statement and general balance sheet of the State (Article 79 of the Constitution).
(2) These are essentially administrative statements representing income and expenditure, monies owed to and by the State. However, they are embodied in the guise of a statute in order to ensure publicity and transparency of the management of public funds. It is asserted that Parliament must vote on the Budget because otherwise, the provisions related to state revenue and expenditure would be without force (*see infra* Nos 492 et seq.).
(3) Parliament approves programmes of economic and social development (Article 79 paragraph 8 of the Constitution).
(4) These programmes feature long-term proposals for the economic future of the country. In contrast to the Budget, the programmes are not mandatory.
(5) Parliament votes on its own budget and accompanying financial statement (Article 120 of the Standing Orders).
(6) Parliament elects its own Speaker (*see infra* No. 157).
(7) Parliament elects the President of the Republic (*see supra* Nos 93 et seq.).
(8) Parliament determines the inability of a President of the Republic to carry out his duties (*see supra* No. 97).

(9) Parliament consents to its suspension beyond a period of thirty days or to a repeated suspension according to Article 40 paragraphs 2 and 3 of the Constitution (*see infra* No. 164).
(10) Parliament determines the inability of a Prime Minister to carry out his duties (*see infra* No. 184).
(11) Parliament decides on referenda (*see supra* Nos 106 and *infra* Nos 173 et seq.).

Chapter 4. Organization

§1. The Presiding Body and the Conference of Parliamentary Chairmen

I. The Presiding Body

157. Parliament is constituted as a body by electing the Speaker, seven Deputy Speakers, three Rectors and six Secretaries. The opposition is always represented in this presiding body of Parliament (Article 6 of the Standing Orders).

The members of the presiding body are elected by secret ballot, without individuals putting themselves forward as candidates and without prior discussion. An absolute majority of the entire Parliament is required for the election of each member of the presiding body. If such a majority is not secured, a second ballot is held between the two candidates who have received the most support, in which he who receives the most votes is elected (Articles 7 and 8 of the Standing Orders).

The tenure of the Speaker and his Deputies is for the whole parliamentary term. The other members of the presiding body are elected for the ordinary parliamentary session (Article 9 paragraph 1 of the Standing Orders).

A premature termination of office of the members of the presiding body is provided for if Parliament approves a motion of censure against them upon the proposal of fifty Members, as well as if they are incapable of exercising their duties (Articles 9 paragraph 3, 150 and 152 of the Standing Orders).

The Speaker directs and coordinates all activities of Parliament, represents Parliament in all its relations, protects the free functioning of Parliament and the freedom of opinion and expression of its members, exercises disciplinary power, and other like matters. Deputy Speakers, Rectors and Secretaries assist the Speaker in the exercise of his duties (Article 65 of the Constitution, Articles 11 and 12 of the Standing Orders).

II. The Conference of Parliamentary Chairmen

158. The Conference of Parliamentary Chairmen has been introduced by the Standing Orders of 1987 (Articles 13 and 14). It is composed of the Speaker and former Speakers, provided they have been elected as Members of Parliament, the Deputy Speakers, the Chairmen of the Permanent Committees, the Chairman of the Committee for Institutions and Transparency, the leaders of parliamentary groups and one independent member of Parliament representing the independents. A Minister representing the Government may participate in the sittings.

It is convoked once a week in order to decide upon the agenda of the following week and upon the total duration of debates, and in order to express opinions as to matters not provided for in the Standing Orders. A significant competence of the Conference of Chairmen is the power to select the members of the Independent Authorities, by unanimous decision if possible or else by at least a four-fifth majority of its members. The Conference of Chairmen is also empowered to summon members of the Independent Authorities to appear before it, to select the President, the Vice President and two members of the Hellenic Statistical Authority, and to express its opinion regarding the selection of the Presidents and the Vice Presidents of the Supreme Courts of Greece.

§2. The Plenum, the Recess Section, the Committees, the Scientific Service of Parliament

I. The Plenum

159. The Parliament conducts its legislative business in plenary session (Article 70 paragraph 1 of the Constitution). This is not an absolute rule, since in paragraph 2 of the same article and Article 71 provision is made for the work of legislation to be carried out by the Recess Section and by the standing parliamentary committees, in accordance with the provisions of the Standing Orders, and under the constraints set out in Article 72 of the Constitution. Article 72 paragraph 1 of the Constitution provides for the exclusive competence of the plenary session concerning bills and law proposals of major importance, such as the exercise and protection of fundamental rights and freedoms, the operation of political parties, ministerial responsibility, the state of siege (emergency), the authentic interpretation of statutes, the relationship between church and State, change in frontiers of the State and the stationing on Greek soil of foreign military forces. Other areas where only the plenary session may pass legislation are the Budget and all other matters which, according to the special provision of the Constitution, are the competence only of the plenary session, or which can only be determined by special majority. Such matters would include the revision of the Constitution, a decision to hold a referendum, and so on.

In the Constitution of 1975/1986, Article 70 provided for the establishment of two sections, by decision of overall majority of all deputies at the beginning of each parliamentary session, for the carrying on of legislative work. These sections never actually functioned and were abolished finally in the Revision of 2001.

The Council of State – though with a remarkable minority opinion – has judged (Rulings 902–3/1981) that the violation of Article 72 paragraph 1 of the Constitution is not subject to judicial review, since any unconstitutionality pertains to the internal workings of Parliament. Any violation of this rule is thus to be reviewed only by the President of the Republic in the exercise of his competence to send back bills to Parliament according to Article 42 of the Constitution (*see supra* No. 106).

Parliament exercises its judicial and administrative powers in the plenary session. This is not explicitly laid down, as is the case in Article 70 paragraph 1 in respect of the work of legislation, but is derived from individual provisions which either require explicitly a decision of the plenary session or majorities of the whole body of deputies.

The power to exercise parliamentary control is also exercised by the plenary session, with provision for the possibility of some of the functions of control being performed by the Recess Section and the standing parliamentary committees (Article 70 paragraph 6 of the Constitution). Only a plenary session can put a motion of censure in the Government or set up investigating committees (Articles 84 paragraph 2 and 68 paragraph 2 of the Constitution).

II. The Recess Section

160. If Parliament is in recess, legislative business as well as parliamentary control are conducted by a special section comprising one-third of the total number of deputies (Articles 71 and 70 paragraph 6 of the Constitution, Article 29 of the Standing Orders). Parliamentary practice has been to divide the summer recess into three parts, with one Recess Section for each so that all Members of Parliament participate in the legislative work during recess. Membership in these sections reflects the proportions of parties and independent Members in the full Parliament, as decided by the Speaker. In principle, the Recess Section meets during the summer period – but can also convene at any other time when Parliament is not sitting. This arrangement ensures continuity in the work of Parliament, allowing it to pursue its functions of legislation and control without interruption.

III. Parliamentary Committees

161. In the Revision of 2001, there was a marked tendency to strengthen the powers of the parliamentary committees in relation to those of the plenary session. The remit of these committees is to assist Parliament in carrying out its work more conveniently and efficiently.

All parliamentary committees are composed of Members of Parliament in proportion to the strength of parliamentary groups and groups of independent deputies. They meet for business both when Parliament is in plenary session, and during the period when the Recess Section is meeting.

The Constitution makes provision for standing parliamentary committees and investigating committees (Article 68 as revised in 2019), as well as a special committee for conducting preliminary investigation of charges against members of the Government (Article 86 paragraph 3) and a special committee to investigate charges following the suspension of a non-completed criminal prosecution, (Article 86 paragraph 5).

The Standing Orders also provide for the establishment of other committees.

(a) Standing Committees. Standing committees consist of one-eighth to one-sixth of the total number of Members of Parliament of the plenum or of one-seventh to one-sixth of the total number of Members of Parliament of the Recess Section. They are set up at the beginning of each regular parliamentary session or during the functioning of the Recess Section, their composition reflecting the proportions of parliamentary groupings and independent deputies. Their basic competences are the elaboration, discussion and voting of Bills and law proposals, subject to the restrictions laid down in Article 72 paragraph 1, as well as the exercise of parliamentary control of Ministers (Articles 31 and 32 of the Standing Orders).

Standing Orders provide for six standing committees:

- cultural and education affairs;
- national defence and foreign affairs;
- economic affairs;

- social matters;
- public administration, public order and justice; and
- production and trade.

The Standing Orders provide also for a number of special standing committees:

- public finances and the implementation of the state budget (Article 31A);
- armament programmes and contracts (Article 31B);
- monitoring of the social security system (Article 31C);
- European affairs (Article 32A). (This offers guidance on EU and European policy matters.)

(b) Special Committees. Where the needs of the legislative work of Parliament so require, special committees may be established ad hoc, in order to elaborate specific bills or law proposals if the Government so requests. These special committees will consist of one-tenth to one-fifteenth of the entire body of Members of Parliament (Article 42 of the Standing Orders).

(c) Special Permanent Committees. Nine special permanent committees are set up at the commencement of each session of Parliament:

- Greeks abroad;
- environmental protection;
- research and technology;
- equality, youth and human rights;
- the regions;
- road safety;
- parliamentary ethics;
- prisoners' rehabilitation and other matters relating to incarceration;
- monitoring of the case law of the ECtHR. Additionally, the special permanent committee on institutions and transparency is set up at the commencement of the parliamentary term for its entire duration. Each special permanent committee is mandated to oversee and offer advice in its specific area (Article 43A of the Standing Orders).

(d) Committees on matters of national significance or general interest. Parliament, upon proposal of the Government, the Speaker or of the leaders of parliamentary groups, may establish committees for the study and elaboration of national matters or matters of general public interest. They remain in existence for as long as the study of the subject assigned to them requires. These committees submit their reports to Parliament (Articles 44 and 45 of the Standing Orders).

(e) Committees on Parliament's internal affairs. The Standing Orders provide for the workings of three committees on internal affairs: the Committee on Standing Orders, which elaborates proposals for amendments to the Standing Orders, the Committee on Parliament's finances, which monitors parliamentary spending, and the Committee on Parliament's library. The Speaker may decide the formation of other such committees (Articles 46 and 47).

(f) Parliamentary Foreign Relations Committees. Foreign relations committees are established to promote international cooperation between the Parliament, the European Parliament, the parliaments of other countries and other international organizations. Provision is made for persons outside Parliament to participate in these committees (Article 49 of the Standing Orders).

(g) Committee on state-owned enterprises, banks, public utility enterprises and social security agencies. This committee is established at the commencement of the parliamentary term for its entire duration. It has fifteen members, among them the Speaker and Deputy Speakers of the Parliament. Its remit is to issue an opinion on the suitability of persons recommended for appointment to the positions of Chairman of the Executive Board, Director or Managing Director or General Manager of state-owned enterprises, banks, public utility enterprises and social security agencies. The Committee's opinion must be formulated and issued before the competent Minister proceeds to make the appointment. The Committee also issues its opinion on the management and progress of the above legal persons, indicating any measures it deems should be taken in the public interest (Article 49A of the Standing Orders).

(h) Parliamentary friendship groups. The Speaker may establish parliamentary friendship groups, following a written request of Members of Parliament. The task of these groups is to enhance parliamentary diplomacy at an international bilateral level and to promote and disseminate the positions of Greece on national and international issues (Article 49C of the Standing Orders). Eighty-four parliamentary friendship groups have been established during the current parliamentary term.

(i) Investigating Committees. On the Investigating Committees *see supra* No. 153.

(j) Special Committees for prosecution of members of the Government and Undersecretaries. On the Special Committees for prosecution of members of the Government and Undersecretaries, *see infra* Nos 197 et seq..

IV. The Scientific Service of Parliament

162. The Scientific Service of Parliament is provided by the Constitution (Article 65 paragraph 5) and is organized by the Standing Orders (Articles 160 et seq.). The Scientific Service of Parliament consists of the first and second directorates of scientific studies as well as the directorate of scientific supervision. Supervised by a nine-member committee (the Scientific Council, consisting of professors of public law, civil law, European law, penal law, political science, economics, statistics and informatics) the Scientific Service of Parliament assists Parliament in the exercise of its legislative and other competences. Its main task is the elaboration of bills and the assistance of Parliament with comparative law reports and other relevant information.

Chapter 5. Workings of Parliament

§1. Parliamentary Term

163. Parliament is elected for a period of four years commencing from the date of parliamentary elections. On the completion of the fourth year, Parliament ceases *ipso iure* to exist. Parliamentary elections must be held within the next thirty days and the new Parliament must be convoked in ordinary session within another thirty days (Article 53 paragraph 1 of the Constitution).

The four-year parliamentary term may be shortened in case of a premature dissolution of Parliament. It may also, exceptionally, be extended in case of war for the entire duration of hostilities. If Parliament has been dissolved, it is recalled *ipso iure* and elections are postponed until the termination of the war (Article 53 paragraph 3 of the Constitution).

A Parliament whose term has expired will also re-convene, its authority renewed, in order to approve the decree declaring the country to be in a state of siege or to approve the renewal of such a decree (Article 48 paragraphs 2 and 3 of the Constitution).

A dissolved Parliament may also be recalled in order to decide if the circumstances warrant the election of a new President of the Republic, in the event of protracted incapacity of the incumbent President to perform his duties (Article 34 paragraph 2 of the Constitution).

§2. Parliamentary Sessions

164. Parliament does not work continuously. It is convened in sessions. Sessions are ordinary, extraordinary and ad hoc:

(1) Parliament is convened by the President of the Republic or *eo ipso* in an ordinary session once a year. The Constitution specifies the first Monday in October as the date for the official opening of Parliament, when the year's work commences. The duration of the session is at least five months. Parliament usually remains in session until June of the following year. It is compulsory for Parliament to exercise its competence on voting the State budget during the ordinary session and it may certainly exercise any other competence as well (Article 64 of the Constitution).

(2) The President of the Republic convenes Parliament in an extraordinary session whenever he considers it appropriate (Article 40 paragraph 1 a of the Constitution). The order to convene takes the form of a Presidential Decree, countersigned by the Cabinet. Parliament does not have to confine itself to the particular object of its convocation; it may exercise other competences too with the exception of voting on the State budget. The extraordinary session will necessarily cease when Parliament convenes for its ordinary session.

(3) Parliament is convened by the President of the Republic in an ad hoc session, when it is not in ordinary or extraordinary session, in order to exercise only one specific competence. Ad hoc sessions are provided for in the Constitution

in the case of presidential elections (Article 32 paragraph 5 of the Constitution), in case of the protracted incapacity of the President of the Republic, in order to decide whether the circumstances warrant the election of a successor (Article 34 paragraph 2 of the Constitution), in case of emergencies (Article 48 paragraphs 2, 3 and 5 of the Constitution) and in case of formation of a new Government for the purpose of the vote of confidence (Article 84 paragraph 1 of the Constitution).

The President of the Republic, or the Prime Minister in his place, opens the first ordinary session of each parliamentary term. Ordinary and extraordinary sessions are declared closed by Presidential Decree (Article 40 paragraph 1 of the Constitution). Ad hoc sessions close after Parliament decides on the topic for which it has been convoked. In this case, too the relevant Presidential Decree or Cabinet order must be issued.

The President of the Republic may also suspend (prorogue) a parliamentary session but only once, either by postponing its opening or by interrupting the continuance of its working. Such suspension may neither exceed a period of thirty days nor be repeated during the same session without the consent of Parliament (Article 40 paragraphs 2 and 3 of the Constitution). This is a power which the President of the Republic has never actually used.

§3. The General Principles of Parliamentary Proceedings

I. Sittings

165. Parliament convenes on the basis of the agenda. The Speaker opens and closes sittings with the consent of Parliament. He may also interrupt sittings (Articles 50 and 59 of the Standing Orders).

Members of Parliament, the Prime Minister, Ministers and Undersecretaries may participate in the sittings in the main hall. The Speaker may also allow civil servants and other officials to be present if so requested (Articles 58 and 60 of the Standing Orders).

Article 66 paragraph 1 of the Constitution acknowledges the principle that parliamentary proceedings should be held in public. But they may be held *in camera* on request of the Cabinet or of fifteen Members of Parliament if a majority in a closed sitting so decides. Thereafter it decides whether debates ought to be repeated in a public meeting (Article 66 paragraph 1 of the Constitution). A similar provision was added in the Revision of 2001 to cover the sittings of parliamentary committees (Article 66 paragraph 3 of the Constitution).

II. Legislative Proceedings

166. The ordinary proceedings have already been laid down in outline (*see supra* Nos 36 et seq.).

The Constitution (Articles 76 paragraphs 4 et seq.) and the Standing Orders (Articles 108 et seq.) provide also deviations from the ordinary procedure, that is, for summary or special proceedings.

(1) Bills or law proposals may be voted without debate or after limited debate. Objections must be heard before the voting. Also, Bills or law proposals may be voted without debate or after limited debate, if they are brought to Parliament following the relevant decision by Parliament or a unanimous proposal of the Conference of Parliamentary Chairmen (Article 108 of the Standing Orders).
(2) Bills or law proposals designated by the Cabinet as very urgent may be tabled for voting after a limited debate at a sitting of the plenary session or Recess Section (Article 76 paragraph 4 of the Constitution and Article 109 of the Standing Orders). The Cabinet may also request that a bill or law proposal of an urgent nature be debated in a certain number of sittings (Article 76 paragraph 5 of the Constitution and Article 110 of the Standing Orders).
(3) Judicial or administrative codes drafted by special committees established by special statutes may be voted in the plenum by means of a particular statute ratifying them as a whole. Likewise, law provisions in force may be codified by simple re-arrangement and repealed laws may be re-enacted, with the exception of tax laws (Article 76 paragraphs 6 and 7 of the Constitution).
(4) Rapid procedures are available for the enactment of statutes ratifying international treaties and conventions and acts of legislative content as well as for the enactment of the statute on the State budget. There is also a special procedure for passing bills and law proposals referred to Parliament by the President of the Republic (*see supra* No. 63).

III. Other Proceedings

167. Proceedings for the revision of the Constitution, proclamation of referenda, declarations of a state of siege (emergency), the election of the President of the Republic, and so on, are specifically provided for in the Constitution and the Standing Orders and have already been (or will be) dealt with in the relevant paragraphs.

IV. Rules on Quorum and Majority

168. Neither the Constitution nor the Standing Orders include provisions on quorum.

In particular, under Article 67 of the Constitution, 'Parliament cannot resolve without an absolute majority of the present members, which in no case may be less than one-fourth of the total number of the Members of Parliament.' Furthermore, under Article 70 paragraph 5 of the Constitution, the Recess Section and standing parliamentary committees, in carrying out their work of legislation, cannot pass resolutions without a majority, which may not be less than two-fifths of the total number of their members.

Special provisions of the Constitution require stronger majorities, for example, for a motion of censure, election of the President, revision of the Constitution, and so on.

The Constitution does not require that any minimum number of Members be present as a quorum for the sittings of Parliament. In practice, the debates preceding a vote are attended by a much smaller number of Members of Parliament than that required to secure the necessary majority for a motion to be passed.

Chapter 6. The Dissolution of Parliament

169. Dissolution of Parliament is dealt with separately here due to the significance which even modern Greek constitutional theory attributes to it. The reason for special attention paid by Greek constitutional theory to the process of dissolution of Parliament has historical roots, mainly King Constantine's anti-democratic dissolutions of Parliament in 1915 (*see supra* No. 34). With these unconstitutional dissolutions in mind, the constitutional legislator of 1975 and, even more so, the legislator responsible for the Revision of 1986, defined as rigorously as possible the circumstances in which Parliament may be dissolved.

The practice of self-dissolution of Parliament is unknown in the Constitution. It was provided for in the Constitution of 1927 only.

Parliament is dissolved by Presidential Decree in the following cases:

(1) When two Cabinets have resigned or have been voted down by Parliament and the composition of Parliament cannot guarantee governmental stability (Article 41 paragraph 1 of the Constitution). If the Prime Minister does not countersign the Decree, it may be issued even without countersignature (Article 35 paragraph 2 of the Constitution). In this case, known as presidential dissolution, a slight margin of discretion is entrusted to the President: it is up to the President to judge, after the second Cabinet has resigned or has been voted down, whether Parliament guarantees governmental stability or not.
The constitutional provision on the presidential dissolution of Parliament *stricto sensu* was introduced in 1986. It amended the broad power of discretion to dissolve Parliament which the Constitution had originally awarded to the President of the Republic, after consulting with the Council of the Republic(an institution which has been abrogated by the constitutional amendment of 1986 (*see supra* No. 12)) if Parliament was in obvious discord with public opinion or if its composition could not ensure governmental stability.
Following dissolution, general elections are conducted under the Cabinet already enjoying the confidence of Parliament or – most probably – by a Cabinet of all parliamentary parties or, if the formation of such Cabinet proves to be impossible, by a Cabinet of the politically widest possible acceptance under one of the Chief Justices of the three Supreme Courts, that is, of the Council of State, of the Supreme Civil and Criminal Court or of the Court of Audit (Article 41 paragraph 1 in conjunction with Article 37 paragraph 3(c) of the Constitution).

(2) If the formation of a Cabinet enjoying the confidence of Parliament is impossible (Article 37 paragraph 3(c) of the Constitution, *see infra* Nos 183 et seq.) As with (1), the President of the Republic is obliged to follow the procedure laid down in the Constitution. His role is confined to the performance of the acts involved in that procedure.

(3) On the proposal of a Cabinet enjoying the confidence of Parliament, for the purpose of renewing the popular mandate in order to deal with a national issue of exceptional importance (Article 41 paragraph 2 of the Constitution). The President of the Republic was originally empowered to use his discretion in

accepting or otherwise the proposal of the Government and therefore dissolving Parliament. The constitutional amendment of 1986 changed into a formal competence the discretionary power of the President of the Republic. The President is now, after that amendment, bound to issue the decree of dissolution, if the Government so proposes. The procedure is, therefore, described as 'governmental dissolution'. Dissolution of the new Parliament for the same national issue of exceptional importance is not allowed.

(4) When, in cases where the Prime Minister has resigned or died or is unable for reasons of ill health to perform his duties, it proves impossible to form a government (Article 38 paragraph 2 of the Constitution). In both cases above the procedure to be followed is precisely defined in the Constitution and no discretionary powers are assigned to the President of the Republic.

The new Parliament may not be dissolved before the lapse of one year from its opening session except in the two first cases mentioned above.

In any case, the decree of dissolution must include the proclamation of elections within thirty days and the convocation of the new Parliament within the next thirty days.

Chapter 7. Political Parties, Lobbies and Interest Groups

170. To the democratic process – democracy is not static, it is dynamic – a major contribution is made by political parties, which aim to attract to their ideology and principles a majority of the people in order to represent them as the majority in Parliament or at least to express a certain part of public opinion and contribute to the formation and more specific definition of the political will. Political parties are unions, differing from other unions or associations mainly due to their constitutional status (Council of State Ruling 2145/1979).

The Constitution explicitly acknowledges the existence and importance of political parties. Article 29 reads as follows:

1. Greek citizens possessing the right to vote may freely found and join political parties, the organization and activity of which must serve the free functioning of democratic government.

   Citizens who have not yet acquired the right to vote may participate in youth sections of political parties.
2. Political parties are entitled to receive financial support by the State for their electoral and operating expenses, as specified by law. A statute shall specify the guarantees of transparency concerning electoral expenses and, in general, the financial management of political parties, of Members of Parliament, parliamentary candidates and candidates for all degrees of local government. A statute shall impose the maximum limit of electoral expenses, may prohibit certain forms of pre-electoral promotion and shall specify the conditions under which violation of the relevant provisions constitutes a ground for the forfeiture of parliamentary office on the initiative of the special body of the following section. The audit of the electoral expenses of political parties and parliamentary candidates is carried out by a special body which is constituted also with the participation of senior magistrates, as specified by law. A law may also extend these regulations to candidates for other offices held through election.
3. Manifestations of any nature whatsoever in favour of or against a political party by magistrates and by those serving in the armed forces and the security corps, are absolutely prohibited. In the exercise of their duties, manifestations of any nature whatsoever in favour of or against a political party by public servants, employees of local government agencies, of other public law legal persons or of public enterprises or of enterprises of local government agencies or of enterprises whose management is directly or indirectly appointed by the State, by administrative act or by virtue of its capacity as shareholder, are absolutely prohibited.

The specific content of paragraphs 2 and 3 of Article 29 was introduced in the Revision of 2001. It enshrined in the Constitution the right of political parties to receive financial assistance from the State. This assistance is available for both electoral and operating expenses and is designed to supplement the parties' own finances, not to meet the entirety of their needs.

The addition of clauses (b) to (e) to paragraph 2 of Article 29 introduced into the Constitution the principle of transparency in electoral spending and the finances of parties and deputies. In 2002 Executive Act 3023/2002 was passed implementing Article 29 of the Constitution. It has determined the methods by which parties may be funded, the ceilings on election spending, the methods of auditing party finances and the penalties to which parties and deputies will be subject if found to have breached the relevant provisions. In 2013 Article 7a was added to Act 3023/2002 (Article 23 of Act 4203/2013). It provides for the suspension of a state party's funding when prominent members of it are involved in criminal activities committed in the context of party activities. Its adoption was considered necessary due to the alleged violent acts of a particular party, which was represented in the Parliament, against foreigners and political opponents. The Full Bench of the Council of State in its Ruling 518/2015 confirmed the constitutionality of this provision. Act 3023/2002 has explicitly recognized political parties as legal persons (Article 29 paragraph 6). Before this legislation political parties were not considered as legal persons; nevertheless, there was practically no consequence as to their capacity to act under the law. Act 3023/2002 has been extensively amended by Act 4304/2014.

171. Apart from Article 29 other constitutional provisions refer to political parties too. For example, the appointment of the Prime Minister and of the Cabinet is based on the institution of political parties (Article 37); sections and committees of Parliament consist proportionally of members belonging to parliamentary groups corresponding to political parties (Articles 68 paragraph 3, and 71). Similarly, the Standing Orders and the electoral law acknowledge the importance of political parties.

The multi-party system is considered one of the organizational principles of the form of government. The free establishment and the free activity of political parties is a fundamental principle of the Constitution enabling popular contribution to the formation of the political will. In this sense, party pluralism is an essential element, a *conditio sine qua non* of democracy.

Citizens are free under the Constitution to form unions and associations (Article 12) and trade unions (Article 23); they have the right to resort to strikes (Article 23). Participation in politics has also been encouraged by the institution of local government, which received substantial new powers in the Revision of 2001 (on local government, *see* more detailed account *infra* Nos 239 et seq.).

172. Lobbies and interest groups exercise a large influence on the decision-making of public authorities, contributing thus to the dialogue between authority and society, a dialogue which is also indispensable for democracy. Within this context, a vital role is now played by the mass media. The press, radio and television are now the principal mechanisms involved in forming public opinion. However, the involvement of the media with invisible centres of power, and the priority given to the pursuit of financial profit over the provision of objective information to the public, have led the media ever farther from their proper role as platforms for social dialogue and champions of our democratic institutions. They now tend to be more engaged in attempts to manipulate and disorient public opinion, seeking to control political forces and the political life of the country (*see infra* No. 400 for a more detailed account of measures to limit media involvement in political life).

Recently, with the enactment of Act 4829/2021, for the first time in Greece, a legislative framework has been created to regulate the communication between state institutions and interest representatives, with the ultimate aim of ensuring integrity, transparency and accountability in the exercise of influence.

To summarize the provisions of the Act, it establishes a 'Transparency Register', which is an electronic database maintained by the National Transparency Authority, to which interest representatives are compulsorily registered and to which the public has free electronic access (Article 8). Enrolment in the Register entails rights and obligations for interest representatives as described in Article 7, the breach of which entails sanctions as provided for in Article 12, imposed by the supervisory authority. Another key element is that Article 10 provides that interest representatives shall submit an annual declaration of the exercise of influence activities, which shall include (a) the policy area and the type of decision, (b) the details of the person who exercised the influence activity, as well as his client if he acted on behalf of another person, (c) the manner in which the influence activity was carried out, (d) the institutional body to which the influence activity was addressed.

Chapter 8. Referendum

173. Under Article 44 paragraph 2 of the Constitution as revised in 1986:

> The President of the Republic shall by decree proclaim a referendum on crucial national matters following a resolution voted by an absolute majority of the total number of Members of Parliament, taken upon proposal of the Cabinet. A referendum on Bills passed by Parliament regulating important social matters, with the exception of the fiscal ones shall be proclaimed by decree by the President of the Republic, if this is decided by three-fifths of the total number of its members, following a proposal of two-fifths of the total number of its members, and as the Standing Orders and the law for the application of the present paragraph provide. No more than two proposals to hold a referendum on a Bill can be introduced in the same parliamentary term.

The competence of the President of the Republic to proclaim referenda is merely formal. The aforementioned provision of the Constitution was introduced in 1986; it amended the discretionary competence of the President of the Republic in the Constitution, according to which referenda on crucial national issues could be proclaimed by the President on his own initiative without proposal by the Government and even without ministerial countersignature.

174. Referenda are of two kinds: one refers to matters of crucial 'national' importance, the other to serious 'social' issues.

Both terms are vague in content. Their juxtaposition helps, however, to define national matters as matters beyond and above social or political antagonisms, affecting thus the unity of the nation; foreign affairs and national defence form, without doubt, the core of 'crucial national matters'.

Serious social matters, too, transcend political antagonisms. This may be substantiated by the large majorities that are required in Parliament for the decision to hold a referendum. This requirement of a large majority probably presupposes that division of Parliament, in more or less disciplined political fractions, is *in concreto* of less practical importance than the unifying element of the seriousness of the social matter.

The referendum on crucial national matters may not, due to its significance, be regarded as merely consultative. It has to be considered as decisive and binding on the Government at least as to the direction of the policy on the national matters in question.

The referendum on Bills of crucial social importance, if sanctioned by popular vote, must also be considered binding and probably deprives the President of the Republic of his competence to send back Bills (Article 42 paragraphs 1 and 2, *see supra* Nos 63 and 106). If the Bill is rejected by popular vote, it may probably not be re-submitted, at least not in the same parliamentary session. This interpretation complies with the system of representative government, to which referenda constitute an exception.

A popular initiative for the proclamation of a referendum is not recognized by the Constitution. In academic debates, it is considered desirable. However, it can only be introduced by a constitutional amendment.

Part IV. Public Administration

175. Greece is a unitary State as opposed to a federation. Executive power is vested in the President of the Republic and the Government (Article 26 paragraph 2 of the Constitution). The Constitution lays down certain basic principles governing the organization of the administration, establishing decentralization, independent administrative authorities and local government as the main lines of its organization (Articles 101, 101A and 102). It also proclaims certain principles in respect of the terms of employment of those serving in public administration (Articles 103 and 104). Finally, the Constitution sets out the regime under which Mt Athos shall be administered (Article 105).

Chapter 1. The Government

§1. THE ORGAN OF STATE

176. The 'government' – 'Cabinet' or 'Council of Ministers' – determines and exercises the policy, internal and foreign, of the country (Article 82 paragraph 1 of the Constitution). As the basic organ of the executive power, it is at the head of the public administration. The various legislative and regulatory provisions concerning the mandate, organization and workings of the Government are regulated in a single text by the recent Act 4622/2019 'Executive State: organization, functioning and transparency of the Government, governmental organs and central public administration'. It functions as a handbook on governance which brings together a single text and renews all the fragmented provisions that were spread over hundreds of pieces of legislation, making them difficult to be implemented. However, the legislation caused various reactions as it transferred excessive regulatory powers to the Prime Minister, thus weakening the constitutionally enshrined position of Ministers and causing bureaucratic over-concentration in one single authority.

I. Composition of the Government

177. The Cabinet, is composed of the Prime Minister and the Ministers. One or more Ministers may be appointed as Vice President(s) of the Cabinet (Article 81 paragraph 1 of the Constitution). If no Minister has been appointed as Vice President, the Prime Minister appoints ad hoc one of the Ministers as his provisional deputy, whenever the need arises, otherwise according to the hierarchical order of the Ministers (Article 17 paragraph 1 of Act 4622/2019). Deputy Ministers, Ministers without Portfolio (now named 'Ministers of State') and Undersecretaries may, according to the Constitution, be members of the Cabinet, if the law so provides (Article 81 of the Constitution combined with Article 13 of Act 4622/2019). Undersecretaries are not members of the Cabinet, whereas all other categories of Ministers are. The Prime Minister may ask Undersecretaries to participate in Cabinet meetings but without the right to vote (Article 1 paragraph 2 of Act 4622/2019).

The Constitution, in Article 81, also provides for permanent salaried Undersecretaries. These would be senior civil servants in charge of all the departments of a Ministry, answering only to the Minister and his Undersecretary. To date, no such appointments have been made.

II. Organization of the Government

178. The Government is organized according to the principle of collegiality. However, legislation provided for several government councils and committees, also functioning under the principle of collegiality. Historically, these were the Government Committee *stricto sensu*, the Government Council on Foreign Affairs and National Defence, the Committee on Institutions, the Committee on Financial and

Social Policy, the Committee for Major Projects and Infrastructure, and the Committee for Framing Strategy and IT Development. They were abolished and replaced by the Government Council (Act of Cabinet 2/2015), with the exception of the Government Council on Foreign Affairs and National Defence.

Currently, after the enactment of Act 4622/2019, the collective governmental bodies are divided into Government Councils and Governmental Committees (Article 6).

179. Government Councils have a permanent and continuous function and exercise specific competences defined by law. In addition, they shall exercise any power which, at the discretion of the Council of Ministers or the Prime Minister, is assigned to them. The Government Councils are: (a) the Government Council for Economic Policy, which is responsible for formulating inter-ministerial policies and taking decisions on matters relating to the economic and development policy of the country, and (b) the Government Council for National Security, which is responsible for formulating inter-ministerial policies and taking decisions on matters relating to the security of the country.

180. The Government Committees, on the other hand, have competence over specific issues of government policy that require special management and systematic monitoring and are therefore established on a case-by-case basis by Acts of the Cabinet of Ministers. To date, more than fifteen government committees have been established, such as the Government Committee for the Coordination of Public Enterprise Governance (Act of Cabinet 38/2019), Government Committee for Strategic Investments (Act of Cabinet 41/2020), Government Committee for the Coordination and Management of Coronavirus Vaccination (Act of Cabinet 50/2020), Government Committee for State Aid (Act of Cabinet 4/2022), Government Committee for the Upgrading of the National Archaeological Museum (Act of Cabinet 8/2022), etc.

181. Furthermore, the Constitution provides for two expert bodies to advise the Government: the Economic and Social Committee (Article 82 paragraph 3, revised in 2001, *see infra* No. 228) and the National Council of Foreign Policy (Article 82 paragraph 4, revised in 2001, *see infra* No. 229).

182. The decision and policymaking process in Cabinet is specified primarily by Act 4622/2019, as well as by the Regulations of Cabinet, which are decided upon by the Cabinet itself (Article 4 paragraph 8). However, these regulations have not yet entered into force, with the result that the detailed provisions of Articles 6 et seq. of Act 4622/2019 apply.

III. Cabinet Formation Process

183. The Constitution regulates issues related to the appointment of the Government (Article 37), and the procedure for securing a vote of confidence in that Government (Article 84). The Cabinet is appointed by the President of the Republic.

Two decrees are issued: the first for the appointment of the Prime Minister, the second, on the proposal of the Prime Minister, for the appointment of the members of the Cabinet and eventually of the Undersecretaries (Article 37 paragraph 1 of the Constitution). The former is signed by the President of the Republic alone (Article 35 paragraph 2 a of the Constitution).

The leader of the political party enjoying the overall majority of seats in Parliament is named Prime Minister (Article 37 of the Constitution). The President of the Republic must proceed to make the relevant appointment as soon as he is informed of the balance of the parties in Parliament. This information is conveyed to him officially by the Speaker. Once appointed the Prime Minister is sworn in, together with the other members of the Government, in the presence of the President of the Republic.

Within fifteen days of the date on which the Prime Minister is sworn in, the Cabinet must request a vote of confidence in Parliament (Article 84 of the Constitution). Confidence is given if the Cabinet is approved by the overall majority of the present Members of Parliament, which majority cannot be less than two-fifths of the total number of Members. On this point, the Constitution introduces the concept of a 'tolerance vote', namely the sufficiency, in a vote of confidence, of a majority of those present but not of the full complement of deputies (*see supra* No. 154). If confidence is not forthcoming, the Cabinet has to resign and it is discharged of its duties by Presidential Decree.

If no party has secured an overall majority of parliamentary seats, the President of the Republic gives the leader of the largest party an exploratory mandate so that the possibility of forming a Cabinet enjoying the confidence of Parliament may, within three days, be ascertained. This exploratory mandate is a formal legal act, signed solely by the President of the Republic (Article 35 paragraph 2 b of the Constitution). If it proves possible to form a Government, there ensues the appointment process and the seeking of a vote of confidence.

We may ask ourselves whether the President of the Republic is bound by whatever assertions may be made by the recipient of the exploratory mandate, or is himself responsible for establishing that they are properly grounded. This question has in fact arisen in practice, in 1989, when all provisions of Article 37 of the Constitution (as revised in 1986) were applied, due to the results of two parliamentary elections which did not give absolute majorities in Parliament. The President of the Republic in both cases declined to appoint as Prime Minister the leader of the largest party, ignoring the request of the latter, because there were clear indications from parties and independent deputies which together enjoyed the overall majority in Parliament that they objected to the formation of such a government.

If the first attempt is unsuccessful, the President gives a second exploratory mandate to the leader of the second-largest party and if this does not lead to success within the next three days he gives a third exploratory mandate to the leader of the third-largest party. Should two parties have equal numbers of seats, the first exploratory mandate is granted to the party which polled the most votes in the election. Moreover, an older party will take precedence over a more recently formed party. In no circumstances, however, may more than four exploratory mandates be granted.

If again, within the next three days, it proves impossible to form a Cabinet enjoying the confidence of Parliament, the President invites all-party leaders to meet, under his chairmanship. This meeting may be attended by all-party leaders, even those of the smallest parties which have not even formed a parliamentary group. In practice, however, in 1989, the relevant negotiations were attended only by the three largest parties which had, in turn, received the exploratory mandate. This procedure represents a last attempt to ascertain the possibility of forming a government which will enjoy the confidence of Parliament and the consensus of the parties.

Should this process confirm the impossibility of forming a government, the President of the Republic has to make every endeavour that an all-party government be formed for the purpose of holding elections. If this attempt fails, he asks the Chief Justice of one of the Supreme Courts (Council of State, Supreme Civil and Criminal Court or Court of Audit) to form a Cabinet enjoying the widest possible acceptance to hold elections, and dissolve Parliament.

Article 37 of the Constitution was introduced in 1986 by constitutional amendment. The previous provision gave the President of the Republic a quite broad margin of discretion, since after the failure of the first exploratory mandate he could either proceed to a second exploratory mandate or appoint as Prime Minister any person, even a non-member of Parliament. This discretionary power of the President of the Republic – although it has never been applied since the situation has never arisen – has been much criticized.

Legal scholars have questioned whether the person appointed as Prime Minister must be a Member of Parliament; if it is possible for an individual from outside Parliament to be appointed to the office. From Article 37 paragraph 4 of the Constitution, where it reads in part '… if the leader or party spokesman has not been elected to Parliament, the President of the Republic shall give the mandate to a person proposed by the party's parliamentary group …', it is clear that the Prime Minister should indeed be a Member of Parliament. This seems to apply above all in the case where the leading party has an overall majority, and in the case where exploratory mandates are being granted. But in the case of the formation of an all-party government, there is no such provision and thus in this circumstance a person from outside Parliament may be appointed.

IV. Resignation of the Cabinet

184. The constitutional amendment of 1986 has rightly abrogated the discretionary competence of the President of the Republic to dismiss the Cabinet after consulting with the Council of the Republic (*see supra* No. 12 and No. 169).

Following that amendment, the Cabinet is now discharged from its duties if it resigns or if Parliament withdraws its confidence. The Government will invariably resign at the end of the parliamentary term, after the new Parliament has been elected and before the appointment of the new Prime Minister. However, it is free to resign also during its term of office, if political reasons so dictate.

Confidence is withdrawn if Parliament approves the motion of no-confidence by an absolute majority of the total number of its Members or rejects the motion of confidence tabled by the Government (Article 84 of the Constitution). The Government is relieved of its duties by Presidential Decree, countersigned by the Prime Minister, or without his signature, should he refuse.

After discharging the Cabinet from its duties the President of the Republic proceeds to the appointment of a new Government. He follows the procedure of the exploratory mandates as described above. If the resigning government enjoys an overall majority in Parliament, the procedure set out in Article 37 of the Constitution is adopted at the stage of negotiation among the party leaders in the presence of the Prime Minister (Article 38 paragraph 1(c), in combination with Article 37 paragraph 3(c) of the Constitution).

A distinction must be made between the case of the resignation of the entire government, and the case in which only the Prime Minister resigns, dies or is unable, for reasons of ill health, to perform his duties (Article 38 paragraph 2 of the Constitution). In the latter case, the President of the Republic appoints as Prime Minister the person proposed by the parliamentary group of the party to which the former Prime Minister belonged, provided that this group enjoys an overall majority in Parliament. The parliamentary group has to designate the new Prime Minister within three days. If no political party has an overall majority of the seats in Parliament, then exploratory mandates are issued. The parliamentary group of the departing Prime Minister nominates the recipient of the first mandate (Article 38 paragraph 2(c), in combination with Article 37 paragraphs 4 and 2 of the Constitution).

The decision on whether a Prime Minister is incapable of performing his duties must be taken by the overall majority of the whole Parliament. The motion may be tabled by the parliamentary group of the Prime Minister's own party if it enjoys an overall majority of seats in Parliament, or by two-fifths of the whole complement of Members or Parliament in all other cases (Article 38 paragraph 2 of the Constitution). These detailed provisions were added in the Revision of 2001, in response to the issues raised in 1996 when the then Prime Minister, Andreas Papandreou, was suffering from a prolonged illness. For about three months, the Prime Minister was too sick to perform his duties, but there was no provision for his replacement without his prior resignation. Eventually, Papandreou did resign.

§2. Eligibility, Incompatibilities and Legal Status

I. Eligibility

185. According to the Constitution (Article 81 paragraph 2), 'No person may be appointed a member of the Government or an Undersecretary if he does not possess the qualifications required in Article 55 for Members of Parliament.' One has thus to be Greek, at least 25 years old and legally entitled to vote. One does not, however, have to be a Member of Parliament. In practice, though, Ministers and Undersecretaries are almost invariably Members of Parliament. Besides it was rare for governments to include persons from outside Parliament; in recent years, a significant number of non-parliamentary Ministers and mainly Undersecretaries have participated in the composition of the Government, on the grounds that they are well-experienced and specialized technocrats with deep expertise in their field.

II. Incompatibilities

186. The Constitution prohibits any professional activity by members of the Cabinet and Undersecretaries (Article 81 paragraph 3).

The duties of any person holding an office or function in the public sector are *ipso iure* suspended on his appointment as a member of the Government or Undersecretary. Furthermore, any kind of contractual relationship with the State or legal persons in the public sector is absolutely prohibited; violation of this provision renders the contracts null and void and the member of the Government or Undersecretary responsible under the law on ministerial responsibility (Article 14 of Act 4622/2019).

Members of the Government receive remuneration equivalent to that of an ordinary Member of Parliament – the same as that paid to the President of the Supreme Civil and Criminal Court (7th Parliamentary Resolution of 17/18 February 1975).

III. Legal Status

187. (a) Ministers. Ministers, being at the head of their Ministries, are officials of the highest rank. The basic difference between them and civil servants, who are appointed for as long as their position is not abrogated by law, is that they do not have disciplinary liability; they are instead politically responsible to Parliament. Ministers, Deputy Ministers and Undersecretaries are all of the same rank. They are not subject to any relations of hierarchical precedence. However, there are seniorities of rank among the members of the Government, mainly of political significance.

188. (b) The Prime Minister. The Prime Minister has a special status, enshrined in both the Constitution and the ordinary laws. He ensures the unity of the Cabinet and directs its actions as well as those of the public services in general so that government policy will be implemented according to the law (Article 82 paragraph 2 of the Constitution). Furthermore, according to the definitions of Act 4622/2019, the Prime Minister is the head of the autonomous, executive public agency 'Presidency of the Government', which consists of individual General Secretariats: General Secretariat of the Prime Minister, Legal and Parliamentary Affairs, Coordination of Internal Policies, Economic and Development Policies, Integrated Information Systems, Monitoring of Government Work, and Communication and Information. The task of the Presidency of the Government is to assist the Prime Minister in the exercise of his responsibilities.

The definition and direction of governmental policy is, however, a matter of collective decision-making in the Cabinet, not the business of the Prime Minister alone.

In other words, the Prime Minister is not *primus solus* but *primus inter pares*. Cabinet functions under the principle of collegiality. Nevertheless, a special status is given to the Prime Minister by the Constitution and the law. First of all, he is appointed by a special decree, before the appointment of the Ministers. He presides over Cabinet meetings. He proposes to the President of the Republic the persons to become Ministers or Undersecretaries – and these proposals are binding. He may dismiss them at any time at his own discretion (Article 37 paragraph 1 of the Constitution). He also appoints his own temporary deputy if he deems it necessary. He specifies governmental policy within the framework of the Cabinet's decisions and coordinates its implementation. He arbitrates between Ministers if the situation calls for it. Finally, the Prime Minister represents the Government (Article 11 of Act 4622/2019).

It has been rightly claimed that Act 1558/1985 (as initially codified by the Presidential Decree 63/2005, and finally replaced by Act 4622/2019), as well as the Revision of 1986, have made the role of the Prime Minister too powerful. It is up to political practice to safeguard the leading role of the Cabinet vis-à-vis the Prime Minister. Historically, the only time at which the Prime Minister did not enjoy real power was the two-year period 1989–1990. The election of June 1989 did not produce an overall majority for any party in Parliament. A bipartisan Government was formed, comprising the New Democracy conservative party and the Alliance of the Left, one of whose constituents was the Communist Party. The Prime Minister appointed was not the leader of the marginally (in terms of number of seats) larger party (New Democracy), but a member of it, Tzanis Tzannetakis. In November of the same year, a new election was held, under a Government with a 'caretaker' Prime Minister (i.e., a Prime Minister whose main remit was to oversee the smooth course of the election), former President of the Supreme Civil and Criminal Court, Ioannis Grivas. But this election too failed to produce an overall majority in Parliament for any party. A new coalition Government had to be formed, this time representing all three parties, with the Socialist Party (PASOK) now participating. The former Governor of the Bank of Greece, Professor Xenophon Zolotas, was sworn in as Prime Minister. During this period real power was wielded by an informal council of leaders of the three parties, which essentially dictated all major decisions to the Prime Minister and Government. This irregular situation was brought to an end in April 1990, when the Conservative Party secured a good working majority in a new election and formed a single-party government, under its leader Constantine Mitsotakis.

§3. Competence

I. Collective Competence of the Cabinet

189. Cabinet determines and directs the general policy of the country in compliance with the principle of the rule of law (Article 82 paragraph 1 of the Constitution); that is, its competence is defined by many different sorts of laws. To mention only one example, only with the prior consenting opinion of the Cabinet, may the Minister of Justice defer or suspend for an indefinite period criminal proceedings in the case of political crimes or of crimes which might endanger the international relations of the country (Article 29 of the Code of Criminal Procedure).

The Constitution itself provides specifically for the main governmental competences. These may be legislative (legislative initiative, the proposal for the issuance of acts of legislative content and the implementation of the law on a state of siege), administrative (the administration of the armed forces) and regulatory (proposal and countersignature of the decree dissolving Parliament, the holding of elections, etc.). The Government is also competent to replace the President of the Republic (Article 34 paragraph 1 of the Constitution).

The Cabinet may also decide on political matters of general importance and on any matter within the competence of collective government bodies or of one or more Ministers, should the matter be referred to it by the Prime Minister (Article 1 paragraph 1 (b) and (c) of Act 4622/2019). The relevant decisions of the Cabinet take the place of decisions by the competent bodies (Article 5 of Act 4622/2019). This is an entirely legitimate provision, consistent with the principle of collective action by the Government.

II. Competences of the Prime Minister

190. The competences of the Prime Minister reflect his special position in the overall context of the Government, especially under the provisions of Act 4622/2019 (for more details, *see supra* No. 188).

III. Competences of the Ministers

191. According to Article 83 paragraph 1 of the Constitution, Ministers exercise the competences specified by law. Furthermore, they coordinate, supervise and control the action of the public servants and officials under their authority, on the basis of the competences assigned to them by the statutes in force, as well as oversee and coordinate the actions of the Deputy Ministers appointed to their Ministry. They exercise, in accordance with the Constitution and the Standing Orders, the legislative initiative in matters within their competence and within the framework of the regulatory planning of the Government, propose the adoption of delegated Regulatory Decrees and the decrees necessary for the implementation of the laws within their competence. Finally, Ministers issue regulatory acts under the authority of the law and exercise any other power conferred on them by the Constitution and the law or delegated to them by the Prime Minister.

Specific competences of the Minister of Finance and the Minister of Justice are also mentioned in the Constitution (*see supra* Nos 61 and 110).

192. Deputy Ministers and Ministers of State (or 'Ministers without Portfolio') acquire their specific competences on the basis of a decision of the Prime Minister (Article 83 paragraph 1(b) of the Constitution).

193. Undersecretaries exercise the competences that are awarded to them by a joint decision of the Prime Minister and the competent Minister (Article 83 paragraph 2 of the Constitution). Unless otherwise stipulated in this joint decision, legislative initiative and other parliamentary competences, as well as regulatory authority, in respect of the competences transferred, remain with the Minister. The same decision may also provide that some of the competences assigned to the Undersecretary will continue to be exercised in parallel by the Minister (Articles 13 et seq. of Act 4622/2019).

§4. Workings of the Cabinet

194. The Cabinet is convened in ordinary meetings by the Prime Minister or his deputy once a month following a written or electronic invitation, which is sent to the members of the Government together with the agenda and the venue of the meeting, at least two days before the meeting.

The annual calendar of regular meetings of the Cabinet is determined by its Secretary, approved by the Prime Minister and communicated to the members of the Cabinet of Ministers at the ordinary meeting in December of the previous year. The date of the regular meeting may be changed by decision of the Prime Minister due to extraordinary circumstances which make it impossible to convene and hold the Cabinet of Ministers on the date fixed (Article 2 paragraph 2 of Act 4622/2019).

The order of the day of the Cabinet's regular meetings is drawn up by the Secretary of the Cabinet, after consultation with the Prime Minister and taking into account the proposals of the Ministers. The Cabinet may, with the approval of the Prime Minister, discuss and take decisions on matters not included in the order of the day or may give priority to the discussion of any other matter, whether or not included in the order of the day (Article 2 paragraph 3 of Act 4622/2019).

The Cabinet shall also have extraordinary meetings when necessary, following a written or electronic or oral invitation by the Prime Minister, which shall include, at their discretion, the date, time and place of the meeting. The invitation shall be accompanied by a statement of the items to be discussed (Article 2 paragraph 4 of Act 4622/2019).

Announcements or proposals by the members of the Cabinet for discussion and decision on any matter shall be addressed to the Secretary of the Cabinet no later than forty-eight hours before the regular meeting and shall be accompanied by a brief explanatory note. The above is communicated to the other members of the Cabinet, before the beginning of the meeting (Article 2 paragraph 5 of Act 4622/2019).

By the enactment of Act 4622/2019, the regular Cabinet meetings of April and September were designated for the planning and evaluation of the Government's work.

The April Cabinet meeting is intended for: (a) assessing the implementation of the Government policy of the last seven months by all members of the Cabinet in order to decide on the necessary corrective measures for the rest of the year; (b) the presentation of the Government priorities for the next year by the Prime Minister and (c) the presentation of the draft Medium Term Fiscal Strategy Framework for the current year by the competent Minister.

The September Cabinet meeting is devoted to: (a) the assessment of the implementation of the current year's government policy by all members of the Cabinet in order to decide on the necessary corrective measures for the remainder of the year; (b) the discussion and approval of the Consolidated Government Action Plan and the Action Plans of the Ministries; (c) the discussion and approval of the Government's legislative and regulatory planning for the coming year, and (d) the presentation of the draft Plan of Action of the Government for the coming year.

Meetings of the Cabinet are attended only by Cabinet members, plus the Secretary of the Cabinet and the staff necessary for taking a shorthand record or tape-recording of the discussions, unless the Prime Minister considers that the matters to be discussed are top secret. (Article 1 paragraphs 3 and 4 of Act 4622/2019). Undersecretaries may attend the meetings at the invitation of the Prime Minister, but they are not entitled to vote (Article 1 paragraph 2 of Act 4622/2019). In order to brief the Cabinet on technical or scientific matters, issues of national defence and security or other general or specific political issues, the Prime Minister may invite to the Cabinet meetings functionaries and employees from the civil service and broader public sector, experts from outside the public sector and other persons as appropriate. Such persons will leave the meeting when the Prime Minister decides that the briefing is complete (Article 1 paragraph 5 of Act 4622/2019).

For a quorum to be achieved it is necessary that half of the members of the Cabinet be present. Debates are secret. The Secretary of the Cabinet keeps minutes (Article 4 paragraph 5 of Act 4622/2019). At the end of the meeting, an official communiqué on the issues discussed by the Cabinet and the decisions taken by it is prepared under the supervision of the Secretary of the Cabinet and delivered through the Government representative to the media. However, these minutes are not made public for thirty years (Article 4 paragraphs 4 and 7 of Act 4622/2019). Decisions are taken by roll call and by the absolute majority of the present members. In the event of a tie, that course of action supported by the Prime Minister shall be adopted (Article 3 paragraph 4 of Act 4622/2019).

§5. MINISTERIAL RESPONSIBILITY

195. Pursuant to Article 85 of the Constitution, 'The members of the Cabinet and the Undersecretaries shall be collectively responsible for the general Government policy, and each of them severally for the actions or omissions within his powers, according to the provisions of statutes on the liability of Ministers. A written or oral order of the President of the Republic may in no case whatsoever relieve Ministers and Undersecretaries of their liability.'

The responsibility of ministers can be divided into political, criminal and civil responsibility.

I. Political Responsibility

196. Political (parliamentary) responsibility, collective and individual, is manifested in the subordination of the Government and of each Minister respectively to parliamentary control (*see supra* Nos 145 et seq.). Ministers, individually or collectively, are responsible for acts or omissions in their area of competence or that of the Government, as well as for acts or omissions of the President of the Republic, in case they have countersigned them. This is emphasized in the last sentence of Article 85 of the Constitution, which in other respects has no practical significance since the President of the Republic no longer has the power to address orders to the Government. Ministers have individual responsibility for their own actions and for those of their subordinates at the Ministries, the persons under their supervision, and so on. Undersecretaries also share in this collective responsibility, even though they are not *lato sensu* members of the Government.

The most extreme form, which the charge of political responsibility can take, is the motion of censure against the Government or one of its members. A successful charge of political responsibility will result in the Minister concerned losing his office, being compelled to resign, or as a result of a motion of censure being passed (*see supra* Nos 154 et seq.).

II. Criminal Liability

197. Provisions governing the criminal liability of Ministers are laid down in the Constitution (Article 86), the Standing Orders (Articles 153 et seq.) and the law (Act 3126/2003). They cover all forms of misdemeanour and felony committed by a member of the Government or by the Prime Minister, during the discharge of their duties. It is irrelevant whether the Minister in question remains in office or not. The Special Court described in Article 86 of the Constitution is responsible for hearing these cases of criminal responsibility; related charges of complicity involving any other persons are heard by the same Court.

When the misdemeanour or felony was not committed during the discharge of ministerial duties, the charges will be heard by the regular criminal courts subject directly to the provisions of the Penal Code, the special penal laws and the Code of Criminal Procedure.

The Constitution states that in respect of criminal acts committed in the exercise of ministerial duties, there may be no prosecution, investigation, preliminary investigation or preliminary examination of the Minister without a prior decision by a plenary session of Parliament (Article 86 paragraph 2 of the Constitution).

A criminal prosecution may be initiated if the relevant motion is made in writing by at least thirty Members of Parliament. The petition shall make specific reference to the details of the alleged criminal act and shall specify the provisions of the law which have been breached (Article 86 paragraph 3 of the Constitution and Article 5 paragraph 1 of Act 3126/2003).

When the above petition has been submitted to the Speaker's office, a special parliamentary committee is set up, by decision to be taken with an overall majority of the total number of Members of Parliament, in accordance with the Standing

Orders. The purpose of the committee is to conduct a preliminary examination. If the above majority is not secured, the motion is rejected as manifestly unfounded (Article 86 paragraph 3 of the Constitution and Article 5 paragraph 4 of Act 3126/2003).

The committee has all the powers of a prosecutor attached to the Court of First Instance when he is conducting a preliminary examination and may entrust specific actions related to the subject of the preliminary examination to a prosecutor with the magistrates' court or appeal court. The subject of the motion for prosecution may be invited to appear before the committee to explain himself (Article 5 paragraph 5 of Act 3126/2003). The committee draws up its findings, in which it explains, fully and clearly, whether or not it favours the taking of criminal proceedings against the individual in question (Article 5 paragraph 6 of Act 3126/2003).

The findings are placed before a plenary session of Parliament, where a decision is taken, by absolute majority of the total number of Members of Parliament, whether or not to proceed with a criminal prosecution (Article 86 paragraph 3 of the Constitution and Article 6 paragraphs 1 and 2 of Act 3126/2003). When the Minister in question is also a Member of Parliament, the decision to initiate a criminal prosecution also serves to remove his parliamentary immunity (Article 6 paragraph 3 of Act 3126/2003).

If the motion to proceed is not passed, no new proposal based on the same facts is admissible (Article 6 paragraph 3 of Act 3126/2003). If it is approved, Parliament formulates the accusation and establishes a five-member Judicial Council, consisting of three members of the Supreme Civil and Criminal Court and two members of the Council of State. One of the members of this Judicial Council is appointed as examining magistrate (Article 86 paragraph 4 of the Constitution and Article 8 of Act 3126/2003). When the investigation has been concluded, either the charges against the minister are dismissed and a *nolle prosequi* is entered, or the case is referred to the Special Court (Article 86 paragraph 4 of the Constitution and Article 12 paragraph 1 of Act 3126/2003).

In the event of the case being referred to the Special Court, the Speaker designates by lot seven judges from the lists of the members of the Supreme Civil and Criminal Court and six from the lists of the members of the Council of State, as well as six alternates who form, under the presidency of the highest ranking of the Supreme Civil and Criminal Court members chosen by lot, the Special Court for Ministers mentioned in Article 86 paragraph 4 of the Constitution and Article 12 of Act 3126/2003. The President of the Court fixes the date of the trial, which is carried out according to the ordinary criminal proceedings in public hearings (Article 13 of Act 3126/2003). No appeal is allowed against the ruling of the Court (Article 17 paragraph 1 of Act 3126/2003).

Following the amendment of Article 3 of Act 3126/2003 by Article 1 of Act 3961/2011 the provision for a short (five-year) status of limitations on offences committed by Ministers was abolished. According to Act 3961/2011, the general provisions of Articles 111, 112 and 113 of Penal Code regulating the limitation of offences and their suspension are also applicable to offences committed by Ministers. The limitation can also be suspended only in the following circumstances:

(1) for as long as the duration of the parliamentary term during which the offence was committed;
(2) for as long as the decision of the plenary session of Parliament remains in effect, on suspending the prosecution, preliminary or main procedure.

It is worth mentioning that prior to the Revision of 2019, according to the second sentence of paragraph 3 of Article 86 of the Constitution, no criminal proceedings could be taken for actions by Ministers committed during the discharge of their duties after the conclusion of the second regular session of the parliamentary term commencing after the committing of the criminal act, if by that date Parliament had not decided to initiate a criminal prosecution against the Minister.

This provision, which was repealed by the Revision of 2019, laid down an extremely short time limit after committing the crime, which under certain circumstances was even less than two years. The Constitution introduced a favourable treatment of crimes committed by Ministers which prevailed over the general principle of equality; besides, it was contrary to it.

In the event of a prosecution being initiated but not concluded (due to the status of limitations, for example), the Constitution provides for the possibility of establishing a Special Committee to examine the charges. The Committee is established at the request of the Minister involved or his heirs (Article 86 paragraph 5).

Provisions on the criminal liability of ministers may be traditionally justified by the idea that politicians of the highest level 'can do no wrong', but such an idea is nowadays obsolete. The principle of equality permits governors and governed and has to be applicable as part of the rule of law to all persons irrespective of their political status.

III. Civil Liability

198. Ministers bear full civil liability for acts and omissions not related to the discharge of their duties. In respect of acts related to the discharge of those duties, they are jointly liable alongside the State, as a legal person. The provisions of Articles 104 and 105 of the Introductory Act of the Civil Code cover their liability arising from legal relations in private law and their liability for malfeasance in the exercise of public authority.

Chapter 2. Advisory and Supervisory Institutions

§1. Advisory and Supervisory Tasks of Judicial Organs

199. The most frequently cited independent non-political bodies (‘*les grands corps d’administration*’) are the Council of State, the Court of Audit and the Legal Council of State.

I. The Council of State

200. The Council of State was originally founded in 1835, under King Otto, and was intended to emulate the French *Conseil d’Etat*, with advisory and judicial functions. This first Council was then abolished in the Constitution of 1844 (Article 102). It was revived in the Constitution of 1864 (Articles 83–86) as a forum for preparation of new legislation and then abolished once more in 1865. The Constitution of 1911 (Articles 82–86) reintroduced it, with advisory functions on draft legislation and the drafts of Regulatory Decrees, and as a supreme administrative court for hearing applications for annulment and certain administrative disputes, as well as exercising disciplinary powers over civil servants. However, the Council never actually performed any of these functions, because the administrative act, required by the Constitution for the Council to be established, was never issued. Provision was again made for the Council of State in the Constitution of 1927 (Articles 102–105), and it was finally founded in 1928 (Act 3713/1928) and began its work in 1929. Since then it has functioned continuously as a court and an independent, non-political authority. Its organization and workings are currently governed by Legislative Decree 170/1973, as amended and codified by the Presidential Decree 18/1989.

The Council of State is made up of a President, ten Vice Presidents, fifty-three Councillors (Justices), fifty-eight associate judges and fifty *rapporteurs* (junior judges) (Articles 1 and 3 of the Presidential Decree 18/1989, as it is amended by Act 3514/2006 and Act 4509/2017, respectively). The Council of State hears cases in six sections of five or seven judges or in Full Bench (Articles 7 and 10 of the Presidential Decree 18/1989). Its judicial competences will be set out *infra* Nos 322 et seq.

201. The administrative competence of the Council of State lies in the prior review of Regulatory Decrees, namely the regulations issued by the President of the Republic (*see supra* No. 77), but not of the other organs of the administration. Its fifth section is competent to conduct this elaboration, whether with three or five members (Article 15 paragraph 4 of the Presidential Decree 18/1989). If a question should arise concerning the unconstitutionality of the legislative delegation on the basis of which the decree in question is being issued, the matter must be referred to the Full Bench of the Council (Article 100 paragraph 5 of the Constitution).

These controls check the accord of the Regulatory Decrees with the Constitution, EU law, international treaties and the statutes providing for their issuing. The control leads to the formulation of an opinion which is simple (i.e., not a ‘consenting opinion'), and therefore the administration is not obliged to follow it (although it is almost always followed in practice) but is obligatory in the sense that it must be given consideration before the Presidential Decree is issued (Article 15 paragraph 3 of the Presidential Decree 18/1989). To issue a Regulatory Decree without a prior opinion from the Council of State represents a failure to observe an important formality of procedure, and therefore either entails nullification of the decree where the latter is challenged directly and within the time limit, or its non-implementation in the event of its being challenged later and incidentally, on the occasion of a challenge in the form of an application for annulment of an individual administrative act (on the application for annulment, *see infra* Nos 298 et seq.). Nevertheless, the Minister may set a deadline for the issuing of the opinion; if the deadline passes without the opinion being issued, the decree may be published without an opinion (Article 15 paragraphs 1 and 2 of the Presidential Decree 18/1989).

202. Within the Council of State a three-member council is established, made up of the President of the competent section, one councillor and one *rapporteur* who is responsible for verifying compliance by the administration with the judicial decisions of this Court (Article 2 of Act 3068/2002). If, following a petition by an interested party, this three-member council ascertains some delay, non-compliance or incomplete compliance with a ruling, it calls on the authority obliged to comply to set out its views. If, following investigation, it confirms that the delay or failure to comply fully is without justification, it calls on that issuing authority to comply with the decision within a reasonable period set by the council and which may not exceed three months (Article 3 paragraph 1 of Act 3068/2002). Should the administration persist in its non-compliance, the council may impose financial sanctions, to be paid to the interested party (Article 3 paragraph 3 of Act 3068/2002).

At the end of each year, this three-member council compiles special minutes concerning the cases before it of the administration's non-compliance with judicial decisions. It submits these minutes to the Prime Minister, the Speaker, the Minister for Justice and the Minister of Interior (Article 3 paragraph 7 of Act 3068/2002).

Counterparts to this three-member council have also been set up and function in the Supreme Civil and Criminal Court, the Court of Audit, the Special Highest Court and the regular administrative courts. Their task is to ensure that the public administration complies with decisions taken in their own jurisdiction (Article 2 of Act 3068/2002).

In cases of non-compliance, the civil servant at fault is subject to both disciplinary and civil liability (Article 5 of Act 3068/2002).

II. The Court of Audit

203. The Court of Audit was founded in 1833, along the lines of the *Cours des Comptes* in the French system, and has functioned without interruption since that time, exercising advisory, auditing and judicial competences. Its purpose and main competences are set out in Article 98 of the Constitution. It is composed of its President, ten Vice Presidents, forty councillors, fifty associate judges (associate councillors) and fifty *rapporteurs*/provisional *rapporteurs* (junior judges/provisional junior judges) (Article 13 of Act 4820/2021).

204. According to the Constitution 'bills pertaining in any way to the granting of a pension and the prerequisites thereof shall be introduced only by the Minister of Finance after an opinion of the Court of Audit' (Article 73 paragraph 2).

205. The auditing competences of the Court of Audit are the preventive and the repressive audit of the expenditures of the State and of local government agencies or other public corporate bodies; the supervision of accountable officers; the compilation and submission to Parliament of a report on the State's balance sheet and financial statement (Article 98 paragraph 1 of the Constitution).

The Court of Audit is also competent, according to Article 98 paragraph 1 of the Constitution, for the preventive audit of high financial value contracts in which a contracting partner is a State or any other legal person who in this respect is equated with the State. The Special Highest Court has ruled that the decisions issued by the various teams and sections of the Court of Audit in the context of their preventive audits do not constitute judicial decisions, and therefore do not constitute *res judicata* (Special Highest Court 20/2005). The question of whether these decisions are subject to application for annulment before the Council of State is still to be decided by the plenary session of the Council.

III. Other Courts of Justice

206. The plenum of all courts of justice is competent to express opinions on legal matters and on matters of general interest concerning the organization of justice (Article 15 of Act 4938/2022, 'Code of Organization of the Courts of Justice'). Of major moral authority are the opinions of the Supreme Courts as well as the legal opinions of the Prosecutor of the Supreme Civil and Criminal Court on legal questions of general interest (for the competence of the Prosecutor of the Supreme Civil and Criminal Court and of all other prosecutors, *see* Article 28 of the Code of Organization of the Courts of Justice).

§2. The Legal Council of State

207. The Legal Council of State was set up for the first time in 1882, abolished in 1982 and revived in 1990. Its organization and workings are governed by Act 4831/2021. It is the highest state authority and is the State's legal advisor and advocate (Articles 1, 2 and 4 of Act 4831/2021). It reports directly to the Minister for Finance and is composed of a President, Vice Presidents, councillors, deputies, judicial proxies and provisional judicial proxies (Articles 4 and 5 of Act 4831/2021). Its personnel staff the various departments of the Council, that is, the Office of the President, which functions as a central department, and the offices of legal advisors, operating at the Hellenic Parliament, each Ministry as well as in some public corporate bodies (e.g., the Foundation for Social Security) and in Piraeus (Articles 20 of Act 4831/2021). Judicial offices of the Legal Council of State also function in other major cities (Patras, Larisa, etc.) (Article 21 of Act 4831/2021).

208. The Legal Council of State has been enshrined directly in the Constitution since the Revision of 2001. Article 100A states that the Legal Council of State is responsible for the judicial support and representation of the State and the recognition of claims against it or for the settlement of disputes with the State. Article 4 of Act 4831/2021 specifies other competences, such as guidance of actions by the public administration through the issuing of legal opinions, the elaboration of draft legislation, decrees and regulatory ministerial decisions referred to it, and so on.

The members of the Legal Council of State receive the same pay and conditions of retirement as judicial functionaries. Promotion of members of the Council to the position of President or Vice President is subject to the provisions, *mutatis mutandis*, on promotion of judges to senior positions (Articles 100A and 90 paragraph 5 of the Constitution).

New appointments are made to the Legal Council of State by means of a national competition organized at intervals by the Council itself (Article 16 of Act 4831/2021).

Chapter 3. Constitutional Independent Authorities and Other Independent Administrative Authorities

209. The independent administrative authorities form a part of the Executive Branch, not belonging to the administrative hierarchical structure. In other words, they are not subject to hierarchical control, nor to any other kind of administrative supervision. Greek law recognizes on the one hand, and on the basis of various laws, certain 'independent administrative authorities' (*see infra* Nos 225 et seq.), and, on the other hand, five constitutionally safeguarded Independent Authorities (*see infra* Nos 210 et seq.).

§1. Independent Authorities Enshrined in the Constitution

210. The Greek legal system has long recognized the institution of the independent administrative authority; as far back as 1952 the Constitution enshrined the service councils in what is now Article 103 as an independent administrative authority, although the term itself is not used (Article 101). These service councils have advisory powers in service transfers and decisive competence in cases of demotion or dismissal of civil servants.

Through the Revision of 2001, five Independent Authorities were established or enshrined in the Constitution: the HDPA (Article 9A, *see infra* Nos 215–216), the National Radio and Television Council (Article 15, *see infra* Nos 217–218), the Hellenic Authority for Communication Security and Privacy (Article 19 paragraph 2, *see infra* Nos 219–220), the Supreme Council for Personnel Recruitment (Article 103 paragraph 7, *see infra* Nos 223–224) and the Ombudsman (Article 103 paragraph 9, *see infra* Nos 223 et seq.). Although these five Independent Authorities are not described in the Constitution as 'administrative', they do actually belong to the Executive Branch and issue acts, being characterized as administrative ones.

The Constitution (Article 101A) lays down certain common rules for the establishment and operation of these five Independent Authorities which it authorizes; these rules are more specifically defined in Act 3051/2002.

211. Thus the members of the constitutionally enshrined Independent Authorities enjoy both personal and functional independence. The Constitution states that they will serve a limited term, specified in law as of six years duration (Article 3 paragraph 2 of Act 3051/2002). During this period a member may not be dismissed except in the event of conviction without further right of appeal for a felony or an offence against property or property rights or an offence related to memoranda or the service or an offence against morals (Article 3 paragraph 6 of Act 3051/2002).

The selection of the personnel to staff these Independent Authorities shall be made by a decision of the Conference of Parliamentary Chairmen (*see supra* No. 158) by the increased majority of four-fifths of its members (Article 101A paragraph 2 of the Constitution, as revised in 2019, and Article 3 paragraph 2 of Act 3051/2002). This selection of the members of the Independent Authorities by the Conference of Parliamentary Chairmen endows the relevant bodies of the administration with an indirect democratic legitimacy. It is envisaged that the persons recruited as members of the Independent Authorities will be individuals of acknowledged status with the appropriate education or professional experience in those fields related to the remit and competences of the authorities (Article 3 paragraph 1 of Act 3051/2002).

Furthermore, in order to ensure the personal independence of members of the Independent Authorities, it is envisaged that they will suspend the exercise of their professional activities and other duties and that their remuneration will be decided by the Minister for Finance, after consultation with the authorities themselves, by way of deviation from other provisions (Article 3 paragraphs 5 and 7 of Act 3051/2002).

212. The functional independence of these authorities involves:

(1) the obligation to examine the unconstitutionality of Legislative Instruments and not to implement those whose regulatory content is deemed to contravene the Constitution; and
(2) non-subordination to hierarchical control (whether preventive or repressive, of legality or merit) by government bodies, and more generally freedom from any control by organs of the Executive Branch related to the substance of the work involved in their area of competence (Article 2 paragraph 1 of Act 3051/2002).

213. The Independent Authorities are, however, subject to parliamentary control pursuant to the Standing Orders (Article 101A paragraph 3 of the Constitution and Article 2 paragraph 1 of Act 3051/2002). Article 43A paragraph 2(a) of the Standing Orders (since 2001) assigns the exercise of parliamentary control over the constitutional Independent Authorities to the Special Permanent Committee on Institutions and Transparency. Article 138A paragraphs 1 and 4 of the Standing Orders provides that each Independent Authority shall submit an annual report of its work to the Speaker. This report shall be forwarded to the competent committee of Parliament, which shall discuss the work of the Independent Authority and submit its findings to the Speaker. The findings, including any minority opinion, shall be sent to the appropriate Minister and the Independent Authority being scrutinized. The process of parliamentary control also involves the option of summoning the presidents or members of the Independent Authorities, at the initiative of a parliamentary committee or of the Conference of Parliamentary Chairmen, to appear before them (Articles 14(g) and 138A paragraphs 5 and 6 of the Standing Orders).

214. The Executive Acts of the Independent Authorities are subject to judicial scrutiny before the competent administrative courts (Article 2 paragraph 8 Act 3051/2002). Any illegal act by the authorities will engender civil liability under the rules governing the civil liability of the State (Article 105 of the Introductory Act of the Civil Code).

I. The Hellenic Data Protection Authority

215. The HDPA has functioned as an 'independent administrative authority' since 1997 (Act 2472/1997), by application of Article 28 of European Directive 95/46 on protection of private persons against processing of data of a personal nature and on the free circulation of these data. Under the revised constitutional provision of Article 9A, the Authority is held solely competent for ensuring the protection of personal data, particularly in respect of their collection, processing and use, especially by electronic means.

The Data Protection Authority, according to Act 4624/2019, is responsible for supervising the implementation of the provisions of the EU's General Data Protection Regulation (GDPR), and other regulations concerning the protection of the individual from the processing of personal data (Article 9).

It contributes to the consistent implementation of the GDPR throughout the EU and to this end it cooperates with the supervisory authorities of the EU Member States and with the Commission (Article 51 paragraph 2, recital 123 of the GDPR, and Article 10 of Act 4624/2019). This Authority represents Greece in the European Data Protection Board and other data protection committees and bodies while cooperating with relevant authorities of third countries and international organizations (Article 50 of the GDPR, and Article 10 of Act 4624/2019).

Among the most significant competences of the HDPA (Article 57 of the GDPR and Article 13 of Act 4624/2019) are monitoring the implementation of and enforcement of the GDPR and other regulations concerning the protection of individuals with regard to the processing of personal data; raising public awareness of data protection issues and drawing the attention of controllers and processors to their obligations; giving an opinion on any regulations to be included in a statute or a regulatory act concerning data processing, and providing data subjects with information on the exercise of their rights upon their request. The Authority is further responsible for handling complaints submitted regarding any case of infringement of the GDPR provisions, carrying out investigations or inspections on the application of the legislation on the protection of personal data, and cooperating with other supervisory authorities through exchange of information by providing mutual assistance to them with a view to ensuring a consistent implementation of the GDPR.

216. According to Article 11 of Act 4624/2019, the HDPA operates as a collective body, composed of its President and six members, who are appointed with their respective alternates for a six-year non-renewable term of office.

The selection of members and alternate members is made among individuals of acknowledged status, who are distinguished for their scientific expertise and professional experience in areas related to the mission and competence of the HDPA). The President, the members and their alternates are selected and appointed in accordance with Article 101A of the Constitution. The members are senior state officials, enjoying both personal and functional independence, and are not subject to any hierarchical or administrative control. The President and the Deputy President are employed on an exclusive time basis at the Data Protection Authority. Such status entails the suspension of any public function and professional activity.

The members do not incur third-party civil liability for acts or omissions in the exercise of their powers. They are liable to the Greek State for acts or omissions committed intentionally or with gross negligence. They are not prosecuted for opinions expressed or for acts or omissions committed in the course of carrying out their duties unless they acted fraudulently or with gross negligence. The Authority may reimburse the costs of legal defence of its members in the event of an action or criminal proceedings brought against them in respect of acts or omissions resulting solely from the performance of their duties.

Finally, according to Act 4624/2019, the Data Protection Authority may also act as a single-member body (President) or sit in chambers composed of at least three members or alternates and chaired by the President of the Authority or his/her alternate (Article 17 paragraph 1). Employees of the Auditors Department are allowed to attend sessions and meetings of the plenary and the chambers for cases to which they have been appointed assistant rapporteurs.

The funds required for the working of the Data Protection Authority are entered into a special account in the annual State Budget, while expenditure is officially recognized by the President of the Authority or his deputy (Article 19 of Act 4624/2019).

II. The National Radio and Television Council

217. The Council has operated as an independent administrative authority since 1989 (Act 1866/1989). Provision had been made for the establishment of the Council in Act 1730/1987, but it was never put into effect. Now, according to the Constitution (Article 15 paragraph 2) the main object of the Greek National Council for Radio and Television is to secure freedom of expression and the promotion of radio and television programmes. It exercises 'direct state control' over radio and television for the objective transmission, on equal terms, of information and news, of literature and of the arts as well as for the promotion of the quality of the programmes.

The Council has advisory and decision-making competences. Its responsibilities mainly involve the granting, renewal or revocation of licences to provide radio and TV services, the formulation of instructions, recommendations, suggestions and opinions for public and private-sector agencies and the taking of measures to ensure plurality, transparency and unimpeded competition in the media, the publication of Codes of Ethics and the imposition of administrative sanctions (Article 4 of Act 2863/2000).

In Greece, despite a number of attempts, a public competition for the provision of television licences has never been successfully conducted. Act 4339/2015 constitutes the latest Act of this never-ending story. Article 2A of Act 4339/2015 limits the number of television licences which shall be offered by the State for broadcasting at national level to four. It also states that the first public competition for the provision of the aforementioned licences is to be conducted by the competent Minister who also grants them. The adoption of these provisions by the Parliament and their subsequent application provoked strong reactions from the parliamentary opposition as well as from a number of television channels. The main argument against Act 4339/2015 was that it violated Article 15 paragraph 2 of the Constitution. The Full Bench of the Council of State (Ruling 95/2017) examined the pertinent arguments and ruled that the aforementioned provisions are unconstitutional since they deprive the National and Television Council of its constitutional competences. Thus, it confirmed its previous case law (*see*, among others, Full Bench, Ruling 1901/2014). Therefore, the second Article of Act 4431/2016 has suspended the application of Article 2A of Act 4339/2915.

218. The Council is a nine-member body, consisting of its President, Deputy President and seven members, selected from persons distinguished for their education, professional experience or contribution to public life. There is no requirement for them to have held a particular professional post (e.g., judicial functionary or university professor) (Article 2 of Act 2863/2000). It has a staff of approximately eighty persons (Article 6 of Act 2863/2000 and Article 19 of Act 3592/2007). The Council has its own budget, which it manages in full independence (Article 1 paragraph 2 of Act 2863/2000).

III. The Hellenic Authority for Communication Security and Privacy

219. The Hellenic Authority for Communication Security and Privacy is responsible for ensuring the confidentiality of letters and all other forms of free correspondence or communication (Article 19 paragraph 2 of the Constitution and Act 3115/2003). Its principal duties involve (i) the conducting of inspections of the National Information Service and other public and private-sector agencies and enterprises engaged in providing postal, telecommunications and – in general – communications services, (ii) the gathering of information and the summoning of persons to hearings, (iii) the confiscation of the means used to violate the confidentiality of communications, (iv) the destruction of data or material acquired illegally, and (v) the formulation of opinions and recommendations and the issuing of regulatory acts (Article 6 paragraph 1 of Act 3115/2003).

220. The Authority has seven members: the President, Deputy President and five regular members who shall be persons acceptable to the community as a whole, distinguished for their education and professional competence in the legal or technical aspects of communications (Article 2 paragraphs 1 and 3 of Act 3115/2003). The members of the Authority act collectively in the performance of their duties and are subject to a duty of confidentiality (Articles 3 paragraph 1 and 7 paragraph 4 of Act 3115/2003). The Authority shall appear in its own right in any form of legal proceedings concerning its acts or omissions (Article 2 paragraph 5 of Act 3115/2003). The credits required to fund its workings are registered in a special account in the Budget of the Ministry of Justice. Expenditure is officially authorized by the President of the Authority (Article 7 paragraph 5 of Act 3115/2003). The Authority has a regular and special expert staff of forty persons (Article 8 paragraph 1 of Act 3115/2003).

IV. The Supreme Council for Civil Personnel Selection

221. The Supreme Council for Civil Personnel Selection was established as and functions as an independent administrative authority under Article 2 of Act 2190/1994, as replaced by Article 3 of Act 4765/2021. According to Article 103 paragraph 7 of the Constitution, its remit is to oversee the procedures for recruiting staff in the civil service, local government and the broader public sector, in order to ensure that the relevant selection procedures are underpinned by the principles of selection by merit, objectivity and transparency. Its main duties are to advertise and fill positions or recruit staff for the civil services, local government and other public or private law legal persons; it is responsible for setting up the appropriate committees and overseeing the proper competition or selection procedures. As of 15/5/2021, the personnel selection process has changed in accordance with Act 4765/2021 on the modernization of the public sector, which aims at strengthening meritocracy in the recruitment system in the public sector as well as upgrading and modernizing the function of the Council.

Act 4765/2021 introduces as a central recruitment procedure 'the pan-Hellenic written competition'. This new competition concerns the filling of public sector positions through a uniform way of evaluation and selection. It will be conducted every two years and the first competition is expected to take place in the third quarter of 2022. The new recruitment system focuses on the aforementioned written competition with the aim of selecting staff capable of working efficiently, in order to serve the public interest in a rapidly evolving public sector.

The Council also issues opinions on the constitutionality of the recruitment of staff on the basis of legal relationships in private law and it issues opinions on breaches of constitutionality for the Prime Minister and Parliament (Article 47 of Act 4765/2021).

222. The Council is composed of thirty-five members: the President, four Vice Presidents and thirty Councillors. All members are elected by the Conference of Presidents of the Hellenic Parliament. Its members are senior state functionaries, employed exclusively by the Council (Article 44 paragraph 1 of Act 4765/2021). The staff of the Council numbers approximately 260 (Article 31 of Ministerial Decision 16637/01/2017/4-9-2017).

V. The Ombudsman

223. The institution of the Ombudsman was introduced under Act 2477/1997 and the corresponding position of Administrative Mediator, which was introduced in Act 2266/1994, never having been implemented in practice. The role of the Ombudsman is enshrined in the current Constitution (Article 103 paragraph 9), but no reference is made to his duties.

The role of the Ombudsman is to mediate between the citizen and the civil service, local government and public and private law legal persons in order to protect the rights of the citizen, combat maladministration and ensure compliance with legality. His remit also includes the duty to defend and promote the rights of children and to monitor the application, in both public and private sectors, of the principle of equal treatment of men and women in the workplace, vocational education and advancement, and working conditions. This latter responsibility was included in the Ombudsman's duties in implementation of Article 1 paragraph 7 of Directive 2002/73/EC and the new Article 8a of Directive 76/207/EEC (Article 1 paragraph 1 of Act 3094/2003). The Ombudsman investigates, on his own initiative or following receipt of complaints, individual administrative actions, omissions or material acts by organs of the public administration which violate the rights or compromise the legal interests of natural or legal persons (Article 3 paragraph 3 of Act 3094/2003). A number of areas of state activity fall outside the area of competence of the Ombudsman, e.g., generally, cases pending before a court or other judicial authority (Article 3 paragraph 4 of Act 3094/2003).

When an individual submits a complaint to the Ombudsman they need not necessarily have recourse to other administrative remedies, nor does referral to the Ombudsman suspend or defer the deadlines set by law for the exercise of administrative recourse or for the appropriate judicial remedies. In the case of exercise of quasi-judicial recourse (i.e., administrative recourse the exercise of which is conditioned on an application for judicial protection) the Ombudsman cannot take on the case until the competent administrative body has issued a ruling, or until the appointed deadline has expired without such a ruling, or, if no such deadline is provided for, until three months have passed without a ruling being issued (Article 4 paragraph 4 of Act 3094/2003).

224. A unique feature of this institution is that unlike the Independent Authorities mentioned above the Ombudsman is a single person, not a collective body. However, the Ombudsman is assisted in their work by six Assistant Ombudsmen, who are appointed on the recommendation of the Ombudsman by the Minister of Interior. The Ombudsman and Assistant Ombudsmen generally enjoy exemption from liability and immunity from prosecution in respect of any opinion they formulate or action they commit during the discharge of their duties (Articles 1 paragraph 2 and 2 paragraph 1 of Act 3094/2003).

The Council of State has ruled that the actions of the Ombudsman do not constitute executive administrative acts which can acceptably be challenged through an application for annulment (Ruling 2274/2003, Ruling 3920/2014). It thus remains open to question whether the Ombudsman constitutes an 'authority' in terms of administrative law. However, the Ombudsman is definitely liable in civil terms under the rules of public law for any illegal actions or omissions (Article 105 of Introductory Act of the Civil Code).

The recommendations of the Ombudsman are not binding on the public administration. However, failure to comply with these recommendations may render employees liable in disciplinary terms and may entail public exposure in the annual report published by the Authority (Articles 4 and 3 paragraph 5 of Act 3094/2003).

The Ombudsman maintains a staff of approximately 170 persons pursuant to Article 5 of Act 3094/2003.

§2. Independent Administrative Authorities Provided for in Various Laws but Not Enshrined in the Constitution

225. Many statutes – particularly in the period since 1989 – have provided for independent administrative authorities not otherwise enshrined in the Constitution, with various advisory and decision-making competences. It is usually envisaged that the members of these authorities will enjoy personal and functional independence on the basis of the provisions of the special laws governing their operations. However, although they are described by the law as 'independent administrative authorities', in many cases neither the legal nor the actual conditions for such a description are met, since their members do not, in fact, enjoy independence, and are subject to hierarchical control or to administrative supervision.

226. The Hellenic Competition Commission (Article 12 of Act 3959/2011), the Hellenic Telecommunications and Post Commission (Article 6 of Act 4070/2012) and the Regulatory Authority for Energy (Article 4 of Act 2773/1999) are three characteristic examples. These authorities are responsible for regulating the market in their specific area of competence, issuing opinions, granting licences, imposing sanctions, and so on.

Other administrative authorities described by the law as independent are the National Education Council (Article 1 of Act 2327/1995), the Governor of the Bank of Greece, whose independence is safeguarded in European law (Article 29 of Act 3424/1927), the Hellenic Gambling Commission (Article 16 of Act 3229/2004), the Hellenic Consumer's Ombudsman (Article 1 of Act 3297/2004), as well as the newly established National Transparency Authority (Article 82 of Act 4622/2022) (*see infra* No. 294).

227. Apart from the above authorities, there are other agencies and organizations which have some of the features of an independent administrative authority but are not so characterized in law. They include the National Bioethics Committee (Article 10 of Act 2667/1998), the Hellenic Capital Market Commission (Article 76 of Act 1969/1991 and Presidential Decree 65/2009), the Committee for Conscientious Objectors (Article 62 of Act 3421/2005), the Supreme Council for Resolving Sporting Disputes (Article 123 of Act 2725/1999), the Committee for Health Education Planning (Article 31 of Act 2071/1992), the National Social Security Council (Article 74 of Act 2084/1992) and the Hellenic Ombudsman for Banking-Investment Services, which has not – however – been established in law as an organ of the State but is the result of a private-sector initiative by the Greek Banking Association, as part of the self-regulation of the banking services sector.

Chapter 4. Other Advisory Bodies in the Public Administration

§1. The Economic and Social Committee

228. Provision was made in the Constitution for the Economic and Social Committee following the Revision of 2001 (Article 82 paragraph 3, although it had already been established under Act 2232/1994, along the lines of the Economic and Social Committee of the European Union). It is made up of representatives of workers and employers (Article 3 of Act 2232/1994). Its mission consists of conducting social dialogue for the overall policy of the country and, especially, for the orientations of economic and social policy, as well as formulating opinions on bills and law proposals referred to it (Article 82 paragraph 3 of the Constitution and Article 1 of Act 2232/1994).

§2. The National Council of Foreign Policy

229. The National Council of Foreign Policy is provided for in the Constitution (Article 82 paragraph 4). It has been set up under Act 3132/2003 as an advisory body to the Government, entrusted with the task of elaborating on issues involved in the strategic planning of foreign policy.

§3. National Commission for Human Rights

230. The National Commission for Human Rights (Articles 10 et seq. of Act 4780/2021) advises the Government on issues in its area of competence, namely monitoring respect for human rights and framing recommendations for improvements in protection of human rights where deemed necessary.

§4. The National Commission for Bioethics and Technoethics

231. The National Commission for Bioethics and Technoethics (Articles 30 et seq. of Act 4780/2021) is an advisory body to the State, subordinate to the Prime Minister, in the fields of life sciences and new technologies in general. Its mission is to investigate the ethical, social and legal dimensions and implications in the fields of biology, biotechnology, medicine and genetics, as well as new technologies such as artificial intelligence, advanced algorithms and robotics.

§5. The National Accessibility Authority

232. The National Accessibility Authority (Articles 1 et seq. of Act 4780/2021) is an advisory body of the State, subordinate to the Prime Minister, for the purpose of access for persons with disabilities in all areas of human activity. Its mission is to monitor continuously issues related to the right of access for persons with disabilities and to prepare proposals for the formulation of public policies on issues within its scope.

Chapter 5. Decentralization

§1. History and General Principles

233. After the Greek War of Independence the Governor, Ioannis Kapodistrias, wishing to bring to heel the majority of local leaders and chieftains, proceeded to divide the country into thirteen sections (prefectures), each administered by an appointed 'extraordinary commissioner' (prefect). Each of these sections was further divided into provinces (a total of sixty-two) and each province into cities, towns and villages (communities). In these communities, the vote was granted to all Greek men aged over 25 years old. The right to stand for election was confined to those bearing the greater burden of taxation and aged over 35. This restriction was set in imitation of Western European models. In 1830, Kapodistrias abolished free election of provincial councils, which he converted into advisory bodies. By his reform of the State, his appointment of extraordinary commissioners and his restrictions on the powers of the local authorities, Kapodistrias acquired a direct influence over the administration of these authorities.

The Bavarians (during the regency of King Otto) divided the country into ten prefectures (temporarily replaced by thirty 'administrations' during the period 1836–1845) and forty-seven provinces headed by selected prefects and provincial governors. In 1833, according to the Royal Decree of 26-4/8-5-1833, it was appointed that the prefect, as the regional representative of the State, would exercise the competences of all the ministerial secretariats, and must implement their orders. In order to prevent the prefect from acquiring too much power in his region, the Bavarians also made provision for other state organs in the prefecture: the ephor, the treasurer, the officer of engineering and the bishop. In reality, all these offices were subject to the control of the crown.

The reforms introduced with Act 3200/1955 were of particular significance, involving the abolition of the General Administrations which had been set up during the period 1913–1945 and making the prefecture the main administrative division. The prefect, as the highest organ of administration in the prefecture, was employed for a renewable term of five years. The prefectural council was made of public state functionaries and civil servants, as well as appointed members elected by the mayors and municipal and communal councillors of each province. The competences of the council were purely advisory in nature.

234. As provided by Article 101 paragraph 1 of the Constitution, the administration of the State is organized according to the principle of decentralization. Regional administrations of the State shall have general decision-making authority on matters in their district. The central administrations of the State, in addition to special powers, shall have the general guidance, coordination and review of the legality of the acts of regional administrations, as specified by law (Article 101 paragraph 3).

The main consequence of the constitutional guarantee of decentralization is that competences once awarded by law to regional agencies may not be given back to central agencies. The transitional provision of Article 118 paragraph 3 of the Constitution explicitly prescribes that until the enactment of a special law on decentralization 'provisions in force pertaining to the distribution of authority between central and regional services shall continue to be applied. These provisions may be amended by the transfer of special authority from central to regional agencies'.

Specifically, the Council of State has ruled (Advice 610/1977, Rulings 1974/1991, 1306/2000) that the statute under which competences assigned to a regional agency are returned to the Minister is unconstitutional. However, the Council also ruled (Advice 402–403/2003) that a competence transferred to a regional agency may return to the central administration if it pertains to issues which, because of changed circumstances, must now be regulated by the central state administration.

§2. The Administrative Organization under the Principle of Decentralization

I. The Decentralized Administrations

235. Act 3852/2010 amended extensively the organization of the decentralized administration of the country, as well as the organization of the local government (*see infra* Nos 412 et seq.). Decentralized administration consists of seven new state units under the name of 'Decentralized Administration' (Article 6 paragraph 1 of Act. 3852/2010) which are single administrative units, enjoying administrative independence and control of their own finances. They replaced the thirteen Regions, which were established by Act 2503/1997 in place of the former fifty-four prefectures ('νομοί') which, until 1994, served the objective of administrative decentralization. The new seven Decentralized Administrations now represent the sole form of decentralization.

II. The Coordinator of the Decentralized Administration

236. Before the adoption of Act 4325/2015, the General Secretary of the Decentralized Administration was in charge of all the Decentralized Administration's departments and services. They were a non-permanent high civil servant, appointed and dismissed by order of the Cabinet on the recommendation of the Minister of Interior. The General Secretary of the Decentralized Administration was the representative of the Government and competent to exercise government policy in his Decentralized Administration. He was senior in rank to, and responsible for, disciplining the employees of the Decentralized Administration. They were also in charge of the police, fire and port services based in the Decentralized Administration, while they participated in the exercise of administrative supervision of the local authority agencies and had the overall control of the Decentralized Administration budget (Act 2503/1997). In brief, the General Secretary exercised the competences of the former prefect (organ of decentralization) insofar as these have not been taken over by the first or second-level local government authorities, as well as the competences that have been attributed to the Decentralized Administration by Act 3852/2010 (Article 280).

The General Secretary of the Decentralized Administration answered to the Minister of Interior and those other ministers whose competences he exercised. Control of their actions was exclusively a control regarding their legality, as explicitly provided by Article 101 paragraph 3 of the Constitution. However, as provided by Article 28 paragraph 1 of Act 4325/2015 the position of the General Secretary of the Decentralized Administration has been abolished and has been replaced by the Coordinator of the Decentralized Administration. The latter constitutes an organ appointed by the Minister of the Interior for a five-year tenure. They are civil servants who have been selected by a special service council following an evaluation procedure (Article 28 paragraphs 2 et seq. of Act 4325/2015). The Coordinator represents the Decentralized Administration and supervises its staff. They are responsible for the coordination and control of all its activities. In general, they have the same competences as the former General Secretary of the Decentralized Administration (Article 28A paragraph 1 of Act 4325/2015).

III. The Council of the Decentralized Administration

237. Each Decentralized Administration of the country has its own Council, a collective body consisting of the Coordinator of the Decentralized Administration, the Commissioners of the Regions and representatives of the associations of the municipalities. The Council has both advisory and decision-making competences related to the planning and coordination of regional development (Article 280 paragraph ix of Act 3852/2010).

§3. Other Regional Organs of the State

238. The Minister for Macedonia-Thrace and the Minister for Merchant Marine, the Aegean and Island Policy were the senior representatives of the Government in the regions of Macedonia and Thrace and in the region of the Aegean. They coordinated and monitored the actions of the General Secretaries of these Regions, but were not their superiors in the official hierarchy. These Ministers were also responsible for reporting to the Cabinet, of which they were members, on regional matters. The Ministries for Macedonia-Thrace and for the Aegean and Island Policy were abolished in 2009 (Presidential Decree 187/2009). The Ministry of the Interior has absorbed the services of the former Ministry of Macedonia and Thrace (Article 1 of the Presidential Decree 24/2015). The competences of the latter are currently exercised by the Undersecretary of the Ministry of the Interior. The Ministry of Shipping and the Aegean has been re-established and renamed as the Ministry of Maritime Affairs and Insular Policy (Article 2 of the Presidential Decree 70/2015).

Chapter 6. Local Government

239. The administration of local affairs, according to Article 102 paragraph 1 of the Constitution, shall be exercised by local government agencies of the first and second levels.

In particular, municipalities ('δήμοι', sing.: 'δήμος', 'demos') constitute the first level (*see infra* Nos 246 et seq.), while regions ('περιφέρειες', sing.: 'περιφέρεια', 'periphery') constitute the second level of local government agencies (*see infra* Nos 256 et seq.). Act 3852/2010 ('Callicrates Programme'), as supplemented and amended by Acts 4555/2018 ('Cleisthenes Programme') and 4804/2021, has brought about major changes both in decentralization, as already discussed (*see supra* No. 235), and in the local government agencies. Consequently, the State devolves some of its tasks to functionally decentralized authorities such as public corporate bodies (*see infra* Nos 261 et seq.).

§1. History and General Principles

240. In 1833, in order to weaken the power of local leaders and chieftains, the thousands of small communities of the Ottoman period were abolished; the various communities were administratively combined, and the national territory was divided up into about 750 municipalities (Act of 27 December 1833). The number of municipalities varied over time, being dramatically reduced at certain periods. At the end of the eighty years in which the above Act remained in effect, they numbered 445. The municipality was now the sole, unified type of local government agency. The division into municipalities with the corresponding mergers of communities represented a particularly bold territorial reform, which not only did not rest on but on the contrary ignored the situation as it was then, although it did meet rational criteria. Each new municipality had an average of one thousand inhabitants (a minimum of three hundred). State influence over the municipalities was ensured through numerous provisions, for example, acts of the municipal councils were only to be valid if ratified by the prefect, who in many cases also examined the merit of the councils' actions. The office of mayor was a significant innovation in the old Turkish system of administration. He was selected by the king or prefect from a list of three candidates elected by the 'municipal voting council', which was made up of the members of the municipal council plus an equal number of the higher taxpayers among the local citizens. The members of the municipal council were directly elected by the votes of all citizens with an income above a certain level. This use of income rather than assets as a criterion for voting entitlement was also an innovation, along the lines of the French model of the period as followed by the Bavarians. It was at this time, too, that the principle of self-government for local authorities was introduced (at least in part). The right to participate in elections was made more general in 1864.

There was no provision for a second level of local government. However, there was provision (Royal Decree 3/15-4-1833) for the establishment of provincial and prefectural councils with advisory powers. The members of the provincial councils were elected from the entire register of male citizens of the province. To be eligible for election they had to pay a certain minimum amount of tax each year. The institution of the provincial council survived until 1890.

Significant reforms were introduced by Venizelos, in 1912, which abolished the old municipalities and created smaller municipal areas and communes (Act DNZ'/1912). The new municipalities were prefectural capitals and towns with more than ten thousand inhabitants; a commune was defined as any permanent settlement with at least three hundred inhabitants and an elementary school, or even a community of fewer inhabitants provided it had a school and at least half those inhabitants eligible to vote requested that it be designated a commune.

In 1980 the MCC was issued (Act 1065/1980), which perfected the existing system of local government, without making any significant modifications. This Code has been replaced in 2006 by the new (MCC, Act 3463/2006, *see infra* Nos 246 et seq.).

Important changes were introduced by the 'Ioannis Kapodistrias' Programme of local government reform in 1997 (Act 2539/1997). It involved the merging of many municipalities and communes, bringing about a significant reduction in the overall number of local councils: 900 municipalities and 133 communes were created, whereas before the mergers the figures were 377 and 5,398 respectively. The *Kapodistrias* Programme was followed by the *Callicrates* Programme implemented by Act 3852/2010: communes were abolished and municipalities were merged into 325 bodies in total (Article 1).

Local government first acquired constitutional support in the Constitution of 1927 (Article 107), (provision for the institution of local government had also been made in the Constitution of 1925, Article 104, but this was never implemented) which envisaged at least two levels, the first being that of the commune. The Constitution of 1952 (Article 99) merely stated that the administrative organization of the State was to be based on decentralization and local government, without any other provision, and left to the ordinary legislator the task of defining more specifically the form of the two institutions. The 1975 Constitution, until the Revision of 2001, provided only for the first level of local government, to consist of municipalities and communes (Article 102), while allowing for other levels of local government to be established by law. From the Revision of 2001 onwards there has been constitutional provision for two levels of local government, although these are not defined by name (Article 102 paragraph 1). The first-level local government agencies are today the municipalities, while the second level is composed of the regions (Articles 1 and 3 of Act 3852/2010). Some scholars have argued that the phrasing of the Constitution, with its explicit reference to two levels of local government, entails a prohibition on the creation by legislation of a third level. However, this argument is not persuasive.

241. Local government agencies are public law legal persons. They enjoy both administrative and financial independence (Article 102 paragraph 2(a) of the Constitution). However, the Constitution does not allow full independence to the local government agencies in the sense of the power to introduce their own rules of law.

242. As already mentioned, local government agencies are responsible for the administration of local affairs. They enjoy the relevant presumption of competence.

However, the definition of what constitutes local affairs and the allocation of responsibility for such affairs to the various levels of local government are both left to the legislator (Article 102 paragraph 1 of the Constitution). Given that in the legislation (MCC and SLLGC), there are no special provisions nor any exclusive enumeration of the affairs to be regarded as local in nature (only an indicative enumeration in the MCC, *see infra* No. 247), it is no easy matter to define exactly what is meant by a 'local affair'. The central concept seems to be the promotion and protection of the local interests of the inhabitants of the region covered by the local government agency, and the satisfaction of certain of their needs. The case law of the Council of State indicates that the concept of 'local affair' is first and foremost an empirical one.

The Constitution (Article 102 paragraph 1(d)) provides for the possibility of the delegation to local government agencies of competences constituting the mission of the State. Any transfer of this sort will entail the transfer of the corresponding funds (Article 102 paragraph 5(c)).

243. Article 102 paragraph 5 of the Constitution also lays an obligation on the State to take all necessary legislative, regulatory and fiscal measures to ensure the financial independence and the funds necessary to the fulfilment of the mission and exercise of the competences of local government agencies. But as a matter of fact, local government agencies are financially weak, though the MCC provides for several categories of revenue (Article 157). In an attempt to strengthen the revenues of the local government agencies and thus their financial autonomy Act 3852/2010 (Articles 259 et seq.) brought about, among others, changes to the composition of Central Independent Funds, which constitute subsidies to local government agencies from the state budget.

244. The State shall exercise the supervision of local government agencies, which shall consist exclusively of review of legality and shall not be allowed to impede their initiative and freedom of action (Article 102 paragraph 4(a) of the Constitution). In respect of control of persons, the Constitution provides that disciplinary penalties shall be imposed on local government agencies only with the concurrent opinion of a council composed in its majority of judges, as specified by law (Article 102 paragraph 4(c)).

245. The Hellenic Republic has ratified the 'European Local Government Charter' (Act 1850/1989), but with reservations regarding Articles 5, 7 paragraph 2, 8 paragraph 2 and 10 paragraph 2 thereof. However, it has not yet signed the Additional Protocol to the European Charter of Local Self-Government on the right to participate in the affairs of a local authority nor the European Outline Convention on Transfrontier Co-operation between Territorial Communities or Authorities concerning Euroregional Co-operation Groupings.

§2. First-Level Local Government

I. The Concept of the Municipality

246. According to Act 3852/2010 (Part A), the municipalities are a 'fundamental institution' in the public life of the Greeks. Municipalities are:

(1) those established by law;
(2) those resulting from the merger of municipalities and communes (Article 1 of Act 3852/2010).

II. The Competences of the Municipalities

247. The remit of the first-level local government agencies is to administer and regulate local affairs, in accordance with the principles of subsidiarity and proximity, in order to protect, develop and continually improve the interests and quality of life of the local community (Article 75 paragraph 1 MCC).

The MCC (Article 75 paragraph 1), as supplemented by Article 94 of Act 3852/2010, enumerates the competences of the municipalities by area of activity. For example:

(1) in the area of development: the construction and functioning of water systems, sewage systems and the electricity supply; the expansion of energy systems;
(2) in the area of the environment: the protection and management of water and land resources; combating pollution in the region covered by each local authority and the removal and management of waste;
(3) in the area of quality of life and the smooth running of towns and communities: the construction and management of parking facilities; the public health inspection of retail premises;
(4) in the area of employment: the implementation of programmes and the founding of Vocational Guidance Centers to promote employment and entrepreneurship;
(5) in the area of social protection and solidarity: the implementation of policies to support vulnerable social groups, prevent crime and develop social solidarity;
(6) in the area of education, culture and sport: the construction and management of sports facilities, the implementation of policies to highlight and promote local culture;
(7) in the area of civil protection: coordination of projects and actions to prevent and respond to disasters in their region;
(8) in the area of agricultural development, stock farming and fishing: the preparation and implementation of projects; the linking of agricultural and tourist development; the promotion of programmes for new farmers.

The above list is solely indicative. Any other activity that can be described as a local matter is presumed to fall within the competence of the municipalities.

The municipalities also exercise on the local level competences of a state character delegated to them to ensure better service for the public, such as the keeping of the electoral roll, the registrar's records of births, marriages, deaths, etc., and so on (Article 75 paragraph 2 MCC).

Municipalities are delegated by law (Article 79 MCC) to issue local regulatory acts on issues within their competence. This delegation corresponds to the constitutional provision of Article 43 paragraph 2 b (*see supra* No. 78).

Finally, the municipalities are granted broad advisory competence. Specifically, the central state authorities are obliged to seek the opinion of municipal councils before issuing any administrative regulatory act whatsoever pertaining to the protection of the environment, regulatory urban or land use plans, and so on (Article 77 MCC).

III. The Organization of the Municipalities

248. Municipalities are governed by the municipal council, the financial commission, the commission for the quality of life, the executive commission and the mayor (Article 3 paragraph 1 of Act 4804/2021). Councils are vested with general competence, whereas the mayor and the financial commission have specific competences (Articles 65, 58 and 72 of Act 3852/2010). For example, the mayor represents the municipality in court hearings, implements the decisions of the collective bodies and has overall responsibility for managing the various services provided by the municipality (Article 58 of Act 3852/2010).

Municipalities are divided into municipal communities (Article 2 of Act 3852/2010).

The organs of the municipal communities are the local council and the president, insofar as the municipal communities have more than three hundred inhabitants. The sole organ of smaller local communities is their president (Article 4 paragraphs 1 and 2 of Act 4804/2021).

To each municipal community, the necessary powers are delegated to promote municipal decentralization in order to deal effectively with local affairs. Their competence is mainly advisory; upon delegation by the mayor or the municipal council, the president or the council of the municipal community may acquire further power to take decisions (Articles 83 and 84 of Act 3852/2010).

IV. The Election of Municipal Authorities

249. According to the Constitution, local government officials are elected on the local level by universal and secret ballot (Article 102 paragraph 2). Both local residents and citizens of the EU may stand for this kind of election (Article 13 of Act 3852/2010). However, the conditions to be met for the latter to exercise their right to vote or stand for election are set out in the Presidential Decree 133/1997.

Act 3838/2010, in its initial form (Articles 14–21) had granted the right to elect and stand for election to certain categories of aliens originating from countries other than those members of the EU. The question of the conformity to the Constitution of this right was answered by the Council of State. The Supreme Administrative Court, after its 4th Section had referred the matter to the Full Bench of the Council (Ruling 350/2011), ruled that it was unconstitutional (Ruling 460/2013, Full Bench). Therefore, Article 4 paragraph 1 of Act 4244/2014 (now replaced by Articles 6 et seq. of Act 4804/2021) abolished Articles 14–21 of Act 3838/2010.

For the election of the mayor and municipal council, a majority of 43% + 1 of the total number of valid ballots is required (Article 24 of Act 4804/2021).

If the required majority is not secured, a run-off election is held between the two stronger candidates or combinations so that a majority of 43% + 1 of the total number of valid ballots can be secured. If the two candidates or combinations tie in the run-off election, the Court of First Instance selects the successful candidate or combination by lot (Article 25 of Act 4804/2021). The runners-up are those receiving one seat (Article 24 paragraph 1 of Act 4804/2021).

The candidate of the successful combination is elected mayor (Article 24 paragraph 2 of Act 4804/2021). Municipal councils, on the other hand, are made up of the successful combination (three-fifths) and the combinations which were runners-up (two-fifths). However, if the successful combination in the municipality, regardless of their population, secures more than 60% of the valid ballot papers, then the total number of seats is allocated proportionally among all the combinations which participated in the election (Article 26 of Act 4804/2021).

Local government agencies are elected for a five-year term. Elections take place on the second Sunday of the month of October during the fifth year of each municipal term (Article 5 of Act 4804/2021).

V. Supervision of Municipalities

250. According to the Constitution (Article 102 paragraph 4(a)), state supervision of local government agencies 'shall not be allowed to impede their initiative and freedom of action'. Supervision is exercised over the actions of the collective and single-person organs, as well as over the persons making up these organs.

Supervision of the actions of the organs of local government is exercised by the Independent Supervisory Agency of local government agencies, which is organized in each Decentralized Administration (*see supra* Nos 235 et seq.), headed by the Auditor of Legality (Articles 215 and 216 of Act 3852/2010). The supervision is confined exclusively to scrutiny of legality (Article 102 paragraph 4(a) of the Constitution and Article 215 paragraph 2 of Act 3852/2010). Act 3852/2010 enumerates the administrative acts of the municipalities which should be submitted for scrutiny. In general, the acts of municipal enterprises concerning the increase of the capital share, and sale of fixed assets and loans are also submitted to scrutiny (Article 225 paragraph 1 of Act 3852/2010). The unit may also proceed to the scrutiny ex officio or upon administrative recourse (Articles 226 and 227 of Act 3852/2010). Appeal against the decisions of the Auditor may be filed to the competent courts (Article 230 paragraph 3 of Act 3852/2010).

251. Supervision of persons involves the exercise of disciplinary power for certain disciplinary or penal offences. It is also exercised by the Auditor of Legality, who may impose the disciplinary penalties of suspension or forfeiture with the consent of a council composed of its majority of judges. Interest parties may protest the decision of the Auditor of Legality before the Council of State, using the judicial remedy of recourse (Articles 233 and 234 of Act 3852/2010).

Members of the municipal authorities may also be dismissed on serious grounds of public interest, by decision of the Minister of Interior based on a reasoned report by the Auditor of Legality, and the consenting opinion of a disciplinary council. In the same way, municipal councils may be disbanded. The judicial remedy of recourse against the decision of the Minister of Interior may be filed before the Council of State (Article 237 of Act 3852/2010).

Provision is also made for *ipso iure* forfeiture of office by members of the municipal authorities in the event of their being convicted, after exhausting all appeals (irrevocable decision), of certain offences, losing their civil rights or being deprived of their assets (Article 236 of Act 3852/2010).

Apart from their disciplinary liability, the organs of local government also bear civil liability towards the State for any actual damage they may cause to the assets of the municipality as a result of intent or grave negligence. The damage is imputed to the organs in question by decision of a three-member audit committee constituted by decision of the Coordinator of the Decentralized Administration. The decision may be appealed before the Administrative Court of Appeal (Article 232 of Act 3852/2010).

252. Pursuant to Article 275 of Act 3852/2010 the Court of Audit audits preventively the expenditures of municipalities, Regions, their enterprises as well as those of any public law legal person they have established. Moreover, the Court of Audit conducts sampling repressive audits annually on the accounts of the above-mentioned bodies (Article 276 of Act 3852/2010). Additionally, draft contracts having a budgeted value that exceeds the amount of EUR 200,000 are also submitted before finalization for a legality audit (Article 278 of Act 3852/2010).

VI. Municipal Legal Persons (Entities) and Enterprises

253. Municipalities may establish public law legal entities, such as hospitals, nursing homes, childcare centres, etc. Each municipality is allowed to have one such body in the field of social protection and education and one in the field of culture, sports and environment. Municipalities with a population of over 300,000 people are allowed to establish two bodies on each field. Municipalities are also entitled to establish a body for the management of a port zone (Article 103 of Act 3852/2010). If these take the form of a foundation, they are established by Presidential Decree at the recommendation of the Minister of Interior and other competent minister, and following the prior decision of the municipal or council (Article 226 MCC).

Municipalities may set up enterprises on their own, in the form of a municipal 'public utility', and may also set up *sociétés anonymes*, alone or in partnership with other municipalities, either with Regions or other local agencies or third parties

(Article 252 MCC) but only one of each kind (Article 107 of Act 3852/2010). Both these forms of organization are private law legal persons (Article 252 paragraph 5 MCC).

254. Public utility enterprises are established by decision of the municipal council and by order of the Coordinator of the Decentralized Administration, published in the Official Gazette. Their purpose is to organize functions or activities and to provide services related to or associated with their areas of competence, covering such areas as social protection and solidarity, education, culture, sport and the environment. Under no circumstances may these enterprises have a commercial or industrial purpose (Article 254 MCC).

Sociétés anonymes set up by several municipalities, either with Regions or with other local agencies, are regarded as local government enterprises insofar as these legal persons hold the majority of the corporate capital. The balance of the corporate capital may be held by other natural or legal persons. The public sector or public law legal persons may participate in a company of this form. Local government *sociétés anonymes* function in accordance with the provisions of Article 265 MCC, as well as the provisions of Act 4548/2018 (Article 252 paragraph 3 MCC).

A *société anonyme* may also be set up by a single municipality in order to exploit the municipal real estate or common areas. In these cases, the municipality shall supply the entirety of the corporate capital (Article 266 paragraph 1 MCC).

VII. Associations of Municipalities

255. According to the Constitution (Article 102 paragraph 3), 'Law may provide for compulsory or voluntary associations of local government agencies to execute works or render services or exercise competences belonging to local government agencies; these shall be governed by elected administrations.' In implementation of this article of the Constitution, Article 105 of Act 3852/2010 provide for the possibility of one or more municipalities and the region to which they belong setting up, by decision of their respective municipal councils and regional councils, an association of municipalities and regions as a public law legal person.

§3. Second-Level Local Government

I. General

256. In 1994 the prefectures, which had hitherto been decentralized regional units of the State, were established as the second level of local government under the name 'Second Level Local Government Agencies, SSLGAs' (Act 2218/1994 as amended by Act 2240/1994). Act 3852/2010 established the Regions as the SLLGAs. They are public law legal persons promoting the economic, social and cultural development of their region (Article 3 of Act 3852/2010). The organization and operation of the Regions are now regulated mainly by Act 3852/2010. However, Presidential Decree 30/1996 (SLLGC), which supplemented and codified the preceding legislation, as amended by Act 2503/1997, is still in force as far as it is not contradictory to the provisions of Act 3852/2010.

The two levels of local government agencies, i.e., the Municipalities and the Regions, are independent of one another (Article 4 of Act 3852/2010).

II. Competence

257. The general competence of the Regions is to administer local affairs at the regional level. Article 186 of Act 3852/2010 defines explicitly the competences of the Regions.

It is always possible to transfer competences of the State to the Regions by Presidential Decree, provided that these competences are consistent with the nature and remit of those defined in Article 186 of Act 3852/2010 and insofar they serve needs in connection to development and function of region and they do not pertain to the exercise of uniform state policy (Article 187(a) of Act 3852/2010). It is not permitted, however, to transfer a competence which, under the Constitution, is assigned exclusively to the State, such as urban planning and land use (Council of State Ruling 2319/1999) and the administration and supervision of public education (Council of State Ruling 377/2001). By Presidential Decree, and under the same conditions, competences which belong to public and private law legal persons or public enterprises and utility organizations (with the consent of their board of directors) may be transferred to the Regions (Article 187c of Act 3852/2010). Whenever such a transfer of competences occurs, the corresponding resources required for effective exercise of the competence by the Regions must also be transferred (Article 187b of Act 3852/2010).

III. Organs of the Region

258. The organs of the regions are the Commissioner of the Region, the Deputy Commissioners, the Regional Council, the Financial Commission and the Executive Commission (Article 42 of Act 4804/2021). The Commissioner guides the implementation of the regional development plan and acts in the service of public interest with respect to the principles of transparency and efficiency. (Article 159 of Act 3852/2010). The Regional Council decides on all issues concerning all the local affairs which are assigned by the law to the region except if law provides otherwise (Article 163 of Act 3852/2010).

The Executive Commission is composed of the Commissioner and the Deputy Commissioners. It coordinates and follows the application of the policies of the region (Articles 173 and 174 of Act 3852/2010).

The Financial Commission is composed of the Commissioner (or a Deputy Commissioner appointed by the Commissioner), two other Deputy Commissioners as members appointed by the Commissioner and six to ten members appointed by the Regional Commission (Article 175 of Act 3852/2010).

A 'regional consultation commission' is established in each region (Article 178 of Act 3852/2010). A regional 'ombudsman' is charged to receive the complaints of citizens and enterprises and he mediates for their solution (Article 179 of Act 3852/2010).

All officials of the regions are elected by universal and secret ballot every five years. The election is carried out together with the election of local government agencies of the first level following, generally, the same electoral procedure and system of election (Article 43 of Act 4804/2021, Articles 32 and 33 of SLLGC).

IV. Supervision of Regions

259. The Auditor of Legality (*see supra* Nos 250 et seq.) exercises administrative supervision on the acts of a region; he is also competent for the disciplinary control of the persons composing the organs of the region (Articles 215 and 216 of Act 3852/2010).

Civil liability of the members of organs of the region is regulated in the same way as the civil liability of members of first-level local government agencies (Article 232 of Act 3852/2010).

V. Legal Persons (Entities) and Enterprises of Regions

260. Like first-level local government agencies, the regions are allowed to establish enterprises under the form of a *société anonyme* aiming at the development of the region (Article 194 of Act 3852/2010) by decision of their regional councils which is submitted for review to the Auditor of Legality (Article 195 of Act 3852/2010). Public law legal persons which were established by the former Prefectures, which were succeeded by the regions, are abolished according to the detailed provisions of Article 201 of Act 3852/2010.

Chapter 7. Functional Self-Administration

§1. General

261. While decentralization and local government have general competences and functions within a certain geographical area, there are public corporate bodies which are decentralized in terms of function, that is, with specialized functions. These are usually public law legal persons and public corporations, which do not form part of the central or local or geographically decentralized administration.

Public legal persons (public law legal persons or private law legal persons) may be established by law or by regulatory act following legislative delegation. When they assume the form of a public enterprise they may also be founded on the basis of the provisions of commercial law (Act 2190/1920, as amended by Act 4548/2018).

Their establishment aims at efficacy based on flexibility and expertise. Functionally decentralized authorities enjoy relatively high administrative and financial independence. The degree of independence varies greatly from institution to institution; it is specified in each particular case by the law which establishes it. State supervision is usually quite extensive in the case of public law legal persons (with the exception of the universities, which, although they are public law legal persons, are granted full self-administering status by Article 16 of the Constitution); on the contrary, it is quite restricted as far as public corporations are concerned; these function under the rules of private law and private economy, though they may also belong to the public sector.

§2. Different Kinds of Public Legal Persons (Entities)

262. Public legal persons fall into various categories: public law legal persons, state private law legal persons, and public-owned companies. Public law legal persons exercise public authority and are organized and function in accordance with the rules of administrative law. State private law legal persons are founded using public-owned assets and are active in the business or production sectors, but in order to attain objectives in the public interest; they are subject in principle to private law but do not belong to any of the types of private law legal person recognized in private law, instead representing sui generis legal persons. These public legal persons may be engaged in business activity (public enterprises, like the Hellenic Railways Organization, etc.), they may be institutions or foundations (like the Institute for Geological and Mineral Exploration) or of a corporative nature (like the Land Improvement Organizations, etc.). By now most public enterprises have been converted into *sociétés anonymes* and are classed as public corporations (if they have not been privatized); essentially, in other words, the categories 'public enterprise' and 'public corporation' have now been merged (*see infra* 263 on Act 3429/2005, which refers to 'public enterprises' instead of the correct term 'public corporations'). Public corporations are state-owned legal persons taking corporate form under commercial law (usually that of the *société anonyme*) and seeking exclusively business objectives. Their only shareholders are the State or local government agencies or other public legal persons, not private persons (where there are private shareholders, the corporation is classed as a 'mixed economy' enterprise).

§3. PUBLIC ENTERPRISES AND ORGANIZATIONS

263. Legislation makes special provision for the concept, organization, function and supervision of public enterprises (Act 3429/2005 'Public Enterprises and Organizations,' superseding Act 2414/1996). A public enterprise is defined as 'any *société anonyme* in which the State may exercise, directly or indirectly, a decisive influence, because of its holding in the share capital, because of its financial involvement, or because of the rules governing the *société anonyme*' (Article 1 paragraph 1 of Act 3429/2005). Provision was made for the establishment of a Joint Ministerial Committee for Public Enterprises and Organizations. The Committee was chaired by the Minister for Economy and Finance; its members included the Minister for Development, the Minister for Employment and Social Protection, the Minister for Transport and Communications, and other ministers whose area of competence was involved (Article 10 paragraph 1 of Act 3429/2005). The Joint Ministerial Committee for Public Enterprises and Organizations issued decisions which defined more narrowly the economic policy of each enterprise and approved its strategic and business plans, its budget, and so on. It also scrutinized the implementation of economic policy on the part of each public enterprise and determined their policies on recruitment (Article 10 paragraph 3 of Act 3429/2005). The Joint Ministerial Committee for Public Enterprises and Organization has been abolished. All matters which were regulated by its decisions are now regulated by joint decisions of the Minister of Finance and the Minister whose area of competence is involved (paragraph C, subparagraph C2 of Act 4254/2014).

Of all the public legal persons, judicial control through the administrative courts is applied only to public law legal persons (and, in respect of certain of their actions only, in which they exercise public authority, certain public legal persons under private law, characterized in case law as being 'of dual nature'), while private law legal persons are subject to the control of the civil courts on the basis of private law.

§4. NATIONALIZATION, DE-NATIONALIZATION, PRIVATIZATION

264. Under the Constitution, Greece experienced a period in which a number of businesses were taken into state ownership (nationalized) by the New Democracy governments in 1975–1977, and, from 1981, on the coming to power of the socialist party PASOK. We might cite by way of example the nationalization of Olympic Airways, the city transport companies, and the Water and Sewage Company. Through these nationalizations, the State assumed control of a large number of important industrial companies. They also gave rise to major constitutional questions, mainly related to the method of calculating the net worth of a business, and the protection of the rights of shareholders in a *société anonyme*. Lengthy legal disputes ended in the highest courts in the land (*see* for example, Council of State 1911/1995), and even went to the European Court of Human Rights in Strasbourg (*see* for example, *Kefalas et al. v. Greece*, Ap. No. 40051/02, Judgment of 27 April 2006) and the European Court of Justice (*see* for example, CJEU cases C-19/90 and C-20/90).

Owing to the over-expansion of the public sector, a trend began in 1991 towards the conversion of the legal status of various state agencies and enterprises into *sociétés anonymes* (first under Act 2414/1996, subsequently under Act 3429/2005). Provision was subsequently made for the possibility of de-nationalizing these agencies and enterprises that is, allowing them to leave the public sector (Article 30 of Act 1914/1990, as amended by Act 1947/1991). There followed a whole wave of privatizations, continuing up to the present day, and taking the various forms envisaged in legislation (Acts 2000/1991 and 3049/2002, *see infra* No. 269). It should be noted that in both legislation and legal theory distinction between the terms 'de-nationalization' and 'privatization' is blurred.

265. The concept of the 'public sector' is not defined in the Constitution. The 'public sector' is a term of reference which means the application of certain specific legislation. It was originated by the legislator (Acts 1256/1982 and 1892/1990) when introducing various constraints on agencies belonging to the public sector, beginning with Act 2190/1994 on recruitment (as replaced by Act 4765/2021). The legislation does not offer a general definition of the public sector; each individual law referring to the concept defines it differently. One of the most recent definitions is included in Article 14 paragraph 1 of Act 4270/2014. However, in the most general terms, we can accept that the following bodies and organizations belong to the public sector:

- public services of the State;
- legal persons under public law, with the exception of the Hellenic Capital Market Commission;
- all kinds of State or public enterprises and organizations, and enterprises and organizations operating State concessions, as well as legal persons under private law which have a public character and pursue objectives in the public interest;
- banks belonging to the State; and
- all kinds of subsidiaries of legal persons under public law and public enterprises and organizations, with the exception of local government enterprises.

As it stands today, following the Revision of 2001, the Constitution refers to the concept of the 'wider public sector' (Articles 14 paragraphs 9 and 103 paragraph 7), without, however, offering a more precise definition.

266. The Council of State, in exercising its competence of elaboration of the Presidential Decrees (*see supra* No. 201), has adhered to certain principles concerning the conversion of public organizations into *sociétés anonymes* (public enterprises) and their exit from the public sector (Advice 518/1998 on conversion of an Organization for Management of Public Material into a *société anonyme*, Advice

158/1992, concerning the exit from the public sector of state-owned petroleum refineries with simultaneous increase of their share capital and acquisition of shares by private persons). On the basis of the constitutional provisions of Articles 23 paragraph 2 (possibility of limiting the right to strike of personnel in enterprises of a public character or utility enterprises), 29 paragraph 3 (prohibition on public servants acting on behalf of political parties) and 106 paragraph 3 (*see infra* No. 268), in the view of the Council of State public enterprises offering a commodity of vital importance, such as water supply, energy and telecommunications, are engaged in providing a public service, given the public purpose of ensuring that society has the goods necessary for a decent standard of living, as measured by contemporary criteria, and the opportunity to develop the individual personality. These enterprises are, therefore, subject to the same principle of continuous operation as that applicable to public services – that is, that continuous operation may not be disrupted and is guaranteed by the State. The Council of State, therefore, concluded that the public enterprises offering goods or services of vital importance may be organized in any legal form, even those of private law, but remain always subordinate to and overseen by the State; they cannot be permitted to evade this supervision. Only under these conditions may an enterprise depart from the public sector (likewise, Council of State Advice 33/1998 on the exit of the Piraeus Port Authority from the public sector).

267. In respect of the personnel of the public law legal person undergoing conversion, the Council of State has ruled that its permanent staff will be employed henceforth in a relationship in private law, since the relationship of state employer to public employee is not appropriate within the context of a private law legal person (Council of State 867/2002, concerning an application for annulment of a Presidential Decree converting the Organization for Management of Public Material into a *société anonyme*). Employees in this position are no longer covered by the constitutional guarantee of permanent tenure (Article 103 paragraph 4), since this guarantee applies only to public employees, employees of public law legal persons, local authorities and parliamentary employees. However, those employees of public law legal persons covered, up until the date of the conversion, by the constitutional protection of their permanent tenure, do have in principle (on certain conditions) the right to occupy equivalent posts in terms of duties and formal qualifications, in the new organizational structure, as those they currently hold – but now in a relationship of private law and without constitutionally protected permanent tenure (Council of State Advice 538/1998 on conversion of the Central Athens Market Organization, public law legal persons, into a *société anonyme*).

268. There is no specific constitutional provision for de-nationalization or privatization. Article 106 paragraph 3 of the Constitution refers to the converse procedure, the acquisition by the State of private businesses, on certain conditions (specifically, the monopolistic character of the businesses or their production of goods of vital importance in exploiting national sources of national wealth, or whose main purpose is the provision of services for the good of society as a whole).

The Council of State, reviewing the concession by the Athens City Council to a private company for the organization of car parking in Athens, also involving policing duties, ruled that the Constitution (Council of State 1934/1998) prohibits the privatization of competences belonging at the core of state authority, such as national defence, policing, the administering of justice and the carrying out of punishments (Articles 1 para, 3, and 26 paragraph 2).

269. The main law enabling privatization was Act 2000/1991. De-nationalizations are currently regulated by the more recent Act 3049/2002, as amended by Act 3965/2011. Article 2 of Act 3049/2002 defines the term 'de-nationalization' as the 'once-for-all or gradual release of state businesses from state control'. De-nationalization may be carried out indicatively in one of the following forms:

(1) the sale of the entire enterprise or its assets or parts or sectors thereof;
(2) the listing of the enterprise on the Athens Stock Exchange or other organized stock market;
(3) the sale of all or some of the shares in the enterprise, with or without simultaneous conclusion of a shareholders' agreement; and
(4) the granting of licences or rights to run the enterprise (Article 4 paragraph 1 of Act 3049/2002).

The Joint Ministerial Committee for Restructures and De-Nationalizations is responsible for framing government policy on the de-nationalization of enterprises, and for determining which enterprises shall be de-nationalized. It is chaired by the Minister for Finance and its members include, among others, the Minister for Economy and Development, the Minister for Employment and Social Welfare and whichever minister has oversight of the enterprise to undergo de-nationalization (Article 3 of Act 3049/2002).

270. Since 2010 Greece is following a programme of extensive reforms having been agreed with the EU and the International Monetary Fund as a condition for their financial assistance (*see infra* Nos 512 et seq.). Privatizations are at the heart of this programme. In this context, Article 1 paragraph 1 of Act 3986/2011, as amended by Act 4038/2012, has established the Hellenic Republic Asset Development Fund under the form of a *société anonyme* regulated by private law. The assets transferred to the Fund consist of real estate, company shares and financial rights (Article 2 of Act 3986/2011). This process has not been without problems. For instance, the Full Bench of the Council of State in its Ruling 1906/2014 ruled that the transfer of shares of the Athens Water Supply and Sewerage Company (EYDAP S.A.) from the Greek State to the Fund was unconstitutional since it would result in the privatization of the company to the detriment of citizens. This case law was reaffirmed recently by Rulings 190–191/2022 of the Full Bench of the Council of State. The revenues of the Fund are used exclusively for the payment of the sovereign debt of Greece (Article 1 paragraph 2 of Act 3986/2011). The Fund plays a major role in promoting privatizations throughout the country with the cooperation of the Government.

271. Act 4389/2016 has established the Hellenic Corporation of Assets and Participations also under the form of a *société anonyme* regulated by private law (Article 184 paragraph 1). The Corporation does not belong to the public sector nor the wider public sector (Article 184 paragraph 4). It manages state assets mainly for the implementation of the investment policy of Greece and the payment of the country's sovereign debt (Article 185). Its duration is ninety-nine years (Article 186). The Corporation's sole shareholder is the State (Article 187). It has four subsidiaries: the Hellenic Financial Stability Fund, the aforementioned Hellenic Republic Asset Development Fund, the Public Properties Company and the Public Holdings Company (Article 188). The organs of the Corporation are the General Assembly, the Supervisory Board, the Board of Directors and the Auditors (Article 190). The Supervisory Board has five members. Its President as well as one more members are selected by the European Commission and the European Stability Mechanism with the consent of the Minister for Finance. The other three members are selected by the State with the consent of the European Commission and the European Stability Mechanism. The Supervisory Board elects and appoints the members of the Board of Directors (Article 191). It is expected that the Corporation will accelerate significantly the implementation of the privatizations projects.

The restrictions having been imposed on the governmental and parliamentary powers due to the formation of the Corporation as well as the fact that almost all state assets have been put under its management have raised a number of objections regarding its constitutionality. It has been argued generally that the formation of the Corporation violates Article 1 of the Constitution, enshrining the principle of popular sovereignty as well as Article 26 of the Constitution, enshrining the principle of separation of powers. It has also been said that this unprecedented measure which has been taken under the pressure of Greece's creditors is reminiscent of colonial practices.

§5. 'Mixed Economy' Enterprises

272. Private individuals may participate in 'mixed economy' enterprises (in both their capital and administration) alongside the State, local government agencies or other public legal persons. The establishment of such enterprises is provided for in Article 106 paragraph 3 of the Constitution, in the case of the partial nationalization of private businesses. The State's participation in these businesses is intended to safeguard the public interest.

'Mixed economy' enterprises may take the form of a *société anonyme* or a limited liability company. They are regarded as public legal persons only insofar as the participation of the State or other public legal person in the capital of the enterprise or the opportunities of the State to determine the persons who will manage the enterprise are sufficient to outweigh those of the private individuals participating in the enterprise.

§6. Concession of a Public Service

273. The concession of a public service is the assignment to private persons of a business activity associated with the production of goods or provision of services to meet the basic needs of society as a whole. This concession may take the form of an administrative act or a contract (ratified by statute or approved by administrative act) and will remain in force for a specified length of time. The party contracting to provide the public service will not belong to the public administration unless it is a public legal person. A special case is that of the contract assigning public works (public works concession), which originates in European law.

§7. Public-Private Partnerships

274. One form of privatization is the public-private partnership (PPP), in which public authorities join forces with the private sector to ensure the funding, construction, maintenance or management of an infrastructure, or to provide a service. In essence, PPPs involve the transfer to the private sector of investment schemes which were traditionally executed or funded by the public sector. The intention behind the PPP is to improve the quality of state services to the citizen and to create the necessary infrastructures, taking advantage of additional private resources to complement available state funding and exploiting the expertise and experience of the private sector.

Over recent years, Greece has seen significant participation by the private sector in the construction and management of projects involving major infrastructures or specific construction projects. For example, there have been the contract for construction and operation of the new Athens International Airport (ratified by Act 2338/1995), the contract for construction and operation of the Rio-Antirio Bridge (ratified by Act 2395/1996) and the contract for the construction and operation of the 'Attiki Odos' motorway (ratified by Act 2445/1996).

275. PPPs are regulated by the provisions of Act 3389/2005 'Partnerships between the Public and Private Sector.' They are defined as written contracts of cooperation *oneris causa*, concluded between public agencies and legal persons in the private sector, to carry out projects or provide services (Article 1 paragraph 2 of Act 3389/2005). The scope of the law covers only partnerships with a budget of up to EUR 500 million (Article 2 paragraph 1 of Act 3389/2005). Public agencies are defined as the State, local authorities, public law legal persons and *sociétés anonymes* whose entire share capital is owned by the above agencies (Article 1 paragraph 1 of Act 3389/2005). Private agencies contract with the State through the Special Purpose Companies set up by them ad hoc and exclusively for the purposes of the partnership (Article 1 paragraph 4 of Act 3389/2005).

The law provides for the setting up of a central support mechanism responsible for the organization, coordination and supervision of the implementation of the PPPs. This mechanism consists of: (i) the Joint Ministerial Committee for PPPs, whose members are the Minister for Economy and Development, the Minister for

Infrastructure and Transport, the Minister for Environment and Energy, and (ii) the Special Secretariat for the PPPs (Articles 3 and 4 of Act 3389/2005).

The law also sets out the procedures for selection of the private agency with which the partnership will be forged, as well as the principles to be adhered to in the awarding of the contract (Articles 9–16 of Act 3389/2005). The law adopts exclusively the 'contractual type' of PPP, where the partnership is based solely on contractual ties between the various parties, ruling out the 'statutory type' in which an agency is set up and controlled jointly by the public and private partners (Article 17 of Act 3389/2005).

Another important provision of the law is that any dispute related to the implementation, interpretation and validity of the partnership contract shall be resolved by arbitration (Article 31 of Act 3389/2005).

§8. Ecclesiastical Legal Persons (Entities)

276. Ecclesiastical legal persons, such as the Church of Greece, the metropolitan dioceses and the monasteries, are subject in their capacity as public law legal persons to various legislative provisions, as well as the jurisprudence of the Council of State and the civil courts (Article 1 paragraph 4 of Act 590/1977). It is obvious, of course, that they do not fall within the ambit of public administration. Their inclusion in the category of public law legal persons is intended to safeguard certain of their privileges and offer them more effective protection. Ecclesiastical legal persons are not invariably public law legal persons. Article 68 of Act 4235/2014 provides that all ecclesiastical institutions and museums constitute private law legal persons (for more detail, *see infra* Nos 454 et seq.).

Chapter 8. The Principles of Action and Personnel of the Public Administration

277. The public administration (in the broadest sense of the term) comprehends the central state administration, the regional state administration, the independent constitutional authorities and other independent administrative authorities, the first-level local government agencies and SLLGAs and the various legal persons enumerated above under 'functional self-administration' (*see supra* Nos 154 et seq.).

§1. The Basic Principles of the Organization and Activity of the Administration

I. The Basic Principles of Administrative Action

278. From the Constitution and from case law (mainly that of the Council of State) we can derive three basic principles governing the activities of the public administration. Specifically:

(1) *The constitutional principle of legality.* The constitutional principle of legality derives from popular sovereignty and representative government and consequently from the precedence and presumption of competence enjoyed by the Legislative Branch, made up of the representatives of the electoral body (combination of Articles 26 paragraphs 2, 43, 50, 82, 83 and 95 paragraph 1 of the Constitution). According to this principle, the administration may not proceed to legal acts, that is, the issuing of administrative acts and the concluding of administrative contracts, nor to material actions, except on the basis of the competence granted to it by rule of law and within the limits of that competence. The public administration is bound by the totality of rules of law that govern its organization, operation and generally its activities, from whatever source these rules may originate (Constitution, European law, generally recognized rules of international law, international conventions ratified by statute, statutes, regulatory acts, individual administrative acts, general principles of administrative law). Compliance with the principle of legality is ensured through the exercise of various forms of scrutiny of the actions of the administration (for scrutiny of the administration, *see infra* Nos 286 et seq.).

(2) *Satisfaction of the public interest.* In all its activities the public administration must seek the direct or indirect satisfaction of the public interest, the more precise definition of which is given by the Legislature. The rules of law laid down by the Legislature regulate the organization and activities of the various agencies of the public administration and determine the objectives it must pursue. Those agencies, through the exercise of their regulatory competence or by issuing or refusing to issue individual acts, then proceed to a more detailed definition of the public interest.

(3) *The protection of the person.* The requirement to protect individuals and private legal persons obliges the administrative bodies on the one hand not to

harm the rights and legal interests of the person, and on the other hand to act, through material actions and legal acts, according to the principle of respect for the person's rights and interests. The basic principle of protection of the person can be broken down into a number of individual principles, such as the principle of equality of all persons in dealings with the public services (equality before the public), the principle of reasonable administration, the principle of good functioning of the administration, the right to a prior hearing, the statutory safeguarding of right of administrative recourse, etc.

II. The Basic Principles of Organization and Operation of the Public Services

279. From the constitutional provisions and the case law of the Council of State, certain fundamental principles are derived which govern the organization and operation of public services. For example:

- the *principle of continuity*, implying that the public administration has to function without interruption in a regular and steady way, because of the importance of the fundamental needs which the administration is intended to satisfy. The principle of continuity is complemented by the *principle of the unity of public services*, in the sense that the administration is understood as, and must act as, a single entity;
- the *principle of equality* of all persons in their dealings with the public services and of equal access to public goods and services;
- the *principle of reasonable administration*, which requires of the administrative bodies that they exercise their competences in accordance with the generally prevalent sense of justice, in order to avert formal and harsh conclusions, as well as the *principle of protected confidence* (legitimate expectations of the individual), which protects the faith or confidence of the person that a particular legal relationship or situation which has been created in his favour by the conduct of State organs is not going to be altered by unforeseen action on the part of the administration;
- the *principles of proportionality and leniency* which require that any burden imposed on the person will be proportional to the public interest being served, and, when there are two equally expedient courses of action available, the administration will always opt for the less onerous;
- the *principle of adaptability*, which requires the satisfaction of the basic needs of the person, as these needs develop and evolve in the light of continually changing socioeconomic conditions and needs, as well as the *principle of frugality* in public services, in accordance with which the goods and services must be provided at the least possible economic sacrifice by the person, in view of the public or more general social interest being pursued, and
- the *principle of legal certainty*, which aims to create stable administrative conditions.

§2. The Personnel of the Public Administration

280. Public servants (civil servants *lato sensu*) can be divided into two categories: military and civil (*stricto sensu*). Civil servants are employed under either public or private law. They may also be regular staff, employed on revocable contracts, or hired for a fixed term. Only the first of these enjoy permanent tenure. Those on revocable contracts are employed to fulfil a particular purpose; their employment is terminated once that purpose has been attained. The Constitution also provides for employees on limited-term private law contracts, recruited to meet unforeseen and urgent needs (Article 103 paragraph 2(b)), as well as employees recruited to fill specialized scientific or technical positions or as auxiliary staff personnel (Article 103 paragraph 3).

The Constitution contains several guarantees for administrative agents (Article 103). The constitutional guarantees cover employees of the State and of public law legal persons, whether they are employed on public or private law contracts. By contrast, employees of public legal persons under private law do not enjoy these constitutional guarantees.

281. In principle, public servants are appointed to 'organic' positions, that is, positions established in law meeting permanent needs of the service (regular public employees and specialist staff employed on private law contracts for an unlimited term). Thus civil servants holding organic posts are permanent as long as their posts are not abrogated by law. They may not be transferred without an opinion, lowered in rank or dismissed without a decision of a service council consisting of at least two-thirds of permanent civil servants (Article 103 paragraphs 2 and 4 of the Constitution). These councils have five members, two of which have been selected by the civil servants to represent them. The president of the competent disciplinary council is an independent judge (Articles 146B and 159 of Act 3528/2007).

The Constitution prohibits the conversion of personnel employed in private law for a limited period to personnel employed for an unlimited term (Article 103 paragraph 8).

282. Personnel are recruited for posts in public administration through a competitive entrance examination or by a selection process using predetermined and objective criteria. The selection process and appointment are subject to the scrutiny of the Supreme Council for Civil Personnel Selection (Article 103 paragraph 7 of the Constitution; *see also supra* Nos 223–224).

283. 'Political neutrality' of public service goes together with certain restrictions on the rights of civil servants. Thus civil servants, in the exercise of their duties, may not express themselves in favour of or against political parties (Article 29 paragraph 3 of the Constitution) and their right to be elected in Parliament is subject to special restrictions (*see supra* Nos 130 et seq.). Though the Constitution authorizes the ordinary legislator to impose specific restrictions on civil servants' right to strike (Article 23 paragraph 2(b)), there are no ordinary statutes pertaining to these issues.

284. On service councils, *see supra* No. 210.

285. On the special judicial remedy of the civil servants' recourse, *see infra* No. 303.

Chapter 9. Control of Administrative Action

286. Administrative action must comply with legal rules. The control of administrative action is exercised by Parliament, by the administration itself, by the Ombudsman and by the courts.

§1. Parliamentary Control

287. Parliamentary control is exercised over the Executive (*see supra* Nos 145 et seq.)

§2. Administrative Control

I. Hierarchical Control

288. 'Hierarchical control' is exercised by superior authorities over subordinate authorities. Every administrative agent is subject to hierarchical control with the exception of the President of the Republic, the Prime Minister, Ministers and Undersecretaries. Specific provisions of law may establish further exceptions. Thus committees or agencies which are not incorporated into the hierarchy of state organs and most tax authorities are not subject to hierarchical control.

This control encompasses review of legality (i.e., external and internal legality, and material error (error of facts)) unless this is explicitly excluded or if there is a clear inference that it is excluded, and review on the merits (substantive scrutiny, scrutiny of the advisability or merit of the regulation or measure), provided that it is explicitly provided for or there is a clear inference that it is provided for by the relevant provisions.

Hierarchical control may be preventive in nature (i.e., occurring before the act occurs), in the form of specific or general instructions (circulars, decrees) or repressive (i.e., after the act occurs).

Repressive control is exercised either ex officio or following administrative recourse by a person with a legal interest.

Repressive exercise of hierarchical control may end in annulment or amendment of the administrative act; however, hierarchical subrogation (the issuance by the senior-ranking organ of an act without the subordinate organ having first exercised its competence) is not permitted.

Hierarchical control is implicit in the hierarchical structure of public administration. Thereby the unity of action of the public administration is ensured, and it thus has constitutional support.

Employees of the State and other public legal persons are also subject to disciplinary control.

II. Administrative Recourse

289. Administrative recourse takes the form of a petition from a person affected to the relevant administrative authority or authorities seeking the revocation or annulment or amendment of administrative acts. This recourse is undertaken in the context of the constitutionally safeguarded right of petition (Article 10, for more detail *see infra* No. 413). Administrative recourse may be simple, special or quasi-judicial.

290. For the lodging of a simple administrative recourse, no further legal basis is required beyond that supplied by Article 10 of the Constitution. A recourse petition may be lodged with the authority which issued the act (recourse for redress), or with the superior authority (hierarchical recourse). They may seek either the revocation or the amendment of an explicit individual administrative act. The recourse process will involve scrutiny of the legality and merit (substance) of the act in question.

291. Provision is made in legislation for special administrative recourse, determining the authority before which the recourse will be heard, the relevant deadline and other conditions involved. The recourse process will only involve a scrutiny of legality regarding the act being challenged. The purpose of the recourse is to seek the complete or partial annulment of the individual or Regulatory Act.

Lodging a simple recourse within the period for the application for judicial remedies against the same act, as well as the timely exercise of the special administrative recourse, interrupts the limitations period for judicial remedies.

292. Quasi-judicial recourse is covered by special provisions determining the authority to which petitions will be addressed and the deadline or other conditions for exercising the recourse. These provisions allow scrutiny of both the legality and merit of the act in question. Lodging this recourse is a condition for the admissibility of an application for annulment or judicial recourse (i.e., before the administrative courts), both of which must be directed not against the act in respect of which the quasi-judicial recourse was made, but in respect of the act issued concerning the quasi-judicial recourse.

III. Administrative Supervision

293. Legal persons of the State are supervised by State organs. This supervision must be regulated by special legislative provisions which define the terms on which the supervision will be exercised. It is conducted through administrative acts by the supervising body and covers the bodies (appointment, removal of unsuitable employees, imposition of sanctions) and acts of the legal persons under supervision (preventive supervision with approval of the legality and merit of certain acts, repressive supervision with the option of annulment or suspension of execution of certain acts, with scrutiny of their legality and replacement in the event of refusal by the body under supervision).

The public legal person under supervision or third parties may challenge the acts of administrative supervision by petitioning for their annulment before the relevant administrative courts.

Special provisions may require the legal person being supervised to inform the supervisory body of an exercise of competence and also allow the supervisory body to provide the legal person under supervision with general instructions and guidelines.

294. A special reference should be made to the Corps of Inspectors-Auditors of Public Administration and the General Inspector of Public Administration, as former special advisory-auditing bodies in the public administration.

The Corps of Inspectors-Auditors of Public Administration was a body entrusted with the internal auditing of the public administration. It investigated on its own initiative or on receipt of information cases of maladministration and corruption; it submitted recommendations to the competent departments and sought to improve the quality of the services provided.

The General Inspector of Public Administration was responsible for the general oversight of the work of the various auditing mechanisms of the public administration.

However, under the provisions of Act 4622/2019 (as amended by Acts 4635/2019, 4637/2019 and 4727/2020) both these audit bodies, as well as other advisory and auditing bodies having like competences, and the General Secretariat Against Corruption were merged into the National Transparency Authority, and their competences were transferred to it.

295. The Authority is designated as the 'Hellenic Anti-Fraud Coordination Service', in accordance with Article 3 paragraph 4 of EU Regulation 883/2013, in cooperation with the Financial and Economic Crime Unit, to the extent of its competences.

In particular, it is an Independent Administrative Authority without legal personality. Its main competences are to enhance transparency, integrity and accountability in the action of governmental bodies, administrative authorities, state entities and public institutions, as well as to prevent, deter, and address fraud and corruption.

The Authority enjoys operational independence, administrative and financial autonomy and, apart from parliamentary scrutiny, it is not subject to control or supervision by governmental bodies, state entities or other administrative authorities.

In the context of its competences, the Authority carries out inspections and audits on all general Government bodies and services, including legal entities governed by public law, regional and local authorities, as well as their enterprises and the legal entities governed by public or private law that they supervise, state legal entities under private law and public enterprises or businesses, whose management is directly or indirectly designated by the State through an administrative act or by the State acting as a shareholder.

§3. Intermediate Control of the Administration

296. For more details on the intermediate control exercised by the Ombudsman, *see supra* Nos 223 et seq.

§4. Judicial Control

297. Administrative disputes fall into two categories: substantive administrative disputes and annulment disputes (*see infra* Nos 322 et seq.). They both belong to the jurisdiction of administrative courts. But judicial review of administrative action is not confined to administrative courts and to administrative disputes. Any court must review in the course of the exercise of its jurisdictional duties, (incidentally, or upon application (defence on grounds of illegality) or ex officio) whether the individual or regulatory administrative act is in accordance with higher legal rules. Judgments refusing to apply administrative acts, in the framework of the indirect review, operate only *inter partes*. A defence on the grounds of illegality is not restricted by time limit.

I. The Application for Annulment

298. The application for annulment (referred to as 'annulment upon petition' by the Constitution, Article 95 paragraph 1 a) is a remedy sought before the Council of State or the competent administrative court (mainly the administrative Court of Appeal) by which administrative action is challenged for reasons of external or internal illegality. Decisions of the administrative appeal courts are subject to appeal before the Council of State.

299. The application for annulment is admissible on the following conditions (Article 95 of the Constitution, Articles 45–47 of the Presidential Decree 18/1989):

(1) that it is addressed against an individual or regulatory administrative act or an individual administrative omission;
(2) that the petitioner is affected in his own lawful interest (*actio popularis* is not allowed);
(3) that proceedings have been instituted within sixty days of the notification of the individual act to the petitioner or of the publication of the regulatory act or of the expiry of a three-month period in case of administrative omission;
(4) that a quasi-judicial recourse if established by law has been previously brought before the public authority;
(5) that no other judicial remedy with the same effect as the application for annulment is available.

300. The grounds for annulment of the administrative act or omission are (Article 95 of the Constitution, Article 48 of the Presidential Decree 18/1989):

(1) lack of competence;
(2) infringement of a substantial norm of administrative process (procedural *ultra vires*);
(3) infringement of substantive law; and
(4) abuse of discretionary power.

Under the category 'infringement of substantive law' fall violations of any source of law, violations of res judicata as well as violations of sound reasoning.

301. The application for annulment does not have an automatic effect of suspension. Nevertheless, the court may, upon application, order the suspension or any other suitable (restraining) measure, without being bound by the proposals of the litigants, if the execution of the administrative act causes damage to the petitioner which cannot be otherwise remedied (unless the public interest outweighs the interest of the petitioner), and in the event that the application for annulment is obviously founded (Article 52 of the Presidential Decree 18/1989).

302. Judgments of the Council of State rejecting an application for annulment operate *inter partes*. Judgments declaring the challenged act to be null and void operate *erga omnes*. Public authorities are bound to take positive measures in order to comply with rulings of the Council of State. Violations of such obligation may lead to disciplinary and penal sanctions against the responsible administrative organ and may result in state liability (Article 95 paragraph 5 of the Constitution and Act 3068/2002, for more detail *see supra* No. 202).

II. Other Recourses Before the Council of State

303. Apart from its jurisdiction in annulment disputes the Council of State is competent to judge recourse by civil servants against decisions of councils imposing disciplinary measures of demotion and dismissal (Article 142 paragraph 1 of Act 3528/2007). The provision for a special, constitutionally enshrined (Article 103 paragraph 4 of the Constitution), judicial remedy in respect of the substance (i.e., scrutiny of both legality and circumstances) of the employee's appeal is a uniquely Greek feature with its origins in Greek history. One of the main central squares in Athens still bears the name Klauthmonos Square (Square of Weeping) because formerly, up until 1911, dismissed employees of the various Ministries which used to surround the square would gather here immediately after a general election! The Council of State also hears recourse petitions concerning disputes relating to the disciplinary authority exercised over members of local government agencies (Article 234 paragraph 6 of Act 3582/2010) as well as recourse against undue prolongation of the deprivation of the free use and usufruct of property (Article 18 paragraph 5 of the Constitution).

304. The Council of State is also the forum hearing petitions for reversal, where petitioners seek to overturn final decisions of the administrative courts. These decisions are scrutinized in terms of their legality, not on the substance of the facts involved.

The sole grounds for reversal are:

(1) that the court of substance has exceeded its remit or was not competent to hear the case in question;
(2) that the court was not legally constituted or composed;
(3) that a significant aspect of the proper procedure was breached;
(4) that the law governing the relation in question was erroneously interpreted or wrongly applied;
(5) that there are two or more final decisions concerning the same case and the same litigants which contradict one another (Article 95 of the Constitution, Article 56 of the Presidential Decree 18/1989).

III. Recourse Before the Court of Audit

305. The Court of Audit (in sections) mainly tries the appeals of officials against administrative acts imposing on them payments for accountable deficits, as well as appeals of civil servants concerning pensions. Under the Court's jurisdiction also falls the application of the Court of Audit Commissioner-General of the State or of the representative of a public authority against a civil servant or military officer who has caused damage to the public authority with intent or by gross negligence (Article 98 of the Constitution and Article 8 of Act 4820/2021).

306. Judgments of the sections of the Court of Audit are subject to petitions for revision, heard by the same section which issued the challenged judgment (Article 89 of Act 4820/2021). They are also subject to petitions for cassation before the same court in plenary session for false interpretation, an erroneous application of the law, for violation of an essential procedural requirement, or for the wrong composition of the section which issued the judgment (Articles 8 of Act 4820/2021) (for the auditing competences of Court of Audit *see supra* Nos 203 et seq.).

IV. Recourse Before the Ordinary Administrative Courts

307. The ordinary administrative courts (Administrative Courts of First Instance and Administrative Courts of Appeal) have general jurisdiction to hear substantive administrative disputes (Article 94 paragraph 1 of the Constitution, Article 2 of the Administrative Court Procedure Code, i.e., Act 2717/1999). Specifically, disputes concerning taxation (up to EUR 150,000, otherwise the Administrative Court of Appeal is competent), social security, registration of trademarks, salaries of civil servants, and such like, are initiated by petition recourse before the Administrative Court of First Instance (Article 1 of Act 1406/1983 and Article 6 of Act 2717/1999). Disputes arising out of administrative contracts are initiated by petition recourse' before the Administrative Court of Appeal (Article 6 paragraph 2 a of Act 2717/1999). Claims for damages based on the liability of the State are brought before the Administrative Court of First Instance by way of action (Article 71 of Act 2717/1999). Disputes concerning the collection of public revenues are raised through a 'defence' (or 'opposition') before the same courts (Articles 216, 217 and 218 of Act 2717/1999). Disputes concerning the elections of local government agents and of boards of directors of public-law legal persons are initiated by an 'objection' (Articles 244–246 and 267–269 of Act 2717/1999). Administrative Courts of First Instance are also competent to hear certain annulment disputes initiated by an application for annulment, such as disputes concerning the revocation of compulsory expropriation (Article 11 of Act 2882/2001) and disputes arising from the implementation of law concerning aliens (Article 15 of Act 3068/2002, *see infra* No. 484).

Part V. The Judiciary

Chapter 1. Judicial Organization

§1. General

308. 'The judicial powers shall be exercised by courts of law, the decisions of which shall be executed in the name of the Greek People' (Article 26 paragraph 3 of the Constitution).

In certain exceptional cases, the Constitution does also assign specific judicial functions to other organs apart from the courts. Thus Parliament is competent to impeach the President of the Republic, Ministers and Undersecretaries (Articles 49 and 86 of the Constitution), while the Constitution also allows for prosecution of a Member of Parliament for libel or any other offence committed during the parliamentary term after leave has been granted by Parliament (Articles 61 paragraph 2 and 62 of the Constitution).

There is also provision for the law's assignment of trying police offences punishable by fine to authorities exercising police duties, and of trying petty offences related to agrarian property and private disputes arising thence, to agrarian security authorities (Article 96 paragraph 2 of the Constitution).

309. The basic guarantees are laid down in the Constitution (Article 93 paragraphs 2 and 3) regarding the administration of justice by the courts: hearings shall be held in public; judicial decisions shall be properly reasoned and pronounced in public session; where there is a dissent, it must also be published. The rule that hearings must be held in public may be waived only when a court deems publicity to be detrimental to good practice or when special reasons call for the protection of the private or family life of the litigants. Proceedings involving minors are also held *in camera* in order to protect the children involved (Article 96 paragraph 3 of the Constitution).

§2. The Basic Principles of Judicial Organization

310. The main source on judicial organization and the legal status of judges is the Constitution and Act 4938/2022 'Code of the Organization of Courts of Justice and of the Status of Judicial Functionaries'.

The two basic principles of judicial organization are the following:

(1) Justice is rendered by civil, criminal and administrative courts (Article 93 paragraph 1 of the Constitution). This distinction, however, does not apply equally to judges. Judges fall into two categories. The first are administrative law judges. These may be divided into three groups: those whose entire career is with the Council of State; those whose career is entirely with the administrative courts, with the option, once they have reached the rank of Appeal Court Judge, of promotion to the Council of State, and lastly, those whose career is entirely with the Court of Audit. The second are the civil and criminal judges. The same person alternates between civil and criminal courts.
(2) Judges on the civil and criminal justice side are either ordinary judges or public prosecutors. The latter have a significant role mainly in criminal proceedings, but they also exercise competences in the domain of civil procedure, for example, at the Supreme Civil and Criminal Court or in matrimonial disputes, in cases of non-contentious (voluntary) jurisdiction, and so on.

§3. Categories of Courts

311. Courts are divided into four main categories.

(1) Ordinary courts are subdivided into ordinary civil, criminal and administrative courts. They have general jurisdiction; that is, they adjudicate all sorts of cases apart from those which fall under the jurisdiction of a special court.
(2) Special courts have jurisdiction in concrete (categories of) disputes or cases or over concrete (categories of) persons. Their jurisdiction is determined in outline in the Constitution. Special courts are the 'Special Highest Court' (Article 100), the 'Special Court' for the crimes of the Prime Minister, Ministers, Undersecretaries and the President of the Republic (Article 86), the 'Court of Audit' (Article 98), the juvenile courts (Article 96 paragraph 3), the military, naval and air-force courts, the prize courts (Article 96 paragraph 4) and the special court for suits against judicial functionaries for 'faulty wrongful judgment' (Article 99). The Revision of 2001 also introduced the 'Salary Court' (Article 88 paragraph 2 of the Constitution). The special courts are staffed in part by judges who do not have the status of ordinary judges.
(3) Before the enactment of Act 1406/1983 Enlargement of the Jurisdiction of Ordinary Administrative Courts there were special administrative courts which were competent for hearing disputes in special areas assigned to them by law. These included, among others, the administrative courts for commercial and industrial trademarks and logos and the administrative court for the mining industry. In other respects, until that time, the civil courts had general jurisdiction over substantive administrative disputes. Provision for the creation of administrative courts with general jurisdiction appeared for the first time in the Constitution of 1952. At first, the only such courts to be created were the taxation courts. The Constitution required the creation of administrative courts of general jurisdiction, providing for a gradual transfer to the existing administrative courts of administrative cases heard at that time by other courts (Article 94 paragraphs 1 and 2, before its revision in 2001; in this respect, it had now

become moot). The transition to the general jurisdiction of the ordinary courts took place gradually up until 1985, on the basis mainly of Act 1406/1983. At the same time, the special administrative courts were also abolished, once the cases pending before them had been resolved.

(4) Extraordinary courts are provided for in Article 48 of the Constitution concerning the state of siege (emergency). These are the extraordinary military, naval and air-force tribunals, which, according to Act 566/1977 On the State of Siege acquire jurisdiction also over civilians charged with crimes, mainly crimes against the State (*see infra* No. 507).

(5) Ad hoc courts are those which are established *ex post*, in order to adjudicate a specific case or a specific person. They are absolutely prohibited by the Constitution (Article 8 paragraph 2).

§4. Civil and Criminal Courts

I. Ordinary Civil Courts

312. 'Civil courts shall have jurisdiction on private disputes, as well as on cases of non-contentious jurisdiction, as specified by law' (Article 94 paragraph 2 of the Constitution).

The exclusive competence of the administrative courts over administrative disputes and of the civil courts over private disputes is enshrined in the Constitution, but not in absolute fashion. Thus it is stated that in special cases and in order to achieve a unified application of the same legislation, the law may assign the hearing of categories of private disputes to administrative courts or the hearing of categories of substantive administrative disputes to civil courts (Article 94 paragraph 3 of the Constitution). Any other competence of an administrative nature may be assigned to civil or administrative courts, as specified by law. These competences include the adoption of measures for compliance of the Public Administration with judicial decisions (Article 94 paragraph 4 of the Constitution).

313. The Code of Civil Procedure (Presidential Decree 503/1985) provides for three types of District Court (of first instance): Justices of the Peace, one-member District Courts and three-member District Courts (Article 13 of the Code of Civil Procedure and Article 4 of Act 4938/2022).

314. Appeals from the Justices of the Peace both on the law and on the facts are heard by the one-member District Courts (Article 17A of the Code of Civil Procedure), while appeals from the other trial courts are heard by one- or three-member panels of the Courts of Appeal (Article 19 of the Code of Civil Procedure).

315. The Supreme Civil and Criminal Court (*Areios Pagos*, Άρειος Πάγος) hears the cases in chambers of five judges or by Full Bench. The public prosecutor is present at the sittings of the Full Bench and the criminal chambers. Regarding the hearings by the civil chambers, he is present only if he is a party to the case or has already submitted his written opinion (Article 27 of Act 4938/2022). Petitions for reversal addressed to the Supreme Court concern only the interpretation and application of the material law and of procedural rules (Articles 20, 559 and 560 of the Code of Civil Procedure).

II. Criminal Courts

A. Ordinary Criminal Courts

316. 'The punishment of crimes and the adoption of all measures provided by criminal laws belong to the jurisdiction of ordinary criminal courts' (Article 96 paragraph 1 of the Constitution).

317. Criminal courts are classified according to the Code of Criminal Procedure (Act 4620/2019) with respect to the categories of offences (felonies, misdemeanours, and petty offences): (1) the mixed jury courts, composed of three judges and four jurors, which try felonies such as murder, rape, and so on, as well as political crimes (Articles 8 and 109 of the Code of Criminal Procedure) (*see* Article 97 paragraph 1 of the Constitution); (2) the one-member panels of the Courts of Appeal, which try as first instance courts non-complex felonies such as felonies against intellectual property and felonies concerning gambling (Article 110 of the Code of Criminal Procedure); (3) the three-member Courts of Appeal which try as first instance courts legally complex felonies such as aggravated theft, fraud, forgery, and so on, as well as misdemeanours by judges and lawyers (Article 111 of the Code of Criminal Procedure); (4) the three-member or one-member misdemeanour courts which share their competence according to the gravity of the offence (Articles 112 and 114 of the Code of Criminal Procedure), and (5) the petty violation courts (Article 115 of the Code of Criminal Procedure). Juvenile offender courts, which are special criminal courts, are either one-member or three-member courts of first instance (Article 113 of the Code of Criminal Procedure).

318. Appeals are heard by the one-member or three-member misdemeanour courts, the three-member or five-member Courts of Appeal, the mixed Appeal Court, composed of three Appeal Court judges and four jurors, and the three-member juvenile Appeal Courts (Articles 7–9 and 111–114 of the Code of Criminal Procedure). Most criminal offences may be tried twice *de novo*, once in the Court of First Instance and once in the Court of Appeals.

319. The Supreme Civil and Criminal Court (*Areios Pagos*), as a court of cassation, hears cases on questions of law alone in chambers of five judges or in Full Bench. The public prosecutor is also present, as in any criminal court (Article 28 of Act 4938/2022).

B. Special Criminal Courts

320. The court provided for in Article 86 of the Constitution is a special criminal court for offences committed by members of the Cabinet and by Undersecretaries. The Special Court of Article 86 of the Constitution is also competent for offences committed by the President of the Republic, according to Article 49 paragraph 3.

321. Other special criminal courts are the military courts (army, navy and air force). According to Article 96 paragraph 5 of the Constitution, these courts are composed of a majority of members of the Judicial Branch of the armed forces, enjoying the guarantees of functional and personal independence. Publicity of the sittings, reasoning and public pronouncement of judgments, publication of minority opinions as well as a review of the constitutionality of laws apply to military courts. Nevertheless, according to Article 96 paragraph 5c of the Constitution, these matters, as well as the time upon which they shall enter into force, shall be specified by law (*see* the Military Penal Code, i.e. Act 2287/1995, in particular Article 167).

§5. Administrative Courts

I. The Council of State

322. The Council of State is the supreme administrative court. It is, under Article 95 of the Constitution, competent to receive applications for annulment of individual or regulatory administrative acts and petitions for reversal of judgments of administrative courts in substantive disputes as well as appeals in annulment disputes originally addressed to the Administrative Appeal Court (*see supra* No. 298 and *infra* no. 328). Applications for substantive judicial review also fall under the jurisdiction of the Council of State in cases provided specifically by law, for example, applications of civil servants against disciplinary measures imposed on them (*see supra* No. 303).

The Council of State has general jurisdiction over annulment disputes. The Constitution (Article 95, in combination with Article 8 preventing the removal of the judge assigned, and Article 20 paragraph 1 on the entitlement to legal protection) enshrines a special civil right whose content is each individual's ability to seek the legal remedy of an application for annulment of an illegal administrative act (*see supra* Nos 298 et seq.). The Constitution also safeguards a similar right to petition for reversal of final judgments of ordinary Administrative Courts and a right to lodge a civil servant's recourse (*see supra* Nos 303–304).

323. Judicial review by administrative law courts refers either to substantive disputes or annulment disputes. The difference between them lies in the extent of judicial protection. In the case of annulment disputes a court may either reject the application or may annul the administrative act and consequently oblige the administrative authority to decide anew in compliance with the court ruling. In the case of substantive disputes, a court may also resolve the dispute by altering the unlawful administrative act.

324. The Council of State has, as already emphasized, a general competence in annulment disputes. But the ordinary legislator may transform annulment disputes into substantive administrative disputes by bringing categories of dispute or even isolated disputes under the jurisdiction of the ordinary administrative law courts (Article 94 paragraph 1 of the Constitution). This transformation does not jeopardize the civil right to judicial protection, since the protection extended for substantive administrative disputes is fuller than that provided by annulment disputes. However, this transformation of annulment disputes into substantive disputes is not permitted to go so far as to remove the general annulment competence of the Council of State. According to the case law (Ruling of the Council of State 1095/1987), the legislator may only specifically determine the particular dispute or the particular categories of disputes which may be transformed into substantive administrative disputes.

Petitions for reversal addressed to the Council of State concern only the interpretation and application of material law by lower courts as well as mistakes in the application of procedural law (*see supra* No. 304).

325. In addition to its judicial competences, the Council of State also has administrative competence in respect of checking Regulatory Decrees (*see supra* Nos 77 and 201).

II. Ordinary Administrative Courts

326. The organization and workings of the administrative law courts are governed primarily by the provisions of the Administrative Court Procedure Code (Act 2717/1999), and additionally by Acts 702/1977, 1406/1983, 1756/1988, etc.

According to the general provision of Article 2 of the Administrative Court Procedure Code, all substantive administrative disputes fall under the jurisdiction of the ordinary administrative law courts, apart from those whose hearing, under special provisions, has been placed within the jurisdiction of other administrative law courts.

327. Ordinary administrative law courts of first instance are composed of one-member and three-member panels. Appeals both on the law and on facts are heard by one-member or three-member panels of the Administrative Courts of Appeal (Article 6 of Act 2717/1999). There are currently thirty first-instance administrative courts, most of which run circuit sessions in the main towns of neighbouring areas. There are also nine Administrative Courts of Appeal.

328. The three-member Administrative Court of Appeal is also competent as a first-instance court to hear applications by civil servants for the annulment of administrative acts changing their status, to hear disputes over the granting of city-planning permits, and so on (Article 1 of Act 702/1977). The constitutional basis of the competence of the Administrative Court of Appeal is Article 95 paragraph 3. 'The trial of categories of cases that come under the Supreme Administrative Court's jurisdiction for annulment may by law come under ordinary administrative courts, depending on their nature or importance. The Supreme Administrative Court has the second instance jurisdiction, as specified by law' (*see also supra* No. 307, on the jurisdiction of Administrative Courts of First Instance on annulment disputes). Act 3659/2008 has enlarged the jurisdiction of the ordinary administrative law courts, transferring certain types of cases, formerly falling under the jurisdiction of Council of State, either to the Administrative Courts of First Instance, as substantive administrative disputes, or to the Administrative Courts of Appeal, as annulment disputes.

III. The Court of Audit

329. The Court of Audit functions as both a court and the major auditing corps of the administration (*see* also *supra* No. 203).

330. The competences of the Court of Audit are, according to the Constitution (Article 98 paragraph 1), to advise, audit and act as a court. For more details on its advisory and auditing competences, *see supra* Nos 204 and 205. For its judicial competences, *see supra* No. 305.

331. The Court of Audit hears cases in five-member benches (Article 24 of Act 4820/2021). Appeals of law against the decisions of the chambers are heard by the Full Bench (Article 19 of Act 4820/2021). The Full Bench of the Court of Audit is the third Supreme Court of the State, the other two being the Supreme Civil and Criminal Court and the Council of State. Decisions of the Full Bench are irrevocable and subject to no special legal remedy except a petition that the procedure be repeated (Article 51 of Act 345/1976). The General Commissioner of the State at the Court of Audit participates in the hearings and also has to be heard (Article 7 of Act 4820/2021).

§6. Other Courts

I. The Special Highest Court

332. The Special Highest Court (or Supreme Special Court) is provided for in Article 100 of the Constitution. The procedure before it is determined by Special Act 345/1976. Although its status is separate from and outside the hierarchical ranking of the courts of each sector, the Special Highest Court is not superior to the other three Supreme Courts (Council of State, Supreme Civil and Criminal Court and Court of Audit).

333. The Court is composed of the Presidents of the three Supreme Courts (of the Supreme Civil and Criminal Court, of the Council of State and of the Court of Audit), four members of the Council of State and four members of the Supreme Civil and Criminal Court. In the exercise of its competence to review the constitutionality of statutes and to settle conflicts of competence between courts of different jurisdictions and between the courts and administrative authorities, its composition is enlarged: it also includes two ordinary professors of law at the law schools of the country. Apart from the Presidents of the Supreme Courts, all other members are chosen by lot for a two-year term. The Special Highest Court is presided over either by the President of the Council of State or of the Supreme Civil and Criminal Court, depending on seniority (Article 100 paragraph 2 of the Constitution and Article 1 paragraph 1 of Act 345/1976).

334. Its competence includes, apart from the aforementioned review of the constitutionality of laws and the settlement of conflicts of competence, the review of parliamentary elections and of elections for the European Parliament, of incompatibilities leading to the forfeiture of office of Members of Parliament, the review of the results of referenda and the settlement of controversies related to the designation of rules of international law as generally acknowledged (Article 100 paragraph 1 of the Constitution).

The competence of the Court is laid down in the Constitution as an exclusive competence. The competence to review the elections for the European Parliament is not mentioned in the Constitution but in Article 8 paragraph 2 of Act 4255/2014 On the Election of Representatives to the European Parliament. The Court has also ruled (9–11/1985) that it also has jurisdiction to review the results of European elections.

The decisions of the Special Highest Court are irrevocable and subject to no legal remedy; from the moment of their publication, they take precedence over any other ruling (Article 100 paragraph 4 of the Constitution and Article 21 of Act 345/1976). The only exception is decisions to reject objections to the validity of parliamentary elections, which are deemed res judicata only between the parties to the dispute (Article 33 of Act 345/1976).

II. The Special Court for 'Faulty Wrongful Judgment' and the Special Court for Disputes on Salaries of Judges

335. Suits against judges for wrongful judgment rendered either on purpose or with gross negligence (referred to as 'faulty wrongful judgment' in the official English translation of the Constitution) are tried by a special tribunal composed of the President of the Council of State, as President of the Court, three Supreme Court judges (one from the Supreme Civil and Criminal Court, one from the Council of State and one from the Court of Audit), two ordinary professors of law and two barristers who are members of the Supreme Disciplinary Council for barristers (Article 99 paragraph 1 of the Constitution, Article 1 paragraph 1 and 6 paragraph 1 of Act 693/1977 On Trials of Misconduct Suits, amended by Act 1366/1983). A judge who belongs to the same branch of justice as the defendant judge is excluded from the hearing panel. If the defendant judge belongs to the branch of administrative justice, the Court is presided over by the President of the Supreme Civil and Criminal Court (Article 99 paragraph 2 of the Constitution and Article 1 paragraph 2 of Act 693/1977).

There can be no action for 'faulty wrongful judgment':

(1) against the members of the Special Highest Court of Article 100 of the Constitution;
(2) against members of courts who decide on the validity of local government elections;
(3) against judicial functionaries of participating councils ruling on issues of the general employment status of judicial functionaries and judicial employees;
(4) against the members of the Special Court for decisions on suits for 'faulty wrongful judgment' (Article 7 of Act 693/1977).

This provision is of dubious constitutional status since Article 99 of the Constitution refers generally to judges.

The object of suits for 'faulty wrongful judgment' is compensation for damages caused to the plaintiff intentionally or by gross negligence by the defendant judge during the discharge of his judicial duties (Article 6 of Act 693/1977).

In order to institute a suit for 'faulty wrongful judgment' no permission is required (Article 99 paragraph 3 of the Constitution).

336. With the Revision of 2001, the Court of Article 99 of the Constitution has been made competent to hear disputes relating to all kinds of remunerations and pensions of judicial functionaries, provided that the resolution of the relevant legal issues might affect the salary, pension or fiscal status of a wider circle of persons. In such cases, the composition of the Court includes the participation of one additional full professor and one additional barrister, as specified by law (Article 88 paragraph 2 of the Constitution).

This provision enlarged the competence of the Special Court for suits for 'faulty wrongful judgment', which now functions as a 'Salary Court'. Article 99, however, in violation of the revisionary process, had not been included among the provisions to be amended. Nevertheless, the relevant executive statute has been issued (Act 3038/2002) and the Court is now functioning as a 'Salary Court', without itself questioning the legality of its establishment (Ruling 1/2005).

Chapter 2. Legal Status of Judges

§1. Functional and Personal Independence

337. Judges enjoy functional and personal independence (Article 87 paragraph 1 of the Constitution).

338. Functional independence is specified further in paragraph 2 of Article 87 of the Constitution. 'In the discharge of their duties judges shall be subject only to the Constitution and the laws.' That is, they are not subject to other state powers or judges of higher rank, to social institutions or to litigants.

339. Personal independence of judges is constitutionally guaranteed as a means to serve their functional independence. It pertains to their appointment, their advancement in their careers and their remuneration. Specifically, guarantees of personal independence of judges take the following form:

I. Selection and Appointment

340. According to the Constitution (Article 88 paragraph 1 and Executive Act 4938/2022), judges are appointed by Presidential Decree in compliance with the law determining the qualifications and the procedure for their appointment. Judges are chosen from among graduates of the National Judges School, which candidates enter by means of periodical examinations (Act 4871/2021). The School has a section for civil and criminal judges, a section for administrative law judges and a section for prosecutors. Successful candidates are chosen by a body composed of judicial functionaries assisted by university professors and barristers (Article 18 of Act 4871/2021).

II. Appointment for Life

341. Judicial functionaries are appointed for life: they remain in office until they reach the age specified by law, even if the post to which they are appointed is abolished by law (Article 88 paragraph 1 of the Constitution). This constitutes a major difference between judges and other civil servants, whose tenure as 'permanent' is so as long as their post is not abolished by law. Judges up to and including the rank of a Court of Appeal judge or deputy prosecutor to the Court of Appeal retire at the age of sixty-five. Judges of higher rank remain in office until the age of sixty-seven (Article 88 paragraph 5 of the Constitution). It has recently been argued that the latter provision can be interpreted as permitting the extension of this age limit. Nevertheless, members of the academic community as well as of the judiciary have emphasized that the extension is not possible without a constitutional amendment.

342. According to the Constitution (Article 90 paragraph 5), the tenure of the President of the Council of State, of the Supreme Civil and Criminal Court (*Areios*

Pagos) and of the Court of Audit, as well as of the Public Prosecutor of the Supreme Civil and Criminal Court and of the General Commissioners of administrative courts and of the Court of Audit may not exceed four years, even if the judicial functionary holding this office has not reached the retirement age. In this latter case, the departing President is entitled to continue to serve in the court in the capacity he held before becoming President, or to leave the service, in which case any period of time which remains until completion of the retirement age, shall be calculated as actual pensionable service.

Judges may only be dismissed following a court decision resulting from a criminal conviction or grave disciplinary violation or from illness or disability or professional incompetence (Article 88 paragraph 4 of the Constitution). Authorities competent to impose dismissal are the three Supreme Courts in Full Bench, depending on the branch of justice to which the judge belongs (Articles 67 et seq. of Act 4938/2022).

III. Changes of Post

343. According to the Constitution (Article 90 paragraph 1), promotions, transfers, and so on of judges are effected by Presidential Decree in compliance with a prior decision by the Supreme Judicial Council corresponding to the three Supreme Courts. If the Minister of Justice disagrees with the decision of the Supreme Judicial Council, he refers the matter to the corresponding Full Bench of the Supreme Court which acts as a Judicial Council. Its decision is binding on the Minister, who is obliged to initiate the issuance of the Presidential Decree (Article 90 paragraphs 3 and 4 of the Constitution).

Provision is made for additional members to sit on the Judicial Councils deciding on the promotion of judicial functionaries to positions of Councillors of the Council of State and the Court of Audit, of President Judges of Appeals, and such like (Article 90 paragraph 2 of the Constitution).

An exception to the rule that promotions of judges are effected after a decision of the Supreme Judicial Council is provided for in Article 90 paragraph 5 of the Constitution and concerns promotions to the highest judicial offices. Specifically, the exception pertains to promotions to the post of President or Vice President of the Council of State, of the Supreme Civil and Criminal Court and of the Court of Audit, to the post of Supreme Civil and Criminal Court Prosecutor, to the post of General Commissioner of the Court of Audit as well as to the post of General Commissioner of administrative law courts. The persons filling these posts are selected by the Cabinet, which also proposes the issuing of the relevant Presidential Decree.

These Presidential Decrees are not subject to an application for annulment before the Council of State (Article 90 paragraph 6 of the Constitution). It has been asserted that this latter provision contravenes the constitutional guarantee of the application for annulment (Article 95 paragraph 1) and the entitlement to judicial protection (Article 20 paragraph 1). This view has not been adopted in the cases: according to the latter, all provisions of the Constitution are of equal force and therefore no one provision can outweigh another (Council of State 1339/1988, 4571/1988, Special Highest Court 11/2003).

IV. Remuneration

344. Finally, Article 88 paragraph 2 of the Constitution includes a special provision for the remuneration of judges, which must be commensurate with their office. This constitutional provision has served as a basis for rulings both of the Supreme Civil and Criminal Court and of the Council of State which, by extending the principle of equality of remunerations in the public sector, have increased salaries of judges by bringing them to the same level as salaries of other civil servants, such as hospital doctors. On the same grounds, the case law has extended to judicial functionaries tax exemptions and special benefits granted to functionaries in other sectors. This, despite the fact that the Constitution states explicitly, '[N]o salary, pension, subsidy or remuneration shall be entered in the State budget or granted, unless it is provided for by statute concerning the organization or other special statute' (Article 80 paragraph 1) (*see also infra* No. 432).

§2. Incompatibilities

345. Judges may not perform any other salaried service nor practice any other profession (Article 89 paragraph 1 of the Constitution).

Exceptionally, judicial functionaries may be elected members of the Academy of Athens or teaching staff of university-level institutions, or sit on councils or committees exercising competences of a disciplinary, auditing or adjudicating nature and on bill drafting committees, provided that this participation is specifically stipulated by the law (Article 89 paragraph 2).

Judicial functionaries are also barred from undertaking administrative duties. The only exceptions are the possibility of representing the country internationally, and the training of judges, which is regarded as a judicial competence (Article 89 paragraph 3). The prohibition on judicial functionaries undertaking administrative duties was first introduced in the Revision of 2001. Previously there had been no such constraint and judges had been able to perform administrative duties, on condition, of course, that provision for this existed in legislation.

Judges may not participate in the Government (Article 89 paragraph 4 of the Constitution). But according to Article 37 of the Constitution, governing the appointment of the Prime Minister, the President of the Council of State or of the Supreme Civil and Criminal Court or of the Court of Audit is appointed Prime Minister and forms a Cabinet of the broadest possible acceptance in order to hold elections, if no other Cabinet can be formed (*see supra* No. 183).

§3. Responsibility

346. Judges are liable for criminal, civil and disciplinary misfeasance. Crimes committed by judges belong to the jurisdiction of ordinary criminal courts. Apart from the common crimes in the Penal Code (Act 4619/2019) there is also provision for crimes committed in the course of judicial duties, such as the offence of accepting a bribe (Article 237 of Penal Code).

Holding judges civilly liable in the discharge of their duties is entrusted to the Special Court for 'faulty wrongful judgment' (*see supra* Nos 335 et seq.). The case law does not accept that illegal actions committed by judges can be the subject of claims for civil liability against the State unless they involve the exercise of duties of an administrative nature. Nevertheless, the Full Bench of the Council of State has recently ruled (Ruling 1501/2014) that the State bears civil liability for compensation in accordance with Article 105 of the Introductory Act of the Civil Code (Emergency Act 2783/1941) in cases of an obvious error by a judge. Moreover, the European Court of Justice has ruled that the State does bear civil liability for decisions of courts in cases of flagrant breach of European law (Judgment of 30 September 2003, C-224/01, *Gerhard Köbler v. Republik Österreich*).

Disciplinary measures are imposed by judicial councils composed exclusively or mainly of judicial functionaries. The Supreme Disciplinary Council is competent for exercising judicial authority over judicial functionaries from and above the rank of member of the Supreme Civil and Criminal Court or Deputy Prosecutor of the Supreme Civil and Criminal Court, or a rank corresponding thereto. Depending on the case the disciplinary action shall or may be initiated by the Minister for Justice (Article 91 of the Constitution).

Chapter 3. Judicial Review of the Unconstitutionality of Laws

347. The system of judicial review of the constitutionality of laws is organized as a system of diffuse, specific and incidental scrutiny (*see supra* Nos 33 and 35). Each and every court is competent to examine the consonance of a specific provision, necessary for resolving the dispute before them, with the provisions of the Constitution. Article 93 paragraph 4 of the Constitution is explicit: 'The courts shall be bound not to apply a statute whose content is contrary to the Constitution.' In case that a certain provision of the law is deemed unconstitutional, it is not rescinded but is not applied in the case before the court. In the event of a provision being deemed unconstitutional by one of the Supreme Courts, even though it is not formally deleted from the statute book it has essentially been rendered 'legally expired'.

348. According to paragraph 5 of Article 100 of the Constitution, an exception to the above rule concerns the sections of the Council of State, the Supreme Civil and Criminal Court and the Court of Audit. If they are inclined to the view that a law is unconstitutional, they may not render a final judgment but are obliged to refer the matter to the Full Bench. This exception is justified by the fact that rulings of these Supreme Courts in Full Bench have a high moral value, so that matters of major significance, such as the review of the unconstitutionality of laws, have to be decided in Full Bench.

349. It has been accepted since the middle of the last century by legal scholars and the case law that every court reviews the constitutionality of legal norms which are established by legislation, both as to the enactment of these acts by the organs which are competent in accordance with the Constitution and as to their normative content. The review of the unconstitutionality of laws may be conducted following an objection by one of the litigants, or ex officio. In respect of compliance with constitutionally required forms, only the substantive elements of the law are examined (called 'external formal unconstitutionality') and not the constitutionality of the procedure followed or the *interna corporis* of Parliament (called 'internal formal unconstitutionality') (*see also supra* No. 56). Not only law originating in Parliament (statutes, acts) is subject to judicial review, but also 'material' law.

Exceptionally, 'pensions must be proposed by means of special Bills; the insertion of provisions pertaining to pensions in Bills introduced to regulate other matters is not permitted under penalty of nullity.' (Article 73 paragraph 2(c) of the Constitution)

350. Parallel with Article 93 paragraph 4, Article 100 paragraph 1(e) of the Constitution, which concerns the Special Highest Court, determines that under its jurisdiction falls *inter alia* 'the settlement of controversies on whether the content of a statute enacted by Parliament is contrary to the Constitution, or on the interpretation of provisions of such statute when conflicting judgments have been pronounced by the Supreme Administrative Court, the Supreme Civil and Criminal Court or the Court of Audit.'(*see also supra* No. 84) This provision is a factor which compromises the character of review of constitutionality as diffuse and incidental.

It has been considered necessary for the unification of the Supreme Court's jurisprudence and for the benefit of the certainty of law.

The main difference between the two articles of the Constitution (Articles 93 paragraph 4, and 100 paragraph 1e) concerns the result of a court's ruling. In the case of Article 93 paragraph 4 a court does not apply the unconstitutional statute *in concreto*, but the law remains valid. In the case of Article 100 paragraph 1e, the law declared unconstitutional is abolished. '[I]t shall', according to Article 100 paragraph 4, 'be invalid as of the date of publication of the respective judgment, or as of the date determined by the ruling'. This competence of the Special Highest Court is an exception to the rule of diffuse and incidental review. In practice, the diffuse and incidental character of the system of judicial review of the constitutionality of the laws has to some extent been compromised.

351. If on the basis of Article 93 paragraph 4 a court considers a statute unconstitutional and does not apply it, the question arises – what law it will then apply? In criminal cases the answer is usually quite simple: the accused person has to be acquitted. In cases of administrative annulment disputes against administrative acts based on unconstitutional laws, the answer is not difficult either: the administrative act has to be annulled, due to the unconstitutionality of its legal basis. Difficulties arise in civil cases as well as in cases of substantive administrative disputes, in which the court will either have to apply the constitutional rule itself in case of direct applicability thereof or it will apply the law which was valid before the unconstitutional statute was enacted. However, the declaration that a provision is unconstitutional cannot lead to a refusal to administer justice.

Nevertheless, Greek constitutional theory and jurisprudence are quite cautious about accepting an unrestricted judicial review of laws. They are very close to the theory of 'judicial self-restraint'.

Part VI. Fundamental Rights and Freedoms

Chapter 1. General

§1. Sources

352. The second part of the Constitution is devoted to civil and social rights. The Constitution refers to civil rights as 'individual rights' (*see* the Title of Part Two, Articles 4 et seq.). Political rights are guaranteed in other parts of the Constitution.

In the first paragraph of Article 2, which forms part of Section I (Form of Government) of the Constitution, the latter assigns to the State the primary obligation to respect and protect human dignity. In the following paragraph, it declares that Greece, adhering to the generally recognized rules of international law, pursues the strengthening of peace and justice, and the fostering of friendly relations between peoples and states (Article 2 paragraph 2). The classification of these provisions under the heading 'Form of Government' indicates and underlines the importance of human rights for the constitutional order as well as the humanistic and liberal orientation of the Constitution (*see also infra* No. 382).

353. The Constitution also recognizes that international and European conventions, as of the time they are ratified by statute and become operative according to their respective conditions, shall prevail over any contrary provision of the law (Article 28, which refers more broadly to the generally accepted rules of international law and to international conventions) on condition of reciprocity for aliens. The Hellenic Republic has ratified numerous international conventions covering civil and social rights.

Among the international treaties ratified by Greece, there are a number which have been concluded in the context of the United Nations: the Founding Charter of the United Nations of 1945 (Emergency Act 585/1945); the United Nations Conventions for the Prevention and Repression of the Crime of Genocide of 1948 (Legislative Decree 3091/1954), on the Abolition of Slavery of 1956 (Legislative Decree 1145/1972), on the Elimination of All Forms of Racial Discrimination of 1966 (Legislative Decree 494/1970), on Economic, Social and Cultural Rights of 1966 (Act 1532/1985), on the Elimination of All Forms of Discrimination Against Women of 1979 (Act 1342/1983), Against Torture of 1984 (Act 1782/1988), on the Rights of Children of 1990 (Act 2101/1992), and the International Covenant on Civil and Political Rights of 1966 (Act 2462/1997), among others.

Greece has also ratified conventions agreed in the context of the Council of Europe, such as the European Social Charter of 1961 (Act 1426/1984), the Revised European Social Charter of 1996 (Act 4359/2016), and the European Convention on the Prevention of Torture, Inhuman or Degrading Treatment or Punishment of 1987 (Act 1949/1991). However, the most important agreement signed by Greece – in terms of legal and political significance – is the ECHR. The Convention was first ratified by Legislative Decree 2329/1953, which, however, excluded the provisions on individual recourse to the European Commission of Human Rights and the ECtHR. The dictatorial regime of 1967–1974 denounced the Convention and withdrew from the Council of Europe in 1969, thereby forestalling the imminent expulsion of Greece for systematic violations of human rights. As soon as the dictatorship had fallen the ECHR was ratified again by Legislative Decree 53/1974 and Greece resumed her place in the Council of Europe. Subsequently, an Announcement of 15 January 1985 from the Minister for Foreign Affairs – and renewed each year by decision of the same Minister on the basis of the power granted by Article 1 of Act 1846/1989 – recognized for the first time the option of individual recourse against Member States before the European Commission of Human Rights and the ECtHR.

354. Furthermore, as a member of the EU, Greece is bound by primary and secondary European law, in the context of which the safeguarding and protection of civil and social rights are strengthened and extended. In the jurisprudence of the CJEU, the shared constitutional principles of the European States, particularly those concerning fundamental rights, are a source of European law (CJEU, C-4/73, *Nold II*). In this way, national rules become part of European law and are reintroduced into national law with the reinforcement of the principle of superiority and efficacy. Moreover, in accordance with Article 6 paragraph 2 of the Treaty on the European Union (TEU), the EU will adhere to the ECHR. Nevertheless, this procedure has been stalled, particularly after the ECtHR's negative Opinion 2/2013 (18 December 2014) concerning the related draft agreement.

In 2000, work was completed on the drafting of the Charter of Fundamental Rights of the European Union, which was incorporated in the text of the Treaty of Rome, to form the basis of the 'European Constitution'. Despite the undisputed political significance of the Charter, its binding force depended on the ratification of the Constitutional Treaty by all the EU Member States. It should be noted that Greece had ratified the European Constitution (Act 3341/2005). The European Constitution was abandoned after its rejection by the Dutch and the French referendums in 2005. The Charter of Fundamental Rights of the European Union was once again proclaimed on 7 December 2007. The new Charter replaced the former one, from the date of entry into force of the Treaty of Lisbon (1 December 2009), signed on 12 December 2007.

Of particular significance in Greece is the influence exerted by the jurisprudence of the ECtHR and the CJEU in framing the jurisprudence law of Greek courts in matters relating to human rights.

§2. Civil, Political and Social Rights: Institutional Guarantees

355. Greek constitutional theory accepts the threefold division of fundamental rights into civil, political and social rights, which goes back to the theoretical edifice of Georg Jellinek, *System der subjektiven öffentlichen Rechte* (Tubingen, Mohr, 1905).

(1) Civil rights correspond to the *status negativus* and establish a claim against the State not to intervene in a sphere of free activity of the individual (*nec facere*).
(2) Political rights correspond to the *status activus* or *status politicus* and establish a claim of the individual to participate in the exercise of State power. Participation in the legislative power is exercised through the right to vote and be elected; participation in the executive power is manifested through the right to be appointed as a civil servant; participation in the judicial power is expressed through the right to be appointed either as a judge or as a member of a jury. The right to found and join political parties is also a manifestation of the participation of the individual in the dynamic political process. The right to participation in political life, the freedom of expression, of press, of assembly and association not only are basic rights of the *status negativus* but also pertain to the *status activus*.
(3) Social rights are a result of the evolution of the welfare state and are more recent than civil and political rights. They correspond to the *status socialis* and establish social claims for certain services or privileges to be provided by the State, guaranteeing a decent standard of living. These claims are, however, not legally enforceable unless they are provided for by legislation. The Constitution creates duties for the State corresponding to social rights, but the bearers of social rights cannot force the State to comply with its obligations. Provisions on State duties are interpreted by case law and function more as constitutional directives or goals with no binding force. However, although they provide no basis for actionable rights, in theory, it is asserted that certain consequences are entailed by their proclamation in the Constitution, with the result that we can regard them as having a minimum regulatory content. It is thus maintained that this minimum content of social rights results in the guarantee of a 'relative social acquis', according to which the legislator may not be compelled to proceed to provide social benefits, defining the social right by legislative regulation, but having done so may not subsequently retract and do away with the protective system that has been created, or arbitrarily limit it. However, the case law does not appear to accept a relative social acquis of this kind (*see* Supreme Civil and Criminal Court 7/1992, Council of State 2677/1992; *see also* Council of State 1479/1997, which implies such a minimum). The case law does, however, recognize that when the administration acts at its own discretion it must, in taking its decisions, bear in mind the need to protect social rights (*see* Council of State 2396/1997). Moreover, when social rights are weighed against civil rights to attain the maximum possible protection of conflicting rights, they may offer support for legislative limitation of the latter (*see* Council of State 2412/1993). An exception to the refusal to recognize 'social acquis' is the case of land use and urban planning acquis.

356. The division of fundamental rights and liberties is figurative and relative. Rights and freedoms corresponding to different historical phases of democratic achievements relate in a modern democratic society to one another and supplement each other. To mention only one example, without a social right to education, the civil right to expression which certainly has also characteristics of a political right could not be fully realized.

In any case, some rights have features of two or three different statuses. For example, the right to legal protection (Article 20 paragraph 1 of the Constitution), although in principle a civil right, also has features of the *status activus*: the entitled individual addresses the judicial system and through his participation in the process contributes to the formation of the civil will. It also carries the *status positivus*: an obligation of the State to provide a complex and expensive system for administering justice. Consider also the right to work (Article 22 of the Constitution) which comprises both a prohibition on forced labour and an obligation on the part of the State to create jobs.

357. The Constitution, apart from fundamental rights and freedoms, also contains institutional guarantees, namely guarantees of public or private law institutions. Ownership, commercial competition, marriage, press, radio and television, universities and local self-government are some examples of such institutions. The constitutional protection of these institutions is independent of the protection of the individuals pertaining to them. Freedom of the press (Article 14 paragraph 2), for example, is safeguarded not for the benefit of the individuals (journalists, publishers, etc.) but for the benefit of the press itself. Similarly, by protecting the institution of the family (Article 21 paragraph 1) the Constitution is not interested in the particular rights of the spouses or children, and by setting the foundations for a free market (Article 5 paragraph 1) it does not aim at the protection of particular enterprises.

Institutional guarantees and fundamental rights and freedoms may certainly co-exist. For example, in Article 21 paragraph 1 of the Constitution there co-exist the civil right to protection of the family, the social right to protection of the family and the institutional guarantee of the family.

§3. The Bearers of Fundamental Rights and Freedoms

358. The Constitution as a rule endows every person with civil rights, namely, with fundamental rights and freedoms of the *status negativus*. Nevertheless, an exception is made for the rights of assembly and association (Articles 11 paragraph 1 and 12 paragraph 1) which, according to the wording of the Constitution, are reserved to Greek citizens only, but may be extended by law to aliens, too. In the case of the absence of legislative provision, aliens enjoy a presumption of '*in dubio pro libertate*'. Political and social rights are awarded to Greeks but may be also extended by law to aliens. For more on the protection of aliens, *see infra* Nos 472–476.

359. Minors also enjoy fundamental rights and freedoms. They even enjoy additional rights guaranteed by ordinary legislation, for example, pension rights, due to the need for special care. But it is obvious that the exercise of several rights is related to a certain degree of maturity. Minors are thus entitled to education but the freedom of choice of the school is reserved to the parents.

360. Additional rights are also reserved for families with many children, mothers, widows and orphans, elderly and homeless people, disabled war and peacetime veterans, war victims as well as people suffering from incurable bodily or mental ailments (Article 21 of the Constitution).

361. Other categories of citizens, such as civil servants, judges, officers and soldiers of the armed forces, and imprisoned people, enjoy less freedom in several aspects. For example, judges do not enjoy the right to strike (Article 23 paragraph 2 of the Constitution); civil servants cannot be active in political parties (Article 29 paragraph 3 of the Constitution). These constraints are imposed by law, but the law may not contain provisions which would result in a removal of the essence of the right. On the question of the limits on restrictions to civil rights, *see infra* Nos 376 et seq.

362. Fundamental rights and freedoms are also guaranteed to legal persons, on condition that they are compatible with the nature of the concrete right and with the nature of the concrete legal person. Thus personal liberty and security, the prohibition of torture, religious liberty, protection of family, and so on refer only to individual persons. Ownership, free correspondence, access to courts, etc., are also guaranteed to legal persons.

363. Legal persons in the public sector as a rule do not enjoy fundamental rights and liberties, since they constitute a part or a branch of the State. An exception is made as far as the right of access to the courts (Articles 8 and 20 paragraph 1 of the Constitution) is concerned. There are also legal persons in the public sector, which cannot be considered as forming part of the State. Universities, local self-government agencies and the Church of Greece are bearers of fundamental rights and freedoms, due to their special constitutional status as self-governed institutions. However, public law legal persons, of the nature of associations, are bearers of certain civil rights, since one of their objectives is to serve the interests of their members. These interests may conflict with the interests of the State.

The above public law legal persons, when they are exercising public authority, are recipients of the obligations derived from civil and social rights.

§4. The Bearers of the Obligation to Safeguard Fundamental Rights and Freedoms

364. All bearers of state power are obliged not to violate fundamental rights and freedoms (the negative function of human rights) and positively protect their exercise (the positive function). Specifically, the Constitution states, ‘The rights of the human being as an individual and as a member of the society and the principle of the welfare state rule of law are guaranteed by the State. All agents of the State shall be obliged to ensure the unhindered and effective exercise thereof.' (Article 25 paragraph 1) Not only the State and public legal entities but also corporations organized under private law yet belonging to the public sector are obliged to safeguard human rights.

365. The question of whether private persons are bound to respect human rights has been dealt with in Greek constitutional theory to quite a large extent. Reference is usually made to German constitutional theory ('*Drittwirkung der Grundrechte*'), which has developed the concept of direct applicability of human rights provisions in private law ('*direkte Drittwirkung*') or of their indirect applicability through the general clauses of private law, such as good faith, abuse of rights, etc. ('*indirekte Drittwirkung*').

Greek scholars consider '*Drittwirkung*' either direct or indirect, but Greek courts still waver between the two extremes, sometimes recognizing '*Drittwirkung*' and sometimes rejecting it.

The Revision of 2001 sought to resolve this question by adding to Article 25 paragraph 1 of the Constitution, 'These rights also apply to the relations between individuals to which they are appropriate.' There is no clarification, however, of what form of '*Drittwirkung*' is involved, or of what relations between individuals are meant. Thus even after the revision of the Constitution, the interpretation of the constitutional provision is still dependent on a definition of the action of each right, given that this is still not explicitly defined. The criterion must be the nature of the right, and specifically the possibility of the right being threatened in practice by individuals. The question of '*Drittwirkung*' arises in particular when between private persons a power relationship exists, such as in relations between employers and employees, unions and their members.

366. The Greek Constitution guarantees some human rights which are addressed vis-à-vis private persons, for example, the right to strike (Article 23 paragraph 2) and the right of equal pay for work of equal value irrespective of sex in the private sector (Article 22 paragraph 1). Other human rights, for example, the right to free education (Article 16 paragraph 4), are addressed only vis-à-vis the State. The question of '*Drittwirkung*' does not self-evidently arise in such cases.

§5. Limitations

367. The protection of fundamental rights is not absolute: it is subject to limitations. Some of these arise from the conceptual content of civil rights, as defined in the Constitution. For example, the constitutionally guaranteed 'right of assembly' is a right to 'peaceable and unarmed assembly' (Article 11 paragraph 1), while the constitutional freedom of religion applies to all 'known religions' (Article 13). Other special limitations are placed by specific constitutional provisions on civil rights, because of the special nature of the particular right. For example, the right of assembly may be curbed where there is a threat of serious disruption to the socio-economic life of a particular region (Article 11 paragraph 2). But apart from these special limitations, the scope or protection of most, if not all, civil rights is limited by certain constitutional provisions of more general significance.

368. (a) State of siege (emergency). In the event of the country being declared to be in a state of siege, provision is made (Article 48 paragraphs 1 and 2 of the Constitution) for the suspension of a whole range of civil rights, such as freedom of movement and assembly, of the press, the right to a judge assigned by law, and so on, in order to allow for more effective response to exceptional circumstances, such as war, mobilization owing to external dangers or direct threat to national security, or an armed uprising against the democratic regime. The Constitution contains certain procedural safeguards and limits on the period for which these exceptional measures may remain in place, but there is always the risk of these limitations on rights and freedoms being abused (for the state of siege *see also infra* No. 507).

369. (b) The abusive exercise of a right. The abusive exercise of a civil right is explicitly prohibited by the Constitution (Article 25 paragraph 3). Case law has often combined the application of this constitutional prohibition with that of Article 281 of the Civil Code, which proscribes the exercise of a right if it clearly exceeds the limits set by good faith and good practice or the social and economic purpose of the right. In other words, no civil right may be exercised for a purpose manifestly different from that for which it was granted. The abuse must be substantiated on the basis of objective and indisputable facts. At any event, since Article 25 paragraph 3 of the Constitution does not provide for the sanction of forfeiture of the right, like the German *Grundgesetz* Article 18, no individual may be deprived of or obliged to forfeit the right.

370. (c) Freedom to develop the personality. According to the Constitution, 'All persons shall have the right to develop freely their personality and to participate in the social, economic and political life of the country, insofar as they do not infringe the rights of others or violate the Constitution and the good usages.' (Article 5 paragraph 1). In respect of the three limits set in Article 5 paragraph 1 on the development of the personality, they have been described, though not unanimously, as transcending the boundaries of the specific right to development of the personality and constituting an 'inherent limitation' of all fundamental rights and freedoms in the same way as the general prohibition of the abuse of rights (Article 25 paragraph 3 of the Constitution. These views, however, overlook the principle of speciality (*lex specialis*) according to which only explicitly prescribed limitations on civil rights are to be tolerated. For more detail on the right to develop the personality, *see infra* Nos 388 et seq.).

371. (d) The social limitation of civil rights. Some theorists maintain that Article 25 of the Constitution, which refers to the welfare state rule of law and recognizes as the purpose of protecting civil rights 'achievement of social progress in freedom and justice', entails a general social limitation on civil rights, consisting of prohibition on the exercise of a right when the latter causes direct and serious harm to society as a whole. Furthermore, the Constitution explicitly provides that the State may demand that all citizens fulfil the duty of social and national solidarity (Article 25 paragraph 4). Various individual provisions insist on additional special social limitations. For example, property rights may not be exercised contrary to the public interest (Article 17 of the Constitution); the right to strike may be curbed for employees of public utility enterprises whose functioning is of vital importance in serving basic needs of society as a whole (Article 23 paragraph 2 of the Constitution), and so on. However, these limitations on civil rights must be explicitly provided for in a context of presumption in favour of the law. Invocation of the above general clauses is not sufficient to support a specific limitation on civil rights.

372. (e) Reservation of the law. Limitations do not have to be stipulated in the Constitution itself. In the case of many constitutional provisions safeguarding civil rights, it is explicitly stated that an 'executive statute will be required to bring that right fully into force (an organic or organizational executive statute) or to implement it (a simple executive statute)' (*see supra* No. 66). Through such Executive Statutes limits are usually placed on the exercise of the constitutional right. According to the case law, this executive law need not even be a statute: it may be an administrative law regulation, provided that the constitutional conditions for legislative delegation have been met (Article 43 paragraph 2) (Council of State 4665/1988). Protection of civil rights would be more complete if legislative delegation was excluded in the event of the imposition of particularly significant limitations. Moreover, the Constitution rules out the granting to the administration (through a framework statute) of a general delegation power to issue executive (substantive/material) laws on civil rights (Articles 72 paragraph 1 and 43 paragraph 5 of the Constitution).

Many constitutional provisions containing a reservation of law require that the law be 'special' (Articles 4 paragraphs 4, 16 paragraph 5, 22 paragraph 4, etc.). The 'special' quality lies in the requirement that the law concern exclusively that specific issue, and not contain unrelated provisions.

373. (f) Reservation in favour of administrative and judicial authorities. Certain constitutional provisions contain a reservation in favour of administrative or judicial authorities, usually in combination with a reservation of law. For example, Article 11 paragraph 2 of the Constitution provides that open-air assemblies may, in certain circumstances, be banned by reasoned decision of the police authority. Article 12 paragraph 2 of the Constitution stipulates that an association may be dissolved for breach of the law or of a substantive provision of its statutes only by court judgment.

374. (g) Rights without reservation. In many provisions of the Constitution civil rights are safeguarded with absolutely no reservation. For example, Greek men and women should have equal rights and obligations (Article 4 paragraph 2) and; freedom of religious conscience is inviolable (Article 13 paragraph 1). Such rights may be restrained only if they conflict with other constitutional rights.

375. Limitations may be either preventive or repressive. The Greek system of limitations is basically repressive. However, preventive limitations are not unknown. The exercise of the right of assembly (Article 11 of the Constitution), for example, does not depend on a permission, but it presupposes a prior declaration to the police authorities. An open-air assembly may furthermore be preventively forbidden due to an imminent threat to public safety and the right to free movement abroad (Article 5 paragraph 3 of the Constitution) is subject to permission (viz. a passport).

§6. Restrictions on Limitations

376. Limitations of fundamental rights are not unlimited. They are conditioned by certain constitutional principles (‘*Schranken-Schranken*’). Limitations must thus be objective, general and non-discriminatory, and they must be justified by a serious public or social interest, such as order, safety, prevention of crime and public health. Nevertheless, the latter requirement, namely that there be some issue of general public interest, is often used in case law not as a curb on limitations, but, on the contrary, as a justification for the imposition of limitations (e.g., Council of State 400/1986).

377. Furthermore, pursuant to the principle of proportionality, limitations must correspond to the purpose they are supposed to serve: they have to be adequate and necessary to meet the concrete purpose and demonstrate internal cohesion with the objective being pursued so that the anticipated benefit will not be outweighed by the harm arising from the limitations (*stricto sensu* proportionality or weighing cost against benefit).

Since as far back as 1984 the case law of the Council of State has recognized the principle of proportionality as a curb on the limitations of civil rights, on the grounds that such a principle is inherent in a State organized by the rule of law. The extent of that curb will be determined by the criteria of suitability and necessity of the limitation being set. The Revision of 2001 enshrined the principle in the Constitution (Article 25 paragraph 1). This constitutional guarantee strengthened judicial control of *stricto sensu* proportionality (e.g., Supreme Civil and Criminal Court 10/2003 and Council of State 990/2004).

378. Lastly, limitations may not infringe on the core of civil rights. This requirement is derived from the need to respect and protect the value of a human being as a primary obligation of any system of government. Thus no limitation is permitted to infringe on basic human values. The core of the right comprehends the *a priori* defined minimum elements of the right, which cannot be infringed under any circumstances. The relative core, which is defined on each occasion in light of the specific circumstances, is identified with *stricto sensu* proportionality.

Limitations constitute exceptions to the rules guaranteeing and protecting civil rights. Consequently, they have to be narrowly interpreted.

Chapter 2. The Particular Rights and Freedoms

§1. The Right to Life

379. The right to life is expressly guaranteed in the ECHR (Article 2). The Constitution only indirectly provides for this right in Article 5 paragraph 2: 'All persons living within the Greek territory shall enjoy full protection of their life, honour and liberty irrespective of nationality, race or language and of religious or political beliefs.' It is obvious that the direct and main concern of this article is non-discrimination. The right to life is also provided in Article 7 paragraph 3, according to which the death penalty shall not be imposed, with one exception, however (*see* more detailed account *infra* No. 381). Article 2 paragraph 1 of the Constitution safeguarding human dignity certainly presupposes the right to life, too.

Two main issues are related to the right to life: the first one is abortion, insofar as it involves the right to life of the embryo; the second is the death penalty.

380. According to the Penal Code (Article 304 paragraphs 4 and 5) abortions are permitted, provided they are done with the consent of the pregnant woman by specialized doctors, in hospitals, in one of the following cases: if the pregnancy is less than twelve weeks, if, in case of a pregnancy of less than twenty-four weeks, there are medical indications that the embryo will be born with physiological anomalies, if the life or the physical or psychological integrity of the pregnant woman is endangered, if pregnancy is a result of rape or a similar criminal offence, before the completion of the nineteenth week. If the pregnant woman is a minor, the consent of the parents is also necessary (Article 304 paragraph 5 of the Presidential Decree 283/1985).

381. The death penalty was provided for in the Penal Code until 1993 for very serious crimes, but it had not been pronounced in judicial practice since 1973. The Constitution (Article 7 paragraph 3) prohibited the death penalty for political crimes (except in the case of compound offences, that is, where the act was also a crime under ordinary criminal law). The Legislature abolished the death penalty in 1993 (Article 33 of Act 2172/1993), even without exempting serious military crimes in times of war.

The Revision of 2001 outlawed the death penalty in times of peace, providing for executions only 'in the cases provided by law for felonies perpetrated in time of war and related thereto' (Article 7 paragraph 3, as revised). However, in Act 3289/2004 Greece ratified the Thirteenth Protocol of the ECHR in respect of the total abolition of capital punishment. Under Article 28 paragraph 1 of the Constitution, the Protocol takes precedence over Greek domestic legislation. Thus following the ratification the exception stipulated in the above constitutional provision is essentially bereft of force.

§2. Human Dignity

382. Human dignity is guaranteed in Article 2 paragraph 1 of the Constitution. 'Respect and protection of the value of the human being constitute the primary obligation of the State.' The proclamation of this principle in the chapter on the form of the system of government demonstrates that the constitutional legislator regarded it as absolutely fundamental. Its application is not confined only to civil and social rights. It offers a specific orientation for interpretation of any constitutional or legislative provision while providing a criterion for judging the constitutionality of a legislative or regulatory act.

383. The prohibition on torture (Article 7 paragraph 2 of the Constitution) and the prohibition of any form of compulsory labour (Article 22 paragraph 4 of the Constitution) are special manifestations of this basic right.

The Constitution prohibits not only torture but also any bodily maltreatment, impairment of health or use of psychological violence, as well as any other offence against human dignity (Article 7 paragraph 2). This constitutional provision is specified by Articles 137 et seq. of the Penal Code, as introduced by Act 1500/1984 'Criminal Punishment of Torture'. Torture is classified in the Penal Code in the part on the 'Assaults on the Form of Government', which indicates the gravity of the offence. It is important to emphasize that neither necessity nor orders by a superior may justify the act.

The European Convention for the Prevention of Torture and Inhuman or Degrading Treatment or Punishment was ratified by Greece in 1988 (Act 1782/1988).

An exception to the ban on compulsory labour is laid down in Article 22 paragraph 4(b) of the Constitution, according to which personal services may be requested in case of war or mobilization or defence needs or urgent social emergencies resulting from disasters or endangering public health as well as in case of local needs. In this last case, personal services are to be rendered to local government agencies.

384. The protection of human dignity is supplemented by every individual's right to develop freely his or her personality and participate in the social, economic and political life of the country, insofar as one does not infringe upon the rights of others or violate the Constitution and moral values (Article 5 paragraph 1, *see infra* Nos 388 et seq.). It is also manifested in everyone's right within the Greek territory to enjoy full protection of life, honour and freedom, irrespective of nationality, race and language and irrespective of religious or political beliefs (Article 5 paragraph 2, *see supra* No. 379).

385. The principle of human dignity applies to all individuals, regardless of nationality. Not only the State but private individuals too must respect this principle.

386. A question concerning infringement of human dignity was raised in the case of application of the Greek legislation on custody of a person for debts to the State. Articles 231–243 of the Administrative Court Procedure Code permitted detention as a means of securing payment of debts to the State and provided for such custody to be ordered, for a period of up to a year, by the Presiding Judge of the appropriate Administrative Court of First Instance. This measure was ruled unconstitutional by a section of the Council of State (Rulings 1623/2002, 2611/2004) as well as by its Full Bench (Rulings 250/2008, 251/2008), on the grounds, *inter alia*, that it contravened the principles of human dignity and personal freedom (Articles 2 paragraph 1 and 5 paragraph 3 of the Constitution). The rulings of the Council of State were subsequently confirmed by the Special Highest Court (Ruling 1/2010). In this context, Articles 231–243 of the Administrative Court Procedure Code were abolished by Act 3842/2010.

387. Moreover, Article 2 paragraph 1 entails a prohibition on the use of methods designed to reveal the inner state or intentions of the individual – such methods as truth serums or lie detectors – even when used with the consent of the individual. From the provisions of Article 2 paragraph 1, it was indirectly inferred, until recently, that individuals had a right to protection of their genetic identity and, more generally, protection against biomedical interventions. Since the Revision of 2001, these rights are now explicitly safeguarded (Article 5 paragraph 5 of the Constitution).

§3. Personal Liberty and Security

I. Right to Free Development of Personality and Participation in the Life of the Country

388. According to the Constitution, 'All persons shall have the right to develop freely their personality and to participate in the social, economic and political life of the country, insofar as they do not infringe the rights of others or violate the Constitution and good usages.' (Article 5 paragraph 1). The Constitution is here establishing a general right of freedom, which complements the protection extended by other provisions to rights relating to the personality.

Although the provision guarantees the right to participate in the economic, political and social life of the country, in practice Article 5 paragraph 1 serves above all to protect the first of these, that is, economic freedom, in all its manifestations (for details, *see infra* Nos 420 et seq.). Various individual manifestations of the personality protected by Article 5 paragraph 1 include sexual freedom, the freedom to present oneself to others as one wishes, and so on.

The right of each person to free development of their personality is guaranteed on condition that the exercise of the right does not infringe the rights of others, or contravene the Constitution or good usages. The concept of 'rights of others' must be understood to comprehend not only constitutional rights but those derived from law or convention as well. These restrictions are limited by the principle of proportionality and the prohibition on any infringement of the core of the right (for more details, *see supra* Nos 376 et seq.).

389. The Revision of 2001 (Article 5A paragraph 1) explicitly safeguarded the right to information, which is a more specific facet of the general freedom of expression. Restrictions to this right may be imposed by law only insofar as they are absolutely necessary and justified for reasons of national security, combating crime or protecting the rights and interests of third parties. The concept of national security must be interpreted narrowly, as covering military secrets. The rights of third parties to be protected are largely rights to protection of their family and private lives.

390. The Constitution (Article 5A paragraph 2) also safeguards – as another special facet of the right to information – the right to participate in the information society, or in 'cyber-space'. It elevates to the rank of an obligation of the State the task of facilitating access to information being transmitted electronically, and also facilitating the generation, exchange and dissemination of information, provided always that private and family lives remain inviolable (Article 19 of the Constitution), that persons are protected from the electronic processing of their personal data (Article 9A of the Constitution) and that the confidentiality of communication is preserved (Article 9 of the Constitution). This provision entails an obligation on the State to take positive measures – such as the introduction of information technology into the educational system.

II. Liberty of the Person

391. Personal liberty *stricto sensu*, namely the physical, bodily freedom of the individual, is protected by Article 5 paragraph 3 of the Constitution. 'Personal liberty is inviolable. No one shall be prosecuted, arrested, imprisoned or otherwise confined, except when and as the law provides.'

Personal liberty includes the liberty of movement and domicile, personal security as well as privacy.

392. (a) Liberty of movement and domicile. Liberty of movement may be restricted for the protection of public health; the liberty to travel abroad may evidently be restricted owing to prosecution on criminal charges (interpretative clause under Article 5 of the Constitution).

The main limitation of personal liberty – actually deprivation – is preventive deportation within the country, provided for in Article 5 paragraph 4:

> Individual administrative measures restrictive of the free movement or establishment in the country, and of the free exit and entrance therein of any Greek are prohibited. Restrictive measures of such content may only be imposed as an attendant penalty by a criminal court ruling, in exceptional cases of emergency and only in order to prevent the committing of criminal acts, as specified by law.

This constitutional requirement was incompatible with provisions of Greek legislation which allowed persons with outstanding debts to the national insurance fund, inland revenue, and such like to be prohibited from leaving the country. These provisions, which also ran counter to Article 12 of the International Covenant on Civil and Political Rights (Act 2462/1997), on the freedom to leave any country, were finally repealed (Article 23 of Act 2768/1999 and Article 12 of Act 2873/2000).

The prohibition on the imposition of individual administrative measures limiting free movement or establishment in the country applies only to Greeks, not to aliens, according to the Constitution. However, according to Article 12 of the International Covenant on Civil and Political Rights, aliens too are entitled to freedom of movement and residence.

393. (b) Protection of health and genetic identity. According to the Constitution, 'All persons have the right to the protection of their health and of their genetic identity. Matters relating to the protection of every person against biomedical interventions shall be specified by law.' (Article 5 paragraph 5, added to the Constitution in the 2001 Revision). The provision complements the guarantee of protection of personal liberty *stricto sensu* and safeguards the personal right to health, outlawing changes in a person's genetic makeup made without his consent. Of course, biomedical interventions cannot be banned outright. The protection extended by the new provision is intended to guard against interventions carried out in violation of human dignity (Article 2 paragraph 1 of the Constitution).

394. (c) Personal security. Habeas corpus (Article 5 paragraph 3 of the Constitution) provides, 'Personal liberty is inviolable. No one shall be prosecuted, arrested, imprisoned or otherwise confined except when and as the law provides.' Under Article 6 of the Constitution arrest or imprisonment is prohibited without a reasoned judicial warrant, which must be served at the moment of arrest or detention. For arrest of persons apprehended in *flagrante delicto*, a judicial warrant is obviously not necessary.

These provisions prohibit any form of deprivation of individual liberty, in cases where there is no legislative provision and the detention is not ordered by a judicial authority.

The Greek courts used to favour a narrow interpretation of the above constitutional provisions on personal detention and confined their scope to cases of penal prosecution (e.g., Supreme Civil and Criminal Court 1753/1983). But the course of the case law was altered when it was ruled that the detention of persons owing money to the State by order of the competent director of a public fund was unconstitutional since, in the sense of the constitutional provisions safeguarding the principle of human dignity (Article 2 paragraph 1) and personal liberty (Article 5 paragraph 3) detention must be ordered by a court, which would verify the legality of the measure being taken and its compliance with the principle of proportionality (Council of State 2775/1989, which pertained to the legislation on detention then in force regarding the period when the competent tax official on his own authority could order detention). The subsequent regime of the Administrative Court Procedure Code on detention for debts to the State was also considered unconstitutional and abolished by Act 3842/2010 (*see supra* No. 386).

Detention may also be ordered as a means of compulsory enforcement of a debtor's property, for financial liabilities, in accordance with the Code of Civil Procedure (Articles 1047 et seq.). Among those liable to detention, according to the Code, are merchants or traders, who can be held for commercial liabilities. However, since the ratification of the International Covenant on Civil and Political Rights (Act 2462/1997) the scope of application of the aforementioned provisions has been limited, given that Article 11 of the Covenant (which takes precedence over national legislation) stipulates that no one shall be imprisoned solely for failure to meet a contractual liability.

Another example of deprivation of personal liberty is the incarceration of a patient, against his will, in a mental health unit. For a person to be subjected to involuntary treatment in a mental health unit the law requires a decision of the prosecutor with a Court of First Instance, that decision to be reached on the basis of expert opinions from at least two psychiatrists. Within three days the question must then be placed by the prosecutor to the three-member Court of First Instance, which shall meet within ten days to decide on whether the person shall remain in detention or be discharged immediately. There follows the process of non-contentious jurisdiction, in which the patient is invited to participate, and has the right to appear before the court with his lawyer and a psychiatrist as an expert advisor (Article 96 of Act 2071/1992).

Arrested persons have to be brought within twenty-four hours before the examining magistrate, who has to decide within a time limit of three days whether the detainee will be released or imprisoned pending trial (Article 6 paragraph 2 of the Constitution). Should either of these time limits elapse before action has been taken, any warden or other officer, civil or military servant, responsible for the detention of the arrested person must release him immediately. Violators shall be punished for illegal detention and shall be liable to restore any damage caused to the sufferer and to pay him damages for pain and suffering, as specified by law (Article 6 paragraph 3 of the Constitution). In case of detention pending trial, a warrant of imprisonment has to be issued, stating reasons which must be in accordance with those specified in the Code of Criminal Procedure (Article 282). Detention pending trial is permitted only for grave offences if it is absolutely necessary to prevent further crimes or escape. Pre-trial detention is an *ultimum remedium*, to be applied if other forms of restriction or control such as posting security or bail, requiring attendance at set intervals before certain authorities, prohibiting communication with certain persons, or electronically monitored house arrest, are reasonably considered inefficacious.

The maximum duration of detention pending trial is one year for felonies and six months for misdemeanours. This maximum duration may exceptionally be extended by six or three months respectively (Article 6 paragraph 4(a) and (b) of the Constitution). According to the Constitution, it is prohibited to exceed these maximum limits of detention pending trial, by successively applying this measure to separate acts of the same case (Article 6, paragraph 4(c), added in the Revision of 2001).

395. (d) Legislative definition of crime. Personal security is further protected by the principal of *nullum crimen nulla poena sine lege (praevia, certa, stricta, scripta)* in Article 7 paragraph 1(a) of the Constitution, according to which, 'There shall be no crime, nor shall punishment be inflicted unless specified by law in force prior to the perpetration of the act, defining the constitutive elements of the act.' In other words, for a punishment to be imposed, legislation must have provided for all the elements constituting the objective existence of a crime, the degree of culpability required to establish the existence of that crime, and the appropriate punishment. Laws establishing or increasing culpability may not have retroactive force (Article 7 paragraph 1(b) of the Constitution). On the basis of the same article, the penal laws may neither be interpreted *per analogiam* nor may they be interpreted extensively.

The concept of punishment comprehends the principal and secondary penalties in the Penal Code, but not security measures. Also, in accordance with the jurisprudence of the Greek courts, disciplinary and other administrative sanctions, such as tax penalties, are not comprehended in the constitutional concept of a punishment and thus provision for them in legislation may have retroactive force. Nevertheless, in the light of the principle of the State organized on the rule of law, it must be accepted that the prohibition of the retroactive force of laws should also apply in the field of disciplinary law and the law of administrative sanctions.

396. (e) The inviolability of the home and the protection of private life

(i) *The inviolability of the home.* According to the Constitution, every person's home is a sanctuary (Article 9 paragraph 1(a)). The concept of the home, as safeguarded in the Constitution, comprehends any enclosed space to which entrance is not permitted to anyone unless he has the consent of the person occupying that space (e.g., car, tent, and so on). The concept of the home also covers professional premises. The only spaces not covered by the concept are public areas to which anyone may have access. The protection of the inviolability of the home may be waived only in the case of a search carried out lawfully and in the presence of representatives of the Judicial Power (Article 9 paragraph 1(c)). A search is defined solely as investigative activity directed to the gathering of evidence in respect of the perpetration of criminal acts. However, given that the provision does not allow any distinction to be made in the conceptual scope of the term 'search', it must be allowed to cover any kind of search conducted by organs of the State, such as an investigation into tax matters. The Constitution provides that violators of the preceding provision shall be punished for violating the sanctuary of the home and for abuse of power, and shall be liable to the party suffering the abuse for full damages, as specified by law (Article 9 paragraph 2).

(ii) *Protection of private and family life.* The Constitution states (Article 9 paragraph 1 (b)) that the private and family life of the individual is inviolable. The phrase 'private life' is to be understood to mean an inviolable nucleus defined by each person for his own self, in which he alone is master. In other words, the protection extended lies in the prohibition on publication of information belonging to that nucleus, as would be involved in forcible cohabitation or co-residence, audio-visual surveillance (except where legally permitted) and so on. The inviolability of family life lies in the right of each individual to create a family and to conduct his family life without hindrance, as he sees fit.

Private and family life are closely associated with the freedom to develop one's personality, enshrined in Article 5 paragraph 1 of the Constitution. Specifically, Article 9 paragraph 1(b) complements the protection granted by Article 5 paragraph 1, covering information associated with the individual as regarded in his private, personal existence, not his role as an active member of society at large. The Council of State has ruled that from the conjunction of Articles 9 paragraph 1, and 2 paragraph 1 of the Constitution it follows that individuals' sexual lives too fall within the inviolable sphere of their private lives (Ruling 3545/2002).

(iii) *Protection of personal data*. The Constitution (Article 9A, as added in the Revision of 2001) also provides that [a]ll persons have the right to be protected from the collection, processing and use, especially by electronic means, of their personal data, as specified by law. Essentially this provision safeguards a more specific manifestation of the protection of private and family life.

Furthermore, in accordance with the EU Charter of Fundamental Rights, the processing of personal data must be provided for by law for specific, predetermined purposes, with the consent of the individual involved and only in exceptional cases without that consent. In all events, the person whose data are being recorded must retain the right of access to the data and the right to correct any inaccurate or erroneous data he may find (Article 8 paragraph 2).

On the Data Protection Authority envisaged in Article 9A of the Constitution, *see supra* Nos 215–216.

397. (f) Confidentiality of correspondence. According to the Constitution, secrecy of letters and all other forms of free correspondence or communication shall be absolutely inviolable (Article 19 paragraph 1). The right of confidentiality of correspondence is also guaranteed by Article 8 of the ECHR. These provisions safeguard the freedom of communication as a specific form of the right to disseminate opinions and also the confidentiality of intimate communication. The provisions cover not only those means of communication known at the time the Constitution was enacted but also any means of communication discovered in future (e.g., electronic). Any form of surveillance and recording of communications is regarded as a breach of confidentiality. The Penal Code (Articles 248–250) requires penalties for violation of confidentiality by postal, telegraph or telephone company employees, while Articles 370 and 370A of the Penal Code provide for punishment in the case of breach of the confidentiality of letters as well as telephone calls, and oral conversations respectively.

Restrictions on the freedom of communication and protection of confidentiality are only allowed in the conditions set out in Article 19 paragraph 1(b) of the Constitution. Specifically, the judicial authority shall not be bound by this secrecy for reasons of national security or for the purpose of investigating especially serious crimes, under guarantees, which shall be specified by law. The provision entails that the relevant law will need to set out criteria on the basis of which the judicial authority may grant an order overriding the principle of confidentiality of communication. In no circumstances may the principle be overridden unless there are reasons for national security or the need to ascertain the perpetration of an offence. The relevant procedures, as well as the organizational and technical guarantees, are set out in detail in the Presidential Decree 47/2005, issued as authorized by Article 9 of Act 3115/2003, 'Hellenic Authority for Communication Security and Privacy'. Directive 2002/58/EC, as amended by Directive 2009/136/EC, is also of relevance.

For more details on the Hellenic Authority for Communication Security and Privacy, provided for in Article 19 paragraph 2 of the Constitution, *see supra* Nos 219–220.

398. (g) Prohibition on the use of illegally obtained evidence. The Constitution states that use of evidence acquired in violation of the present article and of Articles 9 and 9A is prohibited (Article 19 paragraph 3, added in the Revision of 2001). The teleological interpretation of the provision leads to the conclusion that there is a prohibition on the use of evidence acquired in contravention of other constitutional provisions, such as the provisions banning torture (Article 7 paragraph 2). The constitutional provision is laid down in absolute terms without any reservation. In the case law, the prohibition may be waived in view of the need to protect human dignity (Article 2 paragraph 1 of the Constitution) and human life (Article 5 paragraph 2 of the Constitution), subject always to the principle of proportionality (Supreme Civil and Criminal Court 42/2004). Article 177 paragraph 2 of the Code of Criminal Procedure states that evidence shall not be admitted if it has been acquired directly by criminal act or indirectly through the commission of criminal acts.

§4. Intellectual Freedoms

I. Freedom of Expression, Press, Radio, and Television

399. (a) Freedom of expression. According to Article 14 paragraph 1, 'Every person may express and propagate his thoughts orally, in writing and through the press in compliance with the laws of the State.' This provision guarantees the civil right to freedom of knowledge and intellectual movement while providing statutory safeguards for free and pluralistic forming of public opinion. The list of means of expression in the Article is indicative only. Constitutionally acceptable curbs on the freedom of expression are provided for in the Penal Code for punishment of offences against honour (Articles 361 et seq.) Article 29 paragraph 3(a) of the Constitution establishes special restrictions on the right of expression for judicial functionaries, military personnel and those serving in the security services. Also, demonstrations or expressions of opinion for or against political parties are not allowed by civil servants in the discharge of their duties but are permissible when they are not engaged in official duties (Article 29 paragraph 3 b of the Constitution, as revised in 2001).

400. (b) The press. The press is free (Article 14 paragraph 2 a of the Constitution). Freedom of the press includes freedom of printing and producing, freedom of publishing as well as freedom of distribution. The provision also covers the freedom to collect information (subject always to other constitutionally safeguarded rights, such as the inviolability of private life, the protection of personal data, etc.), the freedom to staff newspapers, and the freedom of the journalist in dealings with his publisher (internal freedom of the press).

Censorship and all other preventive measures, such as prior permission by administrative authorities, heavy taxation on paper, and limitations on the circulation of the press are forbidden (Article 14 paragraph 2 b of the Constitution). Exceptionally, Article 14 paragraph 3 of the Constitution permits the seizure of printed matter after circulation by order of the public prosecutor in case of offences against a religion and against the Head of State as well as in cases of disclosure of secret information on the armed forces, of attempts at the violent overthrow of the democratic form of government or against the territorial integrity of the State and finally in case of obscene publications obviously offensive to public decency.

The Revision of 2001 amended paragraph 5 of Article 14 to read:

> Every person offended by an inaccurate publication or broadcast has the right to reply, and the information medium has a corresponding obligation for full and immediate redress. Every person offended by an insulting or defamatory publication or broadcast has also the right to reply, and the information medium has a corresponding obligation to immediately publish or transmit the reply. The manner in which the right to reply is exercised and in which full and immediate redress is assured or publication and transmission of the reply is made, shall be specified by law.

Relevant measures had already been included in domestic legislation (Emergency Act 1092/1938 and Act 1178/1981).

In 2001, in an attempt to divorce political power from the influence of economic interests, a new paragraph 9, was added to Article 14 of the Constitution:

> the ownership status, the financial situation and the means of financing of information media must be made known as specified by law. The measures and restrictions necessary for fully ensuring transparency and plurality in information shall be specified by law. The concentration of the control of more than one information media of the same type or of different types is prohibited. More specifically, concentration of more than one electronic information media of the same type is prohibited, as specified by law. The capacity of owner, partner, major shareholder or managing director of an information media enterprise, is incompatible with the capacity of owner, partner, major shareholder or managing director of an enterprise that undertakes towards the public administration or towards a legal entity of the wider public sector to perform works or to supply goods or services. The prohibition of the previous section extends also over all types of intermediary persons, such as spouses, relatives, financially dependent persons or companies. The specific regulations, the sanctions,

> which may extend to the point of revocation of the license of a radio or television station and to the point of prohibition of the conclusion or to the annulment of the pertinent contract, as well as the means of control and the guarantees for the prevention of infringements of the previous sections, shall be determined by law.

Relevant measures had already been included in Act 2328/1995, the provisions of which had been regarded, even before the enactment of Article 14 paragraph 9 of the Constitution, as a justifiable curb on business activity (Council of State 1882/2003).

The constitutionality of various provisions of Executive Act 3021/2002 implementing Article 14 paragraph 9 was fiercely challenged. There were also questions as to whether they were consistent with European law and in particular with Article 24 of Directive 93/37/EEC. The new government of 2004 attempted to introduce an even stricter legislative framework against improper involvement of political and financial interests, in the form of Act 3310/2005. The reaction of the European Commission, on the grounds of conflicts between this law and European law, led to its suspension and eventual modification by the less stringent Act 3414/2005.

Following a reference for a preliminary ruling from the Council of State (Ruling 3670/2006, Full Bench) the European Court of Justice ruled:

> community law must be interpreted as precluding a national provision which, whilst pursuing the legitimate objectives of equal treatment of tenderers and of transparency in procedures for the award of public contracts, establishes an irrebuttable presumption that the status of owner, partner, main shareholder or management executive of an undertaking active in the media sector is incompatible with that of owner, partner, main shareholder or management executive of an undertaking which contracts with the State or a legal person in the public sector in the broad sense to perform a works, supply or services contract. (Case C-213/2007, Judgment of 16 December 2008, ECR 2008 page I-09999)

Thus the CJEU took no position on the compatibility of Article 14 paragraph 9 of the Constitution with European law.

Following this decision, the Full Bench of the Council of State in its Ruling 3470/2011 ruled that in accordance with Article 14 paragraph 9 of the Constitution, constitutional incompatibility can lead to the prohibition of the conclusion of a public contract only if the person involved acted illegally or unfairly during the procedure of concluding the public contract, aiming to achieve its conclusion. It also ruled that the related provisions of Act 3021/2002 were unconstitutional.

Extreme restrictions on the freedom of the press are provided for in paragraph 6 of Article 14 of the Constitution, according to which:

> After at least three convictions within five years for the criminal acts defined under paragraph 3, the court shall order the definitive ban or the temporary suspension of the publication of the paper and, in severe cases, shall prohibit the

> convicted person from practising the profession of journalist as specified by law. The ban or suspension of publication shall be effective as of the date the court order becomes irrevocable.

In practice, however, the provision in question has never been implemented.

Protective provisions for the press are not applicable to films, sound recordings, radio, television or any other similar media for the transmission of speech or images (Article 15 paragraph 1 of the Constitution). The exception of these media from the special protection granted to the press entails mainly that preventive measures are not prohibited.

401. (c) Radio and television. As far as radio and television are concerned, the Constitution in Article 15 paragraph 2 provides:

> Radio and television shall be under the direct control of the State. The control and imposition of administrative sanctions belong to the exclusive competence of the National Radio and Television Council, which is an independent authority, as specified by law. The direct control of the State, which may also assume the form of a prior permission status, shall aim at the objective and on equal terms transmission of information and news reports, as well as of works of literature and art, at ensuring the quality level of programmes mandated by the social mission of radio and television and by the cultural development of the Country, as well as at respect of the value of the human being and the protection of childhood and youth.

On the National Radio and Television Council provided for in this article, *see supra* Nos 217–218.

Article 15 paragraph 2 of the Constitution does not guarantee an individual's right to set up a radio or television station. The role of the State as envisaged in the Constitution is not only confined to the oversight of radio and television stations but also includes the requirement that a licence be granted before a station can be set up and operated, in accordance with the procedures laid down by the legislator. This requirement that a licence be granted is a result of the physical limit on the number of available frequencies in combination with the need to ensure freedom of expression. However, the State's direct control over radio and television does not entail the establishment of a State monopoly (Council of State, Ruling 5040/1987, Full Bench: the Constitution neither requires nor forbids a State monopoly). The previously existing monopoly was brought to an end in 1987 for radio (Act 1730/1987) and in 1989 for television (Act 1866/1989).

Radio and television stations are obliged to broadcast, without charge, the proceedings of Parliament, and to carry party-political broadcasts at election time (Article 15 paragraph 2(d) of the Constitution).

II. Freedom of Art, Science and Education

402. Under Article 16 paragraph 1(a) of the Constitution art and science, research and teaching are free, and their development and promotion is an obligation of the State. The three freedoms are guaranteed without reservation, and without insertion of the clause 'in compliance with the laws of the State', as is the case in Article 14 paragraph 1 of the Constitution.

403. (a) Academic freedom and freedom of teaching. Academic freedom and freedom of teaching are both guaranteed, on condition of a duty of obedience to the Constitution (Article 16 paragraph 1(b)). Of course, university teachers are allowed the freedom to question the rightness of constitutional provisions. University teachers are described by the Constitution as public functionaries (whereas the previous Constitution of 1952 described them as civil servants) and are extended the same personal and functional independence as that enjoyed by judicial functionaries (Article 16 paragraph 6).

404. (b) The constitutional framework of education. According to the Constitution, 'Education constitutes a basic mission for the State and shall aim at the moral, intellectual, professional and physical training of Greeks, the development of national and religious consciousness and at their formation as free and responsible citizens.' (Article 16 paragraph 2). It has been ruled that the reference to the 'State' here implies the central state authority; it thus excludes the possibility of, for example, local government agencies assuming competences in the education sector, such as the establishment of disciplinary councils for functionaries in public education (Council of State 2479/2000). However, since the Revision of 2001, the final clause of Article 102 paragraph 1 of the Constitution now provides for the possibility of assigning to local government agencies, by law, the exercise of competences which form part of the mission of the State.

On issues arising from the constitutional recognition of the development of religious conscience as a purpose of education, in relation to religious freedom, *see infra* No. 461.

Compulsory education has a minimum duration of nine years (Article 16 paragraph 3 of the Constitution). This provision makes no distinction between Greeks and aliens, who, even if resident illegally in Greece, are not only entitled but obliged to ensure that their offsprings attend a minimum of nine years of schooling.

Education on all levels is free of charge (Article 16 paragraph 4(a)). Nevertheless, the Council of State has ruled that the imposition of tuition on post-graduate students is constitutional (Rulings 2714/2010 and 2411/2012 Full Bench). The State shall provide financial assistance to those who distinguish themselves, as well as to students in need of assistance or special protection, in accordance with their abilities (Article 16 paragraph 4(b)). This provision guarantees the social right to education, the longest-standing right in Greek constitutional law, first enshrined in the Constitution of 1864.

405. (c) Private schools. Private schools may be established, but they operate under the supervision of the State. The Constitution provides that the conditions and terms for granting a licence for the establishment and operation of schools not owned by the State shall be specified by law (Article 16 paragraph 8). Private education is not regarded by the constitutional legislator as an ordinary business activity but must serve the objective set out in Article 16 of the Constitution.

406. (d) Universities. According to the Constitution (Article 16 paragraph 5), education at a university level shall be provided exclusively by institutions which are fully self-governed public law legal persons. The requirement laid down by the constitutional legislator that universities be public law legal persons makes it impossible to found a private university. Moreover, Article 16 paragraph 8b states that the establishment of university-level institutions by private persons is prohibited. As the reader will be aware, education is in principle excluded from the provisions of European law (Article 165 Treaty on the Functioning of the European Union (TFEU) [ex Article 149 of the European Community Treaty]: the EU fully respects the competence of Member States in respect of the content of the teaching in and the organization of their own educational systems). However, questions of consistency with Directive 89/48/EEC on mutual recognition of the degrees of Member States in respect of the exercise of professions were raised by Greece's refusal to recognize, through the competent organization invoking the above constitutional provision, the academic equivalence of degrees from foreign universities to acquire which students were taught part of the university course in Greece, within the private facilities of foreign universities in Greece, or within private schools operating in Greece as liberal studies colleges. These degrees were eventually awarded to the students abroad taking into account the credits they had earned from the courses taken in Greece. In order for the competent agency to recognize academic equivalence, without which the graduates in question could not register to practice with the various professional bodies, the graduates had to undergo examination in those subject areas which they were taught in Greece. The Council of State has ruled (Ruling 3457/1998, Full Bench) that the time spent in studies in a department or annex of a foreign university operating in Greece in the guise of a private school or liberal studies college cannot be recognized as equivalent to time spent in a domestic university, on the grounds that to permit such recognition would violate the constitutional prohibition on private universities in Greece. The case also raised the question of conflict between European and Greek constitutional law; however, the Council of State declined to examine this issue.

The European Court of Justice ruled that the non-recognition by Greece of degrees awarded by foreign universities following courses in Greece at Greek liberal studies centres or colleges, on the basis of licensing arrangements, breached EU law regarding the mutual recognition of the degrees of Member States in respect of the exercise of professions (C-274/05, Commission/Greece, Judgment of 23 October 2008). The Council of State has not yet changed its position on this issue from the perspective of academic equivalence (Rulings 1698/2013, 856/2011, 570–574/2010, 2550/2009).

Acts 3696/2008, 3845/2010 (the so-called first memorandum, *see infra* Nos 512 et seq.) and the Presidential Decree 38/2010, which transferred Directive 2005/36/EC concerning the recognition of professional qualifications, into Greek law, have made it possible to take into account the time spent in studies in private 'colleges' in Greece, created by virtue of the pertinent legislation, for the recognition of professional qualifications of the degree holders. Their adoption has resulted in legislative compliance by Greece with the case law of the European Court of Justice. Unfortunately, in practice, the system of recognition has not functioned effectively. Therefore, numerous petitions are still pending before the competent Greek authority.

Apart from the public nature of the universities, the Constitution also guarantees their 'full self-administration' (Article 16 paragraph 5(a)). This power of self-administration is a statutory guarantee intended to promote the development of science and the advancement of education. It consists of the ability of the universities to manage their own affairs with full administrative and economic independence, within the general framework set out by the law. Specifically, they recruit their own teaching staff and administrative bodies and draw up their own curricula. The constitutional guarantee of self-administration from time to time gives rise to questions on the constitutionality of certain measures. For example, Article 42 paragraph 4 of Act 4186/2013 provides that the number of students admitted to university departments each year shall be set by Ministerial Decision, with the number set usually being much higher than that proposed by the universities themselves, thereby creating operational problems. However, the Council of State has so far been of the view that no such problem is created. Another question of contravention of the principle of self-administration was raised by Article 24 of Act 3549/2007, provided that one-third of the members of the electoral body for the election and promotion of members of teaching and research staff had to be members of the teaching and research staff of other universities, even if the number required by the legislation could be supplemented by experts serving at the university in question. The Council of State ruled (Ruling 32/2009) that this requirement was constitutional. Tending in the same direction, Article 19 of Act 4009/2011, which has succeeded Article 24 of Act 3549/2007, sets a similar requirement.

The self-administration of the universities is restricted in that they are subject to State supervision in the form of scrutiny of the legality of the actions of the university authorities by the Minister for Education, Research and Religious Affairs (Article 16 paragraph 5 b of the Constitution and Article 1 of Act 4009/2011).

Until Act 4009/2011 the main piece of legislation regulating the working of the universities was Act 1268/1982, which was amended and enlarged by dozens of other laws. It provided for the founding of universities, their administration and operation, as well as the recruitment and status of teaching, research and administrative staff, the students and their associations. Under this Act the universities were not to be regarded purely as foundations, as the Constitution provides, but as a combination of foundation and association. The Council of State (Ruling 2786/1984) accepted the constitutionality of Act 1268/1982, ruling that the equal participation of each separate group (main and ancillary teaching staff, student representatives) in the collective bodies of the universities reflects current trends in the evolution of the university composed of different groups.

Act 4009/2011 has replaced all previous legislation and provided for a completely new scheme of administrative organization of the universities. Among other things, it has introduced a council of administration of the university, composed of professors elected by their colleagues and by external members appointed by the elected members (Article 8 of Act 4009/2011). Act 4009/2011 has never been fully implemented, mainly because of the strong reaction from university communities. Moreover, since the change of Governmental in January 2015, a number of acts have been adopted (e.g., Act 4350/2015, Act 4386/2016) amending Act 4009/2011 and aiming to resuscitate the abolished provisions of Act 1268/1982. The recent amendments have targeted, among other things, the institution of the council of administration of the university, the role of which has been significantly diminished. Nevertheless, the Full Bench of the Council of State has ruled that the original provisions of Act 4009/2011, in particular those concerning the council of administration of the university, were constitutional (Rulings 519/2015 and 520/2015).

407. (e) Vocational education. Article 16 paragraph 7 and paragraph 8 of the Constitution reads, 'Professional and any other form of special education shall be provided by the State, through schools of a higher level and for a time period not exceeding three years, as specifically provided by law, which also defines the professional rights of the graduates of such schools. The conditions and terms for granting a license for the establishment and operation of schools not owned by the State, the supervision of such and the professional status of teaching personnel therein shall be specified by law.' A question has arisen as to which schools fall within the scope of this provision regarding vocational education, given that in 2001 the existing Technological Educational Institutes or technical colleges were granted full university status (Act 2916/2001). The Council of State has ruled that this conversion did not violate the constitutionally safeguarded distinction between the 'highest' (university) and 'higher' (vocational) education (Council of State 1291/2003).

408. (f) The social right to engage in sporting activities. The Constitution establishes a right to engage in sporting activity, as a social right (Article 16 paragraph 9). There is an earlier reference to sports in paragraph 2 of Article 16, which includes physical education among the objectives of the educational system. Thus paragraph 9 must be understood as referring primarily to sports outside the school. Sport is placed under the protection, and ultimate supervision, of the State. The Constitution provides for the State to make grants to and control sporting associations. This control consists, for example, of the requirement to submit the budgets of athletic federations to the General Secretariat for Sports so that the way in which the State grants are being used can be scrutinized (Article 51 of Act 2725/1999).

III. Religious Freedom

409. The question of religious freedom is examined in the chapter on the relationship between church and State (*see infra* Nos 448 et seq.).

§5. Procedural Rights

410. The Constitution also guarantees certain rights of a procedural nature, necessary to protect other rights enshrined in the Constitution and to exercise control over state and – mainly – administrative action. The most important of these rights are the right to judicial protection (Article 20 paragraph 1), the right not to be deprived of the judge assigned to one (Article 8), the right to petition authorities and to have access to administrative documents (Article 10), and the right to a prior hearing (Article 20 paragraph 2).

I. The Right to Judicial Protection

411. The Constitution safeguards the right to receive judicial protection. Specifically, under Article 20 paragraph 1 of the Constitution, 'Every person shall be entitled to receive legal protection by the courts and may plead before them his views concerning his rights or interests, as specified by law'. The right of access to independent and impartial courts forms part of the fundamental principle of the '*état de droit*'. Without the safeguard of this right, the protection of all rights and freedoms would only be a paper declaration.

This right involves three forms of judicial protection: (i) the requirement that a decision be issued on the substance of the matter, that there be a genuine judicial examination of the facts of the case; (ii) the requirement that judicial decisions or other entitlements be actually enforced; and (iii) the requirement that effective provisional measures be taken until the legal remedy being used has been resolved. It follows from paragraph 1 of Article 20 of the Constitution that the legislator may not exclude or substantively limit any of the three forms of judicial protection. Moreover, this right guarantees the organization of an efficient, full and effective system for administering justice.

With the exception of the '*actes de gouvernement*', there are no other categories of administrative acts, private disputes or criminal cases which cannot be brought before a competent court. '*Actes de gouvernement*' are defined as those acts which have the external characteristics of an administrative act but cannot be challenged by an application for annulment before the administrative law courts. According to the law, governmental acts and orders, derived from the management of political power, are not subject to applications for annulment (Article 45 paragraph 5 of the Presidential Decree 18/1989). However, both the nature and the precise content of this 'government function' have been questioned in theory. The fact is that those acts recognized as 'governmental' by the Council of State are very few in number. They comprise certain acts on the dividing line between political and administrative functions, including, according to the case law of the Council of State, measures concerning the country's international relations (Council of State 352/1938, 885/1946), relations between the Legislative and Executive Branches (Council of State 484/1978, 1116/1997), declaration of a general mobilization, and the granting of pardons. But even in the case of '*actes de gouvernement*' the individual is not deprived of judicial protection, since he has the right to claim, even in the courts, compensation for loss or damage caused by any illegal '*actes de gouvernement*'.

II. The Right Not to Be Deprived of the Assigned Judge

412. According to the Constitution, 'No person shall be deprived of the judge assigned to him by law against his will. Judicial committees or extraordinary courts, under any name whatsoever, shall not be constituted.' (Article 8) By 'extraordinary courts' Article 8 means courts (mainly criminal) established *ex post*; and by 'judicial committees' it also means courts established *ex post* which are not only composed of judges enjoying functional independence but of other persons as well.

In consequence, the appointment of the judges to hear a particular class of cases must be provided for in a general, abstract law, with no place for individual laws for specific circumstances. Changes may be made by the legislator to the competence of the courts, on condition that they are justified and pertain to a particular category of cases. The reference to a judge shall also apply to the process of arbitration. However, in the case of administrative disputes (including disputes over taxation), the arbitral tribunals may issue rulings on the legality of administrative acts which will be binding on the administrative law courts but may not nullify those acts, given that the Constitution reserves this power exclusively for the State administrative courts (Special Highest Court 24/1993).

III. Right to Petition the Authorities and Rights of Access to Administrative Documents

413. According to Article 10 paragraph 1 of the Constitution and Articles 3 and 4 of the Administrative Process Code, each person acting on his own or in conjunction with others has the right to petition public authorities in writing. Authorities are obliged to take prompt action and give a reasoned written reply. Such a petition consists of any document reproaching a public authority for actions or omissions and seeking the making good of material or moral damage. The right of petition entails an obligation on the administrative authorities to take all necessary action to satisfy lawful petitions and to provide a reasoned response to the petitions submitted. Petitions containing a request for the revocation, modification or annulment of administrative acts are known as administrative recourses (for more detail, *see supra* Nos 289–292).

Prosecution of the petitioner for punishable acts contained in the petition is only permitted after the final decision of the authority approached has been served on the petitioner and on the condition that the authority has permitted the prosecution (Article 10 paragraph 2 of the Constitution).

The Constitution requires the competent authority to respond to requests for information or documents – especially certification, supporting documentation and official affirmations – within a specific period of time no greater than sixty days, as prescribed by law. In the event of this period elapsing without action by the authorities, or in the event of their unlawful refusal to comply with the request, a special financial compensation shall be paid to the petitioner, in addition to any other sanctions or legal consequences, as prescribed by law (Article 10 paragraph 3, as in force since the Revision of 2001). In other words, the Constitution guarantees a general right of the person to receive information from the administration, and the right of interested parties to have cognizance of documents related to their case. This right of access to administrative documents is further defined in the Administrative Process Code (Article 5), which, in this respect, represents in essence a codification of previous case law of the Council of State. Specifically, it obliges the administration to concede to demands by the interested party to be granted access, on written application, to administrative documents. It is not necessary that the applicant have any legal interest in order to exercise this right. However, the applicant must demonstrate special legal interest in cases where he seeks access to private documents kept in public departments (Article 5 paragraph 2 of the Administrative Process Code).

The authorities may refuse to produce documents only in cases where they concern the private or family life of a third party or compromise confidentiality provided for in special provisions (such as confidentiality of medical, banking or tax records) or in cases where granting access to the documents would contravene the provisions of the law on personal data. The administration may also decline to meet the request by an interested party in cases where granting this right would substantially impede the inquiries of the judicial, police, military or administrative authorities into the commission of a crime or an administrative offence, as well as where the documents concern the sittings of Cabinet (Article 5 paragraph 3 of the Administrative Process Code). The legislative provisions regarding the right of access to administrative documents have been codified by the Presidential Decree 28/2015. These restrictions on the right of access to documents should be interpreted narrowly.

The refusal by the administration of the person's request for information or access to administrative documents is an executive, administrative, act and may be challenged by an application for annulment before the Council of State.

IV. Right to Prior Hearing

414. The Constitution also guarantees the right to a prior hearing against any unfavourable administrative action or measure (Article 20 paragraph 2). The obligation of the administration to grant the interested party a prior hearing is more narrowly defined in the Administrative Process Code (Article 6), which, in this respect, is, in essence, a codification of previous case law of the Council of State. The right to prior hearing is a specific manifestation of the principle of a State based on the rule of law and is directly related to the right to legal protection, so that failure to grant a prior hearing may be examined ex officio by the court and lead to nullification of the act by reason of contravention of a substantive element of the formal procedure (procedural *ultra vires*). It comprehends the right of the person to explain his views before the administrative authority in advance of any individual administrative act likely unfavourable to his interests, before the taking of any measure or action against him, and the right to be called to present his case, with corresponding obligations on the part of the administration.

The right to a prior hearing is guaranteed, in accordance with the case law of the Council of State, for individual administrative acts which are issued ex officio by the administrative organ in the exercise of its discretion, and are related to the subjective conduct of the individual affected by those acts. In other words, the right does not apply to those acts issued following application by the interested party or on the basis of a mandatory competence of the administrative organ or those issued under the discretionary powers of the organ but resting on objective facts. Nor does it comprehend regulatory acts (established case law; *see e.g.*, Council of State 2040/1977 (Full Bench), 259/1993, 588/2003).

The Constitution supports the provision of the Administrative Process Code (Article 6 paragraph 3) in respect of the possibility of omitting, in exceptional circumstances, the prior hearing of the interested party, provided that the immediate taking of the measure in question is essential to avoid some danger or serve some urgent public interest. But in these circumstances too, the interested party must be heard within fifteen days; failure to hold such a hearing will mean the *ipso jure* suspension of the measure in question.

§6. Right of Collective Action

I. Freedom of Assembly

415. Freedom of assembly is guaranteed in Article 11 paragraph 1 of the Constitution. 'Greeks shall have the right to assemble peaceably and unarmed.' The right of assembly is one of the earliest of all rights of collective action. It was enshrined in the Constitution as early as 1864. Assembly presupposes prior communication, an organization and a common purpose.

The right of assembly comprehends the freedom to appoint the place, time and content of the demonstration, without any requirement of prior permission. No one may be compelled to take part in an assembly against his will. Article 11 of the ECHR, according to which the real and effective freedom to assemble involves an obligation on the State to take the appropriate positive measures to protect the assembled crowd from violent action on the part of those with different views, provides further support for the right of assembly.

The constitutional protection does not extend to all assemblies, only those which are peaceful and unarmed. A peaceful assembly is to be understood as one in which the participants do not indulge in acts of violence against persons or property. An assembly may still be deemed peaceful even if there are acts of violence by isolated individuals or even a small group among the participants, or even if third parties should commit acts of violence against the assembled crowd.

Private and public assemblies in enclosed spaces are free and are protected by the right to privacy.

Public open-air assemblies are subject to restrictions. Under Article 11 paragraph 2 of the Constitution, the police may be present at open-air public assemblies. In all cases, the police presence must respect the restrictions on limitations to civil rights, namely the principle of proportionality and the central core of the right to assembly. Such assemblies may be preventively prohibited by a reasoned decision of the police authority. The decision to ban the assembly may be taken before or during the event and must be adequately justified, with reference to the specific circumstances of each occasion. The Constitution restricts the possibility of prohibition to cases of an imminent serious threat to public security or of a threat of serious disturbance of social and economic life. In the first case, open-air assemblies may be prohibited throughout the country and in the second case only in a particular area. Legislative Decree 794/1971 'On Public Assemblies', which came into force during the last military dictatorship, is still valid. Several provisions thereof have, however, been declared unconstitutional by the courts.

II. Freedom of Association

416. According to the Constitution, 'Greeks shall have the right to form non-profit associations and unions, in compliance with the law, which however may never subject the exercise of this right to prior permission.' (Article 12 paragraph 1). The right of association comprehends the freedom to set up an association, the freedom to choose the form it shall take, the freedom to maintain the association and its freedom of self-administration. Inseparably associated with the freedom to set up an association is the freedom to determine its character and, specifically, its composition, objectives and statutes. Members of the armed forces are not excluded from the right of association (Full Bench of the Supreme Civil and Criminal Court 3/2012).

The Constitution states explicitly that the establishment of an association shall not be subject to a requirement of prior permission, either judicial or administrative. The court's decision, which according to the Civil Code (Articles 78 et seq.) accepts the statutes of the association, is not a permission since it is confined only to a control of legality. This review of legality has led courts to refuse to admit the formation of royalist associations since it has been held that they are contrary to the basic constitutional provisions on the presidential parliamentary democracy. It must, however, be noted that royalist political parties are considered lawful.

One consequence of the freedom of association is the prohibition on compulsory establishment of such associations by the State or compulsion by the State to participate in such associations. Consequently, the enjoyment of certain privileges may not be made dependent on participation in associations of a certain type, or in a specific association, while it is unconstitutional to place economic burdens on a certain category of persons on account of associations which they represent.

Dissolution of associations is only permitted by court judgment for violation of the law or of substantial provisions of their statutes (Article 12 paragraph 2 of the Constitution). A question has been raised as to the constitutionality of the relevant provisions of the Civil Code (Article 105), insofar as they provide, as reasons to dissolve an association, the attainment of the objective of the association or the incompatibility of the purpose or workings of the association with morality or public order, given that on the one hand the constitutional provisions do not cover such reasons for dissolution, and on the other hand, these reasons are extremely vague and general in content. The Full Bench of the Supreme Civil and Criminal Court has, however, ruled that the provisions are constitutional (4/2005). In any event, a dissolution must be the only expedient and, above all, a necessary means to prevent offence to morality or public order and must be ordered by the ruling of a court. An association may not, therefore, be dissolved by administrative act or by law. Consequently, no measure may be taken equivalent in its effect to the dissolution of the organization, such as the compulsory merger of one association with another.

The Constitution also makes reference to cooperatives, private law legal persons not merely economic in character, but also profit-making and socio-cultural (Article 12 paragraph 4). Specifically, the Constitution enshrines the civil right of self-administration of cooperatives, under the supervision of the State, and as a social right, the obligation of the latter being to protect cooperatives and foster their development. The interest shown by the constitutional legislator in making more specific provisions for these cooperatives is linked to the fact that the cooperative economy lies in an intermediate sphere between the private and public economy. More specific regulations are contained in Act 4386/2016 on agricultural cooperatives and Act 1667/1986 on urban cooperatives.

An exception to the freedom of association is provided for in Article 12 paragraph 5 of the Constitution with respect to compulsory cooperatives: they may be established by law in order to serve purposes of common benefit or public interest or common exploitation of farming areas or other wealth-producing sources, on the condition that equal treatment of all participants is assured. Compulsory cooperatives have been established by several laws (e.g., Act 818/1971 'Compulsory Cooperative of Kozani Crocus Producers'). The organization of certain professions in associations having the status of public legal persons (e.g., Bar Associations or Medical Associations) is also based on Article 12 paragraph 5 of the Constitution.

Specific forms of the right of association are the rights to set up and participate in trade unions and political parties. These particular forms of the right of association are regulated by other provisions of the Constitution (Articles 23 and 29 respectively).

III. Freedom to Unionize

417. The Constitution assigns an obligation to the State to safeguard the freedom of trade unions and the unhindered exercise of related rights, that is – above all – the right to collective autonomy (Article 22 paragraph 2) and the right to strike (Article 23 paragraph 2). Trade union freedom comprehends the freedom to set up a trade union, from which the principle of plurality of unions is derived, along with their right to equal treatment. This equality is to be understood as proportional, on the basis of the degree of representation of each union. The constitutional provisions also protect negative union freedom, namely the freedom not to join a union, and the freedom to leave a union (Article 23 paragraph 1).

The principle of freedom to unionize also comprehends their internal autonomy, on which, however, legitimate restrictions may be placed in order to ensure their democratic structure and workings. This issue is related also to the provision of increased protection to trade union officials against the threat of dismissal by their employers.

The notion of freedom to unionize also comprehends the right of individuals and unions to pursue and defend their industrial and professional interests through various activities – chief among them – collective negotiations and strikes.

418. Article 22 paragraph 2 of the Constitution provides: 'General working conditions shall be determined by law, supplemented by collective labour agreements concluded through free negotiations and, in case of the failure of such, by rules determined by arbitration.' Collective labour agreements comprise both contractual and regulatory elements. In their regulatory aspect, the agreements have, in essence, the force of law and are, therefore, taken into account ex officio by the courts and are binding, on certain conditions, on third parties entering into contracts. Despite the grammatical phrasing of the constitutional provision, certain legal scholars have claimed that collective autonomy, and not the law, is the main factor regulating labour relations. However, the case law of the Council of State and Supreme Civil and Criminal Court has conceded substantial regulatory scope to the ordinary legislator, thereby limiting the significance of the institution.

419. The right to strike for the protection and promotion of financial and other labour interests of working people is also guaranteed in the Constitution (Article 23 paragraph 2) and in its executing Act 1264/1982 'On Syndicalism and on the Protection of Related Rights and Freedoms', which has later been amended. A strike declared by a trade union is deemed lawful until such time as it is recognized as unlawful by a court; until that time, it is regarded as legal in respect of its impact on the individual labour relations of the strikers. However, the Supreme Civil and Criminal Court has accepted that the time during which an employee refrains from working, as part of a strike which is definitively ruled illegal or improper, shall be regarded as a period of non-employment, even that period before the issuing of the court's decision (Full Bench of Supreme Civil and Criminal Court Ruling 27/2004).

The most serious issue raised in relation to the guaranteeing of the right to strike is not so much the provision by the law of procedural conditions as the reviewing by the courts of the abuse of the right by trade unions. In practice, case law has contracted the right to strike, often declaring strikes to be unlawful or improper, on the basis of Article 281 of the Civil Code, which prohibits flagrant breaches of good faith or good usages, or abuse of the proper social and economic purpose of the right to strike. One might expect that the courts would confine themselves to examining the question of whether the strike is intended to serve the constitutional objectives set out in Article 23 paragraph 2 of the Constitution, namely the protection and promotion of the financial and the general labour interests of working people. It has thus been ruled (Thessaloniki Court of Appeal 2806/1999) that a strike is an abuse of workers' rights when the demands of the workers are illegal or contravene the rules of public order; nevertheless, a strike organized in pursuit of a reform of the current labour legislation ought, in principle, to be deemed legitimate. It has also been ruled that a strike is abusive when the demands of the strikers are clearly disproportionate to the damage caused to the employer or to society as a whole (thus the ruling of the Athens Court of Appeal 8571/1998); nevertheless, such a disproportion will not necessarily mean that the strike in question did not serve the interests of the workers.

Judges and members of the security corps do not enjoy the right to strike, though members of the armed forces are remarkably not mentioned in the relevant constitutional exception. Even a work stoppage of a few hours by judges has been ruled to be a prohibited strike. The right to strike of civil servants, of employees of public law legal persons and local government agencies, and of the staff of enterprises of a public character or of enterprises of public benefit, the operation of which is of vital importance in serving the basic needs of the society as a whole, may be restricted more than the right of employees of the private sector (Article 23 paragraph 2(c) of the Constitution). In implementation of this constitutional reservation, Act 1264/1982 (Article 21) lays the obligation on unions declaring a strike to make available a minimum number of staff for safety reasons, and also additional staff to meet the basic needs of the community. It also requires that longer notice of a strike be given to the employer (Article 20 paragraph 2 of Act 1264/1982).

§7. Economic Freedom

420. According to Article 5 paragraph 1: 'All persons shall have the right to develop freely their personality and to participate in the social, economic and political life of the country, insofar as they do not infringe the rights of others or violate the Constitution and the good usages.' These provisions extend constitutional protection to economic freedom. The conceptual core of the right to participate in the economic life of the country comprehends the right to free development of business activity, as well as the right to choose one's own profession and more generally the right to work. Both the first and second of these more specific manifestations of the right of economic freedom are developed in the context framed by the freedom of contracts, a necessary precondition of which is the civil right to private property.

I. Freedom of Contracts

421. The freedom of contracts, which is directly derived from the autonomy of personal will, is also enshrined in Article 5 paragraph 1 of the Constitution, as a manifestation of the right to develop one's personality (Supreme Civil and Criminal Court 717/1985, 167/1998). It comprehends the freedom to engage or not engage in a contract, the freedom to select the other party to the contract and the freedom to determine the content of the contract (*see* Article 361 of the Civil Code). It is, however, permissible for the law to restrict this right in order to safeguard other rights and for reasons of public interest. Thus the Council of State has accepted that legislative imposition of certain terms of employment for guides working with travel agencies or drivers of private trucks is not contrary to the freedom of contracts as a manifestation of economic freedom (Council of State 1014/1999 and 1473/1991). The Supreme Civil and Criminal Court has also deemed constitutional the compulsory extension of leases on quarries drawn up at the parties' free will, insofar as such an extension is required for reasons of public interest, provided that a fair balance is secured between the requirements of the public and private interest through adjustment of the rent to be paid (Full Bench of Supreme Civil and Criminal Court 26/2003).

Freedom of contracts presupposes the legal and substantive equality of the contracting parties. In cases where there is in fact inequality between the parties to a contract, which may in certain circumstances completely compromise the equal status of the parties, legislative restraints may be placed on the absolute implementation of the principle of economic freedom, in favour of the weaker parties. Thus, for example, in the case in which one of the contracting parties enjoys a de facto or de jure monopolistic or oligopolistic position in the domestic market, it may be obliged to enter a contract on the grounds that it is providing goods or services vital to society.

Also, in the case of standard 'subscription contracts' (contracts for receipt of regular service – phone, gas, etc.), the legislation extends special protection to the consumers or users of the relevant services entering the contract. Thus contracts should not contain improper general conditions which, in any case, are regarded as invalid and are not implemented (Article 2 of Act 2251/1994).

II. Freedom of Business Activity

422. The Constitution guarantees business freedom in Article 5 paragraph 1 in combination with Article 106, which, by setting limits to private economic initiative, thereby presupposes the existence of that initiative. Article 106 paragraph 1 states that: 'In order to consolidate social peace and protect the general interest, the State shall plan and coordinate economic activity in the Country, aiming at safeguarding the economic development of all sectors of the national economy. The State shall take all measures necessary to develop sources of national wealth in the atmosphere, in underground and underwater deposits, and to promote regional development and to further especially the economy of mountainous, insular and frontier areas.'

Article 106 paragraph 2 states that: 'Private economic initiative shall not be permitted to develop at the expense of freedom and human dignity, or to the detriment of the national economy.' It follows from these provisions that the Constitution does not guarantee a pure free-economy or free-market system, but – permitting State intervention in the field of private economic activity – establishes a mixed-economy system. It, therefore, excludes the possibility of total state ownership of the economy, while not allowing a complete absence of state regulatory activity from the private economy.

423. The freedom of business activity comprehends the freedom to found and operate private businesses and profit-making associations. The State is obliged to establish the appropriate corporate forms for the effective development of economic activity but must refrain from interfering in the way the various companies are organized and run. However, the Council of State has ruled that the Constitution does not forbid state intervention through legislative measures in the running of *sociétés anonymes*, by taking over their administration and implementing a 'recovery plan' through a compulsory increase in their capital, or by special liquidation, bypassing the authority of the general meeting of shareholders of the company in question (Full Bench of Council of State Rulings 1094–1095/1987, on the compulsory takeover of management of 'problem' businesses by the Organization for Business Reconstruction under Act 1386/1983). However, the CJEU has ruled that such provisions contravene the European directive (77/91/EEC), which provides that corporate capital may only be increased with the consent of the general meeting of shareholders (CJEU cases C-134–135/1991, *Kerafina-Keramische und Finanz Holding AG*, Judgment of 12 October 1992).

424. The concept of business freedom also embraces the freedom to advertise, which is a necessary condition for the development of business activity. The legislator has, however, set certain limits on advertising by legal persons belonging to the public sector or broader public sector (Act 2328/1995, Presidential Decree 261/1997). Specifically, such legal persons must draw up each year a detailed (type and budgeted value) programme of planned advertisement of the services and goods they provide to the public, to be submitted for approval to the Ministry of Press and Media. They may enter contracts for promotional advertising with advertising agencies. They are also obliged to dedicate a specific portion of their promotional spending to the print media (at least 40%) and to the radio (at least 10%) (Article 4 of the Presidential Decree 261/1997).

425. One necessary condition for the free development of business activity is freedom of competition, which can be broken down into the following components: freedom of access to the market, freedom of competition within the market, and prohibition of unfair competition. The current statutory framework on freedom of competition is made up of Acts 146/1914 and 3959/2011. Under Article 12 of Act 3959/2011, the Hellenic Competition Commission has been set up as an independent administrative authority, its remit to protect competition (*see also supra* No. 225).

426. The Constitution provides for the possibility of limits being set to the freedom of economic activity for the sake of the general good (Article 106 paragraphs 1 and 2, *see supra* No. 422). In these cases, the limits may extend as far as a complete ban on a certain activity, for example, in the case of suspending by law the operating licence of businesses issuing bills of lading, in order to prevent tax evasion (Council of State 35/1991) (the evasion in question was facilitated by the operation of these businesses). Strict limits are provided in paragraph 3 of the same article, according to which:

> With the reservation of the protection provided in Article 107 in connection with the re-export of foreign capital, the law may regulate the acquisition by purchase of enterprises or the compulsory participation therein of the State or other public agencies, in the event these enterprises are of the nature of a monopoly or are of vital importance to the development of sources of national wealth or are primarily intended to offer services to the community as a whole.

III. Freedom to Work and Practise a Profession

427. Freedom to exercise a profession tends to be the issue when the key element is the offering of personal services, whereas when the key element is the investment of capital – even where personal employment is also being provided – we speak instead of development of business activity.

Freedom to practise a profession means that each of us may choose and change the type, place and time of our employment, and the way we engage in that employment. Legislative restrictions in respect of more specific regulation of labour relations (working hours, insurance) are limits not so much on freedom of labour as on the business activity of the employer. A common restriction is the provision for prior administrative licence to exercise a profession, or the imposition of restrictions on the way the profession will be conducted, in order – for example – to ensure protection of the environment. Case law has thus determined that the imposition of limits on the movement of taxis is lawful since it is intended to combat atmospheric pollution (Council of State 2930/1989). There is a rich, but sometimes contradictory, mass of case law on limits on the free exercise of a profession. For example, it has been ruled by the Council of State that the introduction of an upper age limit for the exercise of a profession, after which a person is obliged to retire, is unconstitutional when applied to pharmacists, but constitutional when applied to certain court officers (Council of State 3828/1997). It is even permissible to ban completely the practice of some professional activity if this is necessary to safeguard some other right enshrined in the Constitution.

IV. The Right to Work and the Prohibition of Forced Labour

428. The right to work is a more narrowly defined facet of the general principle of economic freedom. It is a typical example of a right of mixed character, in that it is both a social (Article 22 paragraph 1 of the Constitution) and a civil right (Article 22 paragraph 4 a of the Constitution). Specifically, in the words of Article 22 paragraph 1(a) of the Constitution, 'Work constitutes a right and shall enjoy the protection of the State, which shall care for the creation of conditions of employment for all citizens and shall pursue the moral and material advancement of the rural and urban working population.'

The positive freedom of labour does not give any individual the right to take legal action against the State in pursuit of employment but represents an obligation on the part of the State to take the necessary steps to create jobs, reduce unemployment and ensure the best possible working conditions for employees. Legal scholars have maintained that these constitutional provisions guarantee a minimum social acquis, in the sense that the provisions of labour and national insurance law may not be entirely repealed without being replaced by others which will, in all essential points, offer protection equivalent to that extended by the former provisions. Case law would not appear to have followed this line of reasoning. Certainly, there is no case in which an employer is obliged to maintain some initial number of jobs, although the improper dismissal of employees is forbidden.

429. The negative freedom of labour is guaranteed in Article 22 paragraph 4 a of the Constitution: 'any form of compulsory work is prohibited'. An exception to this prohibition is the institution of requisition of personal services (Article 22 paragraph 4(b) of the Constitution). Requisitioning of personal services is permissible only in exceptional circumstances, such as war, a general mobilization, urgent social need, or risk to public health. Legislative Decree 17/1974 contains special provisions for requisitioning of services, some of which are of dubious constitutionality.

V. Protection of Property

430. Economic freedom comprises also classical property rights. Under the Constitution property is protected by the State; rights deriving therefrom may, however, not be exercised contrary to the public interest (Article 17 paragraph 1). Property is safeguarded as both a civil right and a statutory guarantee. 'Property' refers, according to the case law, only to real rights and mainly to ownership of immovables and movables. The protection of property does not extend to rights arising out of the law of obligations by which a person is entitled to claim performance from another person. However, the theory is moving more and more in the direction of the interpretation that Article 17 extends protection also to rights arising out of contracts or torts. In this respect, it is important to note Article 1 of the First Protocol to the ECHR guaranteeing all property rights or interests and not only real rights.

In recent years, the Greek courts have moved towards the interpretation of Article 1 of the First Protocol to the ECHR, as formulated by the ECtHR while preferring not to found the protection of private rights of economic value in Article 17 of the Constitution (Full Bench of the Supreme Civil and Criminal Court 40/1998, Court of Audit 2274/1997, Full Bench of the Council of State 542/1999, but the last ruling does not refer expressly to Article 1 of the First Protocol to the ECHR).

The Constitution legitimizes the imposition of limits on the exercise of the right of property (Article 17 paragraph 1). These limits are mainly derived from the relativization of the exclusive use and usufruct of property and do not entail payment of compensation. Imposition of limits is legitimate provided that the relevant law exists, that the public interest is served and that there is no essential limit on, or complete elimination of, the right of property.

Usually, limitations of property rights are allowed under the Constitution in favour of the cultural and natural environment as well as of urban and rural planning (Articles 18 and 24).

431. If a person is to be deprived of property, the conditions set out in Article 17 paragraph 2(a) of the Constitution must be respected, namely: 'no one shall be deprived of his property except for public benefit which must be duly proven, when and as specified by statute and always following full compensation corresponding to the value of the expropriated property at the time of the court hearing on the provisional determination of compensation'.

Deprivation of property is in principle the same as depriving a person of acquired right of ownership. Equivalent to deprivation of property is to tax property at such high rates that it is likely that within a short period of time, the State will have extracted from it its entire financial value.

The first condition for a declaration of compulsory expropriation is that there be some ground of public benefit. The conceptual content of this principle cannot be defined *a priori* but is determined specifically for each set of circumstances. In no circumstances may public benefit be identified with simple financial profit for the State or purely private benefit. However, public benefit comes into play also when compulsory expropriation is to be made on behalf of a private person, but the underlying purpose will serve the more general public interest. Public benefit must be defined by formal law or regulatory act. The actual public benefit involved is to be defined specifically in the administrative act proclaiming the compulsory expropriation, and the Constitution requires that it be justified: 'duly proven'. The justification must make it clear that the requirements of the principle of proportionality are being adhered to. Also, in accordance with the constitutional provision added in the most recent revision, the justification of the act of expropriation must include a special reference to the possibility of covering the expense incurred.

The second condition for compulsory expropriation is the prior payment of full compensation, by which compensation corresponding to the real value of the property should be understood. It should be in cash and free of any taxes, deductions or fees (Article 17 paragraph 4(i) of the Constitution). By deviation from Article 94 of the Constitution, it is the civil, not the administrative courts, which determine the amount of compensation (Articles 19 and 20 of Act 2882/2001).

Compensation in the amount determined by the court must in all cases be paid within one and one-half years at the latest from the date of publication of the decision regarding provisional determination of compensation payable, and in cases of a direct request for the final determination of compensation, from the date of publication of the court ruling, otherwise the expropriation shall be revoked *ipso jure* (Article 17 paragraph 4(h) of the Constitution).

An exception to the rule of prior payment of compensation before occupation of the expropriated property is laid down in Article 17 paragraph 4(f):

> In order for works of a general importance for the economy of the country to be carried out, it is possible that, by special decision of the court which is competent for the final or the provisional determination of the compensation, the execution of works even prior to the determination and payment of the compensation is allowed, provided that a reasonable part of the compensation is paid and that full guarantee is provided in favour of the beneficiary of the compensation, as provided by law.

The compulsory expropriation order must be revoked by the administrative act if the expropriation is not carried out within a reasonable period of time, even if it had originally been lawfully announced. The Council of State has ruled that the passage of nine years (Council of State 642/1998) or more (Council of State 385/1997, 2682/1999, etc.) without the carrying out of the expropriation constitutes a breach of the reasonable period of time. The expropriation order must also be revoked when, after the compulsory expropriation has taken place, the objective of public benefit which represented the original justification is no longer valid.

Detailed provisions on compulsory expropriation are set out in the Legislative Decree 797/1971, and in the more recent Act 2882/2001 (Code of Compulsory Expropriations of Immovable Property), which does not, however, cover significant cases of expropriation, such as those ordered as part of the implementation of urban plans and the development of residential areas, which are governed by other laws.

§8. EQUALITY

I. The General Principle of Equality

432. Under Article 4 paragraph 1 of the Constitution: 'All Greeks are equal before the law.' The meaning of this provision, the wording of which has been the same under all Greek Constitutions, was initially that the administration and courts were bound by the principle of equality in the implementation of the law. The application of the law could, in other words, not be discriminatory. As far back as 1932, the Supreme Civil and Criminal Court (Ruling 261/1932) held that the principle of equality is binding on the legislator too. The Council of State also adopted this interpretation (Ruling 2176/1947). Equality, in the sense of Article 4 paragraph 1, is substantive and proportional, not formal and arithmetical. In other words, similar cases require similar treatment, and different cases different treatment. Violations of the principle of equality are reviewed by the courts.

Particular questions have been raised in relation to the possibility of extended application of a favourable provision to those who have been unfairly excluded from the original application. The courts – specifically both the Supreme Civil and Criminal Court and the Court of Audit, as well as the administrative courts – tend to accept such extended applications, even when the favourable provision was confined to a specific group, with the result that the provision is eventually extended to many more cases than those initially envisaged by the legislator (*see* Full Bench of the Supreme Civil and Criminal Court 13/1991 on the unconstitutionality of a provision establishing a distinction between categories of public employees in respect of receipt of a provisional overtime payment). The Council of State has been more cautious in accepting claims for extended application of favourable provisions, doing so only when in exceptional circumstances one or more categories have been overlooked by the favourable provision (*see* Council of State 653/2000 on the unjustified exclusion of a specific category of employees of the Ministry of Foreign Affairs serving abroad from receipt of the foreign service allowance, and Council of State 3391/2005, on the unjustified exclusion of a category of police officers serving abroad from receipt of the enhanced foreign service allowance payable to employees with children).

The principle of equality is also cited in case law on the equivalence of salaries, benefits, pensions, etc., of judicial functionaries with those of other public servants and functionaries. Specifically, Article 4 of the Constitution is interpreted in combination with Article 88 paragraph 2(a), which states that the remuneration of judicial functionaries shall be commensurate with their office. On the legal basis of the two above provisions, the courts have repeatedly ruled that there is a manifestly unfair discrimination in respect of salary arrangements for judges (who, because of the importance of their role and the need to ensure their independence, enjoy special salary arrangements) and have extended to them favourable legislative provisions in force for other categories of public functionaries. Article 4 paragraph 1 is cited mainly in the case law of the Supreme Civil and Criminal Court (1751/1984, 1939/1984, 14/1988), while the Council of State usually confines itself to invoking Articles 26 (segregation of functions), 87 paragraph 1 (personal and functional independence of judges), and 88 paragraph 2 of the Constitution in order to accept the upgrading of salaries of judicial functionaries to the level of remuneration enjoyed by another category of employees (e.g., Council of State 2477/1987, 3670/1994 [Full Bench], 470/1996). The Revision of 2001 included an addition to Article 88 paragraph 2 of a provision for the hearing by a special court of disputes concerning all kinds of remuneration and pension of judicial functionaries, insofar as the resolution of the questions at issue can affect the salary, pension or tax status of a broader circle of persons. This special court followed previous case law in its rulings. For example, it ordered that the remuneration of judicial functionaries be rendered equivalent to the more favourable remuneration paid to the judicial representatives of the Legal Council of State (1/2005, 36/2006). In these decisions, the court set up under Article 88 paragraph 2 of the Constitution has aligned itself more closely to the case law of the Supreme Civil and Criminal Court than to that of the Council of State, in citing, *inter alia*, the violation of the general principle of equality.

II. Equality of the Sexes

433. The equality of the sexes is enshrined in Article 4 paragraph 2, which states, ‘Greek men and women have equal rights and equal obligations’, in combination with Article 116 paragraph 2, according to which ‘Adoption of positive measures for promoting equality between men and women does not constitute discrimination on grounds of sex. The State shall take measures for the elimination of inequalities actually existing, in particular to the detriment of women.’ A major step for the implementation of equality between men and women was taken in 1983 (Act 1329/1983).

The equality of the sexes can be seen from both a positive and a negative perspective. On the one hand, the provisions on equality prohibit the creation of inequalities of status among citizens on grounds of gender, both in relations between the sexes and in their relations with the State. On the other hand, the Constitution requires the granting of equal opportunities to both sexes to develop their personalities and participate on equal terms in the economic and social life of the nation. Different treatment of the sexes is constitutionally acceptable only when justified by exceptional factors related to the woman’s greater need for protection, particularly in respect of issues of protection of motherhood, marriage and the family, or related to purely biological differences which require the taking of particular measures in light of the object of the relationship under regulation. In this context, the Full Bench of the Council of State in its Ruling 1323/2016 ruled that the principle of equality of the sexes is violated by the unjustified exclusion of women from the operational and technical specialties of professional soldiers. Thus equality of the sexes is not merely a matter of a simple prohibition on arbitrary treatment but lays the most imperative requirement on the State to take all necessary measures to eliminate existing inequalities, most of which operate to the disadvantage of the female sex.

III. Equal Contribution to Public Charges

434. Article 4 paragraph 5 of the Constitution states that 'Greek citizens contribute without distinction to public charges in proportion to their means.' This provision refers mainly to charges in the form of taxation.

It is a consequence of equality in respect of taxation that the tax burden must be universal, that it must fall on all Greek citizens without exception. Furthermore, equality in respect of taxation is a proportional equality: the share of the burden must be proportional to the capacity to pay. Differentiations in tax may also be justified by differences in circumstances and by reasons of public interest. Grounded in the two assumptions above, the principle of tax equality serves the notion of fairness in taxation and provides the necessary condition for a more just tax system.

The question arises of whether the principle of taxation on the basis of capacity to pay necessarily entails the introduction of a system of progressive taxation. It is more correct to agree that paragraph 5 of Article 4 of the Constitution only guarantees proportional equality of taxation, excluding the imposition of poll taxes. Within this constitutional framework, the ordinary legislator may choose between proportional or progressive taxation, depending on the special characteristics of the object and subject of each tax (but taxation of income shall be progressive according to the Constitution, *see* details *infra* No. 489).

From the provisions of paragraph 5 of Article 4, in combination with those of paragraph 1 of Article 20 of the Constitution, the case law of the courts (Supreme Civil and Criminal Court, Full Bench, 13/1992) has ruled that the extra-contractual liability of the State is guaranteed by the Constitution.

IV. Equality of Payment for Work

435. Article 22 paragraph 1(b) prescribes equal payment for work of equal value irrespective of sex or other distinctions. The provision establishes a civil right and allows a person who has suffered discrimination to initiate legal action.

Only those in a dependent relationship of employment in private law are subject to the constitutional provision. The notion of payment comprehends not only salary or wages but also any kind of allowance or other benefits, even the terms and conditions of retirement.

Case law has extended the right established in Article 22 paragraph 1(b) to a general right to equal treatment for all employees.

V. Equality of Obligation to Military Service

436. According to Article 4 paragraph 6: 'Every Greek capable of bearing arms is obliged to contribute to the defence of the Fatherland as provided by law.' This provision allows the ordinary legislator the scope to introduce a system of compulsory enlistment. Should he do so, however, he must frame the system with respect for the principles of universality and equality. Female Greeks are liable to military service under Act 705/1977 in times of war or recruitment. The exemption of women with children, from mandatory service in times of peace is justified in view of the constitutional protection of motherhood, but in respect of other women, the exemption appears unjustified, given that Article 4 paragraph 6 makes no distinction in this respect, and there is no other constitutional provision justifying different treatment for women.

On the conscientious objectors, *see infra*, No. 450.

VI. Equal Access to Public Office

437. According to paragraph 4 of Article 4, one of the provisions of the Constitution which may not be revised (Article 110 paragraph 1 of the Constitution): 'Only Greek citizens shall be eligible for public service, except as otherwise provided by special laws.' This concept of public service comprehends only those public positions which involve the exercise of public authority, such as *par excellence*, the offices of the three powers set out in Article 26 of the Constitution. Equal access to public office generally prohibits related distinctions of Greek citizens based on whether they are of Greek descent or not (Full Bench of the Council of State 3117/2014).

A question of possible conflict between European law and the Greek Constitution arises in relation to the right of aliens from Member States to be elected in first-level local government elections, provided they are resident in Greece (Presidential Decree 133/1997, *see also* Article 51 paragraph 1 of the TFEU, ex Article 45 paragraph 1 of the European Community Treaty). In all circumstances, the occupation of elected office in local government necessarily entails the exercise of public authority.

Finally, it is asserted that in Article 4 paragraph 4 of the Constitution, equal treatment is guaranteed for all Greeks in their access to public services and in their subsequent careers, on the basis of the principles of the constitutionally enshrined principle of promotion by merit.

VII. Other Forms of Equality

438. Article 4 paragraph 7 of the Constitution forbids one particular form of inequality: 'Titles of nobility or distinction are neither conferred upon nor recognized in Greek citizens.'

439. Another special form of equality is the equality of litigants, derived from Article 4 paragraph 1 of the Constitution, in conjunction with Article 20 paragraph 1, which guarantees the right of legal protection. This equality is to be understood in its formal, arithmetical sense. Particular questions have been raised in respect of the granting of procedural privileges to the State. The European Court of Human Rights has ruled in this respect that the suspension of procedural deadlines in favour of the State for longer periods than those allowed for private citizens is in contravention of the principle of equality of means (ECHR, *Platakos v. Greece*, Judgment of 11 January 2001). Following this Judgment, the Council of State has ruled that the period of suspension of a procedural deadline for the exercise of judicial remedies during the judicial vacations shall be the same both for the State and the persons, otherwise, Articles 4 paragraph 1, and 20 paragraph 1 of the Constitution are breached (Ruling 2808/2002).

440. The European Court of Human Rights has also ruled (ECHR, *Meidanis v. Greece*, Judgment of 22 May 2008) that the provision of Article 7 paragraph 2 of the Legislative Decree 496/1974, setting a lower moratory interest rate in favour of public law legal persons, than the rate applicable to individuals, is in breach to Article 1 of the First Protocol to ECHR. However, the Council of State ruled (Ruling 1620/2011) that a lower moratory interest rate for the State is justified on the basis of the need to secure balanced public finances during times of financial crisis. This ruling has been affirmed by the Special Highest Court (Ruling 25/2012, *see also* the Full Bench of the Council of State 2114/2014).

§9. Political Rights

441. Political rights are the right to vote, the right to be elected, the right to be appointed as civil servant, judge, or juror as well as the right to founding and joining political parties. Political rights are guaranteed only to Greek citizens (but *see infra* No. 472, on the political rights of European citizens). The above rights are examined in detail in the section on organizational constitutional law, in light of their connection with the democratic principle.

§10. Social Rights and Obligations

442. Given the non-absolute nature of the distinction between civil and social rights, it is clear that a series of rights, chief among them the right to demand that the State refrain from intervention, at the same time require the taking of positive measures by the State. These rights thus present aspects which resemble social rights. Furthermore, the Greek Constitution enshrines a series of rights whose content consists mainly of the obligation on the State to intervene and regulate in specific sectors of social action.

The development and promotion of arts, science, research and teaching is an obligation of the State (Article 16 paragraph 1 of the Constitution). Further obligations of the State expressly determined in the Constitution are the protection of family, motherhood and childhood (Article 21 paragraph 1), the special care for health (Article 21 paragraph 2 and paragraph 3), the advancement of conditions of employment (Article 22 paragraph 1) and the care for social security (Article 22 paragraph 5) as well as the protection of the natural and cultural environment (Article 24, which is also a civil right, *see* in details *infra* Nos 444 et seq.). To these obligations correspond the social rights to education and information, the right to work and to social care, the right to a healthy environment, etc. Social rights are not legally enforceable; the State cannot be compelled to render performance.

Following the Revision of 2001, Article 25 paragraph 1 now explicitly refers to the principle of the welfare state. The regulatory force of social rights is thus enhanced (on the principle of the welfare state, *see also supra* No. 18).

443. The Constitution does not ignore social obligations of the citizens towards the State. Thus the State may require, according to Article 22 paragraph 4(b), notwithstanding the prohibition of compulsory labour, that citizens render personal services to it or to local authorities. According to Article 25 paragraph 4 citizens must fulfil 'the duty of social and national solidarity'. Similarly, Article 120 paragraph 2 prescribes that 'respect towards the Constitution and the law concurrent thereto, and devotion to the fatherland and to democracy constitute a fundamental duty of all Greeks'.

§11. Protection of the Environment

444. According to the Constitution (Article 24 paragraph 1(a) and (b), as amended in the 2001 Revision): 'The protection of the natural and cultural environment constitutes a duty of the State and a right of every person. The State is bound to adopt special preventive or repressive measures for the preservation of the environment in the context of the principle of sustainable development.' More specific provisions on environmental protection are to be found in Act 1650/1986, as subsequently amended.

These provisions safeguard the right to environmental protection, both as a civil right, allowing individuals to initiate actions against the State to compel it to refrain from measures damaging to the environment, and a social right, in the sense that the taking of positive measures to protect the environment is elevated to the status of a state obligation.

These provisions now enshrine the principle of prevention, which requires the State to take preventive measures and, only when this is not possible, repressive measures. The principle of prevention is related to the principle of sustainable development, which is also enshrined in Article 24. According to the latter principle, each public policy must be framed with respect for the need to protect the environment and bearing in mind the bearing capacity of the ecosystem in which the planned activity is intended to be developed, in order that this activity cause the least possible harm to the environment, and above all not lead to the exhaustion of wealth-generating resources (Council of State 734/1997). By extension of the same principle, it is permissible to prohibit any economic activity in areas with particularly sensitive ecosystems.

One particular manifestation of the principle of sustainable development is the principle of non-aggressive development, which demands the planning of environmentally friendly development for those areas with particular natural characteristics (vulnerable ecosystems); a ruling in this spirit has been issued, for example, for the islands of Cyclades (Council of State 3146/1998). Furthermore, according to this case law, the concept of the natural environment comprehends those ecosystems and biotopes which, because of their physical characteristics, are vital for the survival of their flora and fauna. The protection of the environment entails another principle, that of protection of diversity, on the basis of which special protection is granted to rare species or species threatened with extinction (Council of State 3955/1995).

Even before their explicit guaranteeing in the Constitution, with the Revision of 2001, the principles of prevention and sustainable development had already been recognized by the Council of State, which had developed in its case law positions which were particularly protective of the environment. The Council of State has required increased levels of protection for coastal zones, streams, wetlands and vulnerable ecosystems.

445. Questions arise in the case of conflict between the requirement of environmental protection and the right of economic freedom. On each occasion, the judge resolves the conflict in question by an ad hoc weighing up of the opposing rights. If for reasons of protection not merely a curb on but actual deprivation of property is imposed, or a ban on its use in the manner intended, this must be effected under the constitutional terms applying to compulsory expropriation (Article 17 of the Constitution). However, the Council of State has ruled that the imposition of building-plot ratios so strict (as in the case of a plot of at least 1,500 m^2 on which building permission was granted for only 50 m^2) that in essence they nullified the intended use of the property, did not violate the right of property, in light of the constitutional requirement to protect the environment (Full Bench of the Council of State 695/1986, concerning protection of sea turtle Caretta-Caretta on the island of Zakynthos, Full Bench of the Council of State 4951/1995 and Council of State 3067/2001).

According to Article 24 paragraph 1(c), (d) and (e) of the Constitution: ‘Matters pertaining to the protection of forests and forest expanses in general shall be regulated by law. The compilation of a forest registry constitutes an obligation of the State. Alteration of the use of forests and forest expanses is prohibited, except where agricultural development or other uses imposed for the public interest prevail for the benefit of the national economy.’ Furthermore, according to Article 117 paragraph 3: ‘Public or private forests or forest expanses which have been destroyed or are being destroyed by fire or have otherwise been deforested or are being deforested, shall not thereby relinquish their previous designation and shall compulsorily be proclaimed reforestable, the possibility of their disposal for other uses being excluded.’ In order to dispel any doubts about the meaning of the terms ‘forest’ and ‘forest expanse’, in the interpretative clause of Article 24 the constitutional legislator adopts the definition given by the Special Highest Court (Ruling 27/1999), namely ‘by forest or forest ecosystem is meant the organic whole of wild plants with woody trunk on the necessary area of ground which, together with the flora and fauna co-existing there, constitute, by means of their mutual interdependence and interaction, a particular biocoenosis (forest biocoenosis) and a particular natural environment (forest-derived). A forest expanse exists when the wild woody vegetation, either high or shrubbery, is sparse'.

446. As well as the natural environment, the provisions of Article 24 also protect the cultural environment, particularly listed buildings, traditional villages, and archaeological sites. Protection of the cultural environment entails the imposition of the necessary restraints on owners of listed buildings. Specifically, paragraph 6 provides: 'Monuments and historic areas and elements shall be under the protection of the State. A law shall provide for measures restrictive of private ownership deemed necessary for protection thereof, as well as for the manner and the kind of compensation payable to owners.' These provisions are enacted in legislation in the form of Act 3028/2002, but also of Act 3658/2008 aiming to protect cultural objects.

447. According to Article 24 paragraph 2 of the Constitution:

> [T]he master plan of the country, and the arrangement, development, urbanization and expansion of towns and residential areas in general, shall be under the regulatory authority and the control of the State, in the aim of serving the functionality and the development of settlements and of securing the best possible living conditions. The relevant technical choices and considerations are conducted according to the rules of science. The compilation of a national cadastral constitutes an obligation of the State.

To date, Greece has not had either a comprehensive master plan or specific urban plans and land use plans. The absence of a national cadastral register is one of the fundamental reasons for this state of affairs. In view of the actual situation, the Council of State has accepted the constitutionality of the provisional substitutes for land use planning, such as the Settlement Control Zones, which operate as precautionary measures until comprehensive plans are drawn up (Council of State 114/1994, Council of State Advice 721/1995). However, in the same case law, after the passing of a reasonable period of time, to be defined by the annulling judge, a comprehensive national, regional and local land use plan must be prepared. Of particular interest is the case law of the Council of State in accordance with which if in a region there is serious investment interest in installing wind-power generating stations, before the approval of the environmental terms and conditions and the granting of the permit to set up such a station, a special overall land use study must have been prepared for the area, in order to factor in the energy needs of the region and the impact on the region of installation of the full complement of wind-powered generating stations (Council of State Ruling 2569/2004). The Council of State ruled that Article 24 of the Constitution derives directly the obligation for the State to issue an urban planification for constructions with important environmental impact, such as ports (Ruling 1434/1998), hatcheries (Rulings 2844/1993 and 2489/2006 [Full Bench]), prisons (Ruling 3249/2000, Advice on Presidential Decrees 108 and 405/1999) industries (Ruling 2319/2002).

Land use planning and urban planning of communities are the exclusive competence of the State, which may not be delegated to local or sectoral authorities (*see*, however, Article 102 of the Constitution, concerning the assignment of the State's competences to local government agencies). There is a significant construction in case law – that of absolute planning acquis. In the case law of the Council of State, modifications to planning provisions must be intended to improve living conditions; those which lead to any deterioration of those conditions are unconstitutional (Full Bench of the Council of State 10/1988).

Part VII. Specific Issues

Chapter 1. Religious Freedom, Church and State

§1. Religious Freedom

448. The Constitution guarantees religious freedom: '- 1. Freedom of religious conscience is inviolable. The enjoyment of civil rights and liberties does not depend on the individual's religious beliefs.- 2. All known religions shall be free and their rites of worship shall be performed unhindered and under the protection of the law. The practice of rites of worship is not allowed to offend public order or the good usages' (Article 13 paragraphs 1 and 2(a) and (b)).

Constitutional protection comprehends the principle of religious conscience, in the form of protection of the individual's relationship with his god from any state interference. Freedom of religious conscience is proclaimed to be inviolable, without any limitation. The Constitution also guarantees religious equality, in the sense that all persons must be treated equally in the enjoyment of the rights granted them under law, regardless of their religious convictions. Freedom of religious conscience entails the freedom to assemble for religious purposes (for more detail on religious associations, *see infra* No. 458).

Religious freedom as a manifestation of religious convictions through the rites of worship of any known religion consists in the right of each person to demonstrate his religious convictions without impediment in various ways, alone or in common with others, provided only that no offence is caused to morality or public order.

According to the Constitution proselytism is forbidden (Article 13 paragraph 2 (c)). Proselytism is defined (Article 4 of the Emergency Act 1363/1938, as replaced by Article 2 of the Emergency Act 1672/1939) as an offence in which attempts are made, whether direct or indirect, to intrude on the religious conscience of persons of other faith in order to change their religious convictions by any kind of inducement or promise, or by the use of fraudulent means or by taking advantage of their inexperience or abusing their trust, or by exploiting their need, spiritual or intellectual weakness or folly. In its current form, the article is intended to protect all religions from proselytizing, whereas previously its scope was confined to protection only of the Orthodox Church. The breadth of the legislative definition of proselytism, and its broad interpretation by the Greek criminal courts, have led to the issuing of rulings against Greece by the European Court of Human Rights (e.g., *Kokkinakis v. Greece*, Judgment of 25 May 1993, *Larissis and others v. Greece*, Judgment of 24 February 1998).

449. The Constitution also guarantees freedom of worship, although this freedom extends only to known religions (Article 13 paragraph 2(a)). By the term 'known religion' the Constitution does not mean a religion recognized by an administrative or other act. A 'known religion' is one which does not have secret teachings or dogmas and which does not infringe on public order or the good usages. The term 'known religion' is juxtaposed with the term 'prevailing religion' (Article 3 paragraph 1 of the Constitution), which refers to the Eastern Orthodox Church (*see infra* Nos 451–452). Rites of worship may not offend public order or the good usages (Article 13 paragraph 2(b) of the Constitution). The good usages may not, however, be defined on the basis of the teachings of the prevailing religion.

450. An interesting issue concerning religious freedom in conjunction with compulsory military service is that of the unarmed service to be rendered by conscientious objectors. Under Article 4 paragraph 6 of the Constitution, 'every Greek capable of bearing arms is obliged to contribute to the defence of the Fatherland as provided by law'. It is of course a matter of interpretation whether 'capable' means physically and/or mentally capable of bearing arms. Irrespective thereof, Act 731/1977 'On Military Conscription' had introduced unarmed military service for those objecting on religious grounds, not on ideological or philosophical grounds – although the latter are equally protected under Article 13 of the Constitution. This unarmed military service had a duration twice as long as armed service. Amnesty International vigorously criticized the provisions of the said statute. The latest Act 3421/2005 on conscription recognizes as conscientious objectors those who refuse to perform their military service on grounds of religious, ideological, philosophical or moral conviction (Article 59). Originally, conscientious objectors had to perform unarmed military service (in departments of the Ministry of Defence, but engaged in duties that did not involve the use of arms, or training in the use of arms) or some alternative service (in departments of public sector agencies offering services to the community). Having been amended by Act 3883/2010, Article 61 of Act 3421/2005 currently provides only for alternative service. The latter generally has the double duration of the armed military service (Article 60 paragraphs 1 and 2 of Act 3421/2005).

In the Revision of 2001, an interpretative clause was appended to Article 4, according to which: 'The provision of paragraph 6 does not preclude that the law provides for the mandatory performance of other services, within or outside the armed forces (alternative service), by those having a substantiated conscientious objection to performing armed service or, generally, military duties.'

§2. The Prevailing Religion

451. The Constitution bears on its title page the declaration that it is proclaimed 'In the Name of the Holy and Consubstantial and Indivisible Trinity'. All Greek Constitutions since the rebirth of Greece in modern times have featured this same declaration. During the drafting of the 1975 Constitution, the idea of removing the declaration was considered but eventually rejected. The declaration entails no practical consequences; its significance is confined to a celebratory proclamation of the close ties which the Greek State acknowledges between itself and the Orthodox faith.

Article 3 of the Constitution, which bears the title 'Relations of Church and State' recognizes as the 'prevailing religion' that of the Eastern Orthodox Church of Christ. Article 3 reads as follows:

> 1. The prevailing religion in Greece is that of the Eastern Orthodox Church of Christ. The Orthodox Church of Greece, acknowledging our Lord Jesus Christ as its head, is inseparably united in doctrine with the Great Church of Christ in Constantinople and with every other Church of Christ of the same doctrine, observing unwaveringly, as they do, the holy apostolic and synodal canons and sacred traditions. It is autocephalous and is administered by the Holy Synod of serving Bishops and the Permanent Holy Synod originating thereof and assembled as specified by the Statutory Charter of the Church in compliance with the provisions of the Patriarchal Tome of June 9, 1850 and the Synodal Act of September 4, 1928. 2. The ecclesiastical regime existing in certain districts of the State shall not be deemed contrary to the provisions of the preceding paragraph. 3. The text of the Holy Scripture shall be maintained unaltered. Official translation of the text into any other form of language, without prior sanction by the Autocephalous Church of Greece and the Great Church of Christ in Constantinople, is prohibited.

It should be noted that the current Constitution regulated the relations between the State and church in Article 3, whereas the 1952 Constitution covered these questions in Articles 1 and 2. This attitude of the Constitution has been interpreted as a loosening of the relationship between the State and the Orthodox Church, which forms the basis for a better guarantee of religious freedom in general.

The term 'prevailing religion' does not mean a religious community which prevails over others. It simply has the declaratory meaning that almost all Greeks are Orthodox. The fact is that Greece has one of the greatest degrees of religious homogeneity in Europe. In accordance with a recent poll (Kappa Research, 2015), 81.4% of Greeks are Orthodox Christians, 14.7% are atheists and 2.9% belong to other religions, while 1% do not wish to reveal their religion (on religious minorities, *see infra* No. 472). After the fall of the Soviet Union, a large number (some estimates place it above 2 million) of – mainly – economic migrants and political refugees came to settle in Greece, bringing radical change to the composition of the population and the degree of religious homogeneity. The turmoil in the Middle East has created new waves of refugees and migrants reaching Greece by hundreds of thousands since 2015. The majority of them are Muslims. It is not known yet how many of them will settle in Greece. Nevertheless, it is expected that the religious homogeneity of the country will be once again affected.

The acknowledgement of the Orthodox Church in all Greek Constitutions as a prevailing religion is due to the fact that Orthodoxy and the clergy have made a unique contribution to the preservation of Greek nationality, language and education during the four centuries of Turkish rule as well as a major contribution to the struggle for liberation and independence.

§3. The Autocephaly and Self-government of the Church of Greece

452. The Church of Greece is autocephalous, that is, administratively independent of the Patriarchate of Constantinople (Article 3 paragraph 1 c of the Constitution). The independence was declared by the Royal Decree of 23 July 1833 without prior permission of the Patriarchate of Constantinople. It was thus contrary to the ecclesiastical canons until the Patriarchate consented to the autocephaly. This was done with the issuance of the Patriarchal Tome of 29 June 1850. After the enlargement of the Greek territory following the Balkan wars (for more details, *see supra* No. 34) the Patriarchate permitted, with the issuance of the Synodal Act of 4 September 1928, the annexation of the metropolitan provinces of the new territories to the Church of Greece.

The Church of Greece is administered by the Holy Synod of all Metropolitans. This Synod is its supreme organ. A smaller Synod, the 'Permanent Holy Synod', consisting of the Archbishop and twelve metropolitans – six from the old and six from the new territories, as the Synodal Act of 1828 and the Statutory Charter of the Church (Articles 3 and 7 of Act 590/1977) provide – administers the Church in everyday matters (Article 3 paragraph 1(c) of the Constitution).

The constitutional provision concerning the self-government of the Church of Greece prohibits the 'Synods of the Best', that is, synods consisting of a small number of metropolitans, selected in an arbitrary manner. Such 'Synods of the Best', being contrary to the synodic principle of the administration of the Orthodox Church have, nevertheless, been established in the past by dictatorships.

§4. The Constitutional Guarantee of the Holy Canons and of the Holy Tradition

453. The constitutional guarantee of the holy apostolic and synodal canons as of the holy tradition (Article 3 paragraph 1(b)) has two sides. First, the Church has a right vis-à-vis the State to observe unhindered the canons and the holy tradition and second, canons and traditions are guaranteed vis-à-vis the Church of Greece, that is, the Church of Greece may not deviate from such observance; otherwise, the unity in doctrine with the Ecumenical Patriarchate and the other Orthodox Churches would be lost.

A major issue concerning the constitutional guarantee of the holy apostolic and synodal canons is whether both dogmatic (i.e., canons that repeat dogmas of the Orthodox Church) and administrative canons enjoy the same constitutional protection. Though in theory it is held that no distinction and differentiation ought to be made, the jurisprudence of the Council of State (Rulings 139/1930, 3178/1976, etc.)

restricts the constitutional guarantee only to dogmatic canons. Administrative canons do not have, according to the rulings of the court, the same importance as dogmatic ones; they are changeable and may be amended by the legislator, with the exception of those administrative canons which have established fundamental institutions of the Orthodox Church.

§5. The Current System of Church-State Relations

454. The principle of the religious neutrality of the State is derived from Article 13 of the Constitution. However, both individual constitutional provisions and more specifically domestic legislation have framed a unique system of relations between church and State, in which each party may involve itself in matters of exclusive competence of the other.

I. Legal Status of Ecclesiastical Entities

455. Ecclesiastical legal persons, such as the Church of Greece, the dioceses, monasteries, and so on are generally characterized in various legislative provisions and in the jurisprudence of the Council of State and the civil courts as public law legal persons. It is obvious, however, that they do not belong to the sphere of public administration. They are placed within the category of public law legal persons in order to safeguard certain privileges they enjoy and to offer them more effective protection. Nevertheless, ecclesiastical institutions and museums are characterized as private law legal persons (Article 68 of Act 4235/2014) (on ecclesiastical legal persons *see also supra* No. 276). The Jewish Community, too, is characterized as a public law legal person (Act 2456/1920).

II. The Muslim Church

456. The Muslim minority in Greece was recognized by the Treaty of Lausanne, ratified by the Legislative Decree of 25 August 1923. Act 2345/1920, passed immediately after the annexation of western Thrace by Greece, introduced the institution of the *mufti* as religious leader with both religious and administrative competences, also providing for the procedures to be followed in his election and appointment (the office of the mufti is now regulated by the provisions of Act 1920/1991, which ratified the Act of Legislative Content 24/24.12.1990). Provision was also made for the establishment in each of the *muftiates* (there are three within Thrace – in Komotini, Xanthe and Didymoteicho) of a council to be made up of elected Muslim residents, known as the 'Council of the Muslim Minority' or the 'Administrative Committee', to administer Muslim assets.

III. The Catholic Church

457. A question has arisen as to the legal status of the Catholic Church. Specifically, when the Catholic Church of Hania lodged an action to protect certain property rights, the Greek civil courts refused to recognize the Church as a legal person, thereby denying it the right of access to the courts (Supreme Civil and Criminal Court 360/1994). Yet since the creation of the modern Greek State, the legal status of the Catholic Church had never been questioned, either by the administrative or the judicial authorities. On the contrary, with the passage of time, legal certainty had grown up in this respect, in which the Church quite reasonably trusted when lodging its action. The Court at Strasbourg ruled that the stance of the Greek State contravened not only the right of access of the Catholic Church to the courts (Article 6 paragraph 1 ECHR) but also the right of religious freedom, in combination with Article 14 ECHR, since the Church was the victim of religious discrimination (*Canea Catholic Church v. Greece*, 16 December 1997).

IV. Other Religious Associations

458. The current Constitution does not contain any specific provision on religious association. However, from a combined interpretation of Articles 13 paragraph 1, 2, and 12 paragraph 1 (on freedom of association), it is evident that the establishment of religious unions and associations is permissible, provided that they are dedicated to worship or the promotion of the principles of known religions, and that they do not engage in proselytizing activities.

No licence, approval or similar decision is required from the administrative authorities before one of these associations is established. There is no conflict between the constitutional provision on freedom of religious conscience and the provisions of the Civil Code (Articles 79 et seq.), which require compliance with certain formalities, including judicial control of the legal conditions for the establishment of an association (Thessaloniki Court of Appeal 377/1950). Specifically, the requirement in the Civil Code that associations be entered in the appropriate register (Article 81) makes it easier to ascertain their legal status, which consolidates the security of transactions. In the event of a religious association deviating from the objectives set out in its statutes, or of its objectives and operations proving illegal and contrary to public order and good usages, the association may not be recognized, or an already recognized association may be dissolved, by decision of the courts (Article 105 of the Civil Code), and its assets forfeited to the State (Athens Court of Appeal 7820/1986 and Supreme Civil and Criminal Court 58/2006, where the threat to public order lay in the fact that the name of the association seeking recognition caused confusion as to whether the body in question was a religious or ethnic association of Muslims).

V. The Regulation of Religious Matters by the State

459. Parliament is competent to regulate issues relating to the organization and administration of the Church, within the constitutional framework. The Charter of the Church (Act 590/1977), then, which regulates its organizational, administrative and operational issues, is voted as a law. Thus the Charter's declaration that the Church of Greece is a 'divine institution' with at its head 'Our Lord Jesus Christ' (Article 1), is a declaration by the legislator, who expresses clearly in this way his religious convictions. Representatives of the Church, such as the Metropolitan Bishops, are elected by its organs but are appointed by Presidential Decree (Articles 17 and 26 of Act 590/1977 concerning Metropolitan Bishops). The State, through the Ministry of Education, Research and Religious Affairs, oversees the ecclesiastical organs, while state courts – principally the Council of State – review the legality of the appointment and acts of those organs, these acts being regarded as administrative when they are used to exercise public authority, whether in their internal relations or in their relations with third parties. Priests are paid their salaries and pensions by the State.

VI. Religious Oath

460. The current Constitution reiterates that the elected President of the Republic is sworn in the name of 'the Holy, Consubstantial and Indivisible Trinity', a provision cited by some to claim that only a Greek Orthodox citizen may be elected President of the Republic (Article 33 paragraph 2).

Article 59 paragraph 1 of the Constitution states that the oath sworn by Members of Parliament shall be in the name of 'the Holy, Consubstantial and Indivisible Trinity', while Article 59 paragraph 2 of the Constitution offers the option to Members of Parliament of another religion or creed to swear the same oath in a form appropriate to their own religion or creed. However, the Constitution makes no provision for the case of Members of Parliament who are not adherents of any religion. The established practice is for Members of Parliament who do not wish to swear the religious oath to swear on their honour (*see also supra* No. 135). This practice was also followed by the majority of the members of the current Government. The same provisions hold for the remarkably large number of cases where ordinary legislation provides for the swearing of an oath. The Code of Civil Procedure requires that witnesses should take the oath in civil hearings and allows these witnesses to choose between a religious and secular oath (Article 408). The non-religious oath is also an option in criminal trials (Article 218 of the Code of Criminal Procedure).

VII. Religion and Education

461. According to the Constitution, one of the objectives of education is the development of religious consciousness (Article 16 paragraph 2). This is a more liberal formulation than that in the previous Constitution, which spoke of education following the directions of Hellenic-Christian culture. The current Constitution does not require a specific model to be followed, leaving this to the judgment of the legislator. The lesson of religion is taught in all Greek schools. Concerning the teaching schedule of religion in primary schools, in third and fourth grade the lesson has to be taught for two hours per week while in fifth and sixth grade for one hour per week (Ministerial Decision F12/657/70691/D1/26-4-2016). In lower secondary schools it has to be taught for two hours per week (Ministerial Decision 93381/D2/7-6-2016). In upper secondary schools, the lesson has to be taught for two hours per week in first and second grade and one hour per week in third grade (Article 2 of Act 4186/2013). Concerning the teaching material of religion, traditionally the lesson has been concentrated on the Christian Orthodox religion while a brief presentation of the teachings of other religions has also been attempted, but only in upper school classes. This practice has been in accordance with the pertinent legislation. Article 1 of Act 1566/1985 places among the objectives of primary and secondary education the development of the true elements of Orthodox Christian tradition. Moreover, Article 6 of Act 1566/1985 provides that in upper secondary education, religious teaching should make students aware of the more profound significance of Orthodox Christian morality and its consistent devotion to universal human values. In contrast to that, since 2016, the new religious syllabus has been adopted (Ministerial Decision 143575/D2/7-9-2016, 'Primary and Lower Secondary Education', and Ministerial Decision 143579/D2/7-9-2016, 'Upper Secondary Education'), aiming to abolish the confessional and catechist characteristics of the lesson and to give emphasis to teachings of other religions. The recent change in the religious syllabus has provoked a strong reaction from the Orthodox Church of Greece, of parents and teachers. They support that the new syllabus is unconstitutional, since the mission of the State is, among others, the development of a religious consciousness to the students based on the prevailing religion in Greece which is the Christian Orthodox (Articles 16 paragraph 2, and 3 paragraph 1 of the Constitution). Due to these reactions, the Ministry of Education, Research and Religious Affairs has promised to consider amending it, but only after having been provisionally applied and subsequently evaluated. The matter is now pending before the Council of State which will examine the constitutionality of the changes. The Constitution enshrines (Article 13, on freedom of religious conscience) the right of each child to be excused from the religion class if he so wishes. In the current legislation, this requires a written statement from the parents (Article 13 paragraph 10 of Presidential Decree. 201/1998). According to the latest circular of the Ministry of Education, Research and Religious Affairs (12773/D2/23-1-2015), the parents need only to express such a will and declare that their child is not a Christian Orthodox. Neither the parents nor the students are under the obligation to disclose their religion. School life features many activities associated with the Orthodox faith, such as morning prayers and participation in religious rites and services. Here too if the parents have provided the appropriate declaration the student of another faith may be excused (Article 13 paragraph 10 of the Presidential Decree 201/1998).

VIII. Setting Up of Churches of Other Religions

462. An illustration of the involved relations of Church and State can be found in the provisions of Article 1 of Emergency Act 1363/1938 and Article 1 of Royal Decree 20-5/2-6-1939, which required, before a church of any creed could be erected, the submission of an application from at least fifty families to the local Metropolitan, followed by the granting of a permit by both the Metropolitan and the Minister for Education, Research and Religious Affairs. The latter granted such permission at his own discretion. These requirements were considered to run counter not only to the provisions of Article 13 of the Constitution but also to those of Article 9 ECHR (*European Court of Human Rights, Manousakis and others v. Greece*, 26 September 1996). The aforementioned legislation was ruled unconstitutional for violating Article 13 of the Constitution, by the Council of State (Ruling 2188/2010), which referred the matter to its Full Bench. Nevertheless, the latter ruled (Ruling 4202/2012) that the system of administrative permission for the setting up of a church of any creed which was provided by Article 1 of Emergency Act 1363/1938 and Royal Decree 20-5/2-6-1939 was constitutional, with the exception of the ministerial discretion to refuse the permission on substantive grounds, which was found unconstitutional. These provisions have been amended by Article 27 of Act 3467/2006 which provides that the permission of the Metropolitan is no longer necessary as well as that the related application has to be submitted only to the Minister for Education, Research and Religious Affairs. Also clearly counter to the Constitution are the provisions of the Emergency Act 2200/1940 (*see also* Article 6 paragraph 1 of Regulation 2/1969 of the Holy Synod of the Church of Greece), which state that in the event of a privately owned church intended to cater to the religious needs of the owner and his family being opened to public worship, the church in question may be closed with the assistance if necessary of the police and at the order of the local Metropolitan or compulsorily expropriated to the advantage of the nearest parish church.

It is significant that despite the multicultural nature of modern Greek society there is still no mosque either in Athens or Thessaloniki – in fact, Athens is the only European capital without an official Muslim place of worship. The legislation allowing the establishment of a mosque in Athens has been passed (Act 3512/2006, subsequently amended a number of times, most recently by Act 4414/2016) but to date, there has been no major progress on the relevant procedures. There were complaints concerning the constitutionality of the establishment of the mosque, mainly alleged violations of the freedom of religious conscience (Article 13 of the Constitution) and the principle of equality (Article 4 of the Constitution), but these were rejected by the Council of State (Ruling 2399/2014, Full Bench). Since 2007, there has been a mosque and Muslim cultural centre in the area of Attica, established by the Muslims of the region with capital from Saudi Arabia (Hellenic-Arabic Educational and Cultural Centre).

IX. Marriage and Baptism

463. The Civil Code (Article 1367) provides for civil marriage, in which the two parties together declare their commitment to live as a married couple, or religious marriage in a ceremony conducted by a priest of the Eastern Orthodox Church or by a functionary of another creed or religion known in Greece. Most Greeks still opt for the religious ceremony, which is seen more as a significant social event. Infants are also baptized in a religious ceremony; it is the tradition, both social and religious, that the child should receive its given name at the baptism ceremony, not at the time of declaration of birth to the registrar of births, marriages and deaths. Nevertheless, Articles 25 and 26 of Act 334/1976 distinguish between the act of name-giving and baptism.

X. Holy Scripture

464. According to the Constitution (Article 3 paragraph 3), 'The text of the Holy Scripture shall be maintained unaltered. Official translation of the text into any other form of language, without prior sanction by the Autocephalous Church of Greece and the Great Church of Christ in Constantinople, is prohibited.'

XI. The Participation of the Church in the Workings of the State

465. Apart from any legislative provisions, the Church is also involved in the workings of the State on a symbolic level, in the blessing of the opening session of Parliament, for example, or in the placing of Christian icons or symbols in public offices, courts, schools, and so on. Nevertheless, the latter has raised a number of objections regarding its constitutionality, especially after the ruling of the European Court of Human Rights which considered the presence of religious symbols in the classrooms to violate Article 2 of the First Protocol (right to education) and Article 9 (religious freedom) of the ECHR (*Lautsi v. Italy*, 3 November 2009, which was, however, subsequently reversed by the ruling of the Grand Chamber, 18 March 2011). In this context, the Council of State was called to rule on the constitutionality of the presence of religious symbols and icons in courtrooms. The rejection of the related application for annulment as inadmissible did not permit the examination of the substance of the matter (Ruling 2980/2013). Moreover, important religious events and major occasions in the Orthodox calendar will see political figures, like the President of the Republic, invariably present in their official capacity, as with detachments of the armed forces honouring the occasion. A prominent example would be the reception of the Holy Flame from the Holy Land on the night of the Resurrection, welcomed to Greece with the honours accorded to a Head of State.

XII. Religion and Greek Identity Cards

466. A crisis broke out in the relations between the State and the Orthodox Church, occasioned by a decision of the HDPA (510/2000), which ruled that the stating of the religion of a person on public documents, and particularly on police identity cards, ran counter to the provisions of Act 2472/1997 on protection of the individual from processing of data of a personal nature. This decision led to the wholesale replacement of every single Greek identity card. The Orthodox Church was adamant in its demands that the religion of the individual should remain specified on the cards, linking the issue with the development of religious conscience. To demonstrate the support it could command the Church organized huge rallies in Greece's major cities and gathered more than three million signatures in an unofficial 'referendum'. But all its efforts were in vain; the current identity card has no entry for the individual's religion.

The issue came before the Council of State, which ruled (Ruling 2281/2001, Full Bench) that both mandatory and optional entry of a person's religion on his identity card was contrary to the provisions of Article 13 of the Constitution. On the issue of optional declaration of one's religion, the Church's compromise proposal, the Supreme Administrative Court ruled that there was an infringement of the religious freedom, in the negative sense, of those Greeks not wishing their religion to be stated on their identity cards, given that their refusal would thereby be incorporated in an official document. They would thus be forced to reveal, albeit indirectly, one aspect of their own personal stance towards religion. Moreover, the Council of State also felt that including a person's religion on his identity card might lead to discrimination – whether positive or negative – which would thus infringe on the principle of religious equality. A similar stance was taken by the European Court of Human Rights in its Judgment *on Sofianopoulos v. Greece* (12 December 2002), where it held that a prohibition on the stating (even when optional) of one's religion in an official document such as an identity card did not infringe the right to express one's religion enshrined in Article 9 ECHR. The European Court of Human Rights felt that the purpose of the identity card is not to satisfy the religious sentiments of the card's bearer, nor to designate the religion of a specific community.

In light of the various matters we have set out above, the conclusion can be drawn that relations between Church and State form a unique system (called 'state ruling by law'), but not without certain elements of the separation of Church and State. We should point out, however, that the current constitutional framework does allow the ordinary legislator to regulate individual aspects of the relations of Church and State, as well as the various ecclesiastical privileges, in such a way as to effect full separation to all intents and purposes.

§6. The Constitutional Status of Mount Athos

467. The first monasteries in Mount Athos ('Aghion Oros', 'Holy Mountain') were founded during the tenth century. They enjoyed a special self-governing status recognized by Byzantine emperors and preserved a special status of relative independence even during Ottoman rule. After the Balkan Wars, Mount Athos became part of the Greek State, the self-government of which is recognized by the Constitution. The acquisition of Greek citizenship by novices and monks of the Holy Mountain (*see infra* No. 469) is due to obligations of Greece assumed in international treaties (*see* Article 62 of the Berlin Treaty of 1878 and Article 13 of the Treaty of Sevres of 1920, ratified by the Lausanne Treaty of 1923).

Article 105 of the Constitution reads as follows:

> 1. The Athos peninsula extending beyond Megali Vigla and constituting the region of Aghion Oros shall, in accordance with its ancient privileged status, be a self-governed part of the Greek State, whose sovereignty thereon shall remain intact. Spiritually, Aghion Oros shall come under the direct jurisdiction of the Ecumenical Patriarchate. All persons leading a monastic life thereon acquire Greek citizenship without further formalities, upon admission as novices or monks. 2. Aghion Oros shall be governed, according to its regime, by its twenty Holy Monasteries among which the entire Athos peninsula is divided; the territory of the peninsula shall be exempt from expropriation. The administration of Aghion Oros shall be exercised by representatives of the Holy Monasteries constituting the Holy Community. No change whatsoever shall be permitted in the administrative system or in the number of Monasteries of Aghion Oros, or in their hierarchical order or in their position to their subordinate dependencies. Heterodox or schismatic persons shall be prohibited from dwelling thereon. 3. The determination in detail of the regimes of the Aghion Oros entities and the manner of operation thereof is effected by the Charter of Aghion Oros which, with the cooperation of the State representative, shall be drawn up and voted by the twenty Holy Monasteries and ratified by the Ecumenical Patriarchate and the Parliament of the Hellenes. 4. Faithful observance of the regimes of the Aghion Oros entities shall in the spiritual field be under the supreme supervision of the Ecumenical Patriarchate, and, in the administrative, under the supervision of the State, which shall also be exclusively responsible for safeguarding public order and security. 5. The aforementioned powers of the State shall be exercised through a governor whose rights and duties shall be determined by law. The law shall likewise determine the judicial power exercised by the monastic authorities and the Holy Community, as well as the customs and taxation privileges of Aghion Oros.

'The Charter of Mount Athos' was decided upon by the Synod of the Monasteries in 1924 and ratified by the Legislative Decree of 10–16 September 1926.

The regime of Mt Athos forbids any woman to set foot on the peninsula (Article 186 of the Charter of Mt Athos, the '*avaton*' principle). Men may only visit with official permission (a document known as a *diamonitirio* [permit to stay] must be issued [Article 176 of the Charter of Mt Athos]), and no visit may exceed four days in length. Those not of the Orthodox faith must also supply a letter of reference from their embassy and a special entry permit from the Greek Ministry of Foreign Affairs. The EU has given its approval to this arrangement (Treaty of Accession of Greece to the European Community, 28 May 1979; in a joint statement appended to the Act of Accession the parties agreed on the regime pertaining to Mt Athos). In 2003 the

European Parliament sought (in decision P5_TA[2003]0376) the lifting of the prohibition on women, on the grounds that it contravened the principle of equality of the sexes and of non-discrimination on the basis of gender, and was also contrary to the provisions on free movement of persons included in the Greek Constitution and in European law – but to no avail.

Chapter 2. Citizenship, Minorities, Aliens

§1. Citizenship

I. Constitutional and Statutory Provisions

468. According to Article 4 paragraph 3 of the Constitution: 'All persons possessing the qualifications for citizenship as specified by law are Greek citizens. Withdrawal of Greek citizenship shall be permitted only in case of voluntary acquisition of another citizenship or of undertaking service contrary to national interests in a foreign country, under the conditions and procedures more specifically provided by law.'

The law to which reference is made in this constitutional provision is the 'Code of Greek Citizenship' (Act 3284/2004). Special provisions are also to be found in bilateral treaties as well as in special laws for Greek nationals with Turkish or Egyptian citizenship. Act 536/1977 has ratified the Paris Convention of 10 September 1964 on the Exchange of Information Concerning the Acquisition of Nationality and Act 535/1977 the Berne Convention of 13 September 1973 on the Limitation of Statelessness.

A. *Acquisition of Greek Citizenship*

469. Greek citizenship by birth may be obtained either by *jure sanguinis* or *jure soli*.

A child born to a Greek father or a Greek mother irrespective of the place of birth is Greek. Furthermore, a child born in Greece, which does not obtain another nationality, is also Greek (Article 1 of Act 3284/2004).

After birth, a person acquires Greek citizenship by being:

- student at a Greek school or graduate of a Greek school or university (Articles 1A and 1B of Act 3284/2004);
- recognized as a child of a Greek father before the age of 18 (Article 2 of Act 3284/2004);
- adopted by a Greek adoptive father or mother before the age of 18 (Article 3 of Act 3284/2004);
- naturalized after the age of 18 (Article 5 of Act 3284/2004);
- voluntarily enlisted for military service (Article 4 of Act 3284/2004); and
- admitted to Mount Athos (Holy Mountain) as a novice or monk (Article 105 paragraph 1 of the Constitution (*see supra* No. 467)).

Naturalization is decided by the Minister of Interior upon application (Article 8 of Act 3284/2004).

To be naturalized a foreigner must not only be over 18 but also not have been extradited or sentenced by a Greek court to imprisonment for at least one year regarding crimes committed with malice aforethought or for at least six months regarding crimes of high treason, against morals, property, etc. Generally, a foreigner of non-Greek origin must also have been a resident in Greece for the seven last years before applying. Foreign nationals granted refugee status need only have been resident in Greece for the three last years before submitting their application. The seven-year residence requirement is waived for the spouse of a Greek national who has lived in Greece for at least three years and has a child. The residence duration is not a requirement for the individual who was born and resided continuously in Greece. The applicant should also have a particular legal title of residence (Article 5 paragraph 1 of Act 3284/2004).

To qualify for naturalization a foreigner should demonstrate adequate knowledge of the Greek language as well as participation in the economic and social life of the country and the ability for active participation in the political life of the country (Article 5A of Act 3284/2004).

Special regulations apply to spouses of Greek diplomats (Article 5 of Act 3284/2004).

The requirement of seven years' legal residence in Greece causes problems in practice because of the fact that most aliens have entered the country illegally, and because of the difficulty they experience in securing the necessary residence and work permits required to legitimize their status. Thus the majority of aliens in Greece, who are economic migrants or political refugees, have no legal status; their unlawful presence is in a way tolerated by the Greek authorities but does create an atmosphere of constant insecurity and uncertainty for the aliens. To deal with this situation the laws on the status of aliens enacted from time to time make provision for the legitimization of the status of the aliens residing illegally in Greece (Presidential Decree 359/1997, Act 2910/2001, Act 3386/2005, Act 3536/2007, Act 3907/2011; for more on these laws, *see infra* Nos 478 and 480 et seq.).

The documentation required for naturalization is to be lodged with the Decentralized Administration. From there it is forwarded to the Ministry of Interior (Article 6 of Act 3284/2004).

The decision of the Minister of Interior granting naturalization has to be published in the Official Gazette (Article 8 paragraph 1 of Act 3284/2004). It is based on a thorough investigation of the personality of the applicant by the Naturalization Committee (Article 7 of Act 3284/2004). All decisions on applications for naturalization have to be reasoned in accordance with the provisions of the Administrative Process Code (Article 8 paragraph 2 of Act 3284/2004).

Children of naturalized persons also acquire Greek citizenship, without the need for any further formalities, if they are under 18 and not married (Article 11 of Act 3284/2004). Children who have acquired Greek nationality in this way may renounce it if they submit the appropriate application to the authorities within a year of their 18th birthday. Nevertheless, the application is rejected if the loss of Greek citizenship leads to statelessness (Article 19 of Act 3284/2004).

Naturalization may further be decided under special circumstances of exceptional services rendered to the country. In this case, Greek citizenship is awarded by Presidential Decree on the proposal of the Minister of Interior (Article 13 of Act 3284/2004).

Article 1 of Act 3838/2010 provided that children born in Greece by immigrants parents lawfully residing in Greece for at least five years acquired Greek citizenship if their parents asked for it within three years following their birth. Immigrant children had also the right to ask for Greek citizenship even if they were not born in Greece, but had successfully studied in a Greek school for at least six years and resided lawfully in Greece.

The Supreme Administrative Court, having referred the matter to the Full Bench of the Council (Ruling 350/2011 [4th section]), ruled that the aforementioned provisions of Act 3838/2010 were unconstitutional because of the lack of real bond of these immigrants with the Greek nation (Ruling 460/2013 [Full Bench]). Therefore, Article 1 of Act 4332/2015 abolished them.

Children born in Greece by immigrants as well as foreign children having studied in Greek schools or universities can still acquire Greek citizenship, but due to the case law of the Council of State, the current legislation has imposed stricter conditions (Articles 1A and 1B of Act 3284/2004).

The procedure of naturalization is concluded by taking the Greek citizen's oath within one year from the publication of the ministerial decision in the Official Gazette (Article 9 of Act 3284/2004).

Greek nationals who are not simultaneously Greek citizens, admitted to military academies or voluntarily enlisted for military service, acquire Greek citizenship without additional prerequisites (Article 4 of Act 3284/2004).

The Greek Citizenship Code provides for special cases of acquisition of citizenship, for example, for non-Greek citizens of Greek origin living in countries of the former Soviet Union (Article 15 of Act 3284/2004).

According to Article 30 of the Code of Greek Citizenship (Act 3284/2004, regulation introduced by Article 6 of Act 1438/1984), citizenship is not affected by marriage. No person acquires or loses Greek citizenship as a result of a marriage.

B. Loss of Greek Citizenship

470. Loss of Greek citizenship may be either voluntary or involuntary. The Constitution contains no explicit provision for the voluntary renunciation of citizenship. However, such an option is believed to be derived from the right to free development of the personality. The Code of Greek Citizenship provides for renunciation of citizenship on application by a person who has already acquired foreign citizenship (Article 16). The citizenship is deemed to have been renounced from the day of acceptance of this application. Consent will not be forthcoming if the interested party has not met his military service obligations or is the subject of a prosecution for a felony or misdemeanour. Voluntary loss of citizenship may also follow a declaration of renunciation by an interested adult if he no longer has any genuine ties to the country and lives abroad (Article 18 of the Code of Greek Citizenship). In both cases, the consent of the Minister of Interior is required following the issuing of consent by the Citizenship Council. The Code also makes special provision for renunciation of citizenship by Greek children under the age of 18 adopted by an alien parent, by the children of naturalized Greeks and by a foreign woman who acquired Greek citizenship through marriage with a Greek (Articles 19–21).

A person may be stripped of his citizenship only in the exceptional circumstances of acquisition of the citizenship of another State or the 'undertaking of service' in a foreign country, contrary to national interests (Article 4 paragraph 3 of the Constitution; *see also* Articles 16 and 17 of the Code of Greek Citizenship). One provision of the Code is of dubious constitutionality, that which cites as a reason for forfeiture of Greek citizenship the development of activity in another State to the benefit of a foreign State and against Greek interests (Article 17 paragraph 1 b): the phrase 'committing of actions' is much broader in scope than the Constitution's reference to 'undertaking of service'.

Both in the case of acquisition of other citizenship and in the case of forfeiture of citizenship, the action to remove the individual's citizenship is taken by the Minister of Interior on the recommendation of the Citizenship Council.

According to the Code of Greek Citizenship previously in effect (Article 19 of Legislative Decree 3370/1955), 'Greek citizens of non-Greek origin who have abandoned Greek territory without the intention of returning or are born and domiciled abroad may be deprived of their Greek citizenship by a decision of the Minister of the Interior'. This rule was laid down to prevent the return to Greece of political refugees who had abandoned the country after the Civil War (*see supra* Nos 36–46). This evidently unconstitutional provision was rescinded (Article 9 paragraph 14 of Act 2623/1998), and Greek citizenship was restored to surviving refugees who wished to claim it.

C. *Re-acquisition of Greek Citizenship*

471. The Code of Greek Citizenship (Articles 22–24) allows for re-acquisition of Greek citizenship by Greek women who lost it on marriage to a foreigner and by the children of a Greek mother who lost their Greek citizenship because of recognition by a foreign father. In both cases, a statement of intent is required by the interested party and a decision by the Coordinator of the Decentralized Administration.

The Code of Greek Citizenship has dropped a previous provision on the *ipso jure* re-acquisition of Greek citizenship, for Greek nationals having lost Greek citizenship due to acquisition of foreign citizenship. Provision had been made for re-acquisition of Greek citizenship after two years of residence in Greece if they had lost the foreign citizenship.

II. Relevance of Nationality

472. The exercising of most civil and social rights is safeguarded not only for Greek citizens but for foreigners too. However, the principle of equality before the law is only guaranteed for Greek citizens. Therefore, the legislator and the administration, in the discharge of the functions assigned to it, may treat persons with a foreign citizenship in a more unfavourable or favourable way. However, their freedom in this respect is limited in two ways.

In respect of EU citizens, the power of the legislator is restricted by the prohibition on any form of discrimination on grounds of nationality (Article 18 of the

TFEU), and by the gradual evolution of a European citizenship. The formulation of a concept of European citizenship, since the Maastricht Treaty (ratified by Act 2077/1992) means that it is accepted that the legal consequences and rights associated with European citizenship include freedom of movement and residence in any Member State of the Union (Article 21 of TFEU). They also include the right to diplomatic and consular protection in a third country, where the country of which the person in question is a citizen is not represented by diplomatic or consular authorities, by the corresponding authorities of any other Member State, under the same terms as those applying to subjects of that latter State (Article 23 of TFEU). They also include the rights enshrined in the ECHR, the right to petition the European Parliament and European Ombudsman, and – to a limited extent – certain political rights (Articles 22 and 24 of TFEU). However, European citizenship, despite its continual enrichment in content, is still of secondary character, given that it presupposes the citizenship of a Member State (Article 20 of TFEU).

For foreign nationals not from Member States the power of the legislators is restricted by consideration for the constitutional protection of human dignity (Article 2 paragraph 1 of the Constitution). This provision guarantees to all persons in Greece a minimum level of protection of their civil and social rights, including a prohibition on any form of adverse treatment of a person or group of persons on grounds exclusively of nationality. There is a related provision of the Constitution which states that all persons finding themselves on Greek soil shall enjoy absolute protection of their life, honour and freedom, without discrimination on the basis of ethnic origin, race, language, political or religious convictions or any other criterion that might be used as a basis for discrimination (Article 5 paragraph 2). Even though these provisions refer to rights which are entailed by or guaranteed by other constitutional provisions, they do, nevertheless, retain some importance in that they recapitulate the principle of that favourable treatment of foreigners which the Greek Constitution wished to guarantee. Moreover, a whole series of international treaties on human rights, chief among them the ECHR, have the effect of ensuring that foreigners legally present in Greece will enjoy the same protection as that extended to Greek citizens.

Political rights are reserved to Greek citizens. After the creation of European citizenship and the ratification by Greece of the Maastricht Treaty (Act 2077/1992), European citizens enjoy the right to vote and to be elected to the European Parliament and local government agencies, according to the terms of Article 22 TFEU.

The right of Greek citizens to settle in and reside in the territory of Greece is a consequence of citizenship and is expressly guaranteed by the Constitution: 'Individual administrative measures restrictive of the free movement or establishment in the country, and of the free exit and entrance therein of every Greek are prohibited' (Article 5 paragraph 4(a)). This provision does not apply to foreigners and non-citizens. For them, and specifically for foreigners not from Member States, it is permissible to apply the above measures, given that they have no constitutional right of residence in Greece.

§2. PROTECTION OF MINORITIES

I. Constitutional Provisions

473. The guarantee and protection of fundamental rights and freedoms, especially of the *status negativus*, is basically a protection of minorities. To the principle of majority, which permeates the functioning of state power, human rights manifesting the principle of minority are juxtaposed. Insofar as both principles are parts of the Constitution and enjoy the same degree of validity, equilibrium is created in order that cases where majorities oppress minorities are avoided. In this sense, all human rights provisions protect minorities.

A special provision of the Constitution as to the protection of minorities is Article 5 paragraph 2(a) and (b): 'All persons living within the Greek territory shall enjoy full protection of their life, honour and liberty, irrespective of nationality, race or language and of religious or political beliefs. Exceptions shall be permitted only in cases provided by international law.' By the term 'nationality' the Constitution does not mean 'citizenship' but mainly the belonging to a nation or an ethnic group. Article 5 paragraph 2 protects both individuals and ethnic or other minorities, irrespective of citizenship.

The Constitution also protects the organization and expression of a religious minority vis-à-vis the majority of the members of a community holding different religious beliefs (Article 13) (on this issue, *see infra* No. 472).

It should be noted that the Constitution does not give rise to any state obligation to take positive measures to protect, preserve or promote the cultural identity of minorities, or to recognize the collective rights of minorities per se, or, even less so, to recognize their right of self-determination.

II. Religious Minorities in Greece: International Treaties

474. There are relatively few religious minorities in Greece:

(1) *The Roman Catholic minority.* There are some fifty thousand Roman Catholic Greek citizens in Greece, most of whom live on the Cyclades islands, mainly Syros and Tinos, as well as tens of thousands of foreign Catholics, who reside permanently in the country. The first mention of special protection of the Roman Catholic minority in Greece was included in the London Protocol of 3 February 1830 signed by England, France, and Russia. It was determined, *inter alia,* that the Roman Catholic confession ought to enjoy free and public exercise of rites of worship. The Treaty of Sevres of 1920 released Greece from the obligations it had assumed towards England, France, and Russia. The preamble stated explicitly that Greece had granted to every person equality of rights irrespective of origin, language or religion and thus international obligations of Greece ought to be assumed towards the international community in general and not towards particular countries.
(2) *The Jewish minority.* The number of Greek Jews was drastically reduced after the mass deportations to the death camps during the German occupation (most

of the victims were from Thessaloniki and Chania, in Crete). The Jewish community in Greece now numbers some 5,500, most of whom live in Thessaloniki.

(3) *The Muslim minority.* The Muslims of western Thrace are the largest religious minority in Greece. They are estimated to number around 120,000, some 35% of whom are Pomak in origin.

(4) Following the Greek-Turkish hostilities in 1922 the two opposing sides signed the Treaty of Lausanne of 1923 (ratified by the Legislative Decree of 25 August 1923), which provided, among other things, that the Muslim populations then living in western Thrace would continue to reside there, while the Orthodox populations living at that time in Constantinople and the islands of Imbros and Tenedos (which were under Turkish sovereignty) would also remain in place. The same Treaty (Articles 37 et seq.) guaranteed the civil rights of the Muslim minority of western Thrace, mainly those pertaining to freedom of religion. Moreover, provisions protecting human rights and especially the religious freedom of Muslim Greeks had been included in the Greek-Turkish Peace Treaty of 1 November 1913, which was signed in Athens (ratified by Act 4213/1913).

§3. Legal Position of Aliens

I. Constitutional Rules

475. For a detailed account of the constitutional rules concerning aliens, *see supra* Nos 472 et seq.

II. Statutory Provisions

476. Statutory provisions on aliens can be classed as those embodied in EU law, those found in international treaties ratified by Greece, and those contained in Greek domestic legislation.

In respect of protection of aliens from EU Member States, both primary and secondary European law require the same treatment for nationals and Member state aliens, establishing the principles of free access and settlement on the territory of other Member States and the prohibition of any form of discrimination against aliens from Member States (Articles 18 and 21 of TFEU). Moreover, with the gradual evolution and consolidation of the concept of European citizenship (*see supra* No. 472), the legal position of EU Member State aliens is now more or less identical to that of Greek nationals, the only exception being the reservation to Greek citizens alone of the right to vote and stand for election to Parliament (Article 55 paragraph 1 of the Constitution and Article 4 of the Presidential Decree 26/2012).

EU Directives have been issued regulating the alignment of the various regimes in effect for aliens in different Member States (Directive 2003/86/EC on the rights of families to be reunited, Directive 2004/81/EC on rights of domicile granted to third-country nationals – victims of people trafficking, Directive 2005/85/EC on minimum standards on procedures in Member States for granting and withdrawing refugee status, Directive 2008/115/EC on common standards and procedures in Member States for returning illegally staying third-country nationals and so on).

For the protection of non-European citizens Greece has ratified, *inter alia,* the Convention Relating to the Status of Refugees (Legislative Decree 3989/1959), though with some reservations, the ECHR (Legislative Decree 53/1974), and the European Social Charter (Act 1426/1984).

Article 4 of the Civil Code determines that aliens enjoy the same rights of private law as Greeks. But this rule does not rank higher than other laws; thus exceptions may be introduced and, as a matter of fact, do exist in Greek legislation. Thus, for instance, members of the board of unions must in principle be Greek; exceptionally, if aliens are indispensable for the functioning of the union, their number may not be higher than the number of Greek members of the board (Article 107 of the Introductory Act to the Civil Code). Furthermore, third-country nationals may not acquire land in the border area of the country (Articles 24 et seq. of Act 1892/1990).

The most important internal law concerning aliens is certainly the Code of Immigration and Social Integration (Act 4251/2014). This Act (like its predecessors, Act 2910/2001 and Act 3386/2005) represents an attempt to tackle the wave of economic migrants and frame a proper immigration policy, in the context of the international agreements binding on Greece and the relevant provisions of European law.

III. Categories of Aliens

477. Aliens may be classified into the following categories:

- citizens of the EU;
- persons with no citizenship, who enjoy a greater protection than ordinary aliens (*see* for example, Act 535/1977 'On the Ratification of the Berne Convention of 1973 on the Limitation of Statelessness');
- aliens belonging to the Greek nation, for whom the Constitution (Article 108) provides a special duty of concern by the State (*see supra* No. 23);
- refugees, and persons who have applied to be treated as refugees, who are subject to the special protective regime set out in the Geneva Convention (ratified by Legislative Decree 3989/1959);
- ordinary aliens, that is, aliens who do not belong to one of the aforementioned categories.

IV. The Code of Immigration and Social Integration

A. *The Scope of the Code of Immigration and Social Integration*

478. The Code (Act 4251/2014) applies to ordinary aliens and non-citizens. It does not apply to citizens of the EU, to refugees or persons who have applied for refugee status (in the sense of the Geneva Convention of 1951, ratified by Legislative Decree 3989/1959), to persons who several nationalities, one of which is Greek, and so on.

The Act is applied subject always to any more favourable provisions which might be found in international (bilateral or multilateral) conventions (Articles 2 and 2A of Act 4251/2014).

B. Access to Greek Territory

479. A national of a third country, arriving on Greek soil, must have with him a valid travel documentation recognized by the competent Greek authorities. These documents must show, where required by the current international agreements, European law and national regulations, a visa stamp supplied by the Greek consular authority in the place of residence of the alien. There are three types of visas: the uniform visa (Visa C), the limited territorial validity visa (Visa LTV) and the long-term visa (national visa-Visa D). The national visa is issued on the basis of the legislative provisions for the residence permit (on the residence permit, *see infra* No. 481) and its duration will be related, depending on circumstances, to that of the anticipated stay. Nationals of third countries who are not obliged to show a visa may enter and remain in Greece for up to three months – three months as a whole, or fractions of that three-month period during a six-month period from the date of the first entry into the country (Article 5 of Act 4251/2014).

Rejection of visa applications by the diplomatic and consular authorities needs to be reasoned. Special reason is required in the case of nationals of third countries who are members of the family of a Greek or citizen of another EU Member State, or in the case of recognized refugees, etc., subject always to the existence of grounds of public order and security.

The Greek authorities controlling immigration may forbid, on good grounds, the entry into Greece of a national of a third country, when: (i) he does not have valid travel documentation or documentation which permit him to cross the borders, recognized by Greece; (ii) he does not have a valid visa, as it is provided by the EU Regulation 593/2001; (iii) he cannot justify the purpose and conditions of his staying, he does not have or cannot legally acquire the sufficient means to support himself; (iv) he has been registered in the Schengen Information System as undesirable; (v) he is considered to be a threat to public order, security, public health or international relations of one of the EU Member States; (vi) his passport or other travel document does not guarantee his re-entry into the country of origin or country of citizenship or a third country; (vii) he has arrived with the intention of staying in Greece for reasons which require the issuing of a residence permit and does not have the necessary national visa; (viii) he is in anyway involved with illegal transfer of immigrants by an organized criminal group, in which case his entry visa is recalled and his name is inserted in the register of undesirable aliens; (ix) he has submitted forged travel documentation; (x) he has submitted forged supporting documents or there are reasonable doubts concerning either the accuracy of the content of the supporting documents which were submitted or the credibility of his declarations (Article 4 of Act 4251/2014).

C. Residence Permit

480. A national of a third country who has received an entry visa for Greece may seek, immediately after his entrance into the country, a residence permit for the same reason, provided the conditions laid down in law are met. The application for a residence permit must be made before the entry visa expires (Article 8 paragraph 1 of Act 4251/2014). There is provision for various types of residence permit, such as residence permit to work, for independent economic activity, for study, for the purpose of reuniting a family, and so on, which give the holder the corresponding rights of access to the labour market (Article 7 of Act 4251/2014).

Nationals of third countries entering Greece lawfully have the right of residence under the following conditions: (i) they hold a valid travel document recognized by Greece, (ii) they hold a valid national visa, (iii) that they are not considered a threat to public order, security or international relations and are not registered in national databases as undesirable, (iv) they do not pose a threat to public health, (v) that they have full medical insurance (Article 6 of Act 4251/2014).

The residence permit is granted by decision of the Coordinator of the Decentralized Administration or the Minister of Interior. Before that the alien may be invited by the Immigration Committee to be interviewed (Article 8 paragraphs 8 and 9 of Act 4251/2014). The initial permit, unless the law specifies otherwise, will be valid for two years, renewable for three years, until the conditions are met for the issuing of a long-term residence permit (Article 7 paragraph 5 of Act 4251/2014). When renewing his permit the person in question must submit his application in the two months before the expiry of the old permit (Article 9 paragraph 1 of Act 4251/2014). In other respects, there are more specific regulations governing the granting and renewal of each type of residence permit (Articles 15 et seq. of Act 4251/2014).

A national of a third country living lawfully in Greece for at least two years is entitled to request entry into and residence in the country of members of his family if all the following conditions are met: (i) the existence of a family relationship between him and the members of his family; (ii) he has a residence for him and the members of his family; (iii) he has a personal income, which is regular, stable, sufficient for him and the members of his family, not consisting of welfare benefits received in Greece; (iv) he has full medical insurance, which may also cover the members of his family (Article 70 of Act 4251/2014).

An adult national of a third country living lawfully in Greece continually over the last five years may, in special circumstances, acquire the status of a long-term resident (Article 89 of Act 4251/2014).

Once a national of a third country has lived in the country legally for ten years during a period of twelve years he becomes entitled to a residence permit of ten years' duration. The permit is issued following an application by the interested party and decision by the competent authority; it also provides access to the labour market (Article 138 of Act 4251/2014).

A residence permit is not required when the national of a third country enters Greece for a vacation, conference, cultural or sporting events, or generally any stay of a few days in length. In such cases, he may remain temporarily, without a residence permit, for as long as his consular visa remains valid, or for three months during a six months' period in the case of nationals of third countries allowed entry into Greece without a consular visa (Article 5 paragraph 4 of Act 4251/2014).

A residence permit may generally be revoked by decision of the Coordinator of the Decentralized Administration. Apart from the special grounds for revocation provided for the various types of permit (Article 34 of Act 4251/2014 for the permit to study, Article 55 of Act 4251/2014 for the permit for victims of people trafficking, Article 74 of Act 4251/2014 for the permit to allow family reunification), there is also provision for the possibility of revoking the permit on grounds of public order and security (Article 6 of Act 4251/2014).

A residence permit may also not be granted, or be revoked, or not be renewed in the following conditions: where the requirements set out in Act 4251/2014 are not, or are no longer, satisfied; where it is demonstrated by a formal document of the competent Greek authority that for the issuance of the residence permit false or misleading information or counterfeit or altered documents or other illegal means have been used or fraud has been committed; where the applicant does not respond in a two months' period to a written summons by the competent authority regarding the residence permit (Article 24 of Act 4251/2014).

D. Social Inclusion Programmes

481. Act 4251/2014 follows Act 3386/2005 which placed on the statute book for the first time measures applying to the social inclusion of immigrants in Greek society. Specifically, provision is made for the implementation of social inclusion schemes to promote the participation, on equal terms, of nationals of third countries in the economic, social and cultural life of the country, and to encourage their respect for the fundamental values of Greek society (Article 128 of Act 4251/2014). The basic principles of these programmes are as follows: avoidance of any form of discrimination against nationals of third countries in accordance with the criteria set by the Greek constitution; respect for their fundamental rights and protection of the cultural difference (Article 129 of Act 4251/2014).

E. Administrative Expulsion of a Foreign National, Removal from Greek Territory

482. Unlawful entry to Greek territory results in the expulsion of the alien (Article 76 of Act 3386/2005). Unlawful entry is an offence, which falls under the jurisdiction of Greek criminal courts and is punishable with a prison sentence of at least three months and a fine. In order to avoid criminal proceedings, which necessarily prolong the alien's residence in the country, the law provides for a quick administrative procedure: the district prosecutor with the consent of the prosecutor at the appeal court decides to abstain from criminal proceedings and notifies the police authority, which proceeds to the expulsion (Article 83 of Act 3386/2005).

Aliens whose residence permit has expired must leave the country, otherwise, they are subject to expulsion (Article 76 of Act 3386/2005).

Expulsion may also be ordered by the competent criminal court as a security measure mainly in cases where the foreigner has been sentenced to imprisonment, subject always to the relevant provisions of the international agreements which have been ratified by Greece. Also, certain provisions of the penal code or of special penal laws envisage expulsion as a consequence of conviction and sentence. In both cases, the person in question is expulsed as soon as he has served his sentence (Article 74 of the Penal Code).

Administrative expulsion of an alien is also permitted in the following circumstances:

(1) The person has been convicted without possibility of further appeal and given a custodial sentence of at least a year or, irrespective of the sentence, has been convicted of crimes against the State, treason, crimes associated with distribution of narcotics, legalization of income from unlawful activities, international financial crimes, crimes using high technology, abduction of a minor, crimes against sexual freedom and sexual exploitation crimes, theft, etc., assuming that the expulsion has not been ordered by the competent court.
(2) The person has violated the provisions of Act 3386/2005.
(3) The person's presence on Greek soil represents a danger to public order or the security of the country, or to public health (Article 76 paragraph 1 of Act 3386/2005).
(4) The person's name is included on the list of undesirables kept by the Ministry of Interior, and the person fails to leave the country within the appointed period (Article 82 of Act 3386/2005). Administrative expulsion is ordered by decision of the local Chief of Police after the person in question has been given at least forty-eight hours to lodge his objections (Article 76 paragraph 2 of Act 3386/2005).

When the alien is deemed to be a flight risk or a threat to public order, his temporary detention is ordered until such time as the expulsion decision is issued and, once that decision is issued, the detention will continue until the person is expulsed. However, the person may not be detained in custody for more than six months. This period can exceptionally be extended for twelve more months. The detained alien has the right to lodge objections against the custody decision before the presiding judge of the local administrative Court of First Instance (Article 76 paragraph 3 of Act 3386/2005).

F. Administrative and Judicial Control

483. Expulsion orders of the local Chief of Police are subject to an administrative recourse before the Alternate Minister of Citizen Protection or an authorized body within a period of five days from notification. The Minister decides within three working days of the lodging of the administrative recourse. Once a recourse has been lodged the expulsion decision may not be carried out (Article 77 of Act 3386/2005).

Individual administrative acts issued in implementation of the legislation on aliens (prohibition on entry of aliens into Greece, refusal to grant or renew or revocation of residence permit or work permit, administrative expulsion, etc.), are subject to an application for annulment before the Administrative Court of First Instance. The administrative Courts of Appeal are competent to hear disputes arising from challenges to acts referring to the granting of refugee status and the acquisition or deprivation of Greek citizenship. The rulings of the administrative Courts of First Instance and appeal in these cases may be appealed to the Council of State (Article 15 of Act 3068/2002).

V. Extradition

484. Extradition is provided for in Articles 436 et seq. of the Code of Criminal Procedure, which is applicable if international conventions do not provide otherwise.

The Constitution includes a specific provision prohibiting extradition of aliens prosecuted for their action as freedom fighters (Article 5 paragraph 2 c). The Code of Criminal Procedure prohibits also extradition, *inter alia,* when the act committed abroad belongs to the jurisdiction of Greek courts or constitutes a political, military, tax or press crime, or when it is presumed that the accused person will be prosecuted for acts different from those for which extradition is requested (Article 438).

Extradition is ordered by the Minister of Justice only in case the competent judicial council makes a positive proposal. The proposal is, however, not binding on the Minister, who has discretionary power. However, if the judicial council decides for non-extradition, the case is closed (Article 452 of the Presidential Decree 258/1986).

The judicial council has three members and consists of appeal court judges (Article 448 of the Presidential Decree 258/1986). The person whose extradition is requested or the Prosecutor is entitled to appeal against the judgment before the second section of the Supreme Civil and Criminal Court within a time period of twenty-four hours (Article 451 of the Presidential Decree 258/1986).

Act 4165/1961 has ratified the European Convention on Extradition of 1957, though with some reservations concerning Articles 6 paragraph 1(iii), 7 paragraphs 1, 11, 18 paragraph 4(ii) and 19. Concerning EU Member States the Convention has been replaced by the provisions of the European Arrest Warrant (Act 3251/2004).

By Act 3907/2011 and the Presidential Decree 114/2010 the Asylum Service was established. The Asylum Service is currently regulated by Act 4375/2016. It mainly adjudicates granting refugee status to aliens and persons with no citizenship and generally on application for international protection (Article 1 of Act 4375/2016). The Appeals Committee is competent for the appeals against the Asylum Service's Decisions (Article 4 of Act 4375/2016).

Chapter 3. Taxing and Spending Power

§1. Power to Raise Taxes

I. Constitutional Provisions

485. Article 78 of the Constitution contains the basic constitutional provisions governing taxation. In other respects, taxation is regulated by the constitutional principles and general principles of public law derived from the état de droit.

Article 78 reads as follows:

> 1. No tax shall be levied without a statute enacted by Parliament, specifying the subject of taxation and the income, the type of property, the expenses and the transactions or categories thereof to which the tax pertains. 2. A tax or any other financial charge may not be imposed by a retroactive statute effective prior to the fiscal year preceding the imposition of the tax. 3. Exceptionally, in the case of imposition or increase of an import or export duty or a consumer tax, collection thereof shall be permitted as of the date on which the Bill shall be tabled in Parliament, on condition that the statute shall be published within the time limit specified in Article 42 paragraph 1, and in any case not later than ten days from the end of the Parliamentary session. 4. The object of taxation, the tax rate, the tax abatements and exemptions and the granting of pensions may not be subject to legislative delegation. – This prohibition does not preclude the determination by law of the manner of assessing the share of the state or public agencies in general in the automatic increase on value of private real estate property adjoining the site of construction of public works and resulting exclusively therefrom. 5. It shall, exceptionally, be permitted to impose by means of delegation granted in framework by statute, balancing or counteractive charges or duties, and to impose, within the framework of the country's international relations to economic organizations, economic measures or measures concerning the safeguarding of the country's foreign exchange position.

II. The General Principles of Taxation

A. The Principle of Legality: Content

486. Levying of taxes is only permitted on the basis of a statute, not of an administrative regulation. '*Nullum tributum sine lege*': 'no taxation without representation'. The precise content and scope of the principle of legality of taxation may be derived from Article 78 of the Constitution, in combination with the relevant interpretative solutions in case law, mainly that of the Council of State. Specifically:

- The statute must specify in a certain and clear manner (principle of certainty) all the objectively significant elements of the tax, namely the subject, object, tax rate, abatements and exemptions.

- Parliamentary approval of taxation must be renewed on an annual basis when Parliament votes on the Budget (principle of Annual Parliamentary Consent). Specifically, Article 79 paragraphs 1 and 2 of the Constitution determines that Parliament in the course of its ordinary annual session votes on the State budget of revenues and expenditures for the following year and that all State revenues and expenditures must be entered in the annual budget and the financial statement. Consequently, no revenues may be collected, if they are not mentioned in the Budget. Thus, if during the fiscal year, a new tax is levied by law, it may only be collected if at least the category of the tax is provided for in the Budget. The principle of annual parliamentary consent may be superseded by the principle of biannual consent, if according to Article 79 paragraph 6 of the Constitution, the drafting of budgets for biannual fiscal periods has been established by law (on the Budget, *see infra* Nos 492 et seq.).
- In principle, there can be no regulatory competence for determining the objectively significant elements of taxation. However, since the Revision of 2001 matters pertaining to the determination and collection of local revenues directly from local government agencies shall be specified by law (Article 102 paragraph 5 of the Constitution).
- There may be no retroactive legislative endorsement of regulatory acts determining the objectively significant elements of taxation. It was once common administrative practice for the Minister for Finance to issue decisions on taxation in regard to which not even legislative delegation was permitted, on condition that the decision be ratified by statute. The Council of State, overturning what had been its position in case law up until that time, ruled (Full Bench 3596–3597/1991) that the general practice of retroactive endorsement by law of an administrative act issued without legislative authorization was contrary to the Constitution, since it violated the principle of separation of powers, nullifying the judicial control of the retroactively ratified administrative actions which is enshrined in the Constitution. However, there is no impediment to its application in the future (Council of State 1376/1992, 780/1994, 543/1999 etc.).
- Tax matters may not be regulated by agreement between the State and the taxpayer unless such an agreement is ratified by statute. This constitutional prohibition does not cover the international conventions concluded between Greece and a foreign State, since these come into force on the domestic statute book through the statute ratifying the agreement, pursuant to Article 28 paragraph 1 of the Constitution (*see supra* No. 85).
- The requirement of legislative definition of taxation entails a narrow interpretation of the provisions on taxation. Thus no interpretation *per analogiam* of these provisions can be permitted.
- Wrongly paid tax, in other words, tax whose payment is not provided for by statute or has been levied on the basis of unconstitutional law, etc., must be returned.

B. The Principle of Legality: Limitations

487. The application of the principle of legality of taxation is subject to certain limitations:

- Import or export duties or consumer taxes may be collected not on the basis of a statute but of a bill (loi du cadenas) (Article 78 paragraph 3 of the Constitution). In order words, direct application of the relevant provisions is envisaged by tabling of the legislation in Parliament. If the bill is not passed by Parliament within the determined time limits, taxes collected on the basis of the bill must self-evidently be returned.
- Taxes may also be levied by acts with a legislative content (*see supra* Nos 80 et seq.).
- An explicit exception to the requirement for a statute was also introduced in paragraph 5 of Article 78, which allows the imposition, by means of delegation granted in framework by statute, of balancing or counteractive charges or duties, and the imposition, within the framework of the country's international relations to economic organizations, of economic measures or measures concerning the safeguarding of the country's foreign exchange position. Such acts must be issued using the procedure set out in Article 43 paragraph 4 of the Constitution.
- A particularly widespread practice has been the exercise, on the basis of legislative delegation, of regulatory competence in matters of taxation, through the issuing of Presidential Decrees introducing administrative codes. According to Article 76 paragraph 6 of the Constitution: 'Judicial or administrative codes drafted by special committees established under special statutes may be voted through in the Plenum of the Parliament by a special statute ratifying the code as a whole.' According to Article 76 paragraph 7 of the Constitution: 'Likewise, legislative provisions in force may be codified by simple classification, or repealed statutes may be re-enacted as a whole, with the exception of statutes concerning taxation.' It follows, therefore, that the Constitution now prohibits the administrative codification of tax laws, even those already existing.
- The European Commission is recognized as an agent of primary tax-levying power, which is to say that it may impose taxes directly on Greece, thereby representing an exception to the requirement that tax may only be levied by statute.

C. *The Principle of Equality: Content*

488. The principle of taxation equality is a fundamental principle of Greek public law, enshrined in all the Greek constitutions, in the concept of the universality of taxation (principle of universality) and distribution of public charges on the basis of tax-paying ability. The Greek constitutional texts draw their inspiration from the corresponding formulation of the principle in the Declaration of the Rights of Man and the Citizen, first promulgated during the French Revolution of 1789, and then enshrined in subsequent French Constitutions. The principle of tax equality is a special manifestation of the general principle of equality (Article 4 paragraph 1 of the Constitution), from which it is derived, in combination with the provision (also a special manifestation of the principle of equality) that citizens should contribute without distinction to public charges in proportion to their means. (Article 4 paragraph 5 of the Constitution). Also, in the legislating and applying of tax provisions the equality of the sexes has to be respected (Article 4 paragraph 2 of the Constitution). It follows from the constitutional requirement that tax be based on the ability of the taxpayers to pay that the Constitution requires progressive taxation on income; proportional income tax would be unconstitutional.

According to the principle of universality, every citizen is bound to contribute to public charges irrespective of specific qualifications. Tax exemptions or abatements are not unconstitutional; they comply with the principles of proportionality and universality unless they are arbitrary. Local taxes, for example, municipal or communal taxation, are not unconstitutional either.

D. The Principle of Equality: Limitations

489. The differing circumstances of different taxpayers justify deviations from the principle of equality. Such deviations include the establishment of a minimum threshold of earnings below which no income tax is paid, as well as the variable tax treatment of incomes of salaried workers and the self-employed on the one hand and incomes from farming on the other, and so on.

Deviations from the principle of equality of taxation are also permitted for reasons of the public interest, as is the case when tax incentives are offered in the form of tax exemptions or other tax relief in order to promote investment. It is also legitimate to define tax-paying capacity on the basis of presumptive evidence in order to curb tax evasion. However, taxing income on the basis of conclusive presumptions is of dubious constitutionality, since it reduces the degree of judicial protection (Article 20 paragraph 1 of the Constitution).

Internal double taxation, that is, taxation by two separate bearers of taxing power (e.g., the State and a municipality) of the same object (e.g., income or property) is not contrary to the principle of equality, unless both taxes have the same legal basis. It is also permissible to levy tax taking into account taxes already imposed in calculating the taxable wealth.

E. The Principle of Limited Retroactive Force

490. The burdensome character of taxation, as a drastic intervention by the State in the sphere of economic rights of the citizen, requires very strict regulation of the duration of validity of taxation laws. The retroactive force of tax laws is in principle opposed to the principle of the rule of law, and particularly the principle of the certainty of the law and the protection of the legitimate expectation of the individual, as well as the democratic principle itself. The Constitution establishes the principle of limited retroactive force of tax laws: 'A tax or any other financial charge may not be imposed by a retroactive statute effective prior to the fiscal year preceding the imposition of the tax' (Article 78 paragraph 2) (*see also supra* Nos 64–65). The forms of retroactive force which are not permitted are defined in the wealth of relevant *jurisprudence* of the Council of State.

§2. SPENDING POWER

I. Constitutional Provisions

491. The Constitution contains the basic rules governing the management of the public finances by the State. Specifically, according to Article 79 paragraphs 1 and 2 of the Constitution, in the course of its regular annual session, Parliament shall vote on the State budget of revenues and expenditures for the following year. All State revenues and expenditures must be entered in the annual budget and financial statement. Article 79 paragraph 3 regulates the procedure for voting on the Budget (*see also infra* Nos 503 et seq.).

The Constitution also provides for the drafting of the financial statement and general balance sheet of the State, which shall be laid before Parliament no later than one year from the end of each fiscal year; these are accompanied without fail by the report of the Court of Audit provided in Article 98 paragraph 1 e and are examined by a special committee of Members of Parliament and ratified by the Plenum of Parliament, according to the provisions of the Standing Orders (Article 79 paragraph 7).

492. A constitutional provision relating to the Budget is contained in paragraphs 2 and 3 of Article 73:

> 2. Bills pertaining in any way to the granting of a pension and the prerequisites thereof shall be introduced only by the Minister for Finance after an opinion of the Court of Audit; in the case of pensions burdening the budget of local government agencies or other public law legal persons, Bills shall be submitted by the competent Minister and the Minister of Finance. Pensions must be proposed by means of special Bills; the insertion of provisions pertaining to pensions in Bills introduced to regulate other matters is not permitted, under penalty of nullity. 3. No law proposal or amendment or addition which originated in Parliament shall be introduced for debate if it results in an expenditure or a reduction of revenues or assets for the State or local government agencies or other public law legal persons, for the purpose of paying a salary or pension or otherwise benefiting a person.

493. Furthermore, according to paragraph 1 of Article 75, any bill and law proposal which results in burdening the Budget, if submitted by Ministers, shall not be introduced for debate unless it is accompanied by a report of the General Accounting Office specifying the amount of the expenditure involved; if submitted by Members of Parliament, prior to any debate thereon it shall be forwarded to the General Accounting Office which shall be bound to submit a report within fifteen days. Should this time limit elapse without action, the law proposal shall be introduced for debate without it. According to paragraph 3 of Article 75(a), a Bill resulting in expenditure or reduction of revenues shall not be introduced for debate unless it is accompanied by a special report detailing the manner in which they will be covered, signed by the competent Minister and the Minister of Finance.

494. A constitutional provision relating to the Budget is also contained in Article 80 paragraph 1: 'no salary, pension, subsidy or remuneration shall be entered in the State budget or granted, unless it is provided for by statute concerning the organization or other special statute'. This provision, which was initially introduced in the Constitution of 1911, was intended to put an end to the practice of indirect creation of posts in the public service, for which normally a special law was – and still is under the Constitution (Article 103 paragraph 2(a)) – necessary. This old practice was based on a mistaken opinion as to the nature of the law approving the State budget; it was believed that this law could also extend to other matters, like any other law.

495. The main public finance regulations are to be found in Act 4270/2014 (as amended with Act 4949/2022) concerning State Accounting, which replaced Act 2362/1995, in the Legislative Decree 496/1974 (On Accounting for Public Law Legal Persons) and in other special laws.

Furthermore, the public finances of the Hellenic Republic are subject also to the relevant provisions (enhanced formal validity) of European law and specifically to the rules added with the Maastricht Treaty on the Economic and Monetary Union and the obligation of the Member States to adapt their public finances to certain criteria, specifically to make their central banks independent vis-à-vis the agencies of the broader state sector, and to meet two criteria of fiscal discipline, that is, reducing the public deficit and public debt.

II. The Nature of the Law on the State Budget

496. The law on the State budget could be characterized as *sui generis* regarding its nature. It is a statute, for which the Standing Orders (Articles 121 et seq.) determine a special procedure of enactment. Furthermore, it is a merely statute, not a material law, that is, it is in its substance an administrative act. The two main consequences of the nature of the law on the State budget are, first, that this law may not introduce new legal norms or amend or authentically interpret existing legal norms and, second, it may not impose taxes or other financial charges, such as users' fees, contributions, duties, etc.

Moreover, the Budget is a law with limited formal force since in contrast to ordinary statutes it remains in effect for just one year, or exceptionally for two years, (Article 79 paragraph 6 of the Constitution). Consequently, the law on the State budget is in reality a form of delegation granted by Parliament to the Government so that the latter may proceed to collect income and spend money on behalf of the State in the year in question. The law on the State budget is not the basis but only the condition for collecting revenues and proceeding to incur expenditure. The legal basis for collecting revenues and carrying out expenditures may only be a special law. Both the basis and the condition are necessary in order to receive revenues and proceed to expenditure.

The financial statement and the general balance sheet of the State are laid before Parliament for ratification as specified by Article 79 paragraph 7 of the Constitution and Articles 122 et seq. of the Standing Orders.

III. The General Principles of the State Budget

497. The general principles of the State budget, laid down in the Constitution and the regulations of State Accounting are those of unity, universality, annual consent, and the specific definition of credits. These rules contribute to balanced management of public finances and facilitate Parliament's scrutiny of the management of the finances by the Government. Nevertheless, with the imperative need to modernize public finances, there is provision for numerous deviations from the strict fiscal rules.

A. The Principle of Publicity

498. The principle of publicity is guaranteed by the constitutional rule that the State budget is required to be approved by the parliamentary plenum (Article 79 paragraph 3).

B. The Principle of Unity

499. According to the principle of unity (Article 79 paragraph 2 of the Constitution, Article 49 paragraph 2, and Article 51 paragraph 1 of Act 4270/2014) all revenues and expenditures must be included in one budget. Exceptions are permitted in extraordinary circumstances, for example, disasters, war, etc. requiring extraordinary revenues and expenditures and in the case of major investments, for which an ad hoc budget is drafted and attached to the State Budget.

Act 4270/2014 also allows for deviations from rigorous application of the principle of unity. According to Article 60 paragraphs 1 and 2, the Minister for Finance has the possibility to submit a proposal for the amendment of the Budget's credits by laying a supplementary budget before the Parliament. Furthermore, he is obliged to lay before the Parliament a supplementary budget, mainly when the anticipated expenditure is going to be exceeded as well as when financial or fiscal developments require a significant reduction of the approved Budget's credits.

A basic deviation from the principle of unity, provided for in Greek public finance legislation, is the public investment budget. Specifically, according to Article 57 of Act 4270/2014, the Minister for Finance draws up the Budget for public investments, which contains only expenditures, designed for the execution of productive projects by the State. This budget is financed from special sources of public revenue, chief among which is income from loans.

In addition, local government agencies and public law legal persons draw up special budgets which are not incorporated in the general State budget. Another deviation from the principle of unity is the keeping of special accounts outside the Budget, used to pursue special state objectives.

C. *The Principle of Universality*

500. Pursuant to the principle of universality (Article 79 paragraph 2 of the Constitution, Articles 49 paragraph 2 and 51 paragraph 1 of Act 4270/2014) all State income and expenditures must be shown *in toto*, without interdependence or offsetting of one item against another, within the single text of the State budget.

One deviation from the principle of universality is found in the funding of the public investment budget with income derived almost exclusively from public loans, and another deviation in the procedure which by decision of the Minister for Finance allows the increase of Ministries' and Decentralized Administrations' credits with amounts of equal value to income which had not been provided for in the Budget, e.g., income deriving from the collection of amounts unduly paid (Article 74 of Act 4270/2014).

D. *The Principle of Specialization*

501. The principle of specific definition pertains only to expenditure and does not extend to the income side of the Budget. This principle requires that each credit entered into the State budget must be earmarked for a specific item of spending and may not be used for any other item. A product of the principle of specific definition of expenditure is the rule that the amount of credits referred to in the Budget is a limiting amount in the sense that it may not be exceeded in any way (Article 49 paragraph 2 of Act 4270/2014), in contrast with revenues, whose listing is purely indicative, meaning that the competent authorities may continue to collect the revenues even if they have exceeded the amounts specified in the Budget.

The principle of specific definition of credits is not enshrined in the Constitution but regulated by law. As provided by Article 51 paragraph 2 of Act 4270/2014, according to the principles of budget's specialization and specific definition of credits: (a) the expenses of the Budget are described in accordance with the predetermined analytical codified classification which is decided by the Minister for Finance, (b) the usage of credits for a purpose different from the one mentioned in the Budget is generally not allowed. The method of transfer of credits (increase in the credit of one ministry and a corresponding decrease in the credit of another) is an exception to these rules (Article 71 of Act 4270/2014).

E. *The Principle of Annual Parliamentary Consent*

502. The principle of annual consent is established by the provisions of paragraph 1 of Article 79 of the Constitution and paragraph 1 of Article 49 of Act 4270/2014. This principle comprehends two separate rules:

(1) the process of approval of the Budget must be repeated each year and be completed before the beginning of the financial year it covers; and

(2) the Parliament's delegation to the Government to collect income and commit expenditure shall remain in force for only one financial year; after the passage of that year no expense may be committed and no revenue collected.

Thus the Government is obliged to use the delegation within the financial year for which it is granted; once twelve months have elapsed, the delegation ceases to be valid.

The Constitution provides for the option of voting on a two-year budget (Article 79 paragraph 6), although the option has not to date been used. There is a deviation from the principle of annual consent in the possibility of voting for a special law for the provisional management of State income and spending in circumstances where for some reason voting on the State budget is not feasible (Article 79 paragraph 4 of the Constitution).

Furthermore, in circumstances where voting on the State Budget before the beginning of the financial year is not possible because the parliamentary session has ended or Parliament has been dissolved, the Constitution permits the Government to extend for four months – by Presidential Decree to be issued at the proposal of the Cabinet – the validity of the Budget which has expired or is soon to expire, on condition that the amounts of income and credits do not exceed one-third of the corresponding sums entered in the Budget for this year (Article 79 paragraph 5 of the Constitution and Article 61 of Act 4270/2014).

In addition to these cases, there are other deviations from the principle of annual consent, chief among which are the supply of new credits which originate from the Credit Reserve Account of the Ministry of Finance to deal with emergency expenditure or expenditure originating from the setting up of new departments (Article 59 of Act 4270/2014), the method of credit transfer (Article 71 of Act 4270/2014) and the issuing of provisional financial orders (Article 105 of Act 4270/2014).

IV. The Procedure for Drawing Up and Voting on the State Budget

503. The task of drawing up the State Budget lies in the competence of the Executive Branch, specifically the Minister of Finance. The first stage in preparation of the Budget involves all the individual ministries and Decentralized Administrations, which receive proposals from their own agencies and departments and a recommendation from the Public Finance Audit Services and then proceed to compile an income and spending plan, which they forward to the General State Accounting Office. The latter is a branch of the Ministry of Finance, where officials collate all the individual draft budgets from the ministries and Decentralized Administrations and make the appropriate adjustments to income and expenditure in order to balance the individual budgets (Article 54 of Act 4270/2014).

The final version of the State budget is compiled by the Minister of Finance, after conferring with the competent Ministers. Any disputes which may arise at this stage between the Minister of Finance and other Ministers are resolved by the Prime Minister. Moreover, the Prime Minister and Minister of Finance may, as part of the general framing of government policy, issue guidelines to Ministers on the manner in which their ministerial budgets should be prepared and the criteria to be employed.

One of the innovations in the revised paragraph 3 of Article 79 of the Constitution (Revision of 2001) is the regulation which requires that during the elaboration of the final draft of the Budget, the Minister of Finance will, on the first regular day of parliamentary business, present a draft of the Budget to the competent parliamentary committee, that is, the Standing Committee on Economic Affairs. The Committee then formulates its observations on the draft, which must be taken into account in drawing up the final version. Once the final version is ready it is forwarded to the National Printing Office with orders from the Minister of Finance for its publication. These provisions introduce, for the first time, the participation of organs of the Legislative Branch in the process of drawing up the Budget, even though their contribution is confined to the formulation of an opinion.

The draft budget is submitted by the Minister of Finance to the competent standing parliamentary committee on the first Monday of October and shall be debated, as specified by the Standing Orders. Its concise, introductory report is published on the website of the Ministry of Finance (Article 58 paragraph 1 of Act 4270/2014). The Minister of Finance, taking into account the remarks of the committee, introduces the Budget to Parliament at least forty days before the beginning of the fiscal year. The Budget is debated and voted on by the Plenum in accordance with the provisions of the Standing Orders, which ensure the right of all political factions in Parliament to express their views.

504. The usual procedure (one debate on principle, one clause by clause and one on the bill in its entirety for discussion and voting of statutes) is not followed with the Budget; instead, discussion focuses directly on its content. For Parliament, voting on the Budget is an imperative, not a potential character. During debate and voting Parliament has limited scope for amendment of the individual fiscal figures in the Budget, provided that these amendments do not affect what is known as mandatory or inelastic expenditure.

In May 2008, Article 79 paragraph 1 of the Constitution was revised and it was added that the Parliament may submit proposals for modification of particular items of the State budget during the discussion of the draft budget. These proposals are voted on by the Plenum under the condition that they do not influence the total expenditures and revenues of the State. The Standing Orders provide the specific procedure for the follow-up of the execution of the State Budget by the Parliament.

The vote on the State Budget is intensely political in nature, in the sense that it is seen as a renewal of Parliament's confidence in the Government. Were a budget to be rejected by Parliament, the Government would have no option but to resign, since such a rejection would represent, albeit indirectly, a withdrawal of parliamentary confidence.

V. Judicial Review of the Execution of the State Budget

505. In reviewing the execution of the State budget, particularly its legality and regularity, the principal role is played by the Court of Audit, which is the country's highest Court of Public Finance. The Court of Audit confines itself to a rigorous scrutiny of legality; it does not review the prudent management of the public finances, or the question of whether there is effective and productive return on public spending, in the manner of the European Court of Audit (on the Court of Audit *see supra* Nos 203 et seq., 305–306 and 329–330).

Chapter 4. The State of Siege (Emergency): War

§1. The State of Siege (Emergency)

I. Constitutional Provisions

506. The state of siege (emergency) is provided for in Article 48 of the Constitution. Experience of numerous periods of political upheaval and crisis, with consequent violations of earlier Constitutions, led in 1975 to the introduction of a special constitutional provision relating to the state of siege (emergency). The original provisions of the Constitution came in for fierce criticism, especially from left-wing parties, and finally in 1986, in the first constitutional revision, Article 48 was amended to curb the powers of the President of the Republic. In essence, the amendment introduced a series of statutory deviations from full application of the constitutional provisions, mainly those pertaining to civil rights and rights of collective action.

Specifically, according to Article 48 paragraphs 1 and 7 of the Constitution, in case of war or mobilization on account of external dangers or of an imminent threat to national security, as well as in the event of an armed coup d'état aiming to overthrow the democratic regime, Parliament, upon Government's recommendation, puts in effect throughout the State or in parts thereof the statute on the state of siege (emergency), establishes extraordinary tribunals and suspends constitutional provisions guaranteeing fundamental rights and freedoms. The resolution of Parliament, which is taken by a three-fifths majority of the total number of its members, is published by the President of the Republic.

The duration of the above measures, which may not exceed fifteen days, must be fixed in the resolution of Parliament taken by the aforementioned majority.

If Parliament is not in session or if it cannot convene in time, the state of siege (emergency) may be decided upon by the Government and put into operation by Presidential Decree. In this case, the Presidential Decree must within the next fifteen days be submitted to Parliament for approval (Article 48 paragraph 2 of the Constitution).

If it is necessary to extend the time period of the state of siege (emergency) for more than fifteen days, Parliament decides upon this extension every fifteen days. No substitution of Parliament is allowed for the extension (Article 48 paragraph 3 of the Constitution).

During the state of siege (emergency) the President of the Republic may, on the proposal of the Government, issue acts with legislative content in order to meet the extraordinary emergencies or in order to restore constitutional institutions. These acts must be submitted to Parliament within fifteen days and must be approved by it within the next fifteen days. If these time limits are exceeded, acts with legislative content cease henceforth to be valid.

The statute on the state of siege (emergency) may not be amended during its enforcement (Article 48 paragraph 5 of the Constitution).

No use has to date been made of the provisions of Article 48.

II. Statutory Provisions: The Power of the Military

507. The statute executing Article 48 of the Constitution is Act 566/1977. Many of its provisions, never enforced in practice, have been criticized as unconstitutional.

Specifically, Act 566/1977 'On the State of Siege (Emergency)' determines that all competences and powers concerning the protection of the security of the State and the protection of public order are exercised by military authorities to such an extent as is considered necessary (Article 2 of Act 566/1977). If constitutional provisions on fundamental rights and freedoms are suspended, military authorities may proceed to conduct house searches without the presence of representatives of the Judiciary, restrict free movement, prohibit any kind of assembly, dissolve unions, take preventive measures against the press, prohibit strikes, proceed to arrests without judicial warrants, etc. (Article 3 of Act 566/1977). Military courts may judge criminal cases of civilians applying the Military Penal Code (Article 5 of Act 566/1977).

Even though Act 566/1977 applies in extreme situations, it is, nevertheless, based on the idea of relative autonomy of the military. The same idea also applies in emergency situations, such as mobilizations due to dangers to public order and security, not to national or territorial integrity and safety. It even applies to a state of normality. Act 2292/1995, as amended, 'Organization and operation of the Ministry of Defence, administration and control of the armed forces and other provisions', in accordance with Article 45 of the Constitution, which has deprived the President of the Republic of any decisive competences in relation to the command of the armed forces, entrusts this command to the Government, to the Government Council for Foreign Affairs and Defence and to the Minister for National Defence (Article 1).

§2. Powers Relating to War, Treaty and Foreign Affairs

I. Powers Relating to War

508. The declaration of war belongs to the competences of the President of the Republic; it must be exercised in absolute compliance with the rule of ministerial countersignature. (Article 36 paragraph 1 of the Constitution). Thus the competence of the President to declare war is merely symbolic. It is, as a matter of fact, one of the most important issues of foreign policy which is decided by the Government.

II. Treaties

509. The President of the Republic concludes treaties of peace and alliance and announces them to Parliament with the required explanations whenever the interest and the security of the State thus allow (Article 36 paragraph 1 of the Constitution). Agreements concerning trade, taxation, economic cooperation and participation in international organizations and unions as well as any other agreements for which a statute is necessary are also concluded by the President of the Republic but may not be operative without ratification by statute (Article 36 paragraph 2 of the Constitution). The ratification of international treaties may not be the object of legislative delegation (Article 36 paragraph 4 of the Constitution), because such ratification should be made by virtue of a statute.

The conclusion of treaties by the President of the Republic, in the making of which he does not participate, is merely symbolic competence. Formally it is effected by the promulgation and publication of the statute which ratifies the treaty. In very rare cases, that is, in cases of peace treaties and treaties of alliance, which need not be ratified by statute because they do not contain concessions, obligations or burdens, the conclusion of such treaties is effected by Presidential Decree and has to be announced to Parliament. Secret articles of a treaty may never reverse open articles (Article 36 paragraph 3 of the Constitution).

III. Foreign Affairs

510. The determination of foreign policy belongs to the Government. It falls under the main and broad governmental competence of defining and directing the general policy of the country (Article 82 paragraph 1 of the Constitution). Thus the role of the President of the Republic, who represents the country internationally (Article 36 paragraph 1 of the Constitution), is merely symbolic.

Chapter 5. The Greek Debt Crisis

511. The severe global financial crisis of 2008 had a major negative impact on the economic situation of Greece. The first serious difficulties appeared in 2009. The Greek State was already suffering from a huge public deficit and increased public debt, which led to a general financial crisis, due in a great part to the excessive indebtedness of the private sector. This soon evolved further into a social and political crisis. The Government administration as well as the political system failed to meet the challenges of the new reality. Consequently, Greece was excluded from borrowing in the financial markets. Therefore, it asked for the assistance of the EU and the International Monetary Fund. The latter agreed to provide an emergency bailout package on condition of extensive, structural reforms by the Greek State with the aim of improving public finances. The reforms were provided for by three memoranda which accompanied the respective loan agreements: the first memorandum (Act 3845/2010), the second memorandum (Act 4046/2012) and the third memorandum (Act 4336/2015). In the context of the second memorandum, the Greek debt was significantly reduced through the replacement of Greek bonds with new ones of lower value. This project was named PSI (Private Sector Involvement, Act 4050/2012).

512. The measures which have been adopted in accordance with the three memoranda have provoked major reactions concerning their constitutionality. Those who have opposed the measures have argued that the adoption of the memoranda resulted in the unconstitutional transfer of power to define and direct the general policy of the country to Greece's creditors. It has also been said that due to the Greek fiscal programme the EU and the International Monetary Fund exercise an unconstitutional control over the Greek Government as well as the Greek Parliament. It has to be admitted that the supervision exercised over the work of Greek Ministers by the local representatives of Greece's creditors, especially in the context of their technical assistance, has sometimes been suffocating. Legislative initiatives of the Government are often extensively determined by the involvement and desires of those representatives, while their constant pressure for reforms has led to important measures being brought before the Greek Parliament under emergency legislative procedures or in the form of last-minute amendments to irrelevant bills. The extensive cuts in salaries and pensions in particular have caused strong social reaction. During the last six years, proceedings have been repeatedly instituted raising the unconstitutionality of the measures. The European Court of Human Rights has also been asked to adjudicate on these issues. Concerning the salaries and pensions cuts which were decided mainly in compliance with the first memorandum, it has been ruled that they did not violate the ECHR, especially the right to property (ECHR, *Koufaki v. Greece*, *Supreme Administration of Public Servants' Unions (A.D.E.D.Y.) v. Greece*, Judgment of 7 May 2013).

513. The Council of State has also already ruled on a great number of related issues. During the first period of the Greek debt crisis, the Council of State generally ruled that the reforms were constitutional since they were caused by the extraordinary and emergency conditions of the deep financial crisis and did serve a higher public interest. In a trial of tremendous importance concerning the first memorandum (the so-called Trial of Memorandum) the Full Bench of the Council of State ruled that the first memorandum, particularly its provisions concerning salaries and pensions cuts, were constitutional (Rulings 668/2012 and 1283–1286/2012). In another important decision, the Full Bench also ruled in favour of the constitutionality of an extraordinary tax on real property (Article 53 of Act 4021/2011) which was incorporated into electricity bills (Ruling 1972/2012, *see also* Full Bench, Ruling 3342/2013). Nevertheless, the interruption of electricity supply as a consequence of tax non-payment was considered unconstitutional. The aforementioned PSI, the project of Greek debt reduction, was also found constitutional (Full Bench of the Council of State Ruling 1116–1117/2014, *see also* the recent judgment of the General Court of the EU which ruled that the European Central Bank was not obliged to reimburse the loss suffered by commercial banks in the context of PSI [Case T-749/15, *Nausicaa Anadyomène SAS and Banque d'escompte v. ECB*, 24 January 2017]). Further support to the constitutionality of the measures has also been given with Rulings 2527/2013 (Full Bench, concerning the imposition of an extraordinary tax to freelance professionals), 1901/2014 (Full Bench, concerning the abolition of the Hellenic Broadcasting Corporation (ERT)) and 3170/2014 (Full Bench, concerning the abolition or organic positions in the public sector and the suspension of public servants).

514. The position of the Council of State towards the measures, as it has been particularly expressed in its Ruling 668/2012, currently seems to have changed. In its Ruling 2192/2014 the Full Bench ruled that the retroactive cuts of military and security corps' pensions, which were provided for by the second memorandum, were unconstitutional. The same approach was adopted by the Full Bench in its Ruling 4741/2014 concerning the salary cuts of the universities' teaching staff, also provided for by the second memorandum. In its Ruling 2287/2015, the pension cuts which were decided in 2012 were also considered unconstitutional by the Full Bench. Other matters connected to the austerity measures have been approached in an analogous way. Regarding the system of real estate objective values, which is used by the Greek tax authorities to calculate property tax, the Full Bench of the Council of State in its Ruling 4003/2014 called the Government to comply with the pertinent legislation and review those objective values immediately. The Greek Administration had not done so since 2007, despite the financial crisis which led to the collapse of the real estate market values, in order to keep the tax revenues high. Moreover, the continuing inaction of the Government led to a second decision of the Full Bench (Ruling 4446/2015) with which the related omission was annulled. The real estate objective values were soon afterwards reviewed. However, despite this recent trend, the Full Bench of the Council of State in its Ruling 734/2016 has supported the constitutionality of the lump sum cuts of public sector retirement. Rulings regarding the third memorandum which are still pending will permit further conclusions.

515. The Greek debt crisis has multiplied the voices pushing for an immediate revision of the Constitution. It is thought that the amendment of a significant number of its articles could prove helpful in dealing with the financial problems of the country. Among others, it has been supported that the fiscal elements of the Constitution have to be strengthened. Nevertheless, this is not an easy decision, since financial restrictions posed by the Constitution may limit the freedom of the Government to take decisions with a financial impact regardless of their importance. Consequently, this restriction may potentially harm the protection of fundamental rights and freedoms.

Selected Bibliography

Adamopoulou, P. 'Notes sur la législation relative à la nationalité hellénique et le principe de l'égalité des sexes'. RHDI (1982–1983): 131 et seq.

Akrivopoulou, Ch. 'L'effet horizontal des droits constitutionnels et leur protection judiciaire'. RHDH 30 (2006): 556 et seq.

Alderfer, H.F. 'Modern Greek Government'. *Journal of Central European Affairs* 13 (1952): 331 et seq., (1953): 28 et seq.

Alexander, G.M. *The Prelude to the Truman Doctrine. British Policy in Greece, 1944–47*. Oxford: Clarendon Press, 1982.

Alivizatos, N.C. 'Aspects juridiques de la notion de religion dominante'. REDP 17, no. 1 (2005): 151 et seq.

Alivizatos, N. 'Privacy and Transparency: A difficult Conciliation'. In *Scientific and Technological Development and Human Rights*, edited by L.-A. Sicilianos & M. Gavouneli. Athens: Ant. N. Sakkoulas, 2001, 117 et seq.

Alivizatos, N. 'The "Emergency Regime" and Civil Liberties, 1946–1949'. In *Greece in the 1940s. A Nation in Crisis*, edited by O. Iatrides. Hanover and London: University Press of New England, 1981, 220 et seq.

Anagnostou, D. *Le président de la République d'après la Constitution hellénique de 1975*. Paris, 1982.

Anthopoulos, Ch. 'The Preventive State and the Right to Security'. REDP 18, no. 2 (2006): 773 et seq.

Antoniou, Th. 'Ausgewählte Probleme aus der Anwendung des Gleichberechtigungsgebots zwischen Man und Frau, des Art. 4§2 der Griechischen Verfassung von 1975 am Beispiel der Bisherigen Rechtsprechung'. REDP 2, no. 1 (1990): 115 et seq.

Antoniou, T. *Europäische Integration und griechische Verfassung*. Frankfurt am Main / Bern / New York: P. Lang, 1985.

Auty, Ph. & R. Clogg (eds). *British Policy Towards Wartime Resistance in Yugoslavia and Greece*. London: Macmillan, 1975.

Bacoyannis, C. 'Autonomie régionale et locale et Constitutions (Grèce)'. *AIJC 2006*, XXII (2006), Aix-en-Provence: Economica – Presses Universitaires d'Aix-Marseille, 2007, 201 et seq.

Bacoyannis, C. 'Chronique Grèce 1999 – La faiblesse du contrôle juridictionnel devant l'inconstitutionnalité des deux grandes réformes des années 1990 relatives à l'organisation territoriale'. *AIJC 1999*, XV (1999), Aix-en-Provence: Economica – Presses Universitaires d'Aix-Marseille, 2000, 701 et seq.

Selected Bibliography

Bacoyannis, C. 'Chronique Grèce 1998'. *AIJC 1998,* XIV (1998), Aix-en-Provence: Economica – Presses Universitaires d'Aix-Marseille, 1999, 791 et seq.

Bacoyannis, C. 'Chronique Grèce 1997'. *AIJC 1997*, XIII (1997), Aix-en-Provence: Economica – Presses Universitaires d'Aix-Marseille, 1998, 701 et seq.

Bacoyannis, C. 'Chronique Grèce 1996'. *AIJC 1996*, XII (1996), Aix-en-Provence: Economica – Presses Universitaires d'Aix-Marseille, 1997, 701 et seq.

Bacoyannis, C. 'Chronique Grèce 1995'. *AIJC 1995*, XI (1995), Aix-en-Provence: Economica – Presses Universitaires d'Aix-Marseille, 1996, 771 et seq.

Bacoyannis, C. 'La jurisprudence constitutionnelle du Conseil d'État grec en 1993' (Chronique) & 'La jurisprudence constitutionnelle du Conseil d'État grec en 1994' (Chronique), *AIJC 1995*, X (1994), Aix-en-Provence: Economica – Presses Universitaires d'Aix-Marseille, 1995, 563 et seq. & 588 et seq.

Bacoyannis, C. 'La jurisprudence constitutionnelle du Conseil d'État grec en 1992' (Chronique), *AIJC 1992*, VIII (1992), Aix-en-Provence: Economica – Presses Universitaires d'Aix-Marseille, 1994, 527 et seq.

Bacoyannis, C. 'Le Conseil d'État grec devant deux questions fondamentales liées à l'exercice du contrôle de constitutionnalité' (Chronique Grèce 1991), *AIJC 1991*, VII (1991), Aix-en-Provence: Economica – Presses Universitaires d'Aix-Marseille, 1993, 577 et seq.

Bacoyannis, C. *Le principe constitutionnel de libre administration des collectivités territoriales*. Presses Universitaires d'Aix-Marseille-Economica, 1993.

Bacoyannis, C. 'Chronique Grèce 1990'. *AIJC 1990*, VI (1990), Aix-en-Provence: Economica – Presses Universitaires d'Aix-Marseille, 1992, 683 et seq.

Bacoyannis, C. 'Les bases constitutionnelles de l'organisation universitaire en Grèce selon la Cour Spéciale Suprême – L'influence de la jurisprudence du Conseil Constitutionnel (Chronique Grèce 1985)'. *AIJC 1985*, I (1985), Aix-en-Provence: Economica – Presses Universitaires d'Aix-Marseille, 1987, 457 et seq.

Barbaroussis, N. *La fonction régulatrice du président de la Troisième République hellénique*. Paris: LGJD, Bibliothèque Constitutionnelle et de Science Politique 97, 2000.

Bargiotas, Th. & E. Maganaris. 'Privacy under Attack? The Surveillance Phenomenon in Europe, the Legitimacy of Workplace Monitoring and the Greek Paradigm', REDP 18, no. 3 (2006): 1037 et seq.

Bendermacher-Geroussis, B. & A. Bendermacher-Geroussis, 'Le contrôle juridictionnel du pouvoir discrétionnaire dans l'expulsion et l'extradition des étrangers'. RHDI 38–39 (1985–1986): 375 et seq.

Beys, K. *Prozessuales Denken aus Attica*. Athen: Eunomia Verlag, 2000.

Briolas, D. & Th. Fortsakis. 'L'égalité dans l'éducation en Grèce'. *European Journal for Education Law and Policy, Journal of the European Association for Education Law and Policy* 5, nos 1–2 (2001), 103 et seq.

Calogeropoulos, A. 'Les fondements constitutionnels de l'adhésion de la Grèce aux Communautés européennes'. RDP (1981): 97 et seq.

Campbell, J. & Ph. Sherrard. *Modern Greece*. London: Benn, 1968.

Carey, J.P.C. & A.G. Carey. *The Web of Modern Greek Politics*. New York: Columbia University Press, 1968.

Chalazonitis, K. 'Le droit de la défense devant l'administration en droit hellénique'. RHDI 37 (1984): 255 et seq.

Chryssanthakis, C. 'Le Corps des fonctionnaires'. In *L'Administration publique en Grèce*, Ep. Spiliotopoulos, A. Makrydimitris (dir.) & K. Préface Chalazonitis, Athènes – Komotini: Ant. N. Sakkoulas, 2001, 83 et seq.

Chryssanthakis, C. 'The Civil Service'. In *Public Administration in Greece*, edited by Ep. Spiliotopoulos, A. Makrydemetres & K. Préface Chalazonitis, Athens – Komotini: Ant. N. Sakkoulas, 2001, 81 et seq.

Chryssogonos, K. 'Verfassung und politische Parteien in Griechenland, Betrachtungen zum Defizit demokratischer Repräsentation'. In *Political Parties in the 21st Century*, edited by D. Tsatsos, E. Venizelos, X. Contiades, Centre for European Constitutional Law 'Themistokles and Dimitris Tsatsos Foundation', Ant. N. Sakkoulas – Berliner Wissenschaftsverlag – Bruylant, 2004, 335 et seq.

Chryssogonos, K. 'Chronique de Droit constitutionnel – Grèce'. REDP 13, no. 34 (2001): 1209 et seq.

Chryssogonos, K. 'Chronicle in Constitutional Law, Greece: An Introduction to Greek Electoral Law'. REDP 13 (2001): 1209 et seq.

Clogg, R. A *Concise History of Greece*. Cambridge: Cambridge University Press, 1992.

Clogg, R. *A Short History of Modern Greece*. Cambridge: Cambridge University Press, 1979.

Constitution de la Grèce (1975–1986–2001–2008), Révisée par la Résolution du 27 mai 2008 de la VIIIe Chambre Révisionnelle (sous la direction des professeurs Mavrias, C. et Spiliotopoulos, Ep., traduite par Pantélis, A., Koutsoubinas, S. et Vogin-Fortsakis, F.), Athènes: Parlement Hellénique, 2008.

Constitution de la Grèce (1975–1986–2001), Révisée par la Résolution du 6 avril 2001 par la VIIe Chambre Révisionnelle (sous la direction des professeurs Mavrias, C. et Spiliotopoulos, Ep., traduction Vogin-Fortsakis, F.), Athènes: Parlement hellénique, 2004.

Constitution de la Grèce (texte 1975/1986) (traduite par Koutsoubinas, S., A. Pantelis, Ep. Spiliotopoulos). Athènes: Éditions du service des études de la Chambre des députés, 1992.

Constitution de la Grèce (1975) (traduite par Koutsoubinas, S., A. Pantelis, Ep. Spiliotopoulos). Athènes: Chambre des députés, 1975.

Contiades, X. 'The Relationship Between Political Parties and Independent Authorities: Tension and Supplementarity: Theoretical Remarks on the Basis of the Greek Example'. In *Political Parties in the 21st Century*, edited by D. Tsatsos, E. Venizelos & X. Contiades. Centre for European Constitutional Law 'Themistokles and Dimitris Tsatsos Foundation', Bruylant: Ant. N. Sakkoulas – Berliner Wissenschaftsverlag, 2004, 115 et seq.

Contogeorgis, G. 'Political Science in Greece'. In *The State of Political Science in Western Europe*, edited by H.-D. Klingemann. Opladen: Barbara Budrich Publishers, 2007, 187 et seq.

Contogeorgis, G. (ed.). 'La Grèce du Politique'. *Pôle Sud* 18 (2003): 5 et seq.

Contogeorgis, G. 'Religion et politique dans le monde hellène. Le paradigme grec et les églises "occidentales" et "slaves"', Pôle Sud 17 (2002): 81 et seq.

Contogeorgis, G. 'Le phénomène identitaire en Grèce. Entre le cosmosystème hellénique et l'État nation'. *Revue Internationale de Politique Comparée* 5 (1998): 59 et seq.

Selected Bibliography

Contogeorgis, G. *Histoire de la Grèce*. Paris: Hatier, 1992.

Coufoudakis, V. (ed.). *Greece and the New Balkans: Challenges and Opportunities*. New York: Pella, 1999.

Couloumbis, Th. & J. Latrides. *Greek-American Relations: A Critical Review*. New York: Pella, 1980.

Couloumbis, Th., J. Petropoulos & H. Psomiades. *Foreign Interference in Greek Politics: A Historical Perspective*. New York: Pella, 1976.

Dagtoglou, P. 'Constitutional and Administrative Law'. In *Introduction to Greek Law*, edited by Kozyris Kerameus, 3rd rev. edn. Ant. N. Sakkoulas: Kluwer Law International, 2008, 24 et seq.

Dagtoglou, P. 'The Judicial Review of Constitutionality of Laws, Some Thoughts on the Present State of Constitutional Law in Greece'. REDP 1, no. 2 (1989): 309 et seq.

Damianakos, St. *La Grèce dissidente moderne*. Paris: L'Harmattan, 2003.

Dellis G. 'Administrative Investigations Before the Antitrust Authority and Challenging of the Administrative Procedure'. In *Competition Law in Greece*, edited by D. Tzouganatos. Alphen aan den Rijn: Wolters Kluwer Law and Business, 2015, 241 et seq.

Dellis G. 'Administrative Sanctions in Greece, Country Analysis'. In *Administrative Sanctions in the European Union*, edited by O. Jansen. Cambridge: Intersentia, 2013, 251 et seq.

Dellis G. 'Can You Teach an Old Public Law System New Tricks? The Greek Experience on Good Regulation: From Parody to Tragedy Without (Yet) a Deus ex Machina'. In *Regulatory Impact Assessment*, edited by J.-B. Auby & T. Perroud. Seville: Global Law Press, 2013, 181 et seq.

Dellis G. 'Régulation et droit public "continental". Essai d'une approche synthétique'. *Revue de Droit Public* (2010): 957 et seq.

Dellis G. *Soft Law and Consultation. Two Instruments for the Improvement of Administrative Regulatory Action*. European Public Law Series, XCVIII. London: Esperia Publications Ltd, 2010, 39 et seq.

Dellis G. 'Régulation, service public et intégration régionale en Grèce'. In *Droit de la régulation, service public et intégration régionale*, edited by G. Marcou & F. Moderne, Tome 2, Expériences européennes. Paris: L'Harmattan, 2005, 307 et seq.

Dellis, G. 'Chronique de Droit Administratif 1996–2001 – Grèce'. REDP 13, no. 4 (2001): 1415 et seq.

Dellis, G. 'Chronique de Droit Administratif 2002 – Grèce'. REDP 14, no. 4 (2002): 1579 et seq.

Dellis, G. & N. Sakellariou. 'The Allocation of Gambling Licences, Radio Frequencies and CO2 Emission Permits in Greece'. In *Scarcity and the State II. Member State Reports on the Allocation of Gambling Licences, Radio Frequencies and CO2 Emission Permits*, edited by P. Adriaanse, F. Van Ommeren, W. Den Ouden & J. Wolswinkel. Cambridge: Intersentia, 2016, 87 et seq.

Dimitrakopoulos, G. & G. Kremlis. *A New Constitutional Settlement for the European People*. Athens: Brussels, 2004.

Dimitropoulou, E. *Vorläufiger Verwaltungsrechtschutz in Griechenland*. Schriften zum Öffentlichen Recht, Band 1010, Berlin: Duncker & Humblot, 2006.

Driault, E. & M. Lhéritier. *Histoire diplomatique de la Grèce de 1821 à nos jours.* Paris: P.U.F., vol. 5, 1926.

Economides, C. 'Le Mont Athos et le droit international'. RHDI 38–39 (1985–1986): 286 et seq.

Efstratiou, P.-M. 'Towards a Unified Judicial Protection in Europe?: Greece'. REDP 9, no. 3 (1997): 777 et seq.

Fassoulis, K. 'Autonomy of the University and State Mechanisms of Control: The Case of Greece'. REDP 16, no. 2 (2004): 417 et seq.

Flogaitis, S. 'La notion de principe de légalité'. REDP 10, no. 3 (1998): 655 et seq.

Flogaitis, S. & P. Pavlopoulos. 'Chronique de vie administrative 1988'. *AEAP 1988*, XI (1988), Paris: Éditions du CNRS, 1989, 421 et seq.

Flogaitis, S. & P. Pavlopoulos. 'Chronique de vie administrative 1987'. *AEAP 1987*, X (1987), Paris: Éditions du CNRS, 1988, 493 et seq.

Flogaitis, S. & P. Pavlopoulos. 'Chronique de vie administrative 1986'. *AEAP 1986*, IX (1986), Paris: Éditions du CNRS, 1987, 399 et seq.

Flogaitis, S. & P. Pavlopoulos. 'Chronique de vie administrative 1985'. *AEAP 1985*, VIII (1985), Paris: Éditions du CNRS, 1986, 417 et seq.

Flogaitis, S. & P. Pavlopoulos. 'Chronique de vie administrative 1984'. *AEAP 1984*, VII (1984), Paris: Éditions du CNRS, 1985, 485 et seq.

Flogaitis, S. & P. Pavlopoulos. 'Chronique de vie administrative 1982'. *AEAP 1982*, V (1982), Paris: Éditions du CNRS, 1983, 537 et seq.

Flogaitis, S. & P. Pavlopoulos. 'Chronique de vie administrative 1981'. *AEAP 1981*, IV (1981), Paris: Éditions du CNRS, 1982, 475 et seq.

Flogaitis, S. & P. Pavlopoulos. 'Chronique de vie administrative 1980'. *AEAP 1980*, III (1980), Paris: Éditions du CNRS, 1981, 477 et seq.

Fortsakis, Th. 'La déontologie des fonctionnaires. Rapport national – Grèce'. *AEAP 2015*, Aix-Marseille Université, Faculté de droit et de science politique, CRA, XXXVIII (2015), Aix-en-Provence: Presses Universitaires d'Aix-Marseille, 2016, 85 et seq.

Fortsakis, Th. 'Musique: les collectivités publiques et la musique en Grèce'. *AEAP 2014*, Aix-Marseille Université, Faculté de droit et de science politique, CRA, XXXVII (2014), Aix-en-Provence: Presses Universitaires d'Aix-Marseille, 2015, 91 et seq.

Fortsakis, Th. 'Le secret administratif en Grèce'. *AEAP 2013*, Aix-Marseille Université, Faculté de droit et de science politique, CRA, XXXVI (2013), Aix-en-Provence: Presses Universitaires d'Aix-Marseille, 2014, 65 et seq.

Fortsakis, Th. 'Armée et Administration – Rapport national – Grèce'. *AEAP 2012*, Aix-Marseille Université, Faculté de droit et de science politique, CRA, XXXV (2012), Aix-en-Provence: Presses Universitaires d'Aix-Marseille, 2013, 81 et seq.

Fortsakis, Th. Chronique de vie administrative – Grèce 2012. *AEAP 2012*, Aix-Marseille Université, Faculté de droit et de science politique, CRA, XXXV (2012), Aix-en-Provence: Presses Universitaires d'Aix-Marseille, 2013, 501 et seq.

Fortsakis, Th. Chronique de vie administrative – Grèce 2011. *AEAP 2011*, Aix-Marseille Université, Faculté de droit et de science politique, CRA, XXXIV (2011), Aix-en-Provence: Presses Universitaires d'Aix-Marseille, 2012, 601 et seq.

Fortsakis, Th. 'Crise et fiscalité en Grèce en 2011'. *Revue de droit fiscal* 2012, Hebdomadaire, No. 9, L'année fiscale, Paris: Lexis Nexis, 2012, 154 (23 et seq.).

Fortsakis, Th. 'Les villes et agglomerations en Grèce'. *AEAP 2011*, Aix-Marseille Université, Faculté de droit et de science politique, CRA, XXXIV (2011), Aix-en-Provence: Presses Universitaires d'Aix-Marseille, 2012, 139 et seq.

Fortsakis, Th. Chronique de vie administrative – Grèce 2010. *AEAP 2010*, Université Paul Cézanne – Aix-Marseille III, Faculté de droit et de science politique, CRA, XXXIII (2010), Aix-en-Provence: Presses Universitaires d'Aix-Marseille, 2011, 559 et seq.

Fortsakis, Th. Chronique de vie administrative – Grèce 2009. *AEAP 2009*, Université Paul Cézanne – Aix-Marseille III, Faculté de droit et de science politique, CRA, XXXII (2009), Aix-en-Provence: Presses Universitaires d'Aix-Marseille, 2010, 537 et seq.

Fortsakis, Th. 'Les transformations du contentieux administratif en Grèce'. *AEAP 2009*, Université Paul Cézanne – Aix-Marseille III, Faculté de droit et de science politique, CRA, XXXII (2009), Aix-en-Provence: Presses Universitaires d'Aix-Marseille, 2010, 77 et seq.

Fortsakis, Th. 'Chronique de vie administrative – Grèce 2008'. *AEAP 2008*, Université Paul Cézanne – Aix-Marseille III, Faculté de droit et de science politique, CRA, XXXI (2008), Aix-en-Provence: Presses Universitaires d'Aix-Marseille, 2009, 389 et seq.

Fortsakis, Th. 'Le contrôle des marchés publics en Grèce'. Le contrôle des marchés publics, sous la direction des G. Marcou / L. Folliot-Lalliot / D.I. Gordon / S. L. Schooner / J. Schwartz / C. Yukins, Bibliothèque de l'Institut de Recherche Juridique de la Sorbonne – André Tunc, tome 21, Paris: IRJS Editions, 2009, 323 et seq.

Fortsakis, Th. 'Les autorités indépendantes en Grèce'. *AEAP 2008*, Université Paul Cézanne – Aix-Marseille III, Faculté de droit et de science politique, CRA, XXXI (2008), Aix-en-Provence: Presses Universitaires d'Aix-Marseille, 2009, 75 et seq.

Fortsakis, Th. 'Chronique de vie administrative – Grèce 2007'. *AEAP 2007*, Université Paul Cézanne – Aix-Marseille III, Faculté de droit et de science politique, CRA, XXX (2007), Aix-en-Provence: Presses Universitaires d'Aix-Marseille, 2008, 499 et seq.

Fortsakis, Th. 'L'enseignement supérieur en Grèce'. *AEAP 2007*, Université Paul Cézanne – Aix-Marseille III, Faculté de droit et de science politique, CRA, XXX (2007), Aix-en-Provence: Presses Universitaires d'Aix-Marseille, 2008, 175 et seq.

Fortsakis, Th. 'Chronique de vie administrative – Grèce 2006'. *AEAP 2006*, Université Paul Cézanne – Aix-Marseille III, Faculté de droit et de science politique, CRA, XXIX (2006), Aix-en-Provence: Presses Universitaires d'Aix-Marseille, 2007, 589 et seq.

Fortsakis, Th. 'Parlement et administration en Grèce'. *AEAP 2006*, Université Paul Cézanne – Aix-Marseille III, Faculté de droit et de science politique, CRA, XXIX (2006), Aix-en-Provence: Presses Universitaires d'Aix-Marseille, 2007, 179 et seq.

Fortsakis, Th. 'Chronique de vie administrative – Grèce 2005'. *AEAP 2005*, Université Paul Cézanne – Aix-Marseille III, Faculté de droit et de science politique, CRA, XXVIII (2005), Aix-en-Provence: Presses Universitaires d'Aix-Marseille, 2006, 541 et seq.

Fortsakis, Th. 'Les marchés publics en Grèce'. *AEAP 2005*, Université Paul Cézanne – Aix-Marseille III, Faculté de droit et de science politique, CRA, XXVIII (2005), Aix-en-Provence: Presses Universitaires d'Aix-Marseille, 2006, 195 et seq.

Fortsakis, Th. 'Chronique de vie administrative – Grèce 2004'. *AEAP 2004*, Université Paul Cézanne – Aix-Marseille III, Faculté de droit et de science politique, CRA, XXVII (2004), Aix-en-Provence: Presses Universitaires d'Aix-Marseille, 2005, 487 et seq.

Fortsakis, Th. 'L'administration et l'énergie en Grèce'. *AEAP 2004*, Université Paul Cézanne – Aix-Marseille III, Faculté de droit et de science politique, CRA, XXVII (2004), Aix-en-Provence: Presses Universitaires d'Aix-Marseille, 2005, 253 et seq.

Fortsakis, Th. 'Chronique de vie administrative – Grèce 2003'. *AEAP 2003,* Université Paul Cézanne – Aix-Marseille III, Faculté de droit et de science politique, CRA, XXVI (2003), Aix-en-Provence: Presses Universitaires d'Aix-Marseille, 2004, 479 et seq.

Fortsakis, Th. 'L'évolution de la fonction publique: vers une européanisation? Rapport grec'. *AEAP 2003*, Université Paul Cézanne – Aix-Marseille III, Faculté de droit et de science politique, CRA, XXVI (2003), Aix-en-Provence: Presses Universitaires d'Aix-Marseille, 2004, 101 et seq.

Fortsakis, Th. 'Chronique de vie administrative – Grèce 2002'. *AEAP 2002,* Université de droit, d'économie et de science politique d'Aix-Marseille, Faculté de droit et de science politique, CRA, XXV (2002), Aix-en-Provence: Presses Universitaires d'Aix-Marseille, 2003, 561 et seq.

Fortsakis, Th. '25 ans de réformes administratives en Grèce: pour quel avenir? Bilan et perspectives'. *AEAP 2002*, Université de droit, d'économie et de science politique d'Aix-Marseille, Faculté de droit et de science politique, CRA, XXV (2002), Aix-en-Provence: Presses Universitaires d'Aix-Marseille, 2003, 111 et seq.

Fortsakis, Th. 'Charte des droits fondamentaux de l'Union européenne: Grèce'. REDP 14, no. 1 (2002): 397 et seq.

Fortsakis, Th. 'La gestion administrative des risques en Grèce'. *AEAP 2001*, Université de droit, d'économie et de science politique d'Aix-Marseille, Faculté de droit et de science politique, CRA, XXIV (2001), Aix-en-Provence: Presses Universitaires d'Aix-Marseille, 2002, 89 et seq.

Fortsakis, Th. 'Art Meets Law in Education'. In *Yearbook of the European Association for Education Law and Policy*, edited by J. De Groof, Ch. De Smets & H. Penneman, IV. The Hague / London / Boston: Kluwer Law International, 2001, 197 et seq.

Fortsakis, Th. 'L'administration et la création artistique en Grèce'. *AEAP 2000*, Université de droit, d'économie et de science politique d'Aix-Marseille, Faculté de droit et de science politique, CRA, XXIII (2000), Aix-en-Provence: Presses Universitaires d'Aix-Marseille, 2001, 127 et seq.

Selected Bibliography

Fortsakis, Th. 'Le secteur Public: Contenu, Limites, Privatisations'. In *L'Administration publique en Grèce*, Ep. Spiliotopoulos, A. Makrydimitris (dir.) & K. Préface Chalazonitis, Athènes – Komotini: Ant. N. Sakkoulas, 2001, 141 et seq.

Fortsakis, Th. 'The Public Sector: Contents, Limits, Privatisations'. In *Public Administration in Greece*, edited by A. Makrydemetres, Ep. Spiliotopoulos & K. Préface Chalazonitis. Athens – Komotini: Ant. N. Sakkoulas, 2001, 135 et seq.

Fortsakis, Th. 'Chronique de vie administrative 1999 – Grèce'. *AEAP 1999*, Université de droit, d'économie et de science politique d'Aix-Marseille, Faculté de droit et de science politique, CRA, XXII (1999), Aix-en-Provence: Presses Universitaires d'Aix-Marseille, 2000, 513 et seq.

Fortsakis, Th. 'La médiation, mode alternatif du règlement des litiges entre les autorités administratives et les personnes privées'. In *Les solutions alternatives aux litiges entre les autorités administratives et les personnes privées: conciliation, médiation et arbitrage, Actes, Conférence multilatérale, Lisbonne (Portugal), 31 mai–2 juin 1999*, Strasbourg: Éditions du Conseil de l'Europe, 2000, 89 et seq.

Fortsakis, Th. 'Le régime administratif des cultes en Grèce'. *AEAP 1999*, Université de droit, d'économie et de science politique d'Aix-Marseille, Faculté de droit et de science politique, CRA, XXII (1999), Aix-en-Provence: Presses Universitaires d'Aix-Marseille, 2000, 139 et seq.

Fortsakis, Th. 'Mediation, an Alternative Means of Solving Administrative Disputes'. In *Alternatives to Litigation Between Administrative Authorities and Private Parties: Conciliation, Mediation and Arbitration, Proceedings, Multilateral Conference, Lisbon (Portugal) 31 May-2 June 1999*, Strasbourg: Publications of Council of Europe, 2000, 87 et seq.

Fortsakis, Th. 'Administration et police en Grèce'. *AEAP 1998*, Université de droit, d'économie et de science politique d'Aix-Marseille, Faculté de droit et de science politique, CRA, XXI (1998), Aix-en-Provence: Presses Universitaires d'Aix-Marseille, 1999, 113 et seq.

Fortsakis, Th. 'Chronique de vie administrative 1998 – Grèce'. *AEAP 1998*, Université de droit, d'économie et de science politique d'Aix-Marseille, Faculté de droit et de science politique, CRA, XXI (1998), Aix-en-Provence: Presses Universitaires d'Aix-Marseille, 1999, 529 et seq.

Fortsakis, Th. 'Chronique de vie administrative 1997 – Grèce'. *AEAP 1997*, Université de droit, d'économie et de science politique d'Aix-Marseille, Faculté de droit et de science politique, CRA, XX (1997), Aix-en-Provence: Presses Universitaires d'Aix-Marseille, 1998, 451 et seq.

Fortsakis, Th. 'Chronique de vie administrative 1996 – Grèce'. *AEAP 1996*, Université de droit, d'économie et de science politique d'Aix-Marseille, Faculté de droit et de science politique, CRA, XIX (1996), Aix-en-Provence: Presses Universitaires d'Aix-Marseille, 1997, 381 et seq.

Fortsakis, Th. 'Chronique de vie administrative 1995 – Grèce'. *AEAP 1995*, Université de droit, d'économie et de science politique d'Aix-Marseille, Faculté de droit et de science politique, CRA, XVIII (1995), Aix-en-Provence: Presses Universitaires d'Aix-Marseille, 1996, 443 et seq.

Fortsakis, Th. 'Chronique de vie administrative 1994 – Grèce'. *AEAP 1994*, Université de droit, d'économie et de science politique d'Aix-Marseille, Faculté de droit et de science politique, CRA, XVII (1994), Aix-en-Provence: Presses Universitaires d'Aix-Marseille, 1995, 415 et seq.

Fortsakis, Th. 'Chronique de vie administrative 1993 – Grèce – Généralités'. *AEAP 1993*, XVI (1993), Paris: Éditions du CNRS, 1994, 475 et seq.

Fortsakis, Th. 'Chronique de vie administrative 1992 – Grèce – Généralités'. *AEAP 1992*, XV (1992), Paris: Éditions du CNRS, 1993, 483 et seq.

Fortsakis, Th. 'La protection sociale des agents publics en Grèce'. In *La protection des agents publics en Europe*, Paris: La Documentation française, 1993, 209 et seq.

Fortsakis, Th. 'Chronique de vie administrative 1991 – Grèce – Généralités'. *AEAP 1991*, XIV (1991), Paris: Éditions du CNRS, 1992, 573 et seq.

Fortsakis, Th. 'Chronique de vie administrative 1989 – Grèce'. *AEAP 1989*, XII (1989), Paris: Éditions du CNRS, 1990, 483 et seq.

Fortsakis, Th. 'La formation et le recrutement des agents territoriaux dans l'Europe des douze, Perspectives 1992'. Actes des cinquièmes rencontres d'Angers, 15–16 décembre 1988, *Les Cahiers n° 27/Nouvelle série* (mars 1989), Centre National de la Fonction Publique Territoriale, 56 et seq.

Fortsakis, Th. 'Personne et Communauté – Citoyenneté commune et identité nationale et culturelle'. In *Verso una Constituzione Europea*. Leuzzi, Mirabelli. Italia: Marco Editore, II, 491 et seq.

Fortsakis, Th. (avec la collaboration de Souma, Th.), '*Les autorités administratives indépendantes en Grèce'. In Les autorités administratives indépendantes: évaluation d'un objet juridique non identifié* (par Gelarg, P.), Office parlementaire d'évaluation de la législation, Rapport sur les autorités administratives indépendantes (I & II), no. 3166, Assemblée Nationale (France), no. 404 Sénat, II (2006), 299 et seq.

Fortsakis, Th. & Em. Velegrakis. 'L'instruction religieuse dans l'enseignement public primaire et secondaire en Grèce'. In *Religious Education in Public Schools: study of comparative law,* Yearbook of the European Association for Education Law and Policy, VI, ELA Springer (2006), 235 et seq.

Fortsakis, Th. & P. Pavlopoulos. 'Chronique de vie administrative 1990 – Grèce – Généralités'. *AEAP 1990*, XIII (1990), Paris: Éditions du CNRS, 1991, 397 et seq.

Frangakis, N. 'Digital Democracy and Threat to Privacy'. RHDH 34 (2007): 459 et seq.

Gazeau, D. *La presse sous la dictature militaire grecque, 1967–1974*, Thèse 3e cycle, sc. de l'information, Paris, 1976.

Gerapetritis, G. *Affirmative Action Policies and Judicial Review Worldwide*. Ius Gentium Series Comparative Perspectives on Law and Justice No. 43. Heidelberg, New York, Dordrecht: Springer Publications, 2015.

Gerapetritis, G. 'Europe's New Deal: A New Version of an Expiring Deal'. *European Journal of Law and Economics* 38 (2014): 91 et seq. and *European Review of Public Law* 85 (2012): 1045 et seq.

Gerapetritis, G. *Affirmative Action: A New Challenge for Equality in Values of Global Administrative Law*. Oxford: Hart Publications, 2011, Ch. 12.

Gerapetritis, G. 'Public Interest Versus Freedom of Competition in Sea Ports' Privatizations: The Case of Greece'. In *Competition and Regulation in Shipping and Shipping Related Industries*, edited by A. Antapassis et al. Leiden-Boston: Martinus Nijhooff Publishers, 2009, 153 et seq.

Gerapetritis, G. 'E-Access to State Documents: From Information to Participatory and Dialogic Democracy'. In *E-Government* (European Association of Legislation [EAL]), edited by U. Karpen. Baden-Baden: Deutsche Gesellschaft für Gesetzgebung (DGG), 8 (2005): 79 et seq.

Gerapetritis, G. 'The Hellenic Council of State vis-à-vis the European Court of Justice: From Voluntary Seclusion to Inevitable Constitutional Dialogue'. In *Essays in Honour of Georgios I. Kassimatis*, edited by N. Alivizatos et al. Athens: Ant. N. Sakkoulas – Berliner Wissenschaftsverlag – Bruylant, 2004, 83 et seq.

Gerapetritis, G. 'EU Law *v.* the Hellenic Constitution: The Council of State Non-approach, Decisions 3457/1998 and 1440/2000'. Revue Hellenique de Droit International (2001): 301 et seq.

Gerapetritis, G. 'Non-judicial Resolution of Disputes in Environmental Law – Greece'. In *Non-judicial Resolution of Disputes in Environmental Law*, edited by M. Sancy. Madera: CEDE, 2001, 104 et seq.

Gerapetritis, G. 'Droit d'accès aux documents administratifs'. In *L'Accès aux Normes Juridiques*, Strasbourg: Editions du Conseil de l'Europe, 2000, 31 et seq.

Gerapetritis., G. 'Publicité et entrée en vigueur des normes'. In *L'Accès aux Normes Juridiques*, Strasbourg: Editions du Conseil de l'Europe, 2000, 9 et seq.

Gerapetritis, G. 'The Right of Access to Administrative Documents'. Human Rights (2000): 599 et seq.

Gerapetritis, G. 'Towards a Unified Judicial Protection of Citizens in Europe'. In *Towards a Unified Judicial Protection of Citizens in Europe*, edited by Ep. Spiliotopoulos. London: Esperia Publications, 2000, 811 et seq.

Gerapetritis, G. *Proportionality in Administrative Law: Judicial Review in France, Greece, England and in the European Community*. Athens: Ant. N. Sakkoulas, 1997.

Gerapetritis, G. (in cooperation with Pantelis, A. and Koutsoubinas, S.). 'Elections in Europe-Greece'. In *Elections in Europe – A Data Handbook*, edited by D. Nohlen & P. Stöver. Baden-Baden: Nomos Verlagsgesellschaft, 2010, 807 et seq.

Gerapetritis, G. (in cooperation with Sioutis, G.) 'Access to Justice in Environmental Matters in the EU – Greece'. In A*ccess to Justice in Environmental Matters in the EU*, edited by J. Ebbesson. The Hague – London – New York, 2002, 261 et seq.

Gerapetritis, G. (in cooperation with Spiliotopoulos, E.) 'The EU Charter of Fundamental Rights, Case-Study'. *European Review of Public Law* 14 (2002): 881 et seq.

Gerontas, A. *Das griechische Verwaltungsrecht, Eine Einführung*. Kehl am Rhein: N. Engel, 1993.

Gialitaki, C. 'Le principe constitutionnel d'égalité entre les hommes et les femmes et la Jurisprudence du Conseil d'État hellénique: L'affaire "Gardes-frontières", arrêt 1986/2005 ass'. REDP 18, no. 3 (2006): 999 et. seq.

Gialitaki, C. 'Le Cadre constitutionnel de l'imposition en Grèce: L'impôt sur le revenu'. REDP 14, no. 2 (2002): 981 et seq.

Gratsias, D. 'Protection des droits et libertés de l'individu par le juge administratif'. RHDH 16 (2002): 1001 et seq.

Haberle, P. 'Funktion und Bedeutung der Verfassungsgerichte in vergleichender Perspective'. *EuGrZ* 32, Nr 22–23, 684 et seq.

Hlepas, N.-K. 'Carte administrative et pouvoir politique: les enjeux de la décentralisation en Grèce'. In Contogeorgis, 'La Grèce du politique', *Pôle Sud* 18 (2003), 63 et seq.

Hlepas, N.-K. 'Local Government Reform in Greece'. In *Reforming Local Government in Europe. Closing the Gap Between Democracy and Efficiency*, edited by N. Kersting, A. Vetter. Opladen: Leske & Budrich 2003, 221 et seq.

Hlepas, N.-K. 'La Décentralisation territoriale'. In *L'Administration publique en Grèce*, Spiliotopoulos, Makrydimitris (dir.) Préface Chalazonitis, K., Athènes – Komotini: Ant. N. Sakkoulas, 2001, 61 et seq.

Hlepas, N.-K. 'Local Government'. In *Public Administration in Greece*, edited by A. Makrydemetres & Ep. Spiliotopoulos Preface K. Chalazonitis. Athens – Komotini: Ant. N. Sakkoulas, 2001, 61 et seq.

Hlepas, N.-K. & H. Heinelt. 'Typologies of Local Government Systems'. In *The European Mayor. Political Leaders in the Changing Context of Local Democracy*, edited by Heinelt Back & Wiesbaden Magnier. Wiesbaden: VS Wiesbaden, 2006, 21 et seq.

Hofmann, E. & E. Iliadou. 'Die Hilfspakete für Griechenland und ihre Umsetzung im Bereich der Altersrenten. Zum Urteil des Höchsten Griechischen Verwaltungsgerichts vom 18. Juni 2015 in der Rechtssache Nr. 2287/2015 und seinen Nachwirkungen', *DÖV 2016*, 401 et seq.Iliopoulos-Strangas, J. 'Constitution et droits sociaux: Grèce'. *Annuaire International de Justice Constitutionnelle*, XXX (2015), Paris–Aix-en-Provence: 299 et seq.

Iliopoulos-Strangas, J. 'Les garanties constitutionnelles du suffrage universel et leur mise en œuvre en droit grec'. In Tanasescu, S.E. & Vrabie, G. (eds), *Constitution, Démocratie et Élections*. Bucuresti: 2015, 93 et seq.

Iliopoulos-Strangas, J. 'La multiplication des garanties et des juges dans la protection des droits fondamentaux: coexistence, cohérence et articulation entre les systèmes constitutionnels, internationaux et régionaux? Evolution d'une décennie: Grèce'. *Annuaire International de Justice Constitutionnelle*, XXVIII (2013), Paris–Aix-en-Provence.

Iliopoulos-Strangas, J. 'Das Verhältnis von nationalem Recht und Europarecht im Wandel der Zeit: Der Vorrang des Unionsrechts aus griechischer Perspektive'. In Schwarze, J. (Hrsg.), *Das Verhältnis von nationalem Recht und Europarecht im Wandel der Zeit*. Baden-Baden: 2012, 227 et seq.

Iliopoulos-Strangas, J. 'Der Vorrang des Gemeinschafts-Unionsrechts gegenüber der Verfassung: Eine noch offene und umstrittene Frage in der griechischen Rechtsordnung'. *Festschrift Christian Starck* (2007): 825 et seq.

Iliopoulos-Strangas, J. 'Les décisions de la Cour spéciale suprême grecque et leur mise en œuvre'. In *Colloqui de justicia constitucional del Principat d'Andorra*, edited by Cour Constitutionnelle d'Andorre, 2007, 75 et seq.

Iliopoulos-Strangas, J. 'Constitutions nationales et Constitutions européennes (Grèce)'. *AIJC 2005*, XXI (2005), Aix-en-Provence: Economica – Presses Universitaires d'Aix-Marseille, 2006, 145 et seq.

Iliopoulos-Strangas, J. 'Constitution et élections (Grèce)'. *AIJC 2003*, XIX (2003), Aix-en-Provence: Economica – Presses Universitaires d'Aix-Marseille, Aix-en-Provence, 2004, 179 et seq.

Iliopoulos-Strangas, J. 'Nationales Verfassungsrecht mit Blick auf eine Europäische Verfassung – Rechtsvergleichende Überlegungen unter besonderer Berücksichtigung des griechischen Verfassungsrechts'. In *Staat, Wirtschaft, Finanzverfassung-Festschrift Peter Selmer*. Berlin: Duncker & Humblot, 2004, 123 et seq.

Iliopoulos-Strangas, J. 'Constitution hellénique et Intégration européenne'. In Association des Constitutionnalistes grecs et Association française des Constitutionnalistes (dir.), *Défense nationale – Intégration européenne – Les réponses constitutionnelles*, Athènes – Bruxelles: Ant. N. Sakkoulas – Bruylant, 2002, 69 et seq.

Iliopoulos-Strangas, J. 'Le droit de l'Union européenne et les Constitutions nationales – Rapport hellénique'. *F.I.D.E.* [Fédération Internationale pour le Droit Européen], XX. Congrès, I. Le droit de l'Union européenne et les Constitutions nationales, Londres 30 octobre – 2 novembre 2002, www. FIDE2002.org.

Iliopoulos-Strangas, J. 'Der Schutz der sozialen Grundrechte in der griechischen Rechtsordnung'. In Bundesministerium für Arbeit und Sozialordnung, Max-Planck-Institut für ausländisches und internationales Sozialrecht, Akademie der Diözese Rottenburg Stuttgart, *Soziale Grundrechte in der Europäischen Union*, Baden-Baden: Nomos Verlag, 2000/2001, 149 et seq.

Iliopoulos-Strangas, J. 'Le droit constitutionnel national et l'intégration européenne'. Deutsche Wissenschaftliche Gesellschaft für Europarecht und Nomos Verlagsgesellschaft (Hrsg.), 17. F.I.D.E. Kongress, Fédération Internationale pour le Droit Européen, *I. Le droit constitutionnel national et l'intégration européenne*, Baden-Baden: Nomos Verlag, 1996, 120 et seq.

Iliopoulos-Strangas, J. (Hrsg.). *Grundrechtsschutz im europäischen Raum, Der Beitritt der europäischen Gemeinschaften zur europäischen Menschenrechtskonvention*. Baden-Baden: Nomos, 1993.

Iliopoulos-Strangas, J. 'Der Einfluß des Grundgesetzes auf griechisches Verfassungsrecht'. In *40 Jahre Grundgesetz*, Stern, K. (Hrsg.). Münich: Beck-Verlag, 1990, 259 et seq.

Iliopoulos-Strangas, J. *Rückwirkung and Sofortwirkung von Gesetzen, Eine verfassungsrechtliche Untersuchung unter Berücksichtigung des deutschen und griechischen Steuerrechts*. Baden-Baden: Nomos Verlag, 1986, 376 et seq.

Iliopoulos-Strangas, J. 'Grundrechtsschutz in Griechenland'. *JöR*, N.F. 32 (1983), 395 et seq.

Iliopoulos-Strangas, J. & E. Georgitsi. 'Juges constitutionnels et Parlements: Grèce'. *Annuaire International de Justice Constitutionnelle*, XXVII (2011), Paris–Aix-en-Provence: 2012, 267 et seq.

Iliopoulos-Strangas, J. & E. Georgitsi. 'Constitutions et droit pénal: Grèce'. *Annuaire International de Justice Constitutionnelle*, XXVI (2010), Paris–Aix-en-Provence: 2011, 241 et seq.

Iliopoulos-Strangas, J. & E. Georgitsi. 'Le juge constitutionnel et la proportionnalité: Grèce'. *Annuaire International de Justice Constitutionnelle,* XXV (2009), Paris–Aix-en-Provence: 2010, 213 et seq.

Iliopoulos-Strangas, J. & S.-I. Koutnatzis. 'Constitutional Courts as Positive Legislators'. Greek National Report, XVIIIth International Congress of the International Academy of Comparative Law (Washington D.C., 25 July–1 August 2010). *Revue hellénique de droit international*, 2010: 351 et seq.

Iliopoulos-Strangas, J. & G. Leventis. 'Der Schutz der sozialen Grundrechte in der griechischen Rechstordnung'. In Iliopoulos-Strangas, J. (Hrsg.), *Soziale Grundrechte in Europa nach Lissabon – Eine rechtsvergleichende Untersuchung der nationalen Rechtsordnungen und des europäischen Rechts.* Athens – Baden-Baden – Brüssel-Wien: 2010, 249 et seq.

Iliopoulos-Strangas, J. & E. Georgitsi. 'Constitution et liberté d'expression (Grèce)'. *AIJC 2007*, XXIII (2007), Aix-en-Provence: Economica – Presses Universitaires d'Aix-Marseille, 2008, 265 et seq.

Iliopoulos-Strangas, J. & G. Leventis. 'La protection des droits sociaux fondamentaux dans l'ordre juridique de la Grèce'. In *La protection des droits sociaux fondamentaux dans les États membres de l'Union européenne – Étude de droit comparé,* Iliopoulos-Strangas J. (dir.), 2000, 395 et seq.

Iliopoulos-Strangas, J. 'Le principe de subsidiarité comme principe de droit constitutionnel' [avec la collaboration de G. Kassimatis], RHDI (1994): 327 et seq.

Ioannou, K. 'The Application of the ECHR in the Greek Legal Order'. *Revue Hellénique de Droit Européen* (1996): 229 et seq.

Jecchinis, Ch. *Trade Unionism in Greece. A Study in Political Paternalism.* Chicago: Labor Education Division, Roosevelt University, 1967.

Kaissis, G. & A. Mavromatis (eds). *Advantages of Arbitration in Greece and Balkan Countries.* International Seminar, Thessaloniki 15–16 May 1998, Thessaloniki: Sakkoulas, 1999.

Kaissis, G. & A. Mavromatis (dir.). *Les Avantages de l'Arbitrage en Grèce et dans les pays des Balkans.* Séminaire International, Thessalonique, 15–16 mai 1998, Thessalonique: Sakkoulas, 1999.

Kaloudi, A. 'Personen der Zeitgeschichte und Pressefreiheit in der griechischen Rechtsordnung'. REDP 13, no. 3 (2001): 1083 et seq.

Kaloudi, A. *Pressefreiheit und Personlichkeitschutz. Ein Typischer Grundrechtskonflikt im Vergleich der deutschen, der US-amerikanischen und der griechischen Rechtsordnung.* Hannover, 1996.

Kaminis, G. *La tradition constitutionnelle en Grèce et en Espagne.* Paris: LGDJ, 1993.

Kantianis, An. *Palliativmedizin als Sterbebegleitung nach deutschem und griechischem Recht.* Frankfurt am Main: Peter Lang, 2005.

Kareklas, St. & Ef. Fitrakis. *Umweltstrafrecht in mittel und sυdeuropäischen Ländern, Griechenland.* Beiträge und Materialien aus dem Max-Planck Institut fυr Ausländisches und internationales Strafrecht Freiburg, Gυnter Heine, ed. Iuscrum.

Kassimatis, G. 'Aktuelle Probleme im Verhältnis von Staat und Kirche in Griechenland' (Disskussionsbeitrag), In *Menschenrechte und Bürgerrechte in einer vielgestaltigen Welt, zur Ehre von Thomas Fleiner*, Häberle, Müller (Hrsg.), Institut du fédéralisme, Fribourg, Suisse, 2000, 103 et seq.

Kassimatis, G. 'Origines et évolution de l'État social'. In *La protection des droits sociaux fondamentaux dans les États membres de l'Union européenne*, edited by J. Iliopoulos-Strangas. Athènes – Bruxelles: Bruylant, 2000, 3 et seq.

Kastanas, E. 'Le droit d'accès à la Justice en droit grec'. REDP 13, no. 1 (2001): 383 et seq.

Katrougalos, G.S. 'Le problème du rapport entre droit communautaire et Constitutions nationales, à la lumière du 'dualisme institutionnel' de l'Union européenne'. *REDP* 12, no. 4 (2000): 1235 et seq.

Kerameus, K. 'Judicial Organization and Civil Procedure'. In *Introduction to Greek Law*, edited by K.D. Kerameus & P.J. Kozyris, 3rd rev. Deventor: Kluwer Law International – Ant. N. Sakkoulas, 2008, 341 et seq.

Kiss, A.C. & P. Vegleris, 'L'affaire grecque devant le Conseil de l'Europe et la Commission européenne des droits de l'homme'. *Annuaire français de droit international* (1971): 889 et seq.

Kondylis, V. 'Chronique GRÈCE 2015'. *Annuaire Européen d'Administration Publique* (2015), Presses universitaires d'Aix-Marseille, 2016: 371 et seq.

Kondylis, V. 'GRÈCE Chroniques 2013–2014'. *Annuaire Européen d'Administration Publique* (2014), Presses universitaires d'Aix-Marseille, 2015: 407 et seq.

Kondylis, V. 'Le chemin vers la construction d'un droit européen des autorités administratives indépendantes entre les Symblégades des particularités nationales et de la application du droit de l'Union CJUE, gde ch., 8 avril 2014, Commission / Hongrie, aff. C-288/12'. *Revue des affaires européennes* (2014): 411 et seq.

Kondylis, V. *Forms of cooperation and Dialogue between national and European Judges*. European Public Law Organization, CIX, 2013.

Kondylis, V. 'Vers la construction d'un droit européen des autorités administratives indépendantes CJUE, gde ch., 16 octobre 2012, aff. C- 614/10, Commission / Autriche'. *Revue des affaires européennes* (2012): 829 et seq.

Konidaris, L. 'Legal Status of Minority Churches and Religious Communities in Greece'. In *The Legal Status of Religious Minorities in the Countries of the European Union,* European Consortium of Church – State Research, Proceedings of the Meeting Thessaloniki 1993, Thessaloniki-Milano 1994, 171 et seq. and in: *Issues of Byzantine and Ecclesiastical Law* II, Athens-Komotini: Ant. N. Sakkoulas 2008, 161 et seq.

Konidaris, L. 'Die Beziehungen zwischen Kirche and Staat im heutigen Griechenland'. *Osterreichisches Archiv fur Kirchenrecht* 40 (1991): 131 et seq.

Kotsiris, L. (ed.). *Racism.* Conference on Political, Economic and Social Racism, 14–18 May 1995, Thessaloniki – Greece, Athens / Thessaloniki: Sakkoulas, 2005.

Koukoulis-Spiliotopoulos, S. 'Gender Equality in Greece and Effective Judicial Protection – Issues of General Relevance in Employment Relationships'. *Neue Zeitschrift für Arbeitsrecht* 25, Beilage 2/2008 zu Heft 10/2008, 75 et seq.

Koukoulis-Spiliotopoulos, S. 'Greece: From Formal to Substantive Gender Equality – The Leading Role of the Jurisprudence and the Contribution of Women's NGOs'. In *Essays in Honour of Alice Yotopoulos – Marangopoulos*, edited by A. Manganas. Athens – Brussels: Nomiki Vivliothiki – Bruylant, 2003, 659 et seq.

Koulouris, N. 'Les autorités administratives indépendantes'. In *L'Administration publique en Grèce*, Ep. Spiliotopoulos & A. Makrydimitris (dir.) & K. Préface Chalazonitis. Athènes – Komotini: Ant. N. Sakkoulas, 2001, 97 et seq.

Koulouris, N. 'The Independent Administrative Authorities'. In *Public Administration in Greece*, edited by Ep. Spiliotopoulos, A. Makrydemetres & K. Préface Chalazonitis. Athens – Komotini: Ant. N. Sakkoulas, 2001, 95 et seq.

Koumoulidis, J.T.A. (ed.). *Greece in Transition. Essays in the History of Modern Greece, 1821–1974*. London: Zeno, 1977.

Koutnatzis, St.I. 'Grundlagen und Grundzüge staatlichen Verfassungsrechts – Griechenland'. In *Handbuch des Öffentlichen Rechts in Europa*, edited by Bogdandy, Cruz Villalón, Huber (Hrsg.). Ius Publicum Europaeum, C.F. Müller, 2007, 151 et seq.

Koutnatzis, St.-I. & Kaboğlu, I. 'The Reception Process in Greece and Turkey'. In *A Europe of Rights, The Impact of the ECHR on National Legal Systems*, edited by Keller & Stone Sweet, Oxford: Oxford University Press, 2008, 451 et seq.

Koutsoubinas, S. 'Jurisprudence constitutionnelle – Grèce – Le contentieux électoral'. REDP 11, no. 1 (1999): 279 et seq.

Koutsoubinas, S. 'Jurisprudence constitutionnelle – Grèce'. REDP 7, no. 4 (1995): 1163 et seq.

Koutsoubinas, St. 'Introduction au statut juridique de l'enseignement privé général en Grèce'. REDP 5, no. 2 (1993): 277 et seq.

Koutsoubinas, S. *Le peuple dans la Constitution hellénique de 1975*. Préface de François Borella, Presses Universitaires de Nancy, 1989.

Ktistaki, S. & V. Papadimitriou. 'Le rôle des juges dans la formation du droit public: Activisme ou autolimitation?: Grèce'. *REDP* 10, no. 3 (1998): 925 et seq.

Ktistaki, S. 'Le principe de la transparence de la procédure administrative en droit administratif hellénique'. *REDP*, Spetses Conférences (1993): 167 et seq.

Ktistakis, I. 'School – Religion Relations: Greece'. *REDP 17*, no. 1 (2005): 333 et seq.

Legg, K. *Politics in Modern Greece.* Stanford: Stanford University Press, 1969.

Lyberaki, An. 'Balkan Migration to Greece: A Success Story?'. In *Olympia IV: Human Rights in the 21st Century, Migrants and Refugees*, edited by Kyriakopoulos, V. Athens / Komotini: Ant. N. Sakkoulas, 2004, 95 et seq.

Makridis, R.C. 'Greek Political Freedom and U.S. Foreign Policy'. *The Massachussets Review* (1968): 147 et seq.

Makrydemetres, A. 'Public Administration in the Political System. The Government, the Prime Minister, The Ministers'. In *Public Administration in Greece*, edited by Ep. Spiliotopoulos, A. Makrydemetres & K. Préface Chalazonitis. Athens – Komotini: Ant. N. Sakkoulas, 2001, 19 et seq.

Makrydimitris, A. 'L'Administration publique dans le système politique. Le Gouvernement, le Premier ministre, les ministres, les ministères'. In *L'Administration publique en Grèce*, Spiliotopoulos, Makrydimitris (dir.). Préface Chalazonitis, K., Athènes – Komotini: Ant. N. Sakkoulas, 2001, 19 et seq.

Manolkidis, S.K. *Granting Benefits through Constitutional Adjudication, The Extension of the most Favorable Norm in Greece and Italy*. Thessaloniki: Sakkoulas, 1999.

Marinos, A. 'L'avant-projet de loi hellénique sur la protection des données'. REDP 3, no. 2 (1991): 405 et seq.

Markesinis, B. 'Privacy, Freedom of Expression and the Horizontal Effect of the Human Rights Bill: Lesson from Germany'. *The Law Quarterly Review* 115 (1999): 45 et seq.

Markesinis, B. 'Reflections on the Greek Constitution'. *Parliamentary Affairs* (1973–1974): 8 et seq.

Markesinis, B. *The Theory and Practice of Dissolution of Parliament: A Comparative Study with Special Reference to the United Kingdom and Greek Experience.* Cambridge: Cambridge University Press, 1972.

Massias, J.P. *Droit constitutionnel des États d'Europe de l'Est.* Paris, 1999.

Matthéou, P. 'Chronique de Droit Administratif – Grèce'. REDP 8, no. 2 (1996): 477 et seq.

Matthéou, P. 'L'incorporation de la Charte Européenne de l'Autonomie Locale en droit grec'. REDP 6, no. 2 (1994): 323 et seq.

Mavrias, C. 'Les fonctions de décision et de contrôle. Le cas de la Grèce'. In *Le Parlement aujourd'hui?.* Galatasaray Űniversitesi Yayilari – Presses de l'Université de Sciences Sociales de Toulouse 1, 2005, 273 et seq.

Mavrias, C. 'Les principes constitutionnels régissant le droit des élections législatives en Grèce'. In *Essays in honour of Georgios I. Kassimatis.* Athens: Ant. N. Sakkoulas – Berliner Wissenschaftsverlag – Bruylant, 2004, 201 et seq.

Mavrias, C. 'Mandat parlementaire et réforme du régime des incompatibilités après la deuxième révision (2001) de la Constitution hellénique de 1975'. In *Mélanges Pavle Nicolic.* Belgrade, 2004, 315 et seq.

Mavrias, C. 'Luttes contre le terrorisme et protection des droits fondamentaux (Grèce)'. *AIJC 2002*, XVIII (2002), Aix-en-Provence: Economica – Presses Universitaires d'Aix-Marseille, 2003, 245 et seq.

Mavrias, C. 'Le principe de légalité et la protection des libertés publiques dans l'administration hellénique d'après la Constitution de 1975'. in *Études juridiques et politiques*, Athènes – Komotini: Ant. N. Sakkoulas, 1982, 115 et seq.

Mavrias, C. 'Les garanties accordées aux investisseurs étrangers'. In *Études juridiques et politiques*, Athènes – Komotini: Ant. N. Sakkoulas, 1982, 97 et seq.

Mavrias, C. 'Rôle et pouvoirs du Conseil des Ministres en droit hellénique'. In *Études juridiques et politiques*, Athènes – Komotini: Ant. N. Sakkoulas, 1982, 129 et seq.

Mavrias, C. *Le régime juridique des investissements étrangers en Grèce – Contribution à une théorie de l'investissement international.* Thèse, Paris, Éditions Pédone, 1975.

Mavris, Y. 'Political Parties, Mass Media and Opinion polls in Greece'. In *Political Parties in the 21st Century*, edited by D. Tsatsos, E. Venizelos, X. Contiades. Centre for European Constitutional Law 'Themistokles and Dimitris Tsatsos Foundation', Ant. N. Sakkoulas – Berliner Wissenschaftsverlag – Bruylant, 2004, 153 et seq.

Metaxas, J. 'L'administration grecque devant les transformations économiques et sociales contemporaines'. *AEAP 1978*, I (1978), Paris: Éditions du CNRS, 1979, 41 et seq.

Meynaud, J. *Les forces politiques en Grèce*. avec le concours de P. Merlopoulos et G. Notaras, Lausanne: Études de science politique n°10, 1965.

Michalopoulos, N. 'Méthodes d'administration et d'organisation des relations État-citoyen'. In *L'Administration publique en Grèce*, Ep. Spiliotopoulos, A. Makrydimitris (dir.) & K. Préface Chalazonitis. Athènes – Komotini: Ant. N. Sakkoulas, 2001, 185 et seq.

Michalopoulos, N. 'Methods of Management and State-Citizen Relations'. In *Public Administration in Greece*, edited by Ep. Spiliotopoulos, A. Makrydemetres & K. Préface Chalazonitis. Athens – Komotini: Ant. N. Sakkoulas, 2001, 177 et seq.

Miller, W. *A History of Greek People (1821–1921)*. London: Methuen, 1922.

Mitrou, L. 'The Greek Law on the Protection of Personal Data'. In *Scientific and Technological Development and Human Rights*, edited by L.-A. Sicilianos & M. Gavouneli. Athens: Ant. N. Sakkoulas, 2001, 143 et seq.

Moukiou, Ch. 'Chronique, de Droit Administratif'. REDP 17, no. 4 (2005): 1593 et seq.

Moussourou, L. & P. Petroglou. 'Concilier famille et travail en Grèce: droit et pratiques'. In *Concilier famille et travail pour les hommes et les femmes: droit et pratiques*. Association des femmes de l'Europe Méridionale (AFEM), Bruxelles: Ant. N. Sakkoulas - Bruylant, 2005, 109 et seq.

Mouzelis, N. *Modern Greece. Facets of Underdevelopment*. London: Macmillan, 1975.

Nicot, S. & D. Sidirokastriti. 'Immunités constitutionnelles et privilèges de juridiction en Grèce'. *AIJC 2001*, XVII (2001), Aix-en-Provence: Economica – Presses Universitaires d'Aix-Marseille, 2002, 229 et seq.

Nikolakopoulos, Il., 'The Development of Political Opinion Polling in Greece'. In *Political Parties in the 21st Century*, edited by Tsatsos, Venizelos, Contiades. Centre for European Constitutional Law 'Themistokles and Dimitris Tsatsos Foundation'. Ant. N. Sakkoulas – Berliner Wissenschaftsverlag – Bruylant, 2004, 139 et seq.

Noel-Baker, F. *Greece. The Whole Story*. London: Hutchinson, 1946.

Pagoulatos, G. 'Governing in a Constrained Environment: Policy Making in the Greek Banking Deregulation and Privatisation Reform'. *West European Politics* 19, no. 4 (1996): 744 et seq.

Pantelis, A. *Droit Constitutionnel Hellénique*. Préface B. Pacteau, L'Harmattan, 2018

Pantelis, A. 'Chronique de Droit Constitutionnel – Grèce'. REDP 3, no. 1 (1991): 217 et seq.

Pantelis, A. 'Chronique de Droit Constitutionnel – Grèce'. REDP 2, no. 1 (1990): 231 et seq.

Pantelis, A. 'Chronique de Droit Constitutionnel – Grèce'. REDP 1, no. 1 (1989): 77 et seq.

Pantelis, A. *Les grands problèmes de la nouvelle Constitution hellénique*. Paris: LGDJ, 1979.

Pantelis, A. & S. Koutsoubinas. 'Les régimes électoraux en Grèce'. In *Les régimes électoraux des pays de l'Union européenne*, Pantelis, Koutsoubinas. European

Public Law Series – Bibliothèque de Droit public Européen, Volume II, European Public Law, London: Esperia Publications Ltd (diffusion Bruxelles: Bruylant), 1998, 273 et seq.
Pantelis, A. & M. Triantafyllou. 'A New Electoral System'. REDP 5, no. 2 (1993): 301 et seq.
Papadimitriou, G. 'The Greek National Commission for the Protection of Human Rights'. In *The prevention of Human Rights Violations*, edited by L.-A. Sicilianos. Marangopoulos Foundation for Human Rights. Athens / The Hague / New York / London: Ant. N. Sakkoulas – Martinus Nijoff, 2001, 249 et seq.
Papadimitriou, G. 'Die Institution der politischen Partei in Griechenland'. In *Parteienrecht im europäischen Vergleich*, Tsatsos, Schefold, Schneider (Hrsg.). Baden-Baden: Nomos Verlag, 1991, 261 et seq.
Papadimitriou, G. *Die Stellung der allgemeinen Regeln des Völkerrechts im innerstaatlichen Recht.* Berlin: Duncker & Humblot, 1972.
Papadopoulou, O. 'Aspects de la privatisation en Grèce'. *REDP,* Spetses Conferences, Special Number (1994), 129 et seq.
Papadopoulou, O. 'Le recours quasi contentieux: complément ou entrave à la protection juridictionnelle?'. REDP Spetses Conferences (1993), 191 et seq.
Papadopoulou, O. 'Le statut des réfugiés en Grèce'. *REDP*, Spetses Conferences, 7, no. 3 (1993): 845 et seq.
Papadopoulou, O. *Les garanties du fonctionnaire dans la Constitution hellénique.* Paris: LGDJ, 1992.
Papadopoulou, O. 'Les garanties du fonctionnaire dans la Constitution hellénique'. REDP 3, no. 2 (1991): 415 et seq.
Papapetropoulos, A. *La prise en compte de l'environnement par les procédures du droit de l'urbanisme en France et en Grèce.* Athènes / Komotini: Ant N. Sakkoulas, 2002.
Papassiopi-Passia, Z. 'Le Droit à la nationalité'. In *Essays in honour of Georgios I. Kassimatis.* Athens: Ant N. Sakkoulas / Berliner Wissenschaftsverlag / Bruylant, 2004, 507 et seq.
Papastathopoulos, C. 'Local Government and Administration in Greece, 1952–1962'. *Journal of Central European Affairs* 23 (1963): 333 et seq.
Papathanassiou, Ch. *Le nouveau code de la nationalité hellénique.* Thèse pour le doctorat d'université, Paris 1958.
Pararas, P. 'Le contrôle juridictionnel des actes de contenu législatif du président de la République (art. 44 par. 1 de la Constitution hellénique) (Chronique Grèce 1990)'. *AIJC 1990*, VI (1990), Aix-en-Provence: Economica – Presses Universitaires d'Aix-Marseille, 1992, 733 et seq.
Pavlopoulos, P. 'Administration et environnement en Grèce'. *AEAP 1996*, Université de droit, d'économie et de science politique d'Aix-Marseille, Faculté de droit et de science politique, CRA, XIX (1996), Aix-en-Provence: Presses Universitaires d'Aix-Marseille, 1997, 111 et seq.
Pavlopoulos, P. 'L'administration répressive en Grèce'. *AEAP 1995*, Université de droit, d'économie et de science politique d'Aix-Marseille, Faculté de droit et de science politique, CRA, XVIII (1995), Aix-en-Provence: Presses Universitaires d'Aix-Marseille, 1996, 147 et seq.
Pavlopoulos, P. 'Chronique de vie administrative 1994 – Grèce – Intérêt général et

juridiction administrative'. *AEAP 1994*, Université de droit, d'économie et de science politique d'Aix-Marseille, Faculté de droit et de science politique, CRA, XVII (1994), Aix-en-Provence: Presses Universitaires d'Aix-Marseille, 1995, 429 et seq.

Pavlopoulos, P. 'Chronique de vie administrative 1993 – Grèce – Collectivités locales et intégration européenne: le cas de la Grèce – Des obstacles constitutionnels à l'intégration européenne?'. *AEAP 1993*, XVI (1993), Paris: Éditions du CNRS, 1994, 489 et seq.

Pavlopoulos, P. 'Collectivités locales et intégration européenne: le cas de la Grèce'. REDP 6, no. 2 (1994): 313 et seq.

Pavlopoulos, P. 'Chronique de vie administrative 1992 – Grèce – Les bases constitutionnelles du sursis à exécution dans l'ordre juridique hellénique'. *AEAP 1992*, XV (1992), Paris: Éditions du CNRS, 1993, 495 et seq.

Pavlopoulos, P. 'Chronique de vie administrative 1991 – Grèce – L'arbitrage dans le contentieux administratif en Grèce'. *AEAP 1991*, XIV (1991), Paris: Éditions du CNRS, 1992, 585 et seq.

Pavlopoulos, P. 'L'arbitrage dans le contentieux administratif'. REDP 4, no. 1 (1992): 61 et seq.

Pavlopoulos, P. 'Chronique de vie administrative 1990 – Grèce – La hiérarchie dans l'administration, Vers une analyse systémique'. *AEAP 1990*, XIII (1990), Paris: Éditions du CNRS, 1991, 412 et seq.

Pavlopoulos, P. 'Chronique de vie administrative 1983'. *AEAP*, VI (1983), Paris: Éditions du CNRS, 1984, 527 et seq.

Pavlopoulos, P., A. Calogeropoulos, & S. Lytras. 'Chronique de vie administrative 1979'. *AEAP 1979*, II (1979), Paris: Éditions du CNRS, 1980, 559 et seq.

Pavlopoulos, P., A. Calogeropoulos & S. Lytras. 'Chronique de vie administrative 1978'. *AEAP 1978*, I (1978), Paris: Éditions du CNRS, 1979, 427 et seq.

Pazarzis, P. 'Le statut des minorités en Grèce'. *Annuaire Français de Droit International* 38 (1992): 377 et seq.

Petropoulos, J.A. *Politics and Statecraft in the Kingdom of Greece, 1833–1843*. Princeton N.J.: Princeton University Press, 1968.

Petrou, C.A. 'La gestion du Risque en droit public grec'. REDP 15, no. 1 (2003): 321 et seq.

Pilafas, Ch. 'Wissenschaft vom Verfassungsrecht: Griechenland'. In *Grundlagen des Europäischen Verfassungsrechts*, edited by Bogdandy, Cruz Villalón, Huber (Hrsg.). Band II, C.F. Müller, 2007, 525 et seq.

Pollis, A. 'The State, the Law and Human Rights in Modern Greece'. *Human Rights Quarterly* 9 (1987) (The John Hopkins University Press [USA]), 587 et seq.

Pottakis, A. 'Chronicle in Constitutional Law'. REDP 18, no. 4 (2006): 1389 et seq.

Pottakis, A. 'Chronicle in Constitutional Law'. REDP 17, no. 4 (2005): 1541 et seq.

Pottakis, A. 'Chronicle in Constitutional Law'. REDP 16, no. 4 (2004): 1061 et seq.

Pottakis, A. 'Chronicle in Constitutional Law'. REDP 15 no. 4 (2003): 1227 et seq.

Poulantzas, N. *La crise des dictatures. Espagne, Grèce, Portugal*. Paris: Maspero, 1975.

Poulis, P. *Droit constitutionnel et Institutions helléniques*. Paris: L'Harmattan, 2008.

Richter, H. *Griechenland zwischen Revolution und Konterrevolution (1936–1946)*. Frankfurt: Europäische Verlagsanstalt, 1973.

Rizou, Th. *Zugang zu Gerichten im Umweltrecht. Eine vergleichende Studie des deutschen und griechischen Rechts*. Res Publica, 4, Frankfurt am Main: Peter Lang, 2006.

Rosenberg, Th. 'Reception and Detention Conditions for Economic Refugees and Asylum Seekers in Greece: A major Issue of the Protection of Human Rights'. In *Olympia IV: Human Rights in the 21st Century, Migrants and Refugees*, edited by V. Kyriakopoulos. Athens / Komotini: Ant. N. Sakkoulas, 2004, 125 et seq.

Rotis, N. *Le peuple et l'État. Essai sur la clause des Constitutions helléniques*. Thèse, Paris I, 1974, t. 1–3.

Roucounas, E. 'Le droit international dans la Constitution de la Grèce du 9 juin 1975'. RHDI 29 (1976): 51 et seq.

Samartzis, A. & N. Vadivoulis. *Greece's Ambivalent Turn to Militant Democracy*, VerfBlog, 24 May 2023, https://verfassungsblog.de/greeces-ambivalent-turn-to-militant-democracy/.

Saripolos, N. *Das Staatsrecht des Königreichs Griechenland*. Tübingen: Mohr, 1909.

Sassalos, A. *Le contrôle de la constitutionnalité des lois en Grèce*. Thèse, Paris, 1970.

Sicilianos, L.-A. 'Rapport sur la situation des droits fondamentaux en Grèce en 2004'. RHDH 26 (2005): 493 et seq.

Sicilianos, L.-A. (ed.). *The Prevention of Human Rights Violations*. Marangopoulos Foundation for Human Rights, Athens / The Hague / New York / London: Ant. N. Sakkoulas – Martinus Nijoff, 2001.

Sioutis, G. 'La gestion du risque et la protection de l'environnement'. REDP 15, no. 1 (2003): 133 et seq.

Sioutis, G. 'Decentralisation'. In *Public Administration in Greece*, edited by Ep. Spiliotopoulos, A. Makrydemetres & K. Préface Chalazonitis. Athens – Komotini: Ant. N. Sakkoulas, 2001, 45 et seq.

Sioutis, G. 'La Déconcentration'. In *L'Administration publique en Grèce*, edited by Ep. Spiliotopoulos, A. Makrydimitris (dir.) & Préface Chalazonitis. Athènes – Komotini: Ant. N. Sakkoulas, 2001, 45 et seq.

Sioutis, G. 'Chronique de Droit Administratif – Grèce'. REDP 7, no. 4 (1995): 1085 et seq.

Sioutis, G. 'Chronique de Droit Administratif – Grèce'. REDP 6, no. 2 (1994): 463 et seq.

Sioutis, G. 'Chronique de Droit Administratif – Grèce'. REDP 4, no. 1 (1992): 195 et seq.

Sioutis, G. 'Chronique de Droit Administratif – Grèce'. REDP 3, no. 1 (1991): 289 et seq.

Sioutis, G. 'Chronique de Droit Administratif – Grèce'. REDP 2, no. 1 (1990): 281 et seq.

Sioutis, G. 'Chronique de Droit Administratif – Grèce'. REDP 1, no. 1 (1989): 167 et seq.

Sitaropoulos, N. 'Freedom of Movement and the Rights to a Nationality *v.* Ethnic Minorities: The case of ex. Article 19 of the Greek Nationality Code'. *European Journal of Migration and Law* 6 (2004): 205 et seq.

Sitaropoulos, N. 'Comparative Legal Study on Subsidiary Protection – Greece'. In *Subsidiary Protection of Refugees in the European Union: Complementing the Geneva Convention?*, edited by D. Bouteillet-Paquet. Bruxelles: Bruylant, 2002, 529 et seq.

Sitaropoulos, N. 'Legal Principles and Practice Regarding Race Equality in Greece'. REDP 11, no. 2 (1999): 755 et seq.

Skordas, A. & N. Sitaropoulos. 'Why Greece Is Not a safe Country for Refugees'. *International Journal of Refugee Law* 16, no. 1 (2004): 25 et seq.

Skouris, V. 'The Position of the European Court of Justice in the EU Legal Order and Its Relations with National Constitutional Courts'. *ZÖR* 60, Heft 3 (2005), 323 et seq.

Skouris, V. 'Die Überprüfung staatlicher Akte auf ihre Verfassungsmässigkeit in Griechenland'. RHDI 38–39 (1985–1986): 365 et seq.

Souliotis, Y.M. *Le régime parlementaire hellénique d'après-guerre (1946–1967)*. Thèse, Nice, 1972.

Spanou, C. 'Administration publique et politique publique'. In *L'Administration publique en Grèce*, Spiliotopoulos, Makrydimitris (dir.), Préface Chalazonitis, K., Athènes – Komotini: Ant. N. Sakkoulas, 2001, 165 et seq.

Spanou, C. 'Public Administration and Public Policy'. In *Public Administration in Greece*, edited by Ep. Spiliotopoulos, A. Makrydemetres & K. Préface Chalazonitis. Athens – Komotini: Ant. N. Sakkoulas, 2001, 157 et seq.

Spanou, C. 'European Integration in Administrative Terms: A Framework for Analysis and the Greek Case'. *Journal of European Public Policy* 5, no. 3 (1998): 467 et seq.

Spiliotopoulos, Ep. 'La directive 89/665/CEE et le droit administratif hellénique'. In *Mélanges Louis Dubouis*, Paris: Dalloz, 2012, 451 et seq.

Spiliotopoulos, Ep. 'Le principe de l'État de droit social: considérations pour une interprétation du paragraphe 1er de l'article 25 de la Constitution'. In *Itinéraires d'un constitutionaliste, En Hommage à Francis Delpérée*. Bruxelles-Paris: Bruylant-LGDJ, 2007, 1471 et seq.

Spiliotopoulos, Ep. *Droit Administratif Hellénique*. Préface J. Rivero, Athènes-Bruxelles: Ant. N. Sakkoulas-Bruylant, 2eéd., 2004.

Spiliotopoulos, Ep. *Greek Administrative Law*. Preface by Prof. J. Jowell Q.C., Athens – Brussels: Ant. N. Sakkoulas – Bruylant, 2004.

Spiliotopoulos, Ep. 'La protection de l'administré dans l'ordre juridique hellénique'. In *Mouvements du droit public, Du droit administratif au droit constitutionnel, Du droit français aux autres droits, Mélanges en l'honneur de Franck Moderne*. Paris: Dalloz, 2004, 967 et seq.

Spiliotopoulos, Ep. 'Constitution et secret de la vie privée en Grèce'. *AIJC 2000*, XVI (2000), Aix-en-Provence: Economica – Presses Universitaires d'Aix-Marseille, 2001, 291 et seq.

Spiliotopoulos, Ep. 'La protection supralegislative des droits de créance en Grèce'. In *Le nouveau constitutionalisme, Mélanges en l'honneur de Gérard Conac* (textes rassemblés par J.-C. Colliard et Y. Jegouzo), Paris: Economica, 2001, 299 et seq.

Spiliotopoulos, Ep. 'Le contrôle juridictionnel de l'action administrative'. In *L'Administration publique en Grèce*, Ep. Spiliotopoulos, A. Makrydimitris (dir.)

& K. Préface Chalazonitis. Athènes – Komotini: Ant. N. Sakkoulas, 2001, 123 et seq.

Spiliotopoulos, Ep. 'The Judicial Review of Administrative Action'. In *Public Administration in Greece*, edited by Ep. Spiliotopoulos, A. Makrydemetres & K. Préface Chalazonitis. Athens – Komotini: Ant. N. Sakkoulas, 2001, 119 et seq.

Spiliotopoulos, Ep. 'Constitution et sécurité juridique en Grèce'. *AIJC 1999*, XV (1999), Aix-en-Provence: Economica – Presses Universitaires d'Aix-Marseille, 2000), 193 et seq.

Spiliotopoulos, Ep. 'Les droits et libertés des étrangers en situation irrégulière en Grèce'. *AIJC 1998*, XIV (1998), Aix-en-Provence: Economica – Presses Universitaires d'Aix-Marseille, 1999, 243 et seq.

Spiliotopoulos, Ep. 'Les discriminations positives en Grèce'. *AIJC 1997*, XIII (1997), Aix-en-Provence: Economica – Presses Universitaires d'Aix-Marseille, 1998, 175 et seq.

Spiliotopoulos, Ep. 'L'école, la religion et la Constitution en Grèce'. *AIJC 1996*, XII (1996), Aix-en-Provence: Economica – Presses Universitaires d'Aix-Marseille, 1997, 257 et seq.

Spiliotopoulos, Ep. 'L'entreprise publique et l'intérêt général'. REDP 8, no. 4 (1996): 1083 et seq.

Spiliotopoulos Ep. 'Le statut constitutionnel des juges du siège et du parquet en Grèce'. *AIJC 1995*, Groupe d'Études et de Recherches sur la Justice Constitutionnelle –Équipe associée au CNRS (URA 1392), XI (1995), Aix-en-Provence: Economica – Presses Universitaires d'Aix-Marseille, 1996, 247 et seq.

Spiliotopoulos Ep. 'Constitution et partis politiques en Grèce'. *AIJC 1993*, IX (1993), Aix-en-Provence: Economica – Presses Universitaires d'Aix-Marseille, 1995, 157 et seq.

Spiliotopoulos, Ep. 'La fonction législative de l'administration en Grèce'. *AEAP 1994*, Université de droit, d'économie et de science politique d'Aix-Marseille, Faculté de droit et de science politique, CRA, XVII (1994), Aix-en-Provence: Presses Universitaires d'Aix-Marseille, 1995, 139 et seq.

Spiliotopoulos, Ep. 'Révision de la Constitution et justice constitutionnelle en Grèce'. *AIJC 1994*, X (1994), Aix-en-Provence: Economica – Presses Universitaires d'Aix-Marseille, 1995, 119 et seq.

Spiliotopoulos, Ep. 'Constitution et administration en Grèce'. *AEAP 1993*, XVI (1993), Paris: Éditions du CNRS, 1994, 35 et seq.

Spiliotopoulos Ep. 'Les méthodes de travail des jurisprudences constitutionnelles en Grèce'. *AIJC 1992*, VIII (1992), Aix-en-Provence: Economica – Presses Universitaires d'Aix-Marseille, 1994, 267 et seq.

Spiliotopoulos, Ep. 'Groupes de pression et administration en Grèce'. *AEAP 1992*, t. XV (1992), Paris, Éditions du CNRS, 1993, 181 et seq.

Spiliotopoulos, Ep. 'Administration et fonctionnement de la justice en Grèce'. *AEAP 1991*, XIV (1991), Paris: Éditions du CNRS, 1992, 45 et seq.

Spiliotopoulos, Ep. 'Le principe de non-rétroactivité des lois en Grèce'. *AIJC 1990*, VI (1990), Aix-en-Provence: Economica – Presses Universitaires d'Aix-Marseille, 1992, 375 et seq.

Spiliotopoulos, Ep. 'École et religion en Grèce'. RFDA (1991): 69 et seq.

Spiliotopoulos, Ep. 'La dualité des juridictions en Grèce'. RFDA (1990), 877 et seq.

Spiliotopoulos, Ep. 'La transparence administrative en Grèce'. *AEAP 1989*, XII (1989), Paris: Éditions du CNRS, 1990, 95 et seq.
Spiliotopoulos, Ep. 'Les juges constitutionnels en Grèce'. *AIJC 1988*, IV (1988), Aix-en-Provence: Economica – Presses Universitaires d'Aix-Marseille, 1990, 155 et seq.
Spiliotopoulos, Ep. 'La liberté de l'information en Grèce'. *AIJC 1987*, III (1987), Aix-en-Provence: Economica – Presses Universitaires d'Aix-Marseille, 1989, 345 et seq.
Spiliotopoulos, Ep. 'Le droit de l'audiovisuel en Grèce'. RFDA (1989), 499 et seq.
Spiliotopoulos, Ep. 'Les privatisations en Grèce'. *AEAP 1988*, XI (1988), Paris: Éditions du CNRS, 1989, 81 et seq.
Spiliotopoulos, Ep. 'L'administration publique grecque'. *AEAP 1987*, X (1987), Paris: Éditions du CNRS, 1988, 125 et seq.
Spiliotopoulos, Ep. 'L'interruption volontaire de grossesse (Grèce)'. *AIJC 1986*, II (1986), Aix-en-Provence: Economica – Presses Universitaires d'Aix-Marseille, 1988, 165 et seq.
Spiliotopoulos, Ep. 'Chronique Grèce 1985'. AIJC *1985*, I (1985), Aix-en-Provence: Economica – Presses Universitaires d'Aix-Marseille, 1987, 435 et seq.
Spiliotopoulos, Ep. 'L'administration grecque et l'intégration européenne'. *AEAP 1986*, IX (1986), Paris: Éditions du CNRS, 1987, 129 et seq.
Spiliotopoulos, Ep. 'Le droit de propriété dans la jurisprudence constitutionnelle grecque'. *AIJC 1985*, Groupement d'Études et de Recherche sur la Justice Constitutionnelle (GERJC), I (1985), Aix-en-Provence: Economica – Presses Universitaires d'Aix-Marseille, 1987, 233 et seq.
Spiliotopoulos, Ep. 'Les délégations législatives en Grèce'. RFDA (1987): 729 et seq.
Spiliotopoulos, Ep. 'Inflation législative et réglementaire en Grèce'. *AEAP 1985*, VIII (1985), Paris: Éditions du CNRS, 1986, 25 et seq.
Spiliotopoulos, Ep. *Les formes et structures des entreprises publiques. Les entreprises du secteur public dans les pays de la Communauté européenne*, 1985.
Spiliotopoulos, Ep. 'Radio et télévision en Grèce'. *AEAP 1984*, VII (1984), Paris: Éditions du CNRS, 1985, 169 et seq.
Spiliotopoulos, Ep. 'Contrôle juridictionnel et nouvelles protections en Grèce'. *AEAP 1983*, VI (1983), Paris: Éditions du CNRS, 1984, 107 et seq.
Spiliotopoulos, Ep. 'La spécificité du personnel des collectivités locales'. *Association Internationale de la Fonction Publique* – Institut International de Sciences Administratives (AIFP-11SA), 1984, 173 et seq.
Spiliotopoulos, Ep. 'Judicial Review of Legislative Acts in Greece'. *Temple Law Quarterly 56*, no. 2 (1983), Temple University (Philadelphia, Pennsylvania, USA), 463 et seq.
Spiliotopoulos, Ep. 'L'administration dans le débat politique en Grèce'. *AEAP 1982*, V (1982), Paris: Éditions du CNRS, 1983, 255 et seq.
Spiliotopoulos, Ep. 'Parlement et administration en Grèce'. *AEAP 1981*, IV (1981), Paris: Éditions du CNRS, 1982, 163 et seq.
Spiliotopoulos, Ep. 'Les compétences du pouvoir local en Grèce'. *AEAP 1980*, III (1980), Paris: Éditions du CNRS, 1981, 267 et seq.

Spiliotopoulos, Ep. 'La politique de choix des fonctionnaires en Grèce'. *AEAP 1979*, II (1979), Paris: Éditions du CNRS, 1980, 179 et seq.
Spiliotopoulos, Ep. 'L'abus de pouvoir et de fonction en droit public hellénique (rapport gec)'. Travaux de l'Association Henri Capitant (1977): 473 et seq.
Spiliotopoulos, Ep. 'L'importance de la distinction entre loi formelle et loi matérielle en droit positif grec'. *Recueil d'études en l'honneur de Charles Eisenmann* (1975): 125 et seq.
Spiliotopoulos, Ep. 'La situation juridique de demandeur d'asile en Grèce' (avec A. Bredimas), RFDA (1993), 767 et seq.
Spiliotopoulos, Ep. & A. Makrydemetres (eds). *Public Administration in Greece*. Athens – Komotini: Ant. N. Sakkoulas, 2001.
Spiliotopoulos, Ep. & A. Makrydimitris (dir.). *L'Administration Publique en Grèce*. Athènes – Komotini: Ant. N. Sakkoulas, 2001.
Spiliotopoulos, Ep. & Pavlopoulos P. 'Le fonctionnaire à la retraite (rapport grec)'. AIFP-IISA (1986): 251 et seq.
Spinellis, D. 'Criminal Law and Procedure'. In *Introduction to Greek Law*, edited by K.D. Kerameus & P.J. Kozyris, 3rd rev. edn, Ant. N. Sakkoulas: Kluwer Law International, 2008, 459 et seq.
Spourdalakis, M. 'The Study of the Political Parties in Greece'. *European Journal of Political Research* 25 (1994): 499 et seq.
Spyropoulos, Ph. 'Die Vermutung der Verfassungsmässigkeit der Gesetze und die verfassungskonforme Gesetzesauslegung'. In *Verfassungsgeschichte und Staatsrechtslehre, Griechisch-deutsche Wechselwirkungen*, Kassimatis, Stolleis (Hrsg.), Frankfurt am Main: Klostermann, 2001, 283 et seq.
Spyropoulos, Ph. 'Institutions of Public Law'. REDP 9, no. 4 (1997), 1137 et seq.
Stamoulas, Ar. 'Cultural Democracies and Human Rights: Conditions for Religious Freedom in Modern Greece'. *Journal of Human Rights* 3, no. 4 (December 2004): 477 et seq.
Stathopoulos, M. 'Reviewing the Constitutionality of Laws'. *REDP* 3, no. 1 (1991): 87 et seq.
Stavrianos, L.S. *The Balkans since 1453*. New York: Reinhart, 1958.
Stavrianos, L.S. 'The Greek National Liberation Front (EAM): A Study in Resistance Organization and Administration'. *Journal of Modern History* (1952): 44 et seq.
Svolos, A. 'Grèce: Chronique constitutionnelle'. *Annuaire de l'Institut Européen de Droit Public* (1936): 304 et seq.
Svolos, A. 'Les rapports entre l'État et les partis d'après le droit public grec'. In *Mélanges Négulesco*, Bucuresti: Imprimerie Nationala, 1935, 713 et seq.
Svoronos, N. *Histoire de la Grèce Moderne*. Paris: Presses Universitaires de France, «Que sais-je?» no 578 (1972).
Svoronos, N. 'Esquisse de l'évolution sociale et politique en Grèce'. *Les Temps Modernes* 276 bis (1969), 7 et seq.
Svoronos, N. 'Grèce'. In *Encyclopaedia Universalis*: *The Constitution of Greece (1975–1986–2001–2008)*, as revised by the parliamentary resolution of 27th May 2008 of the VIIIth Revisionary Parliament, edited by K. Mavrias & Ep. Spiliotopoulos, translated by Paparrigopoulos, X., S. Vassilouni, Athens: Hellenic Parliament, 2008.

The Constitution of Greece (1975–1986–2001), As revised by the parliamentary resolution of 6th April 2001 of the VIIth Revisionary Parliament, edited by Mavrias & Spiliotopoulos, translated by Paparrigopoulos, X., S. Vassilouni, Athens: Hellenic Parliament, 2004.

The Constitution of Greece (text 1975/1986). Athens: Greek Chamber of Deputies, 1992.

The Constitution of Greece (text 1975). Athens: Greek Chamber of Deputies, 1975.

The Hellas Constitution, translated by C. Spyropoulos, Kluwer Law and Taxation Publishers off-print, The Netherlands, Kluwer, 1994.

Tsevas, A. 'Unlawful Invasions of Rights of the Third Persons by Radiotelevision: Case – Study'. REDP 8, no. 3 (1996): 1013 et seq.

Tzemos, V. *Das Untermassverbot*, Europäische Hochschulschriften 11 (2006), Frankfurt am Main: Peter Lang, 2004.

Tzitzis, St. 'Minorités culturelles et devoirs de l'homme'. RHDH 28 (2005): 1235 et seq.

Urbano de Sousa, C. 'La directive 2003/86/CE du Conseil, du 22 septembre 2003, relative au droit au regroupement familial: Une histoire sans une issue heureuse?'. In *La politique européenne d'immigration et d'asile: Bilan critique cinq ans après le traité d'Amsterdam*, Julien-Laferriere, Labayle, Edltrom (dir.), Bruxelles: Bruylant, 2005, 127 et seq.

Vacalopoulos, A. *Histoire de la Grèce Moderne*. Paris: Horvatt, 1975.

Valticos, N. 'Droits de l'homme ou droits humains? Petit exercice de terminologie'. RHDH 15 (2002): 665 et seq.

Vegleris, P. 'Le Conseil d'État et l'examen de la constitutionalité des lois en Grèce'. In *Studi in onore di Silvio Lessona*, II, Bologna: Zanichelli, 1961, 597 et seq.

Venizelos, Ev. 'European Constitution: A Challenge for Constitutional Theory, Introduction'. REDP 16, no. 1 (2004): 20 et seq.

Vlachos, G. 'Les décrets législatifs et la loi formelle en droit constitutionnel hellénique'. RDP (1960): 233 et seq.

Voloudakis, E. *Recherche sur le suffrage politique en Grèce, 1910–1975*. Paris, 1977.

Woodhouse, C.M. *Modern Greece: A Short History*. London: Fabor, 1977.

Woodhouse, C.M. *The Struggle for Greece, 1941–1949*. London: Hart-Davis MacGibbon, 1976.

Xydis, St. *Greece and the Great Powers, 1944–1947: Prelude to the Truman Doctrine*. Thessalonique: Institute for Balkan Studies, 1963.

Yalitaki, E. 'Committal to Prison for Debts to the Greek State: Constitutional Limitations in a Comparative Perspective'. REDP 15 (2003): 1199 et seq.

Yessiou-Faltsi, P. 'Judicial Responsibility in Greece'. RHDI 35–36 (1982–1983): 281 et seq.

Yotopoulos-Marangopoulos, Al. *Les Mesures Positives, pour une égalité effective des sexes*. Sakkoulas – Bruylant, 1998.

Ziamou, Th. 'Creating a Single Electricity Market for Europe with an Environmental Approach: The European Challenge and the Greek Legal Response'. REDP 12, no. 3 (2000): 989 et seq.

Zilemenos, C. *Le droit de la presse hellénique*. Paris: LGDJ, 1970.

Selected Bibliography

Index

The numbers here refer to paragraph number.

1. Subject Index

Index

Index

2. The Constitution of the Hellenic Republic and constitutional texts

(in reverse chronological order)

2.1. The Constitution of 1975/1986/2001/2008/2019, 39 et seq.

(Articles)

Index

5. INTERNATIONAL COVENANT ON CIVIL AND POLITICAL RIGHTS

6. CODES

Index

7. Acts

Index

8. LEGISLATIVE DECREES

9. PRESIDENTIAL DECREES

10. ACTS OF LEGISLATIVE CONTENT

11. ACTS OF CABINET

12. MINISTERIAL DECISIONS

13. HELLENIC DATA PROTECTION AUTHORITY

14. CASE LAW

14.1. Court of Justice of the European Union

14.2. European Court of Human Rights

14.7. Court of Audit

14.8. Court of Appeal

15. ADVICES OF COUNCIL OF STATE

16. ADVICE OF LEGAL COUNCIL OF STATE

Index

www.ingramcontent.com/pod-product-compliance
Lightning Source LLC
Chambersburg PA
CBHW071422230926
51846CB00001B/114
9789403504278